Little Red Readings

Little Red Readings

Historical Materialist Perspectives

on Children's Literature

Edited by Angela E. Hubler

UNIVERSITY PRESS OF MISSISSIPPI • JACKSON

Children's Literature Association Series

www.upress.state.ms.us

The University Press of Mississippi is a member of the Association of American University Presses.

First printing 2014

∞

Library of Congress Cataloging-in-Publication Data

Little Red Readings : Historical Materialist Perspectives on Children's Literature / edited by Angela E. Hubler.
pages cm. — (Children's Literature Association Series)
Summary: "A significant body of scholarship examines the production of children's literature by women and minorities, as well as the representation of gender, race, and sexuality. But few scholars have previously analyzed class in children's literature. This definitive collection remedies that by defining and exemplifying historical materialist approaches to children's literature. The introduction of Little Red Readings lucidly discusses characteristics of historical materialism, the methodological approach to the study of literature and culture first outlined by Karl Marx, defining key concepts and analyzing factors that have marginalized this tradition, particularly in the United States. The thirteen essays here analyze a wide range of texts—from children's bibles to Mary Poppins to The Hunger Games—using concepts in historical materialism from class struggle to the commodity. Essayists apply the work of Marxist theorists such as Ernst Bloch and Fredric Jameson to children's literature and film. Others examine the work of leftist writers in India, Germany, England, and the United States. The authors argue that historical materialist methodology is critical to the study of children's literature, as children often suffer most from inequality. Some of the critics in this collection reveal the ways that literature for children often functions to naturalize capitalist economic and social relations. Other critics champion literature that reveals to readers the construction of social reality and point to texts that enable an understanding of the role ordinary people might play in creating a more just future. The collection adds substantially to our understanding of the political and class character of children's literature worldwide, and contributes to the development of a radical history of children's literature"— Provided by publisher.
Includes bibliographical references and index.
ISBN 978-1-61703-987-4 (hardback) — ISBN 978-1-61703-988-1 (ebook) 1. Children's literature—History and criticism. 2. Class consciousness in literature. 3. Historical materialism. I. Hubler, Angela E., editor of compilation.
PN1009.5.S62L58 2014
809'.89282—dc23   2013044120

British Library Cataloging-in-Publication Data available

To Tim Dayton, my favorite Marxist

CONTENTS

INTRODUCTION

The Case for a Historical Materialist Criticism of Children's Literature

ANGELA E. HUBLER

When my son Jack was about three years old, I read Patricia McKissack's *Ma Dear's Aprons* to him. This picture book focuses on two African American characters living in the 1900s, David Earle and his widowed mother who supports her family as a domestic worker, wearing a different, clean apron each day. On Monday, she does laundry, on Tuesday she irons—with David's help—and on Wednesday, they cross "the railroad tracks to the other side of Avery where all the rich people live" to deliver baskets of clean clothes (n.p.). After her work is "carefully" inspected, David's mother is paid a quarter. During the rest of the week, David and his mother visit the sick, clean house for the Alexander family, and sell pies at the train station, before they rest on Sunday. While the book portrays the warm relationship between a mother and son, it also foregrounds economic inequality, and the hard work and low pay endured by African American women. When I finished reading the book, Jack had a question: "Did they pay her very much to clean?" "Probably not," I replied.

Jack's response to this book reveals the way that literature allows readers—even very young readers—to cognitively map social reality: to begin to understand the way in which race, class, and sex structure social inequality. While the term "cognitive mapping" was developed by Fredric Jameson, the idea that literature enables a perception of social reality not often immediately available to us has a long history in literary theory—originating in Aristotle—and is currently most effectively deployed in historical materialist criticism of literature.[1]

Such criticism continues to be necessary because, while social justice movements have achieved some formal legal equality for historically subordinated groups, class continues to dramatically determine the life chances of children today. A 2008 study by the Pew Charitable Trusts reports that the economic position of adults is heavily influenced by that of their parents: "42 percent of children born to parents in the bottom fifth of the income distribution remain in the bottom, while 39 percent born to parents in the top fifth remain at the top" (Isaacs, Sawhill, and Haskins 4). Economic mobility is particularly difficult for poor girls and African Americans. "Close to half (47 percent) of low-income girls compared to 35 percent of low-income boys end up in the bottom fifth upon adulthood" (65), while black children at every income level are less likely than white children to experience upward economic mobility and more likely than white children to experience downward mobility (74). Given these social realities, it is important that a robust critical tradition has developed that analyzes the production of children's literature by women and by African Americans and other racial minorities, and that examines the way that gender and race are represented in children's literature. However, a similarly robust analysis of the significance of class in children's literature is lacking. This collection aims to address this gap in the field of children's literature by defining and exemplifying historical materialist approaches to this body of writing.

Idealism versus Historical Materialism

While historical materialism is centrally engaged with class, its concerns are much broader. Historical materialism is a methodological approach to the study of culture and society first outlined by Karl Marx in *The German Ideology*, in which Marx rejects the idealism that characterized most philosophical inquiry "from Plato to G. W. F. Hegel" (Booker 71): "The premises from which we begin are not arbitrary ones, not dogmas, but real premises from which abstraction can only be made in the imagination. They are the real individuals, their activity and the material conditions under which they live, both those which they find already existing and those produced by their activity" (Marx, *German Ideology* 149). With this, Marx challenged the idealist view that historical change results from the unfolding of reason. Rather, historical materialists insist that social change takes place as a result of class struggle. And reason, they argue, is neither divine, unchanging, nor disinterested but instead imbricated with the interests of "real individuals." At its most basic, a historical materialist approach to children's literature analyzes texts in terms of the material conditions and social relations from which they emerge and upon which they comment.

Thus, while Marx was decidedly not a literary critic but a political economist (broadly understood to refer to an analyst of the relationship between the economic, the social, and the political), an analyst of contemporary history, and a social theorist, historical materialism is a methodology that can be employed by the literary critic. Moreover, key Marxist concepts including class, alienation, reification, commodity fetishism, and ideology have proven central to the critical analysis of culture and society. In exemplifying some of these widely ranging historical materialist approaches to children's literature, this collection aims both to broaden an understanding of historical materialist literary criticism and to remedy the marginal status of this approach, particularly in the United States.

Base and Superstructure

In the social production of their life, men enter into definite relations that are indispensable and independent of their will, relations of production which correspond to a definite stage of development of their material productive forces. The sum total of these relations of production constitutes the economic structure of society, the real foundation, on which rises a legal and political superstructure and to which correspond definite forms of social consciousness. The mode of production of material life conditions the social, political and intellectual life process in general. It is not the consciousness of men that determines their being, but on the contrary, their social being that determines their consciousness. (Marx, *German Ideology* 149)

Robert C. Tucker, editor of *The Marx Engels Reader*, calls this passage "the *locus classicus* of historical materialism" (3). In it, Marx articulates a metaphor that expresses the relationship between the economy (or the mode of production) and social and political institutions including the family, law, and, less directly, ideology and consciousness as that between a base and its superstructure, which is shaped, or more precisely, determined "in the last instance" by the base (Engels, qtd. in Althusser 74). Most broadly, the concept of base and superstructure rejects the position that ideas shape culture, society, and history, insisting instead that material human processes shape consciousness. The relationship between cultural production and the economy is not always, in fact not usually, a direct one. That is, rather than reflecting social reality, art and literature "mediate" social reality, a term that Raymond Williams explains is used "to describe the process of relationship between 'society' and 'art' or between 'the base' and 'the superstructure'" (*Marxism and Literature* 98).[2] This relationship is active rather than static: art does not passively mirror reality but results from a creative process.

A great deal of literary analysis of children's literature ignores the insights of historical materialism and fails to analyze the relationship between art and social and economic reality. Jack Zipes, probably the best-known historical materialist critic of children's literature, however, offers an instructive exception. In *Breaking the Magic Spell*, he argues that "by relocating the historical origins of the folk and fairy tales in politics and class struggles, the essence of their durability and vitality will become more clear, and their magic will be seen as part of humankind's own imaginative *and* rational drive to create new worlds that allow for total autonomous development of human qualities" (27). Thus, a historical materialist analysis is central to Zipes's project: he shows that folk tales reflect "late feudal conditions" and "generally deal with exploitation, hunger, and injustice familiar to the lower classes in pre-capitalist societies" (8). And while the "utopian projections" expressed within the tales should not be understood as revolutionary, "their resolutions allow us to glean the possibility of making the world" (23). But Zipes also shows that, as the folk tale was appropriated "by the aristocratic and bourgeois writers in the sixteenth, seventeenth, and eighteenth centuries," resulting in a new literary genre, that of the fairy tale, a new "ideology of conservatism" reflected the interests of the aristocracy (13).

Ideology

The ideas of the ruling class are in every epoch the ruling ideas, i.e. the class which is the ruling material force of society, is at the same time its ruling intellectual force. . . . The ruling ideas are nothing more than the ideal expression of the dominant material relationships, the dominant material relationships grasped as ideas. (Marx, *German Ideology* 172)

As Raymond Williams explains Marx's discussion of ideology, the mystification of the way that ideas support the material interests of the ruling class, and the extent to which such ideas are represented as abstract, universal truths, results in what Marx terms as "ideology" (*Keywords* 155). Thus, ideology reflects the interest of members of the ruling class in maintaining their dominance and preserving the economic system they benefit from. While Zipes shows how this is the case with the fairy tale, Bob Dixon's *Catching Them Young 1: Sex, Race and Class in Children's Fiction* focuses on literature for older children but also argues that, as a genre, it has the effect of "indoctrinating children with capitalist ideology" (70) in a variety of ways: working-class characters appear primarily in "minor roles and in a very few categories. . . . objects of charity (but only if loyal and obedient workers); repugnant characters, often criminals, who posed a menace to the social structure; or menials who were usually funny. . . . [W]e can simply resolve this into the two categories of the deserving and the undeserving" (48).

Meredith Cherland elaborates on the ideological effect of the way in which canonical children's literature often depicts poverty: "The canon serves the interests of those at the top insofar as it undermines resistance, and makes one's place in society seem inevitable—and therefore not to be questioned. Older Newbery winners like *Onion John* and *Blue Willow* serve both to naturalize poverty, and to assign the responsibility for the relief of such poverty to kind individuals rather than to social programs. More recent Newbery winners have treated racism as something caused by the attitudes of the *individual* (*Maniac Magee* for example), and poverty as the result of individual bad luck (*Shiloh*)" (124). Such representations discourage collective action to bring about social change, undermining resistance and preserving the class hierarchy.

In *The Empire's New Clothes: What the Lone Ranger, Babar, and Other Innocent Heroes Do to Our Minds*, Ariel Dorfman argues that a similar role is played by Jean de Brunhoff's *Babar* books: they present children with a "theory of history, an unconscious method for interpreting the economic and political world" (22). That is, the picture books depict the "Westernization of those barbaric territories"—Africa—minus "all the plundering, racism, underdevelopment and misery" (25, 26). The naked and orphaned elephant leaves the jungle and it taken in by a rich "Old Lady," who clothes and educates him. After adopting bipedalism, Babar returns to the jungle, "a native educated in the ways of men," where he is elected as the new king, converted, as Patrick Richardson notes, to a hereditary monarch (qtd. in Dixon 76).

These issues trouble Herbert Kohl as well and supply the title for his book, *Should We Burn Babar? Essays on Children's Literature and the Power of Stories*. Kohl's primary concern is the way in which "power is distributed among the characters in the text" (4). He argues that "the reader learns that there are different classes of people and the Rich Lady is of the better (that is richer) class" (6). Kohl notes that his own childhood understanding of class was shaped not only by conservative ideological messages conveyed by *Babar* but also by his union-supporting family members, "who talked about the rich and the bosses as if they were morally, intellectually, and otherwise evil and deficient" (7). And while he argues that children can become critical readers of such texts, he issues a plea for radical children's literature: "there is still an almost total absence of books, fiction or nonfiction, that question the economic and social structure of our society and the values of capitalism" (38). Kohl goes on to define radical children's literature and to discuss several examples: Geoffrey Trease's *Bows against the Barons*, "a radical retelling of the adventure of Robin Hood"; Virginia Hamilton's *The Planet of Junior Brown*, a "social-realistic-fantasy"; and Vera Williams's picture books, which present "life within a multiracial and multicultural working-class community" (51–65).

Periodic calls have been issued by historical materialist critics to confront the conservative class character of children's literature. In 1979, in *Breaking the Magic Spell*, Zipes insisted that "literary criticism must become more radical. This means breaking the spell of commodity production and conventional notions of literature so that we can discover our individual and communal potential for infusing our everyday reality with the utopias we glean from the tales" (xiii). But in 1993, Ian Wojcik-Andrews noted, in his introduction to a special issue of the journal *The Lion and the Unicorn* on class, both the "centrality of class" and "the absence of a sustained class analysis in children's literature criticism" (114). Almost a decade later, in his 2002 preface to the revised edition of *Breaking the Magic Spell*, Zipes reiterated his comments from 1979, noting in the study of folk and fairy tales "a strange avoidance to discuss social class, ideological conflicts, and the false assumptions of numerous psychological approaches in a frank and straightforward manner" (ix).

Why We Are Not All Historical Materialists Now

The reasons that historical materialist analyses of society and culture are infrequently taken up are myriad. First, as David Harvey notes in his preface to *A Companion to Marx's "Capital,"* "the past thirty years, most particularly since the fall of the Berlin Wall and the end of the cold war, have not been a very favorable or fertile period for Marxian thought, and most certainly not for Marxian revolutionary politics. As a consequence, a whole younger generation has grown up bereft of familiarity with, let alone training in, Marxian political economy" (vii). An additional and unique obstacle to Marxist theory in general presents itself in the United States, where the ideology of U.S. society insists upon the irrelevance of class. The myth of the United States as an escape from the rigid class societies of the Old World, where every individual has the opportunity to pull himself up by his own bootstraps (or her own bra straps, as the case may be), suggests that U.S. society by its very nature enables the hardworking and talented to rise and that fundamental social change is therefore unnecessary. The continuing power of this ideology is revealed in responses to the recent Occupy movements, which have been rejected as "growing mobs" by House majority leader Eric Cantor (R-VA). While Cantor backpedaled to say that he sympathized with protesters' frustrations, the response of the Republican Party was to continue to push for the extension of the Bush tax cuts, which many analysts argue are partially responsible for growing income inequality in the United States. President Barack Obama's efforts to address income inequality by, in part, eliminating these tax cuts are condemned by conservative pundits as class warfare, and by House speaker John Boehner (R-OH) as "pitting one group against another" (Juan Williams).

To be clear, though, the Republican and Democratic Parties have united in following neoliberal economic policies that have shredded the social safety net at the same time that real wages have eroded. According to Harvey, neoliberal economic policies became dominant not just in the United States but globally, beginning in 1978 with Deng Xiaoping's liberalization of the Chinese economy and continuing with the administrations of Margaret Thatcher and Ronald Reagan, who acted to "curb the power of labor, deregulate industry, agriculture and resource extraction, and liberate the powers of finance both internally and on the world stage" (*Brief History of Neoliberalism* 1). Harvey argues that neoliberalism should be understood less as an economic theory and more as "a *political* project to re-establish the conditions for capital accumulation and to restore the power of economic elites" (19). Harvey's argument is supported by the actions of Republican president Reagan, who cut taxes and social spending and attacked unions. Democratic president Bill Clinton's support of so-called welfare reform instituted a five-year limit on cash assistance and shifted control from the federal government to the states. While these benefits have been limited, the recent economic crisis has led to increasing poverty rates. The U.S. Census Bureau reported that the child poverty rate in 2011 was 21.9 percent, and for black children it was 38.8 percent (DeNavas-Walt, Proctor, and Smith 59). If nothing else, statistics like these demonstrate the continuing relevance of Marx's historical materialist mode of social and literary analysis.

The global economic crisis that began in 2008 may have created a potentially more receptive climate for the kind of scholarship called for by Zipes, Andrews, and others than has been the case in the past. Indeed, this is suggested by the acclaim with which a cluster of recent scholarship—focusing on the literary production of the Left, especially the radical Left—has been met: the 2005 special issue of *Children's Literature Association Quarterly*, "Children's Literature and the Left," edited by Julia Mickenberg and Phil Nel; followed by Mickenberg's *Learning from the Left: Children's Literature, the Cold War, and Radical Politics in the United States*, which reconstructs the role of the Left in shaping the field of children's literature in the United States; and *Tales for Little Rebels: A Collection of Radical Children's Literature*, coedited by Mickenberg and Nel, which makes some of this radical literature available again.

Yet Marxist approaches to the study of literature continue to be poorly understood and marginalized relative to other theoretical traditions. For example, *The Routledge Companion to Children's Literature*, edited by David Rudd, includes no entry for Marx in the "Names and Terms" section, although entries for Sigmund Freud, Carl Jung, and Judith Butler *are* included. An entry for Fredric Jameson references an undefined "Marxism" as his theoretical framework, and the entry for Jack Zipes credits him with introducing the area of folk and fairy tales to the "critical approaches" of the Frankfurt School, without identifying its Marxist foundations. Rudd is not unique, and the result is that while graduate students are well grounded in poststructuralist, postcolonial, psychoanalytic, feminist, and queer approaches to literature, they generally have no idea what a historical materialist or Marxist approach would even be.

The lack of knowledge about historical materialism is in part due to the predominance of poststructuralist, or more broadly postmodernist, theory within the study of literature. Poststructuralist/postmodernist and historical materialist theories conflict in several fundamental ways, as Rudd's comments in his essay in *Owners of the Means of Instruction?* make clear.[3] Rudd takes Marxism to task for a belief in "some unproblematic 'real world' discernible outside ideology. Clearly, the main difference with writers more influenced by postmodernism is that the latter query our access to this bedrock of the real, which is—of course—to query Marxism's hold on the historical pulse, its millenarian trajectory" (44). Despite a number of questionable assumptions, Rudd accurately points to the radically opposed epistemological and ontological premises of Marxism and poststructuralism. Poststructuralism is antirealist, arguing that we must reject the goal of apprehending reality. Reality, the poststructuralist argues, cannot be known—Jane Flax, for example, says: "Perhaps reality can have 'a' structure only from the falsely universalizing perspective of the dominant group" (634).

Historical materialism, however, in its rejection of idealism, is realist. Like poststructuralism, historical materialism rejects positivism; unlike poststructuralism, it seeks to understand social reality as a totality, however difficult that prospect might be. Within the social sciences and philosophy, post-positivist realism and critical realism investigate these possibilities. Justin Cruickshank writes: "Critical realists argue that the self can obtain knowledge of a reality that is separate from our representations of it. This does not mean we have a direct access to a manifest truth, but instead it means that we have access to reality via fallible theories. This view of knowledge holds that there is an objective reality, and instead of hoping that one day we will somehow have absolute knowledge, the expectation is that knowledge claims will continue to be better interpretations of reality. As knowledge claims are fallible, the best we can do is improve our interpretations of reality, rather than seek a definitive, finished 'Truth'" (1–2). This rich body of scholarship and theory, however, is virtually unknown within literary and cultural studies—outside of those working in historical materialist traditions. As Lourdes Benería points out, while poststructuralists have focused on language, identity, and subjectivity, "these tendencies have run parallel, on the material side of everyday life, to the resurgence of neoliberalism across countries and to the globalization of markets and of social and cultural life—generating rapid changes that need to be understood and acted upon. Yet a good portion of postmodern analyses have tended to neglect the dynamics of political economy thus deemphasizing important areas of social concern having to do with the material and more concretely, the economic" (25–26). As Fredric Jameson has argued, as market capitalism has given way to monopoly and now late capitalism, it has become increasingly difficult for individuals to grasp the way that "economic and social form . . . governs . . . experience" (349). However, he argues, the work of art, because it might enable perception of the totality of social reality, can help to span the gap between "essence and appearance, structure and lived experience"

(349). Historical materialism is committed to a view of reality in which spanning this gap is possible, however provisionally and laboriously.

Eschewing the notion of totality, poststructuralists direct attention exclusively to the discursive construction of identity and the politics of difference. Clearly, a theoretical model focused on discourse is well suited to the analysis of literature. Poststructuralists, however, often go beyond the narrowly literary to make claims about the political or even revolutionary significance of literature and theory. But while the discursive is undoubtedly part of the greater social totality, it is only a part, and must be understood in relation to the nondiscursive relations and dynamics characteristic of the parts of social reality that, while they may be discursively mediated, cannot be thoroughly—or even adequately—understood in purely discursive terms. Accounts of subjectivity, identity, sexuality, and race—to say nothing of class—that fail to analyze the way in which they are embedded in material and historical structures are inadequate. While poststructuralism is often promoted as uniquely able to discuss issues of difference, feminist historical materialism addresses gender in intersection with class and race.

But if there is a dearth of historical materialist criticism of children's literature, there is even less a feminist criticism of children's literature that is historical materialist in approach. As in literary criticism in general, the reign of poststructuralism over other theoretical perspectives results in a feminist criticism that is often strangely divorced from historical and political reality, given the origins of feminist theory in political movements. This lack of attention to the material is evident in the scholarship of some of the foremost feminist critics of children's literature. Christine Wilkie-Stibbs, for example, author of *The Feminine Subject in Children's Literature*, notes that French feminism, which provides the theoretical framework for her analysis, has been criticized as ahistorical and apolitical, but her appropriation of this tradition does little to illuminate the relationship between history and subjectivity. It is important, however, to maintain the difference between changing subjectivity and changing society. Bronwyn Davies also fails to make this distinction in her *Frogs and Snails and Feminist Tales*. While this book is significant in its rejection of sex role theory as a viable framework for feminist criticism, insisting that children's agency must be accounted for in understanding how they respond to the way in which gender is represented in literature, Davies collapses the difference between changing discourse and changing reality. She persuasively argues that children might learn the ways in which gender is discursively constructed and calls upon readers to "change the world through a refusal of certain discourses and the generation of new ones" (62). Here, Davies is vulnerable to the criticism that Marx made of the Young Hegelians when he wrote: "As we hear from the German ideologists, Germany has in the last few years gone through an unparalleled revolution. . . . [I]n the general chaos mighty empires have arisen only to meet with immediate doom. . . . [A]nd in the three years 1842–45 more of the past was swept away in Germany than at other times in three centuries. All of this is supposed to have taken place in the realm of pure thought" (*German Ideology* 147). Changing ideas is often central to political projects, whether feminist or Marxist, conservative or revolutionary. It is, however, not sufficient: it is also critical to understand the relationship between ideas—or discourse—and material reality, which must also be analyzed. But as poststructuralism collapses the two and rejects the possibility of knowing reality, as a theory it is inadequate to this task.

Feminist Historical Materialism

Feminist historical materialism, however, offers a theoretical framework that accounts for discursive *and* material realities, subjectivity *and* politics. In addition to Zipes, several feminist historical materialist critics of children's literature merit mention. Lynn Vallone, in "'A Humble Spirit under Correction': Tracts, Hymns and the Ideology of Evangelical Fiction for Children, 1780–1820," analyzes the creation of a "class-and often gender-based literature by Hannah More, Anna Laetitia Barbauld, and Mary Martha Sherwood. These writers were concerned with issues considered to be 'feminine': religion, home and family" (73). Vallone shows the ways in which these writers undertook "a vigorously ideological program of social control" (74) in didactic writing that encourages female working-class readers to identity, for example in More's tracts, with Betty Brown, a character whose obedience to a wealthy woman is rewarded with "material and personal success" in a marriage to "a good man of her own class" (81). J. S. Bratton's "British Imperialism and the Reproduction of Femininity in Girls' Fiction, 1900–1930" examines the seeming conflict in the functions ascribed to females by British imperialism as it was reflected in fiction for girls. On the one hand, women were expected to "contribute to the preservation, perpetuation and enhancement of the race, both physically and spiritually" (Mackay and Thorne, qtd. in Bratton). On the other, women's own demands for greater freedoms, combined with the rigors of life in a colonial setting, called for "greater activity and independence" (197). Bratton analyzes stories from *The Girls' Empire, The Girl Guides' Gazette*, and Girl Guide fiction, concluding: "[I]ncorporating the modern girl's demand for self-determination, for a wider field in which to develop and to excel, it [this fiction] maintains the essential feminine value of instrumentality and subordination" (214). Vallone's and Bratton's analyses show that the discursive construction of gender must be understood in relation to material social reality.

My own historical materialist, feminist critical practice has critiqued the liberal feminist orientation of much feminist children's literature, an orientation that is reflected in the individualistic character of much of that fiction—ranging from series fiction to Newbery winners—which suggests that sexism is the result of ignorance and prejudice that can be transcended by hardworking, spirited girls. All too often, such novels fail to show the ways in which ideologies of gender are related to social institutions—economic, political, legal, religious, familial, and sexual—which must be transformed to liberate women and girls.[4] Thus, despite significant differences between liberal and poststructuralist feminism, each are in their own way idealist: liberal feminism in the view that simply by eliminating bad ideas sexism can be eradicated, and poststructuralism in suggesting that changes in discourse should be the focus of feminist effort. However, some literature for children represents the ways in which ideologies of gender, race, and class justify material inequality, and although these ideologies have developed historically, they are also historically alterable.[5]

Historical Materialist Analyses of Children's Literature: New Contributions

This volume's contribution to the development of historical materialist approaches to children's literature begins with Mervyn Nicholson's "Class/ic Aggression in Children's Literature." Nicholson argues that children's literature often appears to be remote from the themes of Marxian analysis such as class struggle, inequality, and immiserization; children, rather, seem to inhabit a zone of innocence where kings and queens are not the kings and queens of history but figures in a fantasy domain independent of historical reality. Nicholson shows, however, that in many of the great texts of what might be called the "golden age" of children's literature—such as *Alice in Wonderland, Treasure Island, The Railway Children*, and *The Wind in the Willows*—while class struggle is not named, it is represented by ways of speaking and acting that express its underlying social reality. Another important concept in historical materialism, commodification, or the process by which everything—from nature to emotion to human beings to works of art—is reduced to an item that can be sold, is central to Anastasia Ulanowicz's analysis of the ways that the Gossip Girl series and its television spin-off offer the illusion that by purchasing the proper commodity, the "aspirational longing" of readers can be satisfied. In "Precious Medals: The Newbery Medal, the YRCA, and the Gold Standard of Children's Book Awards," Carl Miller analyzes the book as commodity and the role of children's literature in terms of Pierre Bourdieu's and John Guillory's concepts of cultural capital and social stratification.

Several essays argue that texts that appear to be progressive in fact offer hegemonic views of their subject matter. In "'We Are All One': Money, Magic, and Mysticism in *Mary Poppins*," Sharon Smulders argues that while the working-class Mary Poppins seems to triumph over the bourgeois Banks family at the same time that she schools them in Eastern philosophical truths, ultimately the most significant work done by the novel is to reconcile consumerism to antimaterialist belief. Cynthia McLeod analyzes novels that represent the labor movement in the United States in "Solidarity of Times Past: Historicizing the Labor Movement in American Children's Novels" and finds that recent union activism is portrayed in a less favorable light than that of the distant past. The way in which recent labor activism is represented suggests that the decline of the labor movement is due to bullying and violence on the part of unions, or to the success of a postindustrial economy. Daniel Hade and Heidi Brush argue that the picture books of Eve Bunting, while they appear to champion social justice, offer a similarly hegemonic view of poverty and labor. Although the first-person narration of books like *Fly Away Home* implies that the perspective is that of the working class, it is actually a middle-class one, echoing the sentiment of nineteenth-century reform literature.

A number of the essays in this collection participate in the construction of a radical cultural and literary history. In "*The Young Socialist*: A Magazine of Justice and Love (1901–1926)," Jane Rosen analyzes the way in which this magazine, published by the Socialist Sunday School movement, provided an alternative to the jingoist imperialism that characterized British children's literature at the time and sought to shape a future socialist society. Jana Mikota's "Girls' Literature by German Writers in Exile (1933–1945)" discusses novels by German writers who sought to produce an antifascist literature that challenged the authoritarian values promoted by

National Socialism, including the rigidly prescriptive gender roles imposed by the Nazis. Naomi Wood discusses the children's literature published by Anveshi, a women's collective in India that contests the marginalization of low-caste, poor Indian children within the educational system, particularly by producing children's literature that offers a corrective to the ideal child typically represented in Indian children's literature. These books represent Dalit and Muslim children not as objects of pity but as models of resistance. Ian Wojcik-Andrews seeks to restore multicultural children's films to film history in his essay "A Multicultural History of Children's Films," arguing that they reflect class struggle as well as economic and racial discrimination, which are often elided in Hollywood films.

As Zipes does in analyzing the revolutionary capacity of the fairy tale, several essays rely upon the philosophical work of Ernst Bloch. Although Ruth Bottigheimer has convincingly argued that children's Bibles, among the first examples of children's literature, reproduced hierarchical class relations, in "Bloodthirsty Little Brats; or, The Child's Desire for Biblical Violence," Roland Boer argues that "moralizing tales of goodness and obedience" are far less popular with children than the more violent tale of David and Goliath and others that are less well known but that also show the triumph of the smaller and weaker against a stronger oppressor. In "Utopia and Anti-Utopia in Lois Lowry's and Suzanne Collins's Dystopian Fiction," I argue that while Lowry's and Collins's series are similar generically, the world views informing them are radically different. Lowry aligns herself with the forces of anti-utopia, depicting efforts to create a utopian society as incapable of accommodating individual desire, and inevitably failing due to the limitations of human nature. Lowry's Cold War–era skepticism about radical efforts to improve society is shaped by her sense of the shortcomings of the French and Russian Revolutions; and while Collins's representation of the dangers of revolutionary societies demonstrates that she too is mindful of the real precedents to her fictional utopia, she recognizes that people are driven to change the world and remains hopeful that human, collective efforts can create a just society. The utopian is also the focus of Justyna Deszcz-Tryhubczak's "Ursula Le Guin's *Powers* as Radical Fantasy." Deszcz-Tryhubczak argues that Le Guin's novel also responds to the failures of previous revolutionary efforts: although the slave boy Gavir, the protagonist, rejects "faulty forms of collective resistance" as they prove to be "authoritarian and oppressive," he learns that a "better world" founded upon solidarity and mutual aid can be achieved through individual and social change.

Conclusion

A historical materialist methodology is especially critical in the analysis of children's literature, as children often suffer most from the inequalities that capitalism creates. Responding to this situation, some of the historical materialist critics of children's literature in this collection reveal the ways that literature for children has too often functioned to bolster the oppressions of capitalism, while others champion literature that provides readers with an understanding of the construction of social reality, as well as that which might enable an understanding of the role that individuals and groups have and might play in creating a more just future. The project in which these writers and critics are engaged is vital, because children need the vision, hope, and knowledge it affords. In addressing this need, the critics in this anthology, like many of those who take up Marx's historical materialist methodology, reveal their commitment to the project of justice and human liberation. In this they join Marx, whose analysis of political economy was not disinterested—although it was conducted with the highest regard for science; indeed, as he wrote, "the philosophers have only interpreted the world, in various ways; the point, however, is to change it" ("Theses on Feuerbach" 145). As the socialist, lesbian, feminist poet Adrienne Rich wrote,

> *My heart is moved by all I cannot save*
> *So much has been destroyed*
> *I have to cast my lot with those*
> *Who age after age, perversely,*
> *With no extraordinary power,*
> *Reconstitute the world. (264)*

ACKNOWLEDGMENTS

This introduction was greatly improved by the suggestions and editing of Tim Dayton, Michele Janette, and Naomi Wood. Naomi and Tim also assisted with the selection of essays for the collection. Our anonymous reviewer at University Press of Mississippi offered many helpful suggestions about the collection as a whole, as did members of the Publications Committee of the Children's Literature Association. We are very grateful as well to Norman Ware, our copyeditor, who is extraordinarily careful and clever.

NOTES

1. "Historical materialist," "Marxist," and "Marxian" are terms that are commonly used interchangeably (see, for example, the title of the journal *Historical Materialism: Research in Critical Marxist Theory*), and that will be the case in this collection as well. However, "historical materialist" refers specifically to the methods of analysis originated by Marx and Engels and employed by those who follow in the tradition they initiated. "Marxian" typically also refers to the academic applications of Marx's thought, while "Marxist" *may* sometimes have a more narrowly political connotation. I could go on, but for the purposes of this introduction, this brief clarification should be adequate.

2. Williams's *Marxism and Literature* is an excellent introduction to key concepts in historical materialist literary and cultural criticism, as it includes short chapters on literature, ideology, base and superstructure, and other topics.

3. The more established position of historical materialism in Great Britain is suggested by this collection, the proceedings from a 2006 conference on Marxist perspectives in children's literature held at the University of Hertfordshire. The collection includes a useful introductory essay by Michael Rosen on the relevance of Marxist concepts to the analysis of children's literature.

4. For a fuller discussion of this in one of the Sweet Valley Twins series books, see my essay, "Beyond the Image: Adolescent Girls, Reading and Social Reality."

5. In "Girl Power and History in the Dear America Series Books," I analyze a number of titles from the series that reflect liberal feminist views as well as a number that offer a materialist analysis of oppression based on sex, race, and class, and the way in which these are interdependent.

WORKS CITED

Althusser, Louis. *For Marx*. Translated by Ben Brewster. London: Verso, 2005. Print.

Benería, Lourdes. *Gender, Development, and Globalization: Economics as if All People Mattered*. New York: Routledge, 2003. Print.

Booker, M. Keith. *A Practical Introduction to Literary Theory and Criticism*. White Plains, N.Y.: Longman, 1996. Print.

Bratton, J. S. "British Imperialism and the Reproduction of Femininity in Girls' Fiction, 1900–1930." In *Imperialism and Juvenile Literature*, edited by Jeffrey Richards, 195–215. Manchester: Manchester University Press, 1989. Print.

Cherland, Meredith Rogers. *Private Practices: Girls Reading Fiction and Constructing Identity*. London: Taylor & Francis, 1994. Print.

Cruickshank, Justin. Introduction to *Critical Realism: The Difference It Makes*, edited by Justin Cruickshank, 1–14. London: Routledge, 2003. Print.

Davies, Bronwyn. *Frogs and Snails and Feminist Tales: Preschool Children and Gender*. Sydney: Allen & Unwin, 1989. Print.

DeNavas-Walt, Carmen, Bernadette D. Proctor, and Jessica C. Smith. *Income, Poverty, and Health Insurance in the United States: 2011.* United States Census Bureau, September 2012. Accessed January 10, 2013. Website.

Dixon, Bob. *Catching Them Young 1: Sex, Race and Class in Children's Fiction.* London: Pluto Press, 1977. Print.

Dorfman, Ariel. *The Empire's Old Clothes: What the Lone Ranger, Babar, and Other Innocent Heroes Do to Our Minds.* New York: Pantheon, 1983. Print.

Flax, Jane. "Postmodernism and Gender Relations in Feminist Theory." *Journal of Women in Culture and Society* 12:4 (1987): 641–643. Print.

Harvey, David. *A Brief History of Neoliberalism.* New York: Oxford University Press, 2005. Print.

———. *A Companion to Marx's "Capital."* London: Verso, 2010. Print.

Hubler, Angela. "Beyond the Image: Adolescent Girls, Reading and Social Reality." *NWSA Journal* 12:1 (2000): 84–99. Print.

———. "Girl Power and History in the Dear America Series Books." *Children's Literature Association Quarterly* 25:2 (2000): 98–106. Print.

Isaacs, Julia B., Isabel V. Sawhill, and Ron Haskins. "Getting Ahead or Losing Ground: Economic Mobility in America." Pew Center on the States, February 2008. Accessed June 27, 2012. Website.

Jameson, Fredric. "Cognitive Mapping." In *Marxism and the Interpretation of Culture*, edited by Lawrence Grossberg and Cary Nelson, 347–360. Chicago: University of Chicago Press, 1988. Print.

Kohl, Herbert. *Should We Burn Babar? Essays on Children's Literature and the Power of Stories.* New York: New Press, 1995. Print.

Marx, Karl. *The German Ideology.* In *The Marx-Engels Reader*, 2nd ed., edited by Robert C. Tucker, 146–200. New York: W. W. Norton, 1978. Print.

———. "Theses on Feuerbach." In *The Marx-Engels Reader*, 2nd ed., edited by Robert C. Tucker, 143–145. New York: W. W. Norton, 1978. Print.

McKissack, Patricia C. *Ma Dear's Aprons.* New York: Simon & Schuster, 1997. Print.

Mickenberg, Julia L. *Learning from the Left: Children's Literature, the Cold War, and Radical Politics in the United States.* New York: Oxford University Press, 2006. Print.

Mickenberg, Julia, and Philip Nel, eds. "Children's Literature and the Left." Special issue, *Children's Literature Association Quarterly* 30:4 (2005). Print.

———, eds. *Tales for Little Rebels: A Collection of Radical Children's Literature.* New York: New York University Press, 2008. Print.

Rich, Adrienne. "Natural Resources." In *The Fact of a Doorframe.* New York: W. W. Norton, 1984. Print.

Richards, Jeffrey. *Imperialism and Juvenile Literature.* Manchester: Manchester University Press, 1989. Print.

Rudd, David. "On Your Marks with Spit Nolan: Childhood Ideology and Taking Fantasy Seriously. In *Owners of the Means of Instruction? Children's Literature: Some Marxist Perspectives*, edited by Jenny Plastow, 39–54. Hatfield: University of Hertfordshire Press, 2007. Print.

————. *The Routledge Companion to Children's Literature*. London: Routledge, 2010. Print.

Taxel, Joel. "Children's Literature at the Turn of the Century." *Research in the Teaching of English* 37 (2002): 145–197. Print.

Terkel, Amanda. "Eric Cantor on Occupy Wall Street: I'm Upset Democrats are 'Joining in the Effort to Blame Others.'" *Huffington Post*, October 16, 2011. Accessed January 11, 2013. Website.

Tucker, Robert C. Headnote to "Preface to *A Contribution to the Critique of Political Economy*" by Karl Marx. In *The Marx-Engels Reader*, 2nd ed., edited by Robert C. Tucker, 3–11. New York: W. W. Norton, 1978. Print.

Vallone, Lynn. "'A Humble Spirit under Correction': Tracts, Hymns and the Ideology of Evangelical Fiction for Children, 1780–1820." *The Lion and the Unicorn* 15 (1991): 72–95. Print.

Wilkie-Stibbs, Christine. *The Feminine Subject in Children's Literature*. New York: Routledge, 2002. Print.

Williams, Juan. "Obama's Class Warfare Strategy Is Working with Americans." Fox News. com, October 4, 2011. Accessed January 11, 2013. Website.

Williams, Raymond. *Keywords: A Vocabulary of Culture and Society*. Rev. ed. New York: Oxford University Press, 1983. Print.

————. *Marxism and Literature*. Bath: Oxford University Press, 1977. Print.

————. *The Politics of Modernism*. London: Verso, 1989. Print.

Wojcik-Andrews, Ian. "Introduction: Notes toward a Theory of Class in Children's Literature." *The Lion and the Unicorn* 17 (1993): 113–123. Print.

Zipes, Jack. *Breaking the Magic Spell: Radical Theories of Folk and Fairy Tales*. Rev. ed. Lexington: University Press of Kentucky, 2002. Print.

————. *Fairy Tales and the Art of Subversion: The Classical Genre for Children and the Process of Civilization*. London: Heinemann, 1983. Print.

Little Red Readings

Class/ic Aggression in Children's Literature

MERVYN NICHOLSON

Is the child to be considered as an individuality, or as an object to be moulded?
EMMA GOLDMAN[1]

In her little-noticed essay "The Child and Its Enemies," Emma Goldman examined the position of children in capitalist society. "Must not one suppose that parents should be united to children by the most tender and delicate chords?" she asks (135). Isn't it obvious that parents love their children? This is no rhetorical question, as Goldman's answer indicates: "One should suppose it: yet, sad as it may be, it is, nevertheless, true, that parents are the first to destroy the inner riches of their children" (135). How can this be? For Goldman, it is the *negative* attitude, where hurting children is often visualized as helping them, that requires attention, the attitude that children are lesser beings and therefore can be, like other lesser beings, owned.

Capitalism is inherently hostile toward children, as the extent of child poverty makes plain, but this hostility cannot be acknowledged without arousing deep prejudices. This is the theme of Elisabeth Young-Bruehl's *Childism: Confronting Prejudice against Children*. She defines childism as "a prejudice against children on the ground of a belief that they are property, and can (or even should) be controlled, enslaved, or removed to serve adult needs" (37). Young-Bruehl's approach is that of a psychoanalyst and social democrat, but her argument is suggestive for class analysis. Contrary to the common notion that children are indulged, she argues that children are the object of a deep-seated hostility manifest in their actual treatment/ mistreatment/neglect. The key is the concept of "childism" itself: a prejudice that coheres with other forms of prejudice such as racism or homophobia.

3

Young-Bruehl is the kind of thinker who makes us see something that is everywhere yet invisible: something that surrounds us and yet is strangely difficult to perceive. The reason why it is hard to see, despite being plainly evident, is that it is a central area of social conditioning: the refusal to see what is, as it were, obvious. We are conditioned to ignore what we actually know.

From a left perspective, the most important of these ignored but obvious facts is the class nature of society. There are two fundamental classes: one class derives its income from owning, and the other survives by selling its labor. Most work—a few own. A few command—many obey. Those who own derive their income from those who work, from exploitation, which is, above all, *unequal exchange*. What the worker gives is more than what the worker receives. No capitalist is going to hire someone unless the value of what the employee produces is worth more than the wages paid to that employee. Wages are thus paid out of what the worker produces, leaving a surplus for the capitalist, a surplus that takes the form of profit. Capital reinvests this surplus and expands the process of accumulation. Hence unpaid labor is the motor of capitalism.

According to Young-Bruehl, children are understood as "property": they are *owned* by others, and, since they are owned, their needs are subordinate to owners, even though the needs of children ought to come first. In terms of class analysis, there is a curious parallel between the relation of children to adults and the relation of wage labor to the owners of capital. They are not the same but there are significant parallels. Children are not in the technical sense members of the working class, even if their parents are: that is, they are not among those who sell their labor to the owners of capital, owners who in turn capitalize the products of that labor. Unlike the working class—those who sell their labor—children do not produce surplus value. Of course, children do indeed produce surplus value for owners in many countries, including rich ones, in the form of "child labor." But such labor is typically outlawed or restricted, and children are regarded as outside the process of capital accumulation.

In fact, children are viewed not just as outside the circle of labor and capital—but somehow *outside society*. Therefore they must be "trained" to conform. This assumption may be absurd—children are part of society from conception—but irrational assumptions often dominate the way people think, and, as so often with targets of prejudice, children are either idealized or demonized. The child is "Other." The child must be tamed, must be "assimilated," adapted to the real world, the world of adults, of parents. Children do not "become" adults: they must be shaped.

The belief that children must be tamed, reconstructed, is built into traditional Christianity. The central Christian belief is that human beings are fallen. The condition of fallenness is essentially disobedience, caused by the disobedience of Adam and Eve, who originated a rebellion against authority. Hence obedience must be restored: children must be forced to obey. Such forcing is physical and emotional, with an emphasis on hitting and humiliating children in order to force them to do what they are told, as in the formulation of obedience made familiar by the quaint language of King James: to "honor thy father and mother"—a rule so essential as to warrant inclusion on the supreme list of rules known as the Ten Commandments.[2] Beating children beats the devil out of them; hitting them is good for children. Submission is the law of God, and it is a law because children are not naturally obedient but rebellious. The long history of feudalism reinforced these beliefs. But the secular culture that developed under capitalism retained many of the same attitudes. For instance, William Bagley, an education guru popular in the "golden age" of children's literature, wrote an influential textbook for teachers titled *Classroom Management*: "One who studies educational theory aright can see in the mechanical routine of the classroom the educative forces that are slowly transforming the child from a little savage into a creature of law and order, fit for the life of civilized society."[3] Bagley's display of childism is couched in imperial, pseudoscientific rhetoric: "little savage," "creature," "law and order," "fit," "civilized society."[4] Children are outside of "civilization"; they are "wild," like animals.

The conception of childhood began a far-reaching transformation during the Enlightenment, a change toward what Lawrence Stone calls "affective individualism," especially for rich parents who could afford to do without the labor of their children. The argument identified with Jean-Jacques Rousseau that children must be allowed to develop freely became influential.[5] Nevertheless, the notion that children are somehow "outside" society persists, even if manifested in a more liberal form than the Christian obsession with hitting and forcing children. Thus, children, children's literature, and imagination itself occupy a zone outside the "real" world, much as J. M. Barrie's "Neverland" or Lewis Carroll's "Wonderland" (a dream) are outside reality. The real world is what adults have; an unreal zone is what children have. Adults are real people; children are sub-real.

This brings us back to the parallel referred to earlier (child:adult::worker:capitalist). In capitalist society, the ruling class are fully adult; the working class are like children. One group is "real"—the other is not "real." That is, one group understands and is in control. The other group is ignorant, refuses to understand, must be controlled, indeed must be *forced*. One group can be trusted—the other cannot. As Paul Baran and Paul Sweezy put it in *Monopoly Capital*, capital insists that "the wealth and privileges of the few are based on natural, inborn superiority" (315). One group, superior to the other, is in touch with reality—the other, inferior group is not; and the one that is not must be conditioned to learn what reality is. Profits always come first.

The demands of capital accumulation shape all important decisions in society. Every form of authority must be assimilated by capital in order to enhance its power. Any relationship where power is exercised must become an adjunct of capital, including authority of parents over children. The sine qua non of capital accumulation is obedience; therefore, the primary function for parents is the inculcation of obedience. Many labor—a few own. Many obey—a few command. Obedience must be forced when it is not voluntary: this is the basis of what is termed "class struggle."

In what follows I focus on these concerns in children's literature, especially the classics of the "golden age" of children's literature, texts with enormous influence—and which look different when approached from the point of view of class struggle. The period in question is also the period of capitalism as it attains its modern form of giant corporations and imperial domination, the zenith of the European empires and the emergence of the United States as a world power: the opening of the period of what Baran and Sweezy term "monopoly capital." This "golden age" of children's literature cannot be given exact dates, but say roughly from *Alice in Wonderland* to *The Wind in the Willows*, or stretching it a bit, to the publication of *Winnie-the-Pooh* and *The Hobbit*, a period when an amazing number of important books for children appears, when the market for children's writing expands enormously, and when the very conception of "children's literature"—of writing specifically for children—becomes familiar, especially in the form of writing intended to entertain, and not for didactic purposes, in the context of a mass market. The period setting itself, often "an Edwardian world that suggests unlimited comfort and wealth," as Lori Kenschaft puts it (233)—has reinforced associations with an idealized world independent of the workaday reality.

The shift from the didacticism to entertainment is made explicit by L. Frank Baum, especially in the brief manifesto that introduces *The Wizard of Oz*. Baum explains that, nowadays, writing for children is for entertaining children and making them happy, *not* for teaching lessons. It should not frighten children, he states—an important caveat, since, as Baum knew, frightening people is the standard means of controlling people. His point is illustrated by that cute little dog that everybody loves: Toto. Toto, probably the most famous dog in children's literature, is emphatically not a working dog—he is there to play. He is there explicitly to make Dorothy happy. Dorothy herself does not appear to work, either, interestingly, even though her aunt and uncle are practically destitute. Baum emphasizes the desolation of their farm: survival requires incessant dawn-to-dark labor by the prematurely aged farmer and his wife. Toto may well be the first dog to appear in children's literature that is not a working dog; he is certainly the first nonworking dog to occupy such an important position in the plot of the story. Until about the time of *Wizard*, dogs existed in order to work. *The Bremen Town Musicians*, one of the Grimm Brothers' tales, makes the point dramatically clear. As soon as the dog in the story is incapable of working, he is turned out to starve: a nonworking animal is worthless and *should* be dead, as far as earlier culture is concerned.[6] Dogs were not intended for entertaining anybody—apart from the revealing exception of "lap dogs," the property of the wealthy, and hunting dogs kept by the powerful for "sport," a pastime reserved for the leisure class (hence the brutal laws against poaching). Few could afford to keep dogs for nonworking purposes.[7]

Carlo Collodi's great book, *Pinocchio*, illustrates. In *Pinocchio*, dogs *work*, and there are at least two of these work dogs. One, the noble Alidoro, definitely works for his living; if he doesn't work, he doesn't eat (the same lesson constantly drilled into Pinocchio: work, don't play). Alidoro's survival depends upon producing, in effect, surplus value: producing more than the necessities given him in order for survival. This is the "iron law of wages," according to classical economics: wage-labor must be paid no more than what it needs to reproduce itself. In an act of worker solidarity, Alidoro later saves Pinocchio. From the point of view of capital, the working class are indeed work animals and are to be regarded in a similar light. The metaphorical equation here is that working class = animals = children = not fully human = outside reality = must be forced.

The prominence of animals in children's stories of the period is not merely a matter of fantasy but a reminder that children are thought of as in a category not so different from animals. Baum's Toto signals a new era in the social attitude not merely toward dogs, who are to become household "pets," but toward children, too: children are there to play, not to work. They are to be consumers, not producers. Toto is arguably the true hero of *The Wizard of Oz*. Not only does he comfort and sustain Dorothy emotionally—and intimidate the wicked witch—but he uncovers the crucial secret that the "wizard" who rules the metropolis is a con artist; his power is based on manipulating illusory appearances. Thus, ironically, Toto *does* work, but not by obeying an owner: his work is creative and voluntary, work that offers liberation and a better life. This is a different conception of work, and of leisure: it is work that one wants to do and that brings about a better life, not work that is forced and appropriated by others for their benefit and not for the benefit of the worker. Toto is a subversive.

The most revealing text here is also the most famous, *Alice in Wonderland*. For most readers—let us exclude mathematicians and philosophers— *Alice* is fun fantasy, enjoyed by children and adults who appreciate imagination, as though imagination had little to do with social relations and was a private, individual affair, like a dream (*Alice* is, after all, formally "a dream"). But then one notices the "Frog-Footman," with his staring blank eyes, whom Alice meets installed at the entrance to the Ugly Duchess's house, sitting on the ground near the door, "staring stupidly up into the sky."[8]

This footman informs Alice—in fact he speaks to the air as if he could not tell the difference between Alice and vacancy—that he is in effect part of the entranceway, and nothing more: "'I shall sit here,' the Footman remarked, 'till tomorrow . . . or next day, maybe,' the Footman continued in the same tone, exactly as if nothing had happened." (A plate has just been hurled at him, which he pays no attention to: "At this moment the door of the house opened, and a large plate came skimming out, straight at the Footman's head: it just grazed his nose, and broke to pieces against one of the trees behind him.") He sees himself as "stationed" no differently from the equally stationed doorstep and entranceway; he and an inert object fashioned for the use of others are functionally identical. He is conditioned not to notice the bizarre behavior, including the violence, of his owners, as one instinctively calls his "employers." When Alice asks again, "'How am I to get in?'" the Footman "seemed to think this a good opportunity for repeating his remark, with variations. 'I shall sit here,' he said, 'on and off, for days and days'" (344). Not only is he a machine, he *knows* he is a machine. It is not an accident that he is both a "footman" and a "frog," because that is what footmen, real footmen, become: frogs. That is, they are humans who become subhuman. They are alienated.

The footman is not an exception. He is not the only worker in Wonderland who is depicted as an animal, indeed as a reptile, fish, frog—not even a mammal: the Fish-Footman who hands the invitation card to the Frog-Footman is another. Much more conspicuous than either of these footmen is the hapless workman Bill (a lizard), who appears earlier in the story, complete with working-class accent (a working-class Irish accent in the animated Disney version). The scene of the footman at the door of the Duchess's house is, like other brief scenes in this classic text, charged with significance. The nameless Frog-Footman could be an illustration for *Labor and Monopoly Capital*, Harry Braverman's pathbreaking study of the degradation of work under monopoly capital: the dehumanization of people under constant pressure to transform work into meaningless drudgery, a "dull and hideous existence" in Goldman's phrase, because mechanical drudgery (especially if performed by children) is cheaper.[9] The awareness that capitalism degrades work and workers is already recognized by classical economists, notably by Adam Smith in *The Wealth of Nations*. The Frog-Footman in *Alice* is reduced to a frog by a job that is not only boring but inescapable. He cannot leave or move, and he is as "mad" (that is, he is as *damaged*) as other mad people are in *Alice*. As the Cheshire Cat tells Alice, "we're all mad here" (347).

The Frog-Footman is like the enslaved machine-creatures of *Flintstones* cartoons, who furnish much of the interest of that famous TV show. These creatures voice pathetic complaints in the brief asides that they are allowed. Or, in more highbrow terms, he is like Bartleby in Herman Melville's "Bartleby, the Scrivener: A Story of Wall Street." Bartleby is a human Xerox machine, a scrivener in a Wall Street law office. Like the Frog-Footman, Bartleby is a human machine, except that, unlike machines, he is conscious. Consequently, he must cope with—and struggle against—enslavement.[10] The people of Wonderland aren't mad—they are damaged by a social order that is mad, by what Harry Braverman terms "a generalized social insanity" (63).[11]

What the footman makes plain is that we need to reconsider Wonderland in the light of class conflict. Take the interesting scene in which Alice is cast in the role of worker. She has survived the "caucus race" in chapter 4, when the White Rabbit, who earlier incited her curiosity so much that she followed him into Wonderland in the first place, reappears. This time he is looking for something he has forgotten, his gloves. He is as preoccupied with these class accoutrements as he is with his famous timepiece at the beginning of the story. Absorbed in his personal needs, he is oblivious to others; that is, until, of course, he wants to use others. Until then, subordinates are invisible. Actually, they are invisible to him *afterward*, too: "Very soon the Rabbit noticed Alice . . . and called out to her in an angry tone, 'Why, Mary Ann, what *are* you doing out here? Run home this moment, and fetch me a pair of gloves and a fan! Quick, now!' And Alice was so much frightened that she ran off at once in the direction it pointed to, without trying to explain the mistake it had made" (336). The White Rabbit has mistaken Alice for his servant, "Mary Ann." Mary Ann is not where she is required to be; she is not at her station; she has disobeyed and must be disciplined. To the White Rabbit, an elite official, working people are all the same. They are "invisible" in that they are interchangeable with one another. Hence the playing-card soldiers later in Wonderland, differentiated only by the numbers on their back. One is the same as another. Only "face cards" matter—the rulers. The rest are not really people, individual beings with actual identities, apart from their assigned "number." They "look" identical because their *function* is identical. Hence, when he sees Alice, the White Rabbit sees "Mary Ann," i.e., a generic worker he "employs," i.e., *uses*. He doesn't notice that she is not Mary Ann at all, but someone different. In the unlikely case that they should indeed happen to look different, that fact is immaterial and unworthy of notice. There are lots more where they come from. The disdain and contempt of the powerful for those with no power permeates Wonderland.

Not only does the White Rabbit not notice who Alice is but he treats her with angry disrespect, in the manner of those who buy the labor of others and who, now "owning" that labor, feel free to make demands, indeed to be verbally abusive. He owns her time, after all; that is, he owns her life. Alice is already conditioned to obedience: she is so "frightened," the narrator observes, by this absurd authority figure, a rabbit, that she at once acts according to her conditioning—without thinking about it. She obeys. Alice does not even "try to explain the mistake it [the White Rabbit] had made," the narrator explains—no *trying*, even—because, after all, superiors by definition do not make mistakes.

In *Alice in Wonderland*, authority is based on coercion, not ability; this theme is conspicuous in the songs and poems that appear in the book, all of which are satires of familiar poems and songs. For instance, when Alice recites "Father William," a parody emerges that turns the authority father into a bossy ignoramus: what he really is, in other words, from the point of view of those subject to his power. Alice has been required to memorize poems such as Isaac Watts's "Against Idleness and Mischief," which features a worker bee as a model for children, with a reminder that her record will be evaluated and judged by the supreme authority, God, one day. When Alice tries to recite this poem, what she utters instead is a vision of a crocodile "gently smiling" as it "welcomes" "little fishes" into its digestive tract. Alice's conscious mind is fully conditioned; her unconscious but observant mind knows the actual truth. Some eat—others are eaten. Society is a system of predator and prey, those who own and those who produce. One astonishing moment in *Alice* is the celebration of child abuse in the "Pig and Pepper" chapter, where the Ugly Duchess and the Cook sing a song in praise of child abuse and claim that the baby they are "looking after" is crying because it enjoys causing annoyance to adults. Young-Bruehl's sardonic observation "that adults speak the truth while children lie to harm adults" comes to mind (207). Adults are by definition right—children wrong. Children hurt adults, not the other way around.

Alice has thus had two educations: one is the official education, focusing on conformity and rules, where "being good" is equated with obedience. The other is Alice's own education, derived from her own powers of observation. This teaches her that the powerful live by consuming the less powerful: a metaphoric statement of class aggression, and an insight as potent as one can find. Wonderland reveals truths about the "real" world that are silenced and made invisible. The pursuit of the White Rabbit at the outset is also a pursuit of the truth about the world Alice lives in. *Alice* is a profoundly radical book. In the final sequence, Alice confronts and overturns the injustice of the trial, and by extension the social order itself: loudly rejecting it as a travesty, Alice, a child, takes on the king, the queen, and their apparatus of terror, with its lies, manipulated rules, evidence that is irrelevant and meaningless—and obsession with punishment.[12] *Alice* presents actualities of the real world. It illustrates class struggle, but in a displaced form.

It is important to observe how work and workers are visualized. Class analysis is subtle and complex; it is not a mechanical application of a mechanical theory. It draws attention to features of the text that are typically ignored—features that are definitely there but that, for important reasons, are not noticed, thus enlarging our perception generally. In some ways, writing for children is the most appropriate kind of writing for such analysis because it is in childhood that we form our basic conceptions of how things work. Childhood is, therefore, subject to intense conditioning, conditioning that directs children to think and, above all, to act in certain ways and not in others: to see some things, but not other things. It inculcates what Northrop Frye called "adjustment mythology."

Class struggle, according to Marxian theory, is not occasional, like an election or a new moon. It is a continuous, continuing function, by which the owning class of society must constantly force or manipulate those who work to produce more and take less. This picture of society differs from that of neoclassical economics, in which everyone is paid according to his or her contribution, meritocratically as it were, and therefore automatically yielding a harmonious equilibrium by which everyone benefits and by which "class struggle" is reduced to a meaningless conception. But in Marxian analysis, this struggle is a basic, obvious reality: wage-labor must be constantly monitored and pressured if the goal of accumulating more than before is to be attained by the owners of capital. Competition between capitalists exercises an unceasing pressure to increase profits, even apart from the desire of the owning class to extract as much as possible from the system without concern for the consequences. Hence the owning class seeks any means to obtain more from the working class, from those, that is, who must sell their labor in order to buy back their existence.

Children's literature, no less than literature for adults, is shaped by class struggle, in particular by the values of those who are winners in that struggle. The ideas of the ruling class are the ruling ideas in society. Power is not simply physical force, the capacity to make people do what you want. Power also manifests itself in the form of the ideas people accept, the model of reality they work with, the images and thinking that are familiar to them and that they parrot as if they were expressing obvious, uncontested truths. Hence class struggle can be represented in at least two ways: explicitly and implicitly. First, literature can show characters receiving and resisting aggression—or directing and benefiting from that aggression—on the basis of their class position. This is not easy in stories for children; reflecting reality in so direct a way interferes with the happy endings children demand. But such themes are often present in the background.

For example, in George MacDonald's *At the Back of the North Wind*, the suffering of the working class is constantly implied. Where an oppressive struggle to survive is not easy to escape, it is not surprising to find the motif of "the magical exit," as it might be termed. In MacDonald, the "magical exit" is the trajectory of the plot: North Wind takes the little boy Diamond away to her paradise. The motif here recalls a similar use of the magical exit, provided by death, in stories like Hans Christian Andersen's "The Little Match Girl" or even Charles Kingsley's *The Water-Babies*. The child survives by dying, paradoxically, and death is better than living under such conditions. A more sophisticated version of this "magic exit" from hopeless deprivation appears in E. Nesbit's *Harding's Luck*, in which the protagonist travels back in time to a better life than what working-class London offers him.[13] Nesbit was a Fabian socialist and, like others of her progressive impulse, had a profound nostalgia for the Middle Ages and an idealized feudalism. Her intellectual forebear, William Morris, had the same idealized vision—feudalism purged of its poverty and exploitation but emphasizing community and mutual responsibility. The theme of exit from working-class poverty has intense power, but it is difficult to render convincingly. How do you present a child escaping poverty and attaining security and prosperity, and yet be truthful and realistic? One thinks of Dickens's *Oliver Twist* here in which one child escapes the fate that dooms other children because, first, a kind rich person helps him; and second, to reinforce that providential rescue, it turns out that he is actually related to that kind rich person and belongs to his family. This happy fate for Oliver is not that of other children in the story. A few escape—most do not.[14] It is a fairy tale dressed up in the conventions of realism.

In this context, Lucy Maud Montgomery's *Anne of Green Gables* comes into focus. Anne is not merely an orphan when we meet her, an abandoned child. She is already an exploited worker, doomed to a life of drudgery looking after other people's children, while still a child herself. It is only by a fluke that she is rescued from this fate. She is adopted by Marilla and Matthew: they originally wanted a boy, a boy who could, significantly, work for them on their farm—not a girl, since girls cannot provide the work boys can. At first, Marilla is determined to send Anne back to her prior existence as child-care worker, a deprived and impoverished child herself, a fate of impossible pathos. This background is touched by Anne herself—briefly but powerfully. Her dread and anguish over the drudgery she is escaping is one of the most memorable themes of the novel. Unwanted and orphan children, like the thousands of destitute children "exported" from England to Canada (the so-called home children), were often subjected to cruel exploitation. One begins to understand Anne's obsession with books and reading in a new way—her famous "imagination" and her determination to re-create life in the form of her reading. Far from being merely a whimsical eccentricity, a lovable impulse in an unusual child, imagination is Anne's "magic exit" from a miserable life of unrelenting labor—child labor to begin with, and later, as an adult, what would likely be an existence of poverty and marginalized labor.[15] The frequency of orphaned children in stories articulates a powerful fantasy that children should be treated well even though they are not.

Class struggle can be represented in a relatively open way, depicting one group forcing and manipulating another and thus acquiring benefits from the oppressed group. But there is a second, less direct means of representing class struggle, by *attitudes and situations* that express the underlying reality of class struggle without referring openly to that struggle. That is, class struggle is illustrated but not named. The values and practices taken for granted by class society are put on display, often satirically, but in such a manner as to make plain the cruelty and absurdity of these values and practices. It opens to inspection things that are so taken for granted as to be unconscious and undeserving of notice. Class struggle in this sense is aptly illustrated by the White Rabbit's bullying commands to his "servant"—and in another way, by his craven subservience to those who are more powerful in the hierarchy above him. He represents the "professional" class of society, often with aristocratic connections: the immediate servants of the ruling class, the lawyers, officers, high-level bureaucrats, and clerics. As a bureaucratic functionary, the White Rabbit serves the powerful, the King and Queen of Hearts. His terror at the thought of displeasing them is graphically portrayed in his anxiety about being late. The terror of being late is the first thing, as far as Wonderland is concerned, that we see in the story. In a world where time is money, being late can be fatal. Apart from the Cheshire Cat, an independent figure, practically everyone in Wonderland bullies Alice: she seeks conversation but gets verbal abuse.

Wonderland, whatever else it is, is a representation of the waking "real" world of adult power relations. It is the real world of class struggle, but presented satirically. The croquet game is a metaphor for life—you think you know the rules but actually the rules are always changing, changing, that is, according to the wishes of the "rulers." The powerful must be flattered, and by definition they always win. The queen eavesdrops on Alice's private conversations, exercising her right as ruler to monitor every aspect of the lives of her subordinates. But Alice has learned a great deal about how the powerful behave, and she quickly adjusts her words to suit the vanity of this psychopathic boss. Thus she evades the harm that she has witnessed done to others.

Lewis Carroll's poetic counterpart, Edward Lear, presents a similar vision. As Maurice Sendak has said of his own pictures, the monsters (including in *Where the Wild Things Are*) are modeled on adults whose behavior he experienced as a child. The same is true in the case of Lear, except that the caricatures are just that, caricatures—that is, *types*. Frequently, Lear's famous limericks depict two kinds of people: large and large-headed figures (often foregrounded) and figures with small bodies (often sidelined): clearly a representation of adults and children, those with power and those without power. To a child, an adult is a giant, and is especially terrifying when the adult pushes his face into the face of the child and shouts—a not uncommon practice on the part of adults, and a particularly intimidating and humiliating form of coercion. Often the smaller figure in Lear is not

There was an Old Person of Bangor,   whose face was distorted with anger;
He tore off his boots,   and subsisted on roots,
That borascible person of Bangor.

1.1. From *A Book of Nonsense,* written and illustrated by Edward Lear (London: James Miller, 1875), 179.

a caricature, whereas the large-headed "adult" figures are grotesques, with bizarre preoccupations and attitudes. The limerick presents a satiric vision of the adult "normal" world, of the "real" world.

Lear, like Carroll—and like a number of authors for children—can be savagely cynical about adults, about adult power and control. For example, in Lear's nonsense story "The Two Bachelors," the word "sage" ceases to mean a wise old man, an authority with a big book, and is interpreted by two foolish bachelors as an herb used for cooking. For Lear, those who do not conform must leave, like the odd (gay?) couple, the Owl and the Pussy-Cat. In order to marry each other they must sail far away to a magic island. The theme of the magic exit is, again, noticeable. Children's literature is often regarded as a zone of innocence having nothing to do with real-world conflicts, but in fact authors have always used children's literature to express subversive attitudes about power relations in society—disguised, as it were, in the forms of "nonsense" and "fantasy."[16] That is, they depict the cruelty and irrationality of adult class society by presenting it under the guise of meaningless fun suitable for children, who are viewed as incapable of understanding reality.

Class aggression itself costs less when it is disguised or rendered invisible, when for instance it is treated as a process of nature, of impersonal forces or "laws," as if the "law" of gravity and the "law" of supply and demand were the same, or as a mere random background fact without significance, rather than what it is: a powerful force that functions to benefit some at the expense of others. The basic principle that nobody is going to hire someone to do something unless the value of what that person does is worth more than the wages paid to do it was well understood by the classical economists of the nineteenth century. It was well understood even if the economists rationalized this fact away: there is a definite "class struggle" in society, a conflict between the majority, who sell their labor (and whose labor produces everything), and the minority, who have accumulated enough unpaid labor from earlier production to buy that labor now. The need to control labor is the basis of capitalist order—and that means the control of children.

Class issues are expressed in children's literature by the assumptions built into the story, especially its point of view, and sometimes by the language itself. Literature has an old tendency to depict those who labor as inferior to those who control that labor or who, having paid for it, "own" that labor. This is easier to observe at a distance. Compare feudalism here: feudalism is built upon the relation between hereditary landowning nobility and the peasants who work the land—and who are equally "hereditary," since if one's parents are peasants or "commoners," one is also a peasant. Noble parents mean that one belongs to the nobility: social class is determined by birth. These class relations are ordained by God, so that questioning them is to question ultimate authority and risk ultimate violence. In feudal society, working people—people without property—are beasts of burden, considered clowns or cretins—or criminals. Indeed, the word "clown"—someone who makes you laugh—originally was a word for agricultural laborer. Likewise, the word "villain" originally meant "peasant." The words for workers are the words for the defective, the inferior, even the subhuman. Compare the industrial slavery of the nineteenth century, where such attitudes were the norm but were rationalized and indoctrinated by installing theories of racial inferiority: class conflict was screened as race conflict, a function of nature rather than of the social order.

The derogation of workers correlates with the idealization of the ruling class, even in terminology: a point illustrated, once more, by feudalism. Thus the word "noble" means "aristocrat" on the one hand and "wonderful in every way" on the other (is that not what "noble" means?). What Thorstein Veblen termed "invidious distinction" governs the way these classes are presented: one is idealized, the other demonized. Nobles are "betters"—peasants are "social inferiors." In the regime of capital, the ideal-izing terminology survives in expressions such as "the quality" or "a good family" or even the word "gentleman" itself, which no longer means some-one who does not work with his hands (i.e., aristocrat) but simply a man to respect. So many of the surnames that have survived from feudalism reflect the attitude that a human being who works is a function, not a human be-ing. Thus, surnames like "Cook," "Thatcher," "Cooper," "Harper," "Ewing," "Baker," and many others are merely names for occupations. Peasants *are* their occupation: they are not really individuals at all, any more than the numbered cards of *Alice* are. The language is all from the point of view of the ruling class. Things are what the powerful want them to be. The aristoc-racy identified themselves by the property that they owned, not by some work function. Their names identify the estates they possessed, their own-ership power. In Shakespeare, the king of England can be referred to simply as "England." He is what he owns, what he rules. He is his class position.

But it is the *attitude* of class status that matters most here. Those who have no property and must work for a living are often treated as barbaric or as incompletely human. Property ownership means superior capacity, just as the pursuit of "happiness" is covertly the ownership of property. The state of "happiness" *is* property, is property ownership. With the dominance of market capitalism, especially in the period of texts such as *Alice in Won-derland* and *The Wind in the Willows*, the language is not as blunt or crude: the word "capitalist" does not, like "noble," mean "a person wonderful in every way" (although "entrepreneur" comes close). But the assumptions are there nonetheless, since the possession of capital becomes an ideal status. It becomes a condition that only the very worthy in society merit, even if all may aspire to it.

For instance, in *Treasure Island*, the sailors hired to sail the *Hispaniola* to its rendezvous with instant cash are almost all pirates, but, before they are pirates, they are workers—working sailors, "common" sailors that is, not officers. The name of one of the most prominent of them expresses this by way of a conspicuous pun. His name is "Hands." A "hand" is a *worker* (as in "all hands on deck"—i.e., "I want all the workers working"). "Hand" was a standard term in the nineteenth century for factory worker. Robert Louis Stevenson's depiction of these men is revealing. Not only are they drunk-ards incapable of self-control, not only are they murderous—they are *dirty*. They are unclean, with all the profane associations that "unclean" com-municates: *haram*. Much is made of the mess they make of the ship when they seize it—smudge marks left all over the clean walls of the captain's pristine quarters!—ripping out pages of valuable books! and using the torn-out pages for "pipe lights"! (and for who knows what else). On one hand, the pirates are workers; on the other, the workers are pirates. They dare to want the same thing that squire, captain, and doctor—the "entrepreneurs" in the story—want. From the viewpoint of class consciousness, the pirates are a representation of workers. They must be constantly disciplined and controlled. They are naturally dirty, thieving, self-indulgent, untrustworthy, and dangerous. They are epitomized by the character Hands, who is a bad lot all around. Israel Hands is so drunk that Jim mistakes him for dead; he rolls back and forth on the deck in the company of an empty bottle. But Hands is not dead—he is merely shamming. Naturally, Hands tries to murder Jim, a child, after breaking his word to the boy; and he nearly succeeds, the cad. Thank goodness Jim kills him (by accident—sort of). "Hand" is a synecdoche conflating "worker"—and murderous enemy.

By contrast, there are "good" sailors like Abraham Gray who side with established authority, with capital. Workers who submit get special deals. Gray returns to England with a share of the treasure—and, mimicking his betters, he invests it. He works hard and "rises" in life, unlike the lazy, dirty, drunken pirates. Stevenson even provides a glaring contrast here, "good" Gray versus "bad" Ben Gunn. Gunn had been marooned by the evil Captain Flint. But when he meets Jim on the island, Gunn wisely joins the "good guys"; indeed he is responsible for the victory of the Livesey-Smollett-Trelawney group. It is Gunn who makes their success possible. He is, as it were, a worker who sides with the owners against other workers. Nevertheless, the taint of his association with them clings to him. Back in England in the final chapter, Gunn now blows his share of the treasure in less than a month—then he is on the street. Good workers obey their "master" ("master" being the common, even legal term for capitalist in the eighteenth and nineteenth centuries); they work hard and invest their savings in business ventures. By contrast, bad workers are thieves and layabouts who avoid work and do not save; who drink and beg and cheat. When they happen to get hold of some money, they blow it on booze and God knows what else.[17] They are not just bad—they are stupid.

Jim's moralistic verdict on Gunn, which he states in the manner typical of his humorless self-righteousness, is very revealing: "As for Gunn, he got a thousand pounds, which he spent or lost in three weeks, or to be more exact, in nineteen days, for he was back begging on the twentieth" (Stevenson 606). Jim carefully notes the exact number of days it took for Gunn to waste his nest egg. Clearly, if you went to work for Jim, you would be advised to watch your p's and q's and make sure you got to work on time. Jim does not seem to notice that without Gunn, the squire's party would not only *not* have gotten the treasure, they would have perished altogether. He is the one who, having made sure the "good guys" got the treasure, is allowed to live out his life as a kind of pet or, more accurately, a clown: thus he is "something of a butt," in Jim Hawkins's patronizing expression, an object of ridicule. Having blown his "thousand pounds," "he was given a lodge to keep, exactly as he had feared upon the island; and he still lives, a great favourite, though something of a butt, with the country boys, and a notable singer in church on Sundays and saints' days" (606). No longer a deadly pirate, he is a harmless display of the generosity of his betters, those who know how things are done and how they should be done. Again, Stevenson underlines the contrast, and Gray carefully imitates his betters: "Gray not only saved his money, but being suddenly smit with the desire to rise, also studied his profession, and he is now mate and part owner of a fine full-rigged ship, married besides, and the father of a family" (606).

Morally, of course, there is little to differentiate the pirates from the good guys, the "investors" in the expedition, Trelawney, Smollett, Dr. Livesey, in the sense that both groups want the same thing: instant cash. They may want the same thing, the heap of gold and silver buried by the murdering pirates who stole it, but one group is good, indeed ideal, while the other is bad—bad, but also stupid and cunning. Wanting more without working for it is laudable ambition in one group and criminal greed in the other. Meantime, the "treasure" is itself a mass of extorted property. The "good," owning group, headed by the squire (who funds the expedition), benefits from this expropriation—but they do not have to do the dirty work, the killing and robbing, that was required to amass it and that will now benefit them. Others kill and rob for them: that's what thugs are for. Others also shoulder the harmful consequences of that brutality and can be condemned now as criminals. In fact, when the good characters appropriate this mass of plunder, they somehow "cleanse" it. They "launder" it. They do so, essentially, by converting it into capital.[18]

A similar logic informs Mark Twain's *The Adventures of Tom Sawyer*. *Tom Sawyer* climaxes with a display of such treasure, a treasure that is also the result of killing and theft, and it is "laundered"—it is converted into "innocence," into legitimacy—by having been found (or recovered) by two innocent children, Tom and Huck. They then "inherit" the wealth that the violence and crime of others stole, while the criminal who did the dirty work to amass that treasure suffers a terrible death as a consequence of his criminality. He may have murdered the professional man, Doctor Robinson, and then framed the "harmless butt" of the community, the hapless Muff Potter, but he pays with his death, leaving a mass of wealth to be fortuitously appropriated by others. Crime is the hidden basis of wealth.

Treasure Island, whatever else it is, is an allegory of capitalist values and relationships as seen from the point of view of the business stratum of society and their professional allies (physician and sea captain). In this context, Stevenson's presentation of the aristocrat in the story comes into focus. It is notable that the squire, an aristocrat who knows how to shoot but never worked a day in his life, also appears to be the cause of all the problems that afflict the entrepreneurial party. Thanks to his poor judgment, he was fooled by Long John Silver and hired a crew of pirates. He also appears to have been the one who gabbed about the expedition, alerting Long John Silver in the first place. Silver in turn easily duped him and got him to hire a crew that was willing to rob and even kill him. In the culture of capital, the aristocrat is an obsolete feudal relic, one who lives off the work of others but who does nothing except collect economically unproductive rents. He can, however, be redeemed if he supports the party of capital, the party of the entrepreneurs and professionals who are now taking charge of England's grand imperial project: the sea captain and the doctor-scientist.

The ideal man in the world of *Treasure Island* is not the parasitic aristocrat but the man of business: the hard-working entrepreneur or professional whose ambition makes him thrifty and frugal as well as diligent, honest, and, it goes without saying, courageous, someone who dares and risks. It is the values of this stratum of society that the novel glorifies. Jim himself, the chief narrator, comes from a small-business background—his father owned an inn and his mother continued to run it after his father's death. Jim is already a businessman. An independent and hard-working young man, he is markedly more capable than his greedy and confused mother. When they must flee for their lives from the pirates, she dallies, counting money she thinks is owing to her, and when at last she does take off with Jim, she faints at the worst possible moment. Her son, by contrast, knows when and how to act: Jim is a model of what a boy should be. He is determined to "rise" in the world and is destined for success—success in business, of course. Tom Sawyer, the all-American boy, is similarly destined, given the entrepreneurial skills he demonstrates in the famous whitewashing episode, cleverly acquiring things from others that he then turns for a profit. His extraordinary showmanship throughout his "Adventures" marks him as a born salesman, one who rises by manipulating the work of others.

Squire Trelawney in *Treasure Island* does redeem himself, thanks to his shooting ability. Having spent his time aristocratically blasting pheasants and rabbits, he proves his worth in the social order by shooting people, assuming that the pirates can truly be designated as people. Interestingly, Stevenson's other famous book for young people, *Kidnapped*, is far different from *Treasure Island*: it is much closer to the social complexity of Sir Walter Scott's novels, with the communal values of traditional society starkly contrasted against those of commercial property. *Treasure Island* belongs in the tradition of "imperial romance" as it might be called, adventure stories set in exotic places with a strong British-imperial reference, such as *King Solomon's Mines* by H. Rider Haggard. *King Solomon's Mines* was Haggard's response to *Treasure Island*, and, like *Treasure Island*, *King Solomon's Mines* (and *Tom Sawyer*) features an immense treasure, the symbolic goal of imperial enterprise.[19]

The figure of the parasitic aristocrat who does nothing but consume and cause grief for others could hardly be more clearly illustrated in literature than by Toad (of "Toad Hall") in Kenneth Grahame's *The Wind in the Willows*. Like the dirty, thieving pirates of *Treasure Island*, a group of nasty and thieving, and definitely messy, lower-class types with plebeian accents who should be working for their living—the weasels who usurp Toad's property—also appears in *Willows* (see Zanger). They even appropriate Toad's stately home and must be driven out, much as the pirates must be defeated by loyalists to the established order, loyalists who achieve victory, as in *Treasure Island*, heroically, with the odds heavily against them. But of course, whereas *Treasure Island* is deadly earnest, *The Wind in the Willows* is humorous and satiric; Toad is as much a figure of comedy as a parasite on the economic order. Rat and Badger are the equivalent of small-property owners, not exactly professional men like the captain and the physician in *Treasure Island* but representing the same values of frugality, independence, professional skill, temperance, and responsibility, though lacking the impulse for aggression that characterizes them. The fact that they are woodland animals who appear to have no source of income and who are entirely separate from the world of humans (unlike the super-confident and upper-class Toad, who mingles freely with humans) gives them and the values of capital a certain absurdity. But then Grahame's book is a rich and many-sided fantasy, shot through with satire and parody.

Children's literature is often thought of as functioning in a realm of innocence. In the classic period, children's literature typically inhabits a domain in which good triumphs and where death, cruelty, and exploitation may be featured but do not, so to speak, win. It is a world that in many respects makes human sense, unlike the world of "experience," to draw upon William Blake's terminology, the adult world of history, where good often does not triumph and where death, cruelty, and exploitation indeed often do win. In *Tom Sawyer*, for instance, there are no "classes"—there are townspeople-neighbors, all reasonably close in terms of income. The exception—slaves and nonwhites in general—are carefully hidden from view and barely glimpsed in *Tom Sawyer*; and even vagrants—child vagrants no less, like Huckleberry Finn, the child of nature—appear to be happy as well as fed and clothed (bad vagrants like Injun' Joe are a different case). But there are no "rich" people as such—some residents are better off than others, but there are no millionaire/billionaire equivalents. The "innocent" vision in this case is basic to American national mythology, its sense of itself as an almost utopian community: the happy small town where everyone knows everyone else, where everyone cares about everyone else, where nobody is really rich and nobody is really poor.[20]

The equivalent in England is nostalgia for an idealized Middle Ages, with noble lords and loyal peasants working together in harmony. Even in Frances Hodgson Burnett's famous novel, *The Secret Garden*, which features a manor and an aristocratic owner (Archibald Craven) and servants who work for that owner (Martha, Mrs. Medlock, Ben Weatherstaff), "class" as a matter of conflict or struggle is not present, indeed is difficult even to imagine. The important opening scenes set in imperial India are a different matter, however. There we find the irresponsible English rulers and their semislave Indian "servants": a social arrangement to get away *from*, not an arrangement in any way desirable to imitate. Instead, Misselthwaite Manor allows for and even invites a nostalgic fantasy of an idealized society, what literary scholars call a "pastoral vision." In such a vision, the landowning aristocracy are aristocrats in the sense of being true leaders, good people who put the interests of the community ahead of private interests, let alone commercial ones, and who are skilled, responsible, and large hearted.

That is, the "superior" people are "superior" in the sense of character and duty, not in the sense of possessing the power to coerce others. They are leaders who take their responsibility as leaders seriously in looking after an extended family of tenants, workers, and servants who appreciate and support their hereditary leader; who make sure that everyone is cared for and that no one is neglected, as in a benign clan of extended families linked by tradition and shared work. It is an idealized, utopian vision quite common in the "golden age" of children's literature. It is the world that the horse

Beauty finally attains in Anna Sewell's great novel *Black Beauty*, after a life of appalling slavery. (A significant portion of *Black Beauty* is concerned, in contrast to the pastoral vision with which it concludes, with the struggles of working people to survive, just as it is concerned with the struggles of the horse Beauty to survive.)[21] In *The Secret Garden*, the goal is a utopian vision of class harmony, a "Red Tory" vision, a happy, idyllic scene of mutual support and harmony, as opposed to a society based on the cash nexus where some people command others, buying and selling their labor and reducing the people who sell their labor to nonentities, like the nameless "Ayah" of *Garden*'s imperial India. The setting of this harmonious society is typically not urban but rural, like the idyllic landscape Anne attains in *Anne of Green Gables*, or, occasionally, a prosperous village. In short, an "Innocent" vision, in Blake's terms.

In such a context, it is not surprising that a recurring convention is that of the figure of the benign rich man, usually a courtly gentleman with a heart of gold—and a whole lot of cash. Laurie's grandfather in Louisa May Alcott's *Little Women* comes to mind here; he may be crusty, but he proves vital to the March family, whose house, surprisingly, is next door to his splendid mansion.[22] Another example, and the pivot of E. Nesbit's *The Railway Children* (of which a superb movie was made in 1972), is a powerful capitalist: the director of the railway line referred to in the title. He helps not only with supplies for the children but ultimately by redeeming and freeing their wrongly imprisoned father. Nesbit is a subtle and profound writer, and it is interesting that the relationship between the benign rich gentleman and the "railway children" is not simply one of patronage. That is, the kind rich man does not simply do good things for the children—the children do some very important things for him.

Specifically, they avert a railway crash: not bad. They are rewarded with a special gift, so that the relationship between the two parties is somewhat balanced. In fact, in terms of money, what the rich man does for the children is far less than what the children do for the rich man. Such is the genius of E. Nesbit. Preventing a train wreck means a lot more in terms of cold hard cash than the special requests the children make. The rich man is there, but he is not simply idealized. He is not simply the means of making everything OK in the end after all. On the contrary, the reader discovers that, rich though he is, he needs the children. Again, in this "Red Tory" vision, the social order is one of reciprocity, not exploitation.

Frances Hodgson Burnett also uses the convention of a redemptive rich man in *A Little Princess* (he lives next door, like Laurie's grandfather in *Little*

Women). Interestingly, the basis of the plot of Burnett's *The Secret Garden* is the *conversion* of a rich man. The plot is not simply the renewal of Mary and Colin, two children who have been neglected and emotionally (and physically) damaged. The plot is built around the transformation of a man who is a rich and powerful property owner. Archibald Craven, in the manner of the "1 percent," is narcissistic, irresponsible, self-indulgent, indeed cruel, to the point of even willing his son's death. Only his interests matter. But he changes: he becomes a loving parent and a responsible adult. From the point of view of childism, this is a child fantasy of converting an abusive parent into a loving and responsible one. The transformation of the owner takes a miracle: he hears his dead wife calling him to his duty. He has to be, so to speak, tamed, recalling the grandfather figure of Burnett's *Little Lord Fauntleroy*, "the fabulously rich earl of Dorincourt," in Alison Lurie's phrase (*Don't Tell the Grown-Ups* 140). The ruling figure in Eleanor Porter's *Pollyanna*, Miss Harrington, follows a similar trajectory: such figures embody a shift from the values of capital itself and its despotic self-absorption to commitment to genuine community.

The Wizard in *The Wizard of Oz* is a kind of parody of this type of transformational figure (as is, in a different way, Toad in *Willows*). Rather than benevolently assisting the child protagonist, the Wizard is a trickster who artfully avoids all responsibility: he isn't there when his help is most needed, help he promised to give, as when he manages to exit Oz—without Dorothy. Indeed, the Wizard openly exploits Dorothy and her companions. They are not exactly wage labor, of course—but he does get them to do work that is vital, and he cannot pay them what he owes them, except by chicanery. Indeed, he comfortably sends them to almost certain death, as he later explicitly acknowledges—this, after lying to them—and he again lies to them when they return from the near death his task had destined them for. The Wizard's Emerald City, a capitalist fantasy of consumer abundance, turns out to be an illusion. The ruler of this glittering display is another born salesman, a kind of immoral adult Tom Sawyer. Apparently, looking through green-tinted glasses changes one's perspective on things, and it's not so bad, given the advantages of not seeing the truth. Creating illusions is a preoccupation of *The Wizard of Oz*, as it was of its promoter-author. That author, L. Frank Baum, was an early advertising guru: he wrote the first book about shop window display (a book that is, by the way, highly technical and concerned with the minutiae of practical design techniques). The Wizard in the first Oz book is a genuinely evil man, despite his jolly "image" in popular culture.[23]

Children's literature enjoyed a great efflorescence in the period before and after the turn of the twentieth century. This efflorescence is part of something larger, part of a revolt against realism in literature. It was an opportunity for those who wanted to write outside the realist tradition, whatever their interest in children—or lack of interest.[24] From a literary point of view, this was a period of remarkable innovation in terms of genre; in moving away from the conventions of realism, its results were important and numerous, including the development of science fiction (H. G. Wells), detective fiction (*The Moonstone*, Sherlock Holmes), utopian and dystopian writing (Bellamy's *Looking Backward*; Butler's *Erewhon*), horror and ghost stories (*Dracula*, *The Turn of the Screw*). A central figure here is the socialist William Morris, who wrote a key utopian novel, *News from Nowhere*. The narrator of *News* travels in time to the socialist society of the future, and this future vision is the inspiration for the visit made by the children in E. Nesbit's *The Story of the Amulet* to a socialist society of the future. Like the mother in *Amulet*, the inhabitants of the future in Morris's *News* are appalled by the conditions of Morris's own backward time. One explains: "In the nineteenth century, society was so miserably poor, owing to the systematized robbery on which it was founded, that real education was impossible for anybody." Hence: "No one could have come out of such a mill [i.e. a factory] uninjured; and those only would avoid being crushed by it who would have the spirit of rebellion strong in them. Fortunately most children have had that at all times, or I do not know that we should ever have reached our present position" (246).

It is easy to miss the real point of the future socialist here. It is, he says, "the *spirit of rebellion in children*" that makes social progress, if not revolution, possible, recalling Alice's revolution at the end of *Wonderland*. How different this view is from the common attitude that the spirit of rebellion in children must be tamed, if not actually broken, as standard religious doctrine has long insisted ("spare the rod and spoil the child"). Furthermore, Morris decisively repudiates the notion that children are somehow outside reality and need to be brought into the social structure by forced socialization, making "teaching lessons" the purpose of children's literature—which is, in practice, indoctrination. Morris will have none of it. He regards this rebelliousness on the part of young people as vital to social improvement if not human survival. He makes clear that it is children—the spirit of children—that makes transformation possible. It is a striking and, shall we say, revolutionary notion. Note the way that the speaker in *News from Nowhere* aligns poverty, exploitation—and the mis-education of children—with each other. One requires the other. Keeping people ignorant is essential not only to education but to the maintenance of capital accumulation. This is a key theme, interestingly, in Frederick Douglass's exposition of slavery in his *Narrative*, a text preoccupied with children and the practice of crushing the consciousness of children in a society based on naked class aggression.[25] In the words of Noam Chomsky, "People are supposed to be passive and apathetic and doing what they're told by the responsible people who are in control. That's elite ideology across the political spectrum—from liberals to Leninists, it's essentially the same ideology: people are too stupid and ignorant to do things by themselves so for their own benefit we have to control them."

I have focused on the "golden age" of children's literature, but the same issues persist. What makes this a golden age is not just that the classics are remarkable literary works. It is a golden age because so many of its authors take the viewpoint of children rather than of adults, and in this respect they offer not merely a protest against the harms inflicted upon children by an irrational social order but a protest against the mistreatment of human beings generally.

The way children are treated and conceptualized has parallels to the way wage labor is treated and conceptualized. The worker is treated as child-like, in the sense of never knowing as much as the authority figures and having to be told what to do, trained—and controlled. The relation of parents and adults to children, in turn, parallels the relation of capital to labor. There is a practical reason for this parallel: children must be conditioned to the regime of capital, to their destiny as adult workers. Capital is to labor as adult is to child. Furthermore, the deforming effects of capital on adults are, inevitably, projected onto children by a familiar psychological principle. The stresses of a system that coerces adults are inflicted, in turn, upon children, in a process that went unchecked and barely noticed in the social order of the "golden age" period (the late nineteenth and early twentieth centuries[26]). As Young-Bruehl puts it, "Shamed and humiliated men need to shame and humiliate, as later do their shamed and humiliated sons" (181). Unless we are aware, we do to others what was done to us. "Sad as it may be," says Emma Goldman, "it is, nevertheless, true, that parents are the first to destroy the inner riches of their children." But that is because the law of capital is submission.

NOTES

1. Emma Goldman, *Red Emma Speaks: An Emma Goldman Reader*, 3rd ed., ed. Alix Kates Shulman (Amherst, N.Y.: Prometheus Books, 1998), 131.

2. The child abuse recommended, in fact demanded, by the Book of Proverbs, is well known (e.g., Prov. 10:13, 19:18, 23:13). See John Shelby Spong's analysis of prejudice against children in the Bible (143–180).

3. Bagley's thinking remains hegemonic; see the special issue of *Monthly Review* (63:3 [July–August 2011]).

4. Cf. Bill Ayers and Rick Ayers: "The dominant neoliberal metaphor of the rich and powerful posits schools as businesses, teachers as workers, students as products and commodities. It also leads to thinking that school closings and privatizing the public space are natural events; relentless, standardized test-and-punish regimes are sensible; and zero tolerance is a reasonable proxy for justice. This is what the true-believers call 'reform.'"

5. See C. John Sommerville's *Discovery of Childhood in Puritan England*: "In the history of childhood, things do not necessarily get better with time," he sardonically observes (15). Changing religious views matter here, but less than the needs of capital accumulation: the children of owners are different from the children of workers. One group has a "value" that the other does not.

6. Compare slaves who can no longer work. When Frederick Douglass's grandmother was too old to be of use to her "owner," he abandoned her in the woods to die.

7. Nonworking animals such as thoroughbred horses function as "conspicuous consumption" in Thorstein Veblen's analysis in *The Theory of the Leisure Class*, published within a year of Baum's *Wizard of Oz*. The dogs in Hans Christian Andersen's *The Tinder-Box* are not really dogs but supernatural beings, not unlike the cat in *Puss-in-Boots*. (For the cats in *Alice in Wonderland*, see my "Food and Power.")

8. For convenience I cite a standard anthology, John Griffith and Charles Frey's *Classics of Children's Literature* (344).

9. The phrase comes from Goldman's "Anarchism: What It Really Stands For" (66).

10. Commentary on Melville's story rarely emphasizes its obvious theme: demeaning work turns people into machines. Some, like Bartleby, resist. His dignified "I would prefer not to" is the utterance of one equal to another, not of one who is forced to obey. "Bartleby, the Scrivener" appeared in 1853 in the era of slavery, when slaves were kept illiterate and penalties were enforced on those who taught slaves to read. Human machines work better when they are like inanimate machines: unconscious. Compare Melville's near contemporary Charles Dickens, whose *A Christmas Carol* features a clerk treated not unlike Bartleby and whose liberation dramatizes that story's central action.

11. Braverman adds: "that which is neurotic in the individual is, in capitalism, normal and socially desirable for the functioning of society"—the "society" of capital, that is.

12. The radical implications of *Alice in Wonderland* have often been noted. See, for instance, the version of the trial scene by Walt Kelly (of *Pogo* fame) in Nel and Mickenberg, 209–232. Apart from the Cheshire Cat, Alice is "the only wholly decent and sensible person" in Wonderland, as Alison Lurie notes (*Don't Tell the Grown-Ups* 6).

13. E. Nesbit used this motif in *The Story of the Amulet*: an abandoned child in working-class London is taken back in time to a loving mother who receives her as her own child. The past in Nesbit is often better than the present, as in *Harding's Luck*.

14. Esther Forbes's *Johnny Tremain* furnishes a contrast. In this story, the rich relatives whom the boy seeks for rescue turn out to be loyal to the king—i.e., for Americans, they are traitors. There is no "magic exit" because the story celebrates revolution—the boy must win independence from his (rich) relatives, not rely on them.

15. Cf. the "lost boys" of *Peter Pan*: destitute children who magically exit from misery to the freedom of Neverland.

16. Alison Lurie is an astute observer, but for left analysis, see Jack Zipes, especially his preface to *Sticks and Stones*.

17. For a study of "reversions"—revisions that also are also deconstructions—of *Treasure Island* (and *The Wind in the Willows*) from the point of view of the "bad guys," see John Stephen and Robyn McCallum's *Retelling Stories, Framing Culture* (268–290).

18. The time frame of the story—pre–Industrial Revolution—is the era of what Marx termed "the so-called primitive accumulation," "primitive accumulation" being the expression in classical economics for the original capital required for capital accumulation, and which, as Marx demonstrates in *Capital*, volume 1, is the plunder of other countries and peoples (see part 8, "So-Called Primitive Accumulation," 873–940). Child labor is a not insignificant theme of *Capital*.

19. See Patrick Brantlinger, who emphasizes the influence of the English push in the nineteenth century to dump "surplus population" in the colonies.

20. This vision—the happy small town where everyone knows everyone else and supports everyone else ("Main Street, U.S.A.")—is fundamental to American national mythology: "The American myth of innocence, goodness, and determination . . . so much a part of *The Wizard of Oz*," as Ruth Moynihan notes. In Frank Capra's great movie *It's a Wonderful Life*, Clarence, the angel, leaves a copy of *Tom Sawyer* with Jimmy Stewart: a vision of community and mutual support.

21. *Black Beauty* is a variation on Harriet Beecher Stowe's *Uncle Tom's Cabin*. Sewell's point is that animals like "black" Beauty are treated as "black" slaves were. The exploitation of enslaved animals is a crime, just as the exploitation of enslaved workers is. A related text is George MacDonald's *At the Back of the North Wind*, in which the cab horse and the child are identified by shared name and shared occupation.

22. A late example in this tradition is the wise—and wealthy—Professor of C. S. Lewis's *The Lion, the Witch, and the Wardrobe*. Narnia is a classic "Red Tory" vision of variety, freedom, and order without coercion or tyranny. Hostility to commercial relations is written all over the Narnia books, a fact that conservative devotees of the series miss. Lewis was a Red Tory and not a "conservative" in the contemporary sense.

23. "I think you are a very bad man," says Dorothy (Baum 124), helplessly—then she is tricked by the Wizard yet again. Dorothy does not come across as top heavy in the IQ department.

24. Jack Zipes comments on this "great tradition of refusal. . . . In this tradition, writers and artists refuse to let their imaginations and their imaginative works be co-opted by those forces seeking to instrumentalize the fantasy for profit or power. In my opinion, the

essential quality of all great fantasy works is linked to their capacity to subvert accepted standards and to provoke readers to re-think their state of being and the institutions that determine the nature of existence" (*Breaking the Magic Spell* 230).

25. Douglass's *Narrative* is about slavery, but of course slavery was the basis of capital accumulation in the northern United States and in Great Britain. In other words, American slavery was *capitalist* slavery, based on industrial-scale agriculture. It was very different from the prefeudal slavery of antiquity.

26. The culture of child abuse is a significant factor in the genesis of fascism; see Alice Miller's *For Your Own Good*, which examines the child-rearing beliefs that predominated in Germany in the prefascist period.

WORKS CITED

Ayers, Bill, and Rick Ayers. Introduction to "Education under Fire." Special issue, *Monthly Review*, July 7, 2011. Accessed July 23, 2011. Website.

Bacon, Betty, ed. *How Much Truth Do We Tell the Children? The Politics of Children's Literature*. Minneapolis: Marxist Educational Press, 1988. Print.

Baran, Paul, and Paul Sweezy. *Monopoly Capital*. New York: Monthly Review Press, 1966. Print.

Baum, L. Frank. *The Wonderful Wizard of Oz*. Edited by William R. Leach. Belmont, Calif.: Wadsworth, 1991. Print.

Brantlinger, Patrick. *Rule of Darkness: British Literature and Imperialism, 1830–1914*. Ithaca: Cornell University Press, 1988. Print.

Braverman, Harry. *Labor and Monopoly Capital: The Degradation of Work in the Twentieth Century*. Rev. ed. New York: Monthly Review Press, 1998. Print.

Carroll, Lewis. *Alice's Adventures in Wonderland*. In Griffith and Frey, *Classics of Children's Literature*, 322–334. Print.

Chomsky, Noam. "Work, Learning and Freedom." Z Communications, December 26, 2012. Accessed December 30, 2012. Website.

Goldman, Emma. *Anarchism and Other Essays*. Edited by Richard Drinnon. New York: Dover Publications, 1969. Print.

———. "Anarchism: What It Really Stands For." In Goldman, *Anarchism and Other Essays*, 63–72.

———. *Red Emma Speaks: An Emma Goldman Reader*. 3rd ed. Edited by Alix Kates Shulman. Amherst, N.Y.: Prometheus Books, 1998. Print.

———. "The Child and Its Enemies." In Goldman, *Red Emma Speaks*, 131–139. Print.

Griffith, John W., and Charles H. Frey. *Classics of Children's Literature*. 6th ed. Upper Saddle River, N.J.: Pearson, 2005. Print.

Kenschaft, Lori. "Just a Spoonful of Sugar? Anxieties of Gender and Class in 'Mary Poppins.'" In *Girls, Boys, Books, Toys: Gender in Children's Literature and Culture*, edited by Beverly Lyon Clark and Margaret Higonnet, 227–242. Baltimore: Johns Hopkins University Press, 1999. Print.

Leach, William. "A Trickster's Tale: L. Frank Baum and *The Wizard of Oz*." In Baum, *The Wonderful Wizard of Oz*, 157–188. Print.

Lear, Edward. *A Book of Bosh: Lyrics and Prose of Edward Lear*. Edited by Brian Alderson. Harmondsworth, England: Penguin, 1975. Print.

Lurie, Alison. *Boys and Girls Forever: Children's Classics from Cinderella to Harry Potter*. New York: Penguin, 2003. Print.

———. *Don't Tell the Grown-Ups: The Subversive Power of Children's Literature*. Boston: Little, Brown, 1998. Print.

Marx, Karl. *Capital*. Vol. 1. Translated by Ben Fowkes. Harmondsworth, England: Penguin, 1976. Print.

Morris, William. *News from Nowhere*. In *Three Works by William Morris*, edited by A. L. Morton. New York: International Publishers, 1968. Print.

Nel, Philip, and Julia Mickenberg, eds. *Tales for Little Rebels*. New York: New York University Press, 2008. Print.

Nicholson, Mervyn. "Alfred Hitchcock Presents Class Struggle." *Monthly Review* 63:7 (December 2011): 33–50. Print.

———. "Food and Power: Homer, Carroll, Atwood and Others." *Mosaic* 20:3 (1987): 37–55. Print.

Sommerville, C. John. *The Discovery of Childhood in Puritan England*. Athens: University of Georgia Press, 1992. Print.

Spong, John Shelby. *The Sins of Scripture*. New York: Random House, 2005.

Stephen, John, and Robyn McCallum. *Retelling Stories, Framing Culture: Traditional Story and Metanarratives in Children's Literature*. New York: Garland, 1998. Print.

Stevenson, Robert Louis. *Treasure Island*. In Griffith and Frey, *Classics of Children's Literature*, 496–606. Print.

Twain, Mark. *The Adventures of Tom Sawyer*. In Griffith and Frey, *Classics of Children's Literature*, 375–493. Print.

Young-Bruehl, Elisabeth. *Childism: Confronting Prejudice against Children*. New Haven: Yale University Press, 2011. Print.

Zanger, Jules. "Goblins, Morlocks, and Weasels: Classic Fantasy and the Industrial Revolution." In Bacon, *How Much Truth Do We Tell the Children?*, 74–84. Print.

Zipes, Jack. *Breaking the Magic Spell: Radical Theories of Folk and Fairy Tales*. Rev. ed. Lexington: University Press of Kentucky, 2002. Print.

———. Introduction to *Spells of Enchantment: The Wondrous Fairy Tales of Western Culture*, edited by Jack Zipes, xi–xxx. New York: Viking, 1991. Print.

———. Introduction to Nel and Mickenberg, *Tales for Little Rebels*, vii–ix. Print.

———. *Sticks and Stones: The Troublesome Success of Children's Literature from Slovenly Peter to Harry Potter*. New York: Routledge, 2001. Print.

Shopping Like It's 1899

Gilded Age Nostalgia and Commodity Fetishism in Alloy's Gossip Girl

ANASTASIA ULANOWICZ

In an essay featured in the *Huffington Post* on December 21, 2010, Melissa Terzis annotates a Christmas wish list her brother had found on a New York City train bound to Connecticut. This list, apparently composed by a twenty-something-year-old woman and addressed to her presumably wealthy boyfriend, contains the following items: noise-canceling earphones; a bicycle; Louis Vuitton city guides; "whatever the newest Chanel makeup is (as long as I don't already have it)"; a Mulberry oversized Alexa bag (priced at approximately $1,200); a Cartier large Tank watch (priced at approximately $2,000); and a Cartier Love bracelet (priced at approximately $6,200) (2–3). As Terzis comments on the list's contents, her tone becomes increasingly irate. "Honey," she addresses the list's unknown author, "I know you're living in a bubble . . . a purse and Cartier-filled bubble with your noise-canceling earphones on, but we're in a recession. RECESSION. Do you know how many people will claim less than $6,200 in income this year on their taxes? Probably one for each perfectly coiffed hair on your head" (3). Certainly, Terzis's displeasure seems justifiable, at least to those who are not impervious to the hardship created by the ongoing economic recession. The list itself, however—as well as the aspirational desires it communicates—should not be unfamiliar to readers acquainted with the latest contributions to young adult, or YA, fiction. Indeed, it reads like a boiled-down plot of one of the many teen novels packaged by the company Alloy Entertainment.

A division of Alloy Marketing, Alloy Entertainment develops plots for adolescent audiences that it in turn sells to major publishing houses. The books packaged by this firm—including such series as *The A-List*, *The Au*

Pairs, The Clique, The Luxe, and, most notably, *Gossip Girl*—tend to follow the same narrative template. Each of these series features a cast of attractive and stock characters—queen bees, good-girls-gone-bad, teenage lotharios, and ruthless Becky Sharp–type aspirants—who enjoy the privileges of wealth and who, predictably, become involved in one another's amorous affairs. Character driven and marked by sharp, witty dialogue, the books can be quite entertaining, and they occasionally (and perhaps unwittingly) offer insight into cultural perceptions of adolescent girl culture. Engaging though they might be, however, Alloy's books are ultimately concerned not so much with plot, character development, or social commentary as they are with encouraging habits of consumption. Not unlike episodes of daytime soap operas and prime-time dramas, the novels are constructed to provoke envy in a largely middle-class audience by touting the so-called lifestyles of the rich and famous—lifestyles that involve the acquisition of frequently name-dropped high-end consumer goods. Throughout the books, readers are prompted to identify with spoiled, brand-obsessed heroines—and in turn, they are encouraged to recognize, if not purchase, the consumer items favored by these characters. Indeed, the books might be read as mass-produced, well-elaborated, and very readable versions of the Christmas list lampooned by Terzis's essay.

Of all the series produced by Alloy, *Gossip Girl* remains the most popular and the most easily recognizable, even though its plot, characters, and advertising strategies are nearly identical to those employed by most of the company's other offerings. *Gossip Girl* charts the misadventures of the newest generation of New York's Brahmin class. At the center of the series is Serena van der Woodsen, the heiress of a seventeenth-century Dutch shipping company (*GG*[1] 87). Orbiting Serena are Blair Waldorf, her archrival and sometimes friend; a host of lovers and sycophants; and at least one middle-class aspirant to her coveted position at the top of twenty-first-century New York high society. The activities of Serena and her friends and rivals are assiduously documented by a blogger known only as Gossip Girl, who annotates the gossip generated by denizens of the Upper East Side in order to provide an ostensibly official document of the affairs of the rich and famous.

Since 2007, the success of the *Gossip Girl* series has been buoyed by its adaptation into a popular prime-time soap opera, also packaged by Alloy and broadcast on the CW network. Like the book series, the television program features attractive actors, including starlets Leighton Meester and Blake Lively, who sport many of the brand names featured in the books;

thus, like the books, the program is committed to peddling the latest commodities and trends. The secret of the franchise's success, I argue, lies not only in its provocation of class envy and aspirational longing but also in its production of nostalgia. Both the novels and the television program, which are mutually concerned with the promulgation of a consumer consciousness, seek to convince young audiences that they might achieve the social status of the series' charmed heroines through the accumulation of the high-priced items touted by the franchise. These texts amplify this bid for audience attention, moreover, by appealing to nostalgic tastes and desires. As both the novels and television program make clear, the heroes and heroines of *Gossip Girl* are not simply members of the twenty-first-century nouveau riche—as are the protagonists of other Alloy series such as *The Clique*. Rather, they are heirs to veritable American royalty: that is, they are descendants of the robber barons of the nineteenth-century Gilded Age. In this way, the franchise substantiates its key characters' tastes and consumer choices as "timeless" and "classical" in such a way that it intensifies the allure of the commodities these characters favor—and, in turn, readers' desire for such goods.

Crucially, however, even as the franchise whets audiences' desire for the high-cost consumer goods to which it alludes, it simultaneously reminds them that the social status communicated by these objects is prohibitively difficult, if not impossible, to acquire. Like fashion magazines published in both in the nineteenth century and today, the series is committed to touting an upper-class lifestyle that it acknowledges is governed by social codes and proscriptions that are not easily mastered or overcome by the average middle-class reader. Indeed, the appeal of the series derives in part from its depiction of upper-crust existence as rarefied, if not exotic. In this way, it hopes not so much to thwart readers' desires as to intensify their envy. By employing a rhetorical tactic akin to reverse psychology, the series challenges readers to overcome the class-based obstacles it has imposed precisely by tempting them to ramp up their purchasing power. Here, the series' deployment of nostalgia is particularly effective. Nostalgia, as I will argue below, implies a certain insatiability: that is, it depends upon a vision of a past that never actually existed, and that therefore can never be reclaimed or satisfied. Thus, by peppering its narratives with nostalgic allusions to the Gilded Age—allusions that it rather disingenuously posits as historically accurate—*Gossip Girl* tantalizes its young audience, encouraging them, in effect, to buy their way into embodying a historical image or ideal that in fact never existed in the first place.

The purpose of this discussion, then, is to examine precisely *how* the *Gossip Girl* franchise provokes and deploys nostalgia for the purposes of provoking ultimately insatiable consumerist desires. Such an examination, I propose, involves the analysis not only of the texts' narrative contents but of their form. The mode of Alloy's production of teen fiction, as I will demonstrate, can be traced back to strategies employed by publishers of nineteenth-century pulp fiction; moreover, Alloy's narratives draw on literary conventions used in nineteenth-century sensational fiction. What distinguishes the *Gossip Girl* series from Alloy's other offerings, however, is its canny awareness of its nineteenth-century (quasi-) literary heritage: the writers of both the books and the television program signal their indebtedness to earlier forms of literary production by incorporating into their texts allusions to an earlier era. Although such self-reflexivity initially appears to be critical, if not subversive, it is ultimately misdirected. Instead of parodically exposing the time-honored marketing tactics exploited by Alloy, the books and program instead color their allusions to the nineteenth century in the rosy hues of nostalgia, thus intensifying and directing the desires of aspirational readers.

Manufacturing Desire

In order to consider the uses of nostalgia in *Gossip Girl*, it may first be helpful to account for its production by Alloy Entertainment. This company—itself an arm of a larger company, Alloy Marketing—specializes in packaging novels, television programs, and films for a primarily adolescent demographic. Alloy employs writers to concoct potential plots that might attract young audiences, which they in turn pitch at weekly development meetings attended by other writers and editors. Once a writer's project is approved by the committee and by the company's president, Leslie Morgenstein, the writer is charged with drafting a sample chapter. Once this chapter is approved, the writer receives a contract for a full-length book project informed by suggestions from a brainstorming team. The completed text is then sent to various publishing houses and sold to the highest bidder (Mead 62). Although, according to Rebecca Mead, "Alloy authors generally own a fifty per-cent stake in their work," the company nevertheless "retains the property rights to all the work, with a view to generating a movie or a TV show from the same title" (69).

In the case of series fiction such as *Gossip Girl*, the work of producing successive installments is outsourced to Alloy's subsidiary, 17th Street

Productions. Utilizing the same writing-by-committee strategies that its parent company does, 17th Street hires young writers, many of them recent college graduates, to brainstorm and produce new episodes in the series. Although they receive compensation for their work on a series, the writers employed by Alloy and 17th Street do not receive formal, public acknowledgment for their efforts. Rather, the texts they produce are attributed to the series' initial creator. For example, the *Gossip Girl* books are attributed to the series creator, Cecily von Ziegesar, even though von Ziegesar herself reputedly only penned the first few installments of the thirteen-novel series; the rest of the series was composed by an anonymous, uncredited team of writers at 17th Street.[2]

According to Mead, Alloy thus has become a veritable "teen-entertainment factory," which has developed a "process with an industrial level of efficiency" (62). In part, Alloy's success is due to its preservation of property rights with the express intention of developing further lucrative television series and film adaptations. Moreover, its grip on teen publishing has to do with savvy marketing. Alloy Entertainment, after all, is ultimately an arm of a much greater company, Alloy Marketing, which researches the consumer choices and trends of Alloy's targeted demographic. Alloy's marketing research results in something of a (very lucrative) feedback loop. That is, once Alloy identifies the tastes and inclinations of adolescent consumers, it draws on such data to develop plots that might be attractive to such audiences; this, in turn, helps to ensure the market viability of Alloy's packaged plots and the subsequent production of future, teen-targeted books.

As Amy Pattee has demonstrated, *Gossip Girl* serves as a particularly effective case study of Alloy's modus operandi. For example, the narrative of *Gossip Girl*'s genesis explains a great deal about how the company develops and sells its products—and how, moreover, it manipulates public perception of its processes of production. According to Alloy lore, *Gossip Girl*'s creator, von Ziegesar, was already an editor at Alloy and 17th Street when she pitched the idea of a series charting the misadventures of two young Upper East Side socialites at a fictional private girls' school, Constance Billiard. Von Ziegesar was then charged with composing the "pilot" book of the series, entitled simply *Gossip Girl*. Subsequent installments were outsourced to writers at 17th Street. According to Pattee, the attribution of the series solely to von Ziegesar was a strategic move on the part of Alloy. Von Ziegesar, herself a graduate of a posh New York private school, has lent the series an aura of authenticity. Alloy's promotional materials as well as interviews with von Ziegesar in the *New York Times* and the London *Telegraph* in effect have sold the series by calling attention to her intimate acquaintance

with the exclusive, albeit back-biting, "lifestyles" of New York's rich and famous.[3] Thus, these texts reaffirm von Ziegesar's authority insofar as they
confirm her credibility as an Upper East Side "insider" and insofar as they
work to validate her status as the series' author (Pattee 162–163). Simultaneously, however, Alloy's attribution of *Gossip Girl*'s production squarely to
von Ziegesar "intentionally mask[s]" her actual "collaboration with a committee of advisors and conceptual 'owners'" (163)—thus obscuring the fact
that the series is ultimately an "artifact of a literary machine" (164). Such
"masking"—or branding of a quasi-authorial name—also works to ensure
the increased consumption of the titles with which this name is associated. According to Pattee, the fact that the "name Cecily von Ziegesar is
associated both with the series and with the lifestyle described within the
novels further increases the opportunities for readers to 'attach' themselves
to a product they believe is a genuine expression of a familiar personality"
(164). These "opportunities" for "attachment" thus ensure the production
and consumption of still more ghostwritten titles published under the same
author/brand.[4]

Inasmuch as *Gossip Girl* demonstrates Alloy's penchant for yoking
ghost/committee–written narratives to easily recognizable author/brands, it
also makes evident the company's investment in encouraging habits of consumption in a teenage demographic notorious for possessing discretionary
income. *Gossip Girl* might be characterized as what Diane Carver Sekeres
calls "branded fiction," or books "created synergistically, tethered to other
products . . . that draw on literacies other than reading words on printed
paper" (400). Brands, Sekeres explains, "are built by corporations mostly to
create associations in consumers' minds between branded products and a
desirable lifestyle; books are simply one product among many that attract
the consumer to the brand" (400). Alloy's primary objective, then, is to promote a brand it initially established with the publication of von Ziegesar's
first installment of the series. It fulfills this objective, first, by advertising
additional *Gossip Girl* books within each individual installment. A reader
who opens a given book immediately sees advertisements for other installments to the series on the inside front cover; she also sees advertisements
for *Gossip Girl* spin-off series (*It Girl* and *Gossip Girl: The Carlyles*) as well
as for other titles produced by Alloy (for example, *The Clique* and *The A-
List*). Further advertisements are located in the end pages and the inside
back cover. Additionally, books often conclude with excerpts from other
books: *All I Want Is Everything*, for instance, includes a "teaser" excerpt
from the first installment of the spin-off *It Girl*. Recent editions of the series

also come with detachable book covers featuring scenes from the Alloy-produced television program; these book covers, which double as posters for bedrooms or lockers, function as advertisements for the books and the TV show. Such cross-marketing works both ways: for example, the DVD collection of the TV show's first season includes an audio recording of the first novel narrated by actress Christina Ricci.

Alloy sustains consumption of its *Gossip Girl* brand, moreover, by maintaining websites that readers can access for more information about the books and the television show. Fans of the series—which revolves around a fictional website, www.gossipgirl.net—can in turn access an *actual* website with the same address[5] (which features information about the series and its television spin-off). Crucially, this address also serves as an online catalog featuring Alloy's print and DVD offerings; thus, fans who come to the site out of curiosity are enticed to purchase more books, DVDs, and other products associated with the series. Finally, *Gossip Girl* audiences can access Alloy's website (www.alloy.com) to learn more about the company's books, television programs, and films—as well as to keep up to date with Hollywood gossip, style trends, astrological forecasts, and insights about "guys." Fans can also use Alloy's website to order clothes. Not insignificantly, of all the headings spangled across Alloy's banner, the keyword "SHOP" is prominently displayed in all-caps. Although the website is officially intended to publicize the company's literary, televisual, and filmic offerings—and to elaborate on the entertainment and "guy"-related "lifestyle" topics that tie into these products—its primary purpose appears to involve the marketing of consumer items, including those with direct ties to the company.

Such a marketing focus is as present within the series' narratives as it is in the paratextual and extratextual sources that seek to promote them. Indeed, as Pattee argues, the various relationships "among the series organizers—the packager, the publisher, the author" are "reproduced within the text itself" (156). Much like www.gossipgirl.net and www.alloy.com, the installments of *Gossip Girl* feature so-called lifestyle products to readers who presumably possess disposable income. The first few pages of the book series' "pilot" installment, for example, serves as a veritable catalogue of consumer brands: here, the reader encounters references to the cable channel Nickelodeon[6] (*GG* 5); a "black cashmere cardigan" (5); "ballet flats" (5); Saks Fifth Avenue (6); Takashimaya, "the Fifth Avenue luxury goods store" (7); and "gold Cartier cuff bracelets" (8). Initially, these references appear simply to characterize the key players in the *Gossip Girl* saga. The black cardigan sweater and ballet flats, for example, belong to the "bow-tie proper preppy" character Blair Waldorf, who imagines herself as the reincarnation of the stylish Audrey Hepburn (8). Likewise, the Cartier cuff bracelets characterize Blair's gauche stepfather, who should know better that such items were "very popular in the 1980s and not so popular now, unless you've bought into that whole '80s revival thing. *Hello?*" (8). In the logic of *Gossip Girl* (as well as Alloy's other offerings), consumer items become synecdochal expressions of key characters. Certainly, this is not a trend unique to Alloy's teen fiction. Indeed, as David Foster Wallace argued, contemporary fiction often associates characters with name brands with the express intent of gesturing ironically toward the superficial categories that regulate postmodern notions of identity.[7] In *Gossip Girl*, however, the posited relationships between characters and name brands appear earnest rather than ironic. Readers are encouraged to rest assured, for example, that Blair Waldorf is *essentially* an Upper East Side princess precisely because she wears black cardigans, just as they are convinced that her stepfather, Cyrus, is irremediably socially awkward because he wears cuff bracelets. In turn, *Gossip Girl* readers are encouraged not only to shop, but to shop judiciously, since their purchases might betray their inborn, and presumably fixed, personalities.

In this way, the *Gossip Girl* series is not unlike Alloy's website—or, for that matter, magazines such as *Teen Vogue* and *CosmoGirl*. Initially, Alloy's website and these teen glossies appear to be resources on issues presumably of interest to "average" teenage girls: for example, they address such topics as relationships, exercise, and celebrity gossip. However, they are primarily devoted to promoting brand-name clothing and accessories that they guarantee will help each reader assemble her own "unique" and "personal" style—an assembly, of course, that requires the purchase of those items touted in advertisements and "informational" articles. Likewise, although each *Gossip Girl* installment narrates Serena and Blair's newest misadventures (e.g., college interviews, runway modeling stints, spring break shenanigans), the narrative is little more than a broad framework into which allusions to consumer goods and "helpful" style "pointers" might be easily inserted. Each stock character—Serena the free-spirited heiress, Blair the princess, Jenny the ingenue, Vanessa the bohemian—suggests a "unique" personality with which the reader is invited to identify. Once she has inserted herself into a chosen role—just as a magazine reader identifies with a celebrity or supermodel—the reader is prompted to recognize the accoutrements that define her heroine's personality and in turn her own. If the reader is especially intent upon embodying her chosen heroine, she might even be able to find some of the character's accessories at www.alloy.com.

Ultimately, however, the books are not so much invested in promoting discrete items as they are in developing a particular consumer consciousness. After all, the items and trends breezily alluded to by the books are ephemeral: for example, PalmPilots, much touted by the first installment, are now "out," while the bracelets favored by Blair's tacky stepfather currently appear to be back "in." In the final analysis, however, these items are of comparatively little consequence. What matters for *Gossip Girl*—and for Alloy's literary and televisual offerings more generally—is the cultivation of the reader's self-awareness as a consumer. The scrupulous descriptions of characters' possessions and appearances prompt the reader toward a similarly scrupulous evaluation of her own possessions and appearance; such descriptions and allusions encourage an examination of consumer consciousness. Indeed, as Pattee argues, the books instill "us with a certain awareness of the power of self-display, which, with certain appropriate purchases and attitude, can place us on a track running parallel to that of the series characters" (167).

Pattee's expression "a track running parallel to that of the series characters" is especially significant. Crucial to *Gossip Girl*'s procedure of in-text advertisement is a subtext—a fine-print disclaimer, as it were. Middle-class readers, the series suggests, will never actually achieve full equality with the quasi-aristocratic characters whose fictional lives *Gossip Girl* documents. Although a reader might be able to purchase a Prada bag favored by a character (or at least a knockoff) in order to gain proximity to her beloved heroine, she most likely cannot enjoy, for example, that character's access to limitless credit. Her ability to "become" an heiress like Serena or Blair is limited to the imaginative acts she performs by reading the books or by watching the programs—or by buying a pricey goodie here and there. Nevertheless, the reader's purchase of the accoutrements favored by the series' heroines might render her at least a Platonic shadow of her idols. Crucially, however, the reader must rest content with remaining merely a shadow. Indeed, the *Gossip Girl* books encourage fantasies of aspiration even as they suture readers to positions within a reified class structure. Like teen magazines, which Alissa Quart argues "help to solidify feelings of economic and taste inadequacy in girls" by touting items that readers often cannot afford, the *Gossip Girl* books "construct an unaffordable but palpable world of yearning" (5). It is precisely by producing such longing, however, that *Gossip Girl* (or, more to the point, Alloy) exploits adolescent readers, assuring them that even if they cannot be "just like" Blair or Serena, they might at least purchase the wish-fulfilling books or the token baubles peddled by Alloy's website.

Gossip Girl's Literary Ancestors

As Mead and Pattee both note, however, Alloy's mode of production is not at all new. Rather, its origin may be traced to the efforts of the American writer and entrepreneur Edward Stratemeyer, who, in 1899, produced the adventure series *The Rover Boys* (Mead 68). Banking on the success garnered by this series, Stratemeyer went on to establish Stratemeyer Syndicate, which employed ghostwriters to pen installments in such iconic series as *The Hardy Boys* and *Nancy Drew*. Later, in the 1980s, publisher Daniel Weiss of 17th Street Productions followed Stratemeyer's model by packaging the YA romance series *Sweet Dreams*—"Harlequin romances for kids," as Mead characterizes it (68)—which in turn cast the model for 17th Street's immensely popular *Sweet Valley High* series. Weiss's 17th Street was acquired by Alloy in 2000.[8]

Although this genealogy offers an effective narrative framework through which to understand the emergence of Alloy franchises such as *Gossip Girl*, it may nevertheless be useful to consider earlier narrative forms, as well as preceding strategies of publishing and marketing, that implicitly inform Alloy's own modus operandi. *Gossip Girl* is, after all, ultimately characterized as popular fiction: never conventionally associated with proper "literature," it is rather classified (or dismissed) as simply "chick lit." In this respect, it differs surprisingly little from earlier popular literary forms. Like nineteenth-century dime novels and penny papers, the *Gossip Girl* books are cheap and disposable, sold for purchase by readers with moderate-to-little disposable income; moreover, like these earlier works of pulp fiction, they are intended more for entertainment than for any lofty purposes of "enlightenment" or sophisticated aesthetic pleasure. Furthermore, like the nineteenth-century potboilers penned by the "d——d mob of scribbling women" so famously disparaged by Nathaniel Hawthorne,[9] they will probably be remembered (if at all) less for their literary pretensions than for their elaboration of domestic dramas. It may be useful, then, to examine the ways in which Alloy's series have been shaped by conventions initially established in the nineteenth-century United States.

The promotion and dissemination of the *Gossip Girl* books, for example, draws at least indirectly from the nineteenth-century practice of publication by subscription. As Gregg Camfield points out in his afterword to the Oxford edition of Mark Twain and Charles Dudley Warner's *The Gilded Age*—a novel to which I will refer later in this essay—the process of publication-by-subscription served as an "alternative to trade publication"

(25). Publication through subscription, Camfield explains, involved employing "peddlers [to] hawk a prospective book door to door where no bookstores existed, and then, once a sufficient number of books had been subscribed, to publish" (25). Such a technique, he continues, "had been practiced since colonial times but never developed into a mass-production business until manufacturers could produce high volumes of relatively inexpensive books, until literacy had become widespread and highly valued, and until a sufficient labor pool could be tapped to sell books throughout the country" (25). Curiously, the strategies employed by subscription publishers resemble those employed by Alloy today. Publishers' agents who "canvassed the country soliciting sales" would offer their potential buyers a prospectus, "a radical abridgement of the book, includ[ing] a table of contents, a list of illustrations, sample illustrations, and fragments of chapters—just enough to pique interest but never enough to satisfy" (28). Not unlike the "teasers" for other installments and publications offered at the conclusion of each *Gossip Girl* book, these prospectuses were provocative enough to ensure high sales.[10] Needless to say, the practice of door-to-door book sales is now defunct. Nevertheless, it has reemerged in uncanny form through the cataloging of purchasable books online, such as at the website www.gossipgirl.net.

Gossip Girl and its sister publications also resemble another nineteenth-century favorite, the "magazine novel." Although, as Patricia Okker argues, the trend of publishing successive installments of novels in magazines and newspapers is most commonly associated with British literary culture—most notably with the production of works by Charles Dickens, Wilkie Collins, and Arthur Conan Doyle—it was also popular in the United States. Harriet Beecher Stowe's *Uncle Tom's Cabin*, for example, was initially published in serial form by the antislavery paper the *National Era*; other prominent writers such as Henry James and Edgar Allen Poe published serial installments in popular American magazines. Although these serialized novels took materially different forms from contemporary series such as *Gossip Girl*—they were, after all, initially published in periodicals rather than in books immediately available at bookstores or online—they nevertheless set a production standard that these later books would follow. Like these later novels—and like the earlier subscription novels—they depended heavily on "teasers" that ensured the consumption of later installments. According to Okker, magazine editors struck a "balance between postponement and gratification" by publishing installments featuring "cliff-hangers" either in their middle or at their end (18–19); moreover, editors published simultaneous installments of multiple novels in order to guarantee that readers would continue to buy issues, even once the initial story that had attracted them had concluded (19).

Magazine editors also encouraged subscriptions by creating cults of celebrity authorship. Thus, for example, long before Alloy attached the name Cecily von Ziegesar to its *Gossip Girl* franchise, magazines such as *Ladies' Companion* and *Frank Leslie's Ladies' Gazette* banked on the celebrity status of writer Ann Stephens, whose fashion-forward historical romances guaranteed the purchase of multiple subscriptions (Okker 56). The celebrity of authors like Stephens was built up "through such popular features as book reviews, biographical sketches of contributors, autograph series, portraits of authors, and sometimes even engravings of their homes" (63)—even when, as Okker points out, some of the magazine installments were actually written by ghostwriters rather than by the "celebrities" themselves (22). Moreover, such cultivation of celebrity was enhanced by the authors' stylistic habit of directly addressing their "dear readers," which—not unlike Gossip Girl's apostrophizing her audience, to be discussed below—fostered a sense of intimacy between writer and reader and forged a sense of community among readers (63). Indeed, as Okker argues, the sense of community generated by celebrity-penned (or, sometimes, ghostwritten) installments resembled that of contemporary soap opera fan communities. Like present-day soap opera fans, Okker writes, readers of magazine novels enjoyed the "satisfaction of gossip without the guilt because the people aren't real and can't be hurt or betrayed by what one says about them" (17).[11] Not insignificantly, such pleasurable, harmless gossip seems to characterize the conversations among *Gossip Girl* fans, although such exchanges might just as well take place at online chat rooms as in person.

The parallels between late-nineteenth-century magazine novel installments and contemporary "chick-lit" series like *Gossip Girl* are apparent as well in their shared preoccupation with fashion. It is not insignificant, Okker writes, that the "same magazines that supported writers like Edgar Allan Poe and encouraged patronage of American authors also published fashion plates" (56).[12] Indeed, nineteenth-century magazines were richly intertextual insofar as they published not only poems, short stories, and novel installments by high- and middlebrow writers but also illustrations of the latest trends in clothing and advertisements for consumer commodities. Such close attention to clothing and accessories, Okker continues, was also evident *within* magazine novel installments as well; indeed, she argues that a nineteenth-century author like Stephens has been "criticized for her extended 'descriptions of female clothing' that make passages of her stories 'read like modern advertising copy'" (57). It is not difficult, at this point, to remark upon the similarity between charges leveled against nineteenth-century texts by Stephens and others and those applied to contemporary novels like *Gossip Girl*, which also tend to read like advertising copy. The parallels do not end here, however. According to Okker, the fashion-conscious stories published by magazines such as *Peterson's* "ultimately offered readers a way of masking what they were and instead promoting what they might want to be" (61). As Okker explains, the "kind of social status marked by fashion need not be real; indeed fashion promises its followers a chance to mark themselves by the social class they desire. Even when that promise remains unfulfilled, as it nearly always does, fashion magazines offer the illusion that change is possible with a different set of clothes" (61). Certainly, such fashion consciousness, as well as the class insecurities and desires it exploits, is as evident in such twenty-first-century books as *Gossip Girl* as it was in nineteenth-century magazines such as *Peterson's*.

Finally, one might trace *Gossip Girl's* literary ancestry to another late-nineteenth-century source: sensational literature. According to Shelley Streeby, sensational literature "began to proliferate in the 1840s" and was "roughly classified as a 'low' kind of literature in relation to a more middle-brow popular sentimentalism as well as to the largely nonpopular writing that would subsequently be enshrined as the classic literature of the American Renaissance" (27). Such literature depicted, among other subjects, frontier adventures, urban conflicts, and grisly crimes. Moreover, as David S. Reynolds argues, it also extended to voyeuristic accounts of erotic exploits; indeed, as Reynolds argues, "enough evidence survives" within preserved works of popular nineteenth-century fiction "to explode the long-standing myth that there was an all-powerful cult of domesticity that governed daily behavior and kept America a prudish, highly moralistic culture" (211). These descriptions of sensational literature reveal parallels between the sensational novels of the nineteenth century and popular twenty-first-century fiction such as *Gossip Girl*, especially in light of the emphasis made by both on feminine desire. Not unlike the heroines of Louisa May Alcott's minor but nevertheless popular—literary contributions, including "Pauline's Passion and Punishment" (1863) and the novella *Behind a Mask; or, A Woman's Power* (1866), the heroines of *Gossip Girl* struggle to conquer their male objects of desire, even when doing so entails a transgression of class boundaries—and especially when doing so prompts them to resort to subterfuge. Moreover, as in some especially racy nineteenth-century sensational stories, the *Gossip Girl* heroines are "either willing partners or actually aggressors in the sex act" (Reynolds 217).

It is not surprising, then, that the *Gossip Girl* series has met with the same kind of moral-minded criticism to which its American nineteenth-century predecessors were made subject. Charles Dickens, visiting the United States in 1842, accused American sensationalists of "pimping and pandering for all degrees of vicious taste, and gorging with coined lies the most voracious maw; [and] imputing to every man in public life the coarsest and vilest motives" (qtd. in David Reynolds 172). Likewise, Alcott—despite having earned her bread and butter from penning lurid tales—forced her literary avatar, Jo March in *Little Women,* to destroy her sensational scribblings after having learned from her love interest, Professor Bhaer, that such stories were morally endangering "trash" (333). Accusations against "voracious maw" and "trash" reemerge in contemporary reactions against the *Gossip Girl* series. In a review published in the *Wall Street Journal,* for example, Sally Beatty's admonishment of her audience is summarized in the subtitle of her essay: "It's Summer Book Season: Do You Know What Your Child Is Reading?" Clearly, this statement is intended to warn parents of the morally deleterious effects of the series. Likewise, feminist author Naomi Wolf accuses the series of promulgating a "value system in which meanness rules, parents check out, conformity is everything, and stressed-out adult values are presumed to be meaningful to teenagers" (22). Wolf insists that *Gossip Girl* is akin to "*Lord of the Flies,* set in the local mall, without the moral revulsion" (23). Not insignificantly, Wolf's article is accompanied by a sidebar entitled "What's a Girl to Read?" which lists apparently preferable young adult titles including Laurie Halse Anderson's *Speak* (1999) and John Green's *Looking for Alaska* (2005); such works, the sidebar proclaims, foster the "developing moral intelligence of both their characters and their audience" in ways that *Gossip Girl* presumably does not (23). Each of these criticisms—Beatty's, Wolf's, and the *Book Review's* sidebar alike—echoes a nineteenth-century, quasi-Arnoldian reaction against sensational popular fiction.[13] That is, each critique makes a claim against the presumably morally dangerous effects of the series. In so doing, each piece implies a divide between the "lowbrow" sensationalist logic of the series and the implicitly more morally enlightening efforts of superior works of fiction.

Gossip Girl and the Gilded Age

Gossip Girl invites accusations of sensationalism; indeed, it courts them. It is not insignificant, for example, that the series creator, Cecily von Ziegesar, was not only a graduate of a tony preparatory high school but an alumna of Colby College—a prestigious New England institution where the author no doubt received solid training in literary history. Nor is it insignificant, for that matter, that von Ziegesar's later ghostwriters graduated from universities that boast internationally renowned literature programs. It is no wonder, then, that the writers involved in this series—von Ziegesar and her ghostwriters alike—are especially attentive to its literary antecedents. Indeed, *Gossip Girl* acknowledges its debt to underappreciated, yet nevertheless thriving, nineteenth-century modes of storytelling and production. Von Ziegesar and the writers who extend her series insert historical and literary allusions into the novels as they do references to consumer goods. Moreover, the series' use of language is so hyperbolic, and its plots so contrived, that its allusions serve in effect as winks at the careful and appreciative reader.

Consider, for example, the opening passage of von Ziegesar's first installment of the *Gossip Girl* series, which features the inaugural post of the eponymous blogger, Gossip Girl. Not unlike a narrator of a nineteenth-century magazine novel, the blogger begins by apostrophizing her "dear reader"; crucially, however, she employs the more democratic, albeit more impersonal, "hey people!" (*GG* 3). Immediately thereafter, she resorts to a tactic also employed by certain magazine novel installments, particularly those intended for fashion-conscious female readers: provoking envy and desire in her presumably middle-class audience. "Ever wondered what the lives of the chosen ones are really like?" Gossip Girl asks in her opening sentence (3). Here, the reader is directly situated as an outsider to the lives of wealthy "chosen ones": the narrator assumes that the reader has only "wondered" about lives of privilege but has not actually experienced such life herself. The second line—"Well, I'm going to tell you, because I'm one of them"—reinstates the class divide that separates the reader from the narrator and her subjects. The blogger clearly demarcates a line between "you" (the lowly reader) and "I" and "them" (the privileged class); moreover, she situates herself in a position of authority from which she can instruct her humble audience. In the paragraph that follows, Gossip Girl complacently sketches the lives of those who "have everything anyone could possibly wish for and who take it all for granted":

Welcome to New York City's Upper East Side, where my friends and I live and go to school and play and sleep—sometimes with each other. We all live in huge apartments with our own bedrooms and bathrooms and phone lines. We have unlimited access to money and booze and whatever else we want, and our parents are rarely home, so we have tons of privacy. We're smart, we've inherited classic good looks, we wear fantastic clothes, and we know how to party. Our shit still stinks, but you can't smell it because the bathroom is sprayed hourly by the maid with a refreshing scent made exclusively for us by French perfumers. (3)

Like the first two lines of the novel, this paragraph establishes a clear divide between "we" and "you," with the express intention of mocking the imagined relative disadvantages experienced by the middle- or working-class reader. *You*, the text implies, do not have your own bedroom and bathroom; *you* do not have unlimited access to money; *your* shit stinks and *you* can't disguise the smell like *we* can.

One might expect that the snobbery of the novel's first paragraphs would turn away any self-respecting reader, even if such a reader has little knowledge of, or interest in, class struggles. After all, these lines are insulting, since they posit the reader as little more than a smelly yokel-ignoramus. And yet, judging from the immense popularity of the series, it seems as though audiences have managed to shrug off this preliminary offense to embrace Gossip Girl's self-touted authority. A reader's inclination to read on might be accounted for as an act of envy, wish-fulfillment, or abjection facilitated by false consciousness. What seems more likely, however, is that readers are taken by the pseudo-anthropological discourse of the eponymous blogger. As unpleasant as Gossip Girl's introduction might be, it nevertheless promises a voyeuristic glimpse into the lives of a slim demographic—a glimpse whose authenticity is reaffirmed by creator von Ziegesar's own acquaintance with rarefied Upper East Side culture. The reader is bidden, in other words, to see how the other half (or, more precisely, the top 1 percent) lives.

My allusion to Jacob Riis's *How the Other Half Lives* is intentional. In addition to employing the rhetorical tactics of the magazine novel and the lush, envy-inspiring imagery of the sensational novel, *Gossip Girl* also draws—subtly and perhaps paradoxically—on Riis's photojournalistic document of nineteenth-century New York City slums. Published in 1890, *How the Other Half Lives* allowed members of the American middle and upper classes to witness, from a comfortable distance, the working and living conditions faced by a predominantly immigrant urban workforce. Although Riis's photographs of crowded tenements, sweltering sweatshops, and street urchins were intended to stir readers' consciences and thus mobilize their correction of class injustices, it nevertheless was often read as a curiosity piece. Indeed, as Susan Sontag argues in *On Photography* (1977), Riis's text, like the later photojournalistic projects it inspired, "was an instrument of that essentially middle-class attitude, both zealous and merely tolerant, both curious and indifferent, called humanism—which found slums the most enthralling of decors" (56). According to Sontag, then, Riis's text shores up a normative, middle-class identity by positioning that identity against the images of poverty portrayed within the text. *Gossip Girl*, for its part, may be read as a funhouse mirror image of Riis's text. Written at the dusk, rather than at the dawn, of the twentieth century, it promises to reveal the hidden lives of the most—rather than the least—privileged members of U.S. society. In turn, it establishes a fixed boundary between its middle-class audience and its fictionalized upper-class subjects.

I also refer to Riis's text because it was published during an era that *Gossip Girl* seems intent upon evoking: that is, the so-called Gilded Age. The term "Gilded Age"—originally coined by Mark Twain and Charles Dudley Warner in their 1873 satirical novel, *The Gilded Age*[14]—is generally used by historians and literary critics to designate the last quarter of the American nineteenth century, an era marked by both fabulous wealth and incredible poverty. On the one hand, the development of new technologies—ranging from railroads to heavy machinery to commodities such as sewing machines, phonographs, and processed foods—aided in the emergence of a distinct middle class, which both oversaw production and enjoyed its fruits. Notably, it also lined the pockets of so-called captains of industry—less charitably known as robber barons—who consolidated monopolies and spent their profits on lavish estates, forbiddingly expensive commodities, and further stock holdings. On the other hand, however, this era witnessed the growth of a substantial working class, composed of immigrants and native-born citizens alike, who, realizing their exploitation by the owner class, began to unionize and strike.[15]

Gossip Girl shows absolutely no interest in the dramatic, and often tragic, history of the Gilded Age working class. It is positively obsessed, however, with the late-nineteenth-century robber barons, whom it intimates are the ancestors of its cast of spoiled characters. Indeed, the upper-class subjects whom *Gossip Girl* features could be just as much at home in the late nineteenth century as they are in the twenty-first. Unlike Alloy's other series, which take place in suburban gated enclaves, *Gossip Girl* is set in New York City—the proverbial heart of the Gilded Age. Moreover, the series takes pains to remind its readers that its upper-crust, Upper East Side heroines and heroes owe their privilege to fortunes amassed by their nineteenth-century ancestors. As the narrator announces in her inaugural post, the novels' characters are unique simply because they are "chosen" (3). "I'm not talking about beautiful models or actors or musical prodigies or mathematical geniuses," the narrator declares (3). Rather, she explains, "I'm talking about people who are *born into it*—those of us who have everything anyone could possibly wish for and who take it all for granted" (3). Besides inspiring envy in the reader, this post makes clear that heritage trumps all. The phrase "born into it"—emphatically italicized in the text—implies that the heroines of the novel have the privilege of emplotting themselves within genealogies unavailable to self-made artists or the upstart nouveau riche; theirs is an inheritance that stretches across generations. The post suggests, moreover, that although beauty might fade, talent might waver, and fortunes might be made and lost, one's blue-blood pedigree is a currency whose value rarely diminishes over time. In an era of makeshift celebrity and cut-and-paste trends, the heroines of *Gossip Girl* maintain a well-established status simply by virtue of their surnames—veritable calling cards that gain them entry into institutions and events forbidden to the novels' hoi polloi readership.

Moreover, the surnames *Gossip Girl* assigns to its principle characters, Serena and Blair, are thinly veiled allusions to the ostensible heroes of the Gilded Age. Serena van der Woodsen's surname, for example, substantiates her Dutch heritage and thus her claim to "original" European ownership of Manhattan: little wonder, then, that the series posits her as New York royalty. Moreover, and perhaps more significantly, Serena's surname provokes associations with the Gilded Age name of Vanderbilt: the Vanderbilt family owed its incredible fortunes to nineteenth-century railroad trusts and was for a time the wealthiest family in the United States. Likewise, Blair Waldorf's surname calls to mind the luxury Waldorf Hotel, opened in 1893 on Fifth Avenue by William Waldorf Astor. Thus, like the vintage Burberry coats donned by Serena or the black cardigans favored by Blair, their very surnames are veritable commodities that bespeak their essential, "chosen" natures. Their names are, as it were, especially high-cost brands that link them to Gilded Age dynasties. Simultaneously, their branded surnames remind readers of the impossibility of accessing the "lifestyle" touted by the novels. As the series suggests, unless one is a "van der Woodsen" or a

"Waldorf"—that is, unless one can attach oneself to a family that can trace back its wealth for at least a century—then one cannot possibly posit equality with the novels' "chosen ones."

Admittedly, the series' allusions to the Gilded Age are subtle: unless a reader is familiar with the historical and social weight carried by certain surnames, she might miss some of the book's references to a bygone era. The series' preoccupation with the Gilded Age becomes more apparent, however, once readers consider it alongside the CW network's primetime television adaptation of *Gossip Girl*. The series' pilot, for example, might as well be a modern-day adaptation of Edith Wharton's iconic depiction of upper-class Gilded Age culture, *The Age of Innocence*. The episode begins with a montage of establishing shots of New York's most fashionable spots (Bergdorf Goodman's, Madison Avenue, Park Avenue) and then closes in on a shot of Serena (the actress Blake Lively) as she gazes melancholically on her native city from the window of a train. By the next scene, which features Serena's arrival at Grand Central Station (once again, she gazes wistfully, this time from a balcony), it is clear that she is the series' tragic heroine, a social outcast returning to the circle that once nurtured her but now might well reject her. Not unlike Wharton's beautiful but scandal-stricken Countess Olenska, whose return to late-nineteenth-century New York is met by swirling rumors of her supposed marital infidelities, Serena's reentry to New York's Upper East Side is marked by energetic posts to Gossip Girl's website. As the former queen bee Serena walks into a soiree at a lavishly decorated penthouse—the mise-en-scène rivals that of Martin Scorsese's 1993 film adaptation of Wharton's novel—she is summarily snubbed by the guests, who whisper rumors of rehab and pregnancy. Ultimately, she is rebuffed even by her best friend, Blair (Leighton Meester), who gives Serena's invitation to a "Kiss on the Lips" party to the ambitious upstart, Jenny Humphrey (Taylor Momsen). The pilot thus frames the trajectory of the rest of the series, marking *Gossip Girl* as a reformulation of melodramatic plots of nineteenth-century intraclass warfare.

Subsequent episodes reaffirm the original's allusion to the Gilded Age. For the most part, these references are tacit: bad-boy Chuck Bass, for example, sports ascots; Serena takes up rooms at the Palace Hotel (a stand-in for New York's Plaza Hotel, established in 1906 near the mansions of Gilded Age millionaires); and queen bee Blair Waldorf barks commands from beneath a portrait of a Victorian-clad forebear. Other references, however, are comparatively heavy handed. The first season's tenth episode, for example—entitled "Hi, Society"—concerns Serena's and Blair's debutante ball at the Palace Hotel. Although Serena's love interest, the bohemian Dan Humphrey (Penn Badgley), dismisses the ball as "antiquated [and] a remnant of a different age"—and although Serena herself causes a scene at the cotillion—the audience is prompted to appreciate the nineteenth-century glamour of the whole affair. Indeed, wide-angle shots of carefully choreographed dances beneath chandeliers and sumptuous bouquets recall for the viewer scenes from costume dramas and period pieces and convince her that, as aspirant Jenny Humphrey puts it, such events are "totally legendary." In the second season, the series amplifies its allusions to the Gilded Age. In the eighteenth episode of this season, entitled "The Age of Dissonance," the cast takes part in a stage production of Wharton's *The Age of Innocence*.[16] The brilliance of this episode, gratuitous though it might be, depends upon a clever act of inversion. Here, the twenty-first-century characters' assumption of nineteenth-century roles reveals the secret formula of the entire series: namely, that *Gossip Girl* is itself a contemporary rehearsal of a familiar, nineteenth-century melodramatic plot.

Plus ça change, plus c'est la même chose

No doubt, *Gossip Girl* and its televised adaptation on the CW network promises a certain economy of pleasure. Audiences with even the slightest acquaintance with the social and literary culture of the Gilded Age are rewarded by these texts for their recognition of occasionally abstruse historical allusions. Audiences are rewarded as well with the gratifying suspicion that the *Gossip Girl* franchise may be more self-aware and subversive than it initially appears. After all, *Gossip Girl*—unlike many of Alloy's other offerings—appears to acknowledge its creators' deployment of nineteenth-century modes of production by making tacit, even sneaky, references to the mythical Gilded Age that gesture simultaneously to myths of extravagant wealth and to the underlying modes of production that make such wealth possible. A reader may be tempted, then, to consider the radical potential of a series that exposes, and thus ironically comments on, the ways in which its industrial means of production are gilded over by a pleasing historical metamyth.

It is crucial, however, not to assign too much significance to these apparently self-conscious moments of *Gossip Girl*. As Alissa Quart argues in her study of brands sold to adolescent consumers, the cleverness of self-referential and apparently self-parodic teen flicks such as *Clueless* and *10*

Things I Hate About You masks their ultimate objective of selling branded "lifestyles" to impressionable audiences. Adult critics, argues Quart, are often entranced by the gratifying cultural references made by these texts: they are captured, for example, by the ways in which Amy Heckerling's *Clueless* restages Jane Austen's *Emma* or the ways in which Gil Junger's *10 Things I Hate About You* repurposes Shakespeare's *The Taming of the Shrew*. Thrilled by these clever allusions, which they mistake for an aesthetic and political self-awareness, critics overlook the ways in which these films communicate an "exaltation of high-end goods and opulence" and offer a "sharp-edged satire camouflaging an ardor for consumption" (Quart 85). In the end, after all, *Clueless* celebrates the consumer habits of its spoiled heroine, just as *10 Things I Hate About You* concludes with a traditional, heteronormative pairing that implies the acquiescence of its headstrong female protagonist.

Likewise, it is important to recognize the ways in which *Gossip Girl*, for all its moments of self-reference, ultimately underscores, rather than undermines, Alloy's production of desire—desire that, in the logic of Alloy and its nineteenth-century predecessors, can be satisfied through the purchase of discrete commodities. Such desire is amplified, rather than dampened, by the series' presentation of traditional class structures as natural and therefore immutable. That is, by presenting its characters as undisputed heirs to earlier quasi-aristocratic claims, the series effectively erases the memory of historical movements—for example, labor strikes or later calls for gendered and racial enfranchisement—that challenged the entitlement preserved by an upper-crust, white, Anglo-Saxon Protestant ruling class.

Such rationalizing, reactionary logic works so brilliantly for *Gossip Girl* and its adaptations because it is steeped in nostalgia. Nostalgia, as Svetlana Boym argues, involves a "longing for a home that no longer exists or has never existed" (xiii). Moreover, she maintains, nostalgia can be politically conservative or even reactionary. "Restorative" nostalgia, as Boym puts it, seeks a "transhistorical reconstruction of the lost home"; such a form of nostalgia, which does not even "think of itself as nostalgia, but rather as truth and tradition," seeks to obliterate memory of the conflicts and contradictions of the past (and present) in order to present a unified vision of contemporary social relations (or *nostos*) (xviii).[17] Such nostalgia is, in other words, a form of fantasy. Certainly, *Gossip Girl* and its adaptations are fantasies not the least because they depend upon a view of late-nineteenth-, twentieth-, and twenty-first-century American history conveniently purged of social conflict. Moreover, they depend upon an idealized image of the Gilded Age as an era of enviable wealth and profligate play, rather than one that was marked by deplorable poverty and bloody class struggles. Such an image seduces the reader into coveting a point of time—indeed, a state of existence—that never actually existed in the first place. Once she is drawn into this fantasy, the reader is prompted to imagine that she could occupy the position of a Serena van der Woodsen or a Blair Waldorf, and therefore that she could transgress her own proscribed position. That is, by identifying with these heroines and occupying the idealized realm in which they live, the reader can imagine her life, and the historical context in which she lives, as other than what they actually are. However, such nostalgic acts of identification and aspirational desire are precisely what allow *Gossip Girl* and its adaptations to promulgate an essentialized and reified notion of class. Ultimately, readers are bidden to work out their desires within a nostalgic and ahistorical fantasy space, rather than to confront class disparities directly within their own lived moment. The logic guiding *Gossip Girl* is carnivalesque: by night, readers might entertain fantasies of Gilded Age sumptuousness, if only by day they concede to their humble, "real," and reified class positions.

Such channeling of nostalgic fantasy is lucrative indeed. Nostalgia, as Boym reminds her readers, is insatiable: it tantalizes one with the image of an ever-receding past, just out of reach. Certainly, insatiable desire has long been exploited by advertisers who depend on time-honored practices of "bait and switch." Once they have tempted audiences with objects of desire (for example, a scantily-clad woman or a pristine Caribbean beach), advertisers then harness such desire and project it toward the acquisition of comparatively lackluster commodities (for example beer, iced tea, or dryer sheets). The same strategies are demonstrable in *Gossip Girl*. Dazzled by the nineteenth-century "mystique" of the series' characters—and encouraged to perceive this mystique through the series' allusion-laden adaptations and spin-offs—the reader is prompted to covet those items that might place her "on a track running parallel to that of the series characters" (Pattee 167). In other words, the series exploits the very nostalgic yearnings it inspires by redirecting them toward the commodities it brazenly advertises within its pages. It is not entirely surprising, furthermore, that the *Gossip Girl* franchise should exploit such desires at a historical moment of dire economic distress—at a moment, as Melissa Terzis puts it, when the number of indigent American citizens equals the number of hairs on a spoiled girl's perfectly coiffed head—since its fantasies of aspiration waylay the potential of actual, material, albeit messy, challenges to a class-bound status quo. In this way, then, the series appears not so much to self-reflexively subvert nineteenth-century literary-qua-advertisement strategies as it does to reappropriate them. Like the nineteenth-century magazine novels that preceded it, *Gossip Girl* only offers the illusion that, as Patricia Okker puts it, "change is possible with a different set of clothes" (61).

NOTES

1. *GG* refers to the first installment of the series, entitled simply *Gossip Girl* (Von Ziegesar), published in 2002.

2. According to an article published in the *New York Times* in April 2006 (Rich and Smith), von Ziegesar composed the first eight novels in the series. However, accounts made by authors such as Rebecca Mead and Amy Pattee suggest that von Ziegesar's contributions were less substantial than those offered in this official statement. If nothing else, the uncertainty regarding von Ziegesar's actual contributions to the series should place into relief the ambiguity of its installments' authorship.

3. See, for example, Bellafante and Mechling.

4. Other Alloy-packaged series also depend on author biographies to authenticate the contents of their novels. The back cover of the first installment of *Pretty Little Liars* proclaims its author, Sara Shepard, to be a native of Philadelphia's Main Line—the setting of the series. Moreover, as Mead notes, the *Clique* series author Lisi Harrison maintains her celebrity authorship by writing a blog that receives up to a thousand reader responses per week (69).

5. When a user types this address into her browser, she is redirected to Alloy's *Gossip Girl* homepage (gossipgirl.alloyentertainment.com).

6. Juliet Schor identifies the Viacom-owned channel Nickelodeon as a particularly influential source of child-oriented marketing. The allusion to Nickelodeon in *Gossip Girl*, then, reveals a (perhaps unintentional, yet nevertheless significant) marketing nexus.

7. Wallace discusses the influence of television—including commercials, on which television programs depend—on American fiction written in the 1980s and 1990s. He writes, for example, that "there's something sad about the fact that young lion David Leavitt's sole description of certain story characters is that their T-shirts have certain name brands on them. But the fact is that, for most of the educated young readership for whom Leavitt writes, members of a generation raised and nourished on messages equating what one consumes with whom one is, Leavitt's descriptions *do the job*" (167, italics in original).

8. See the press release posted on www.publishersweekly.com on January 17, 2001.

9. Hawthorne's infamous phrase, meant to condemn the female writers whose works outsold his own, originally appeared in the author's 1855 letter to his British publisher, William D. Ticknor. Cited in Larry John Reynolds (33).

10. Indeed, critics of Twain and Warner's *The Gilded Age* were quick to point out that the novel, although it famously "attacked greed," was written by authors who "intended their attack to make them rich" from high subscription sales (Camfield 24).

11. Okker takes this quotation—attributed to a soap opera aficionado—from C. Lee Harrington and Denise Bielby's *Soap Fans: Pursuing Pleasure and Making Meaning in Everyday Life*, which, in part, studies the development of soap opera fan communities.

12. Okker's statement here is a loaded one, since she is addressing what she perceives to be biased scholarly responses to magazine novels. Contemporary literary critics, she argues, are quick to observe the commingling of fiction and advertising copy within magazines targeted toward female audiences (e.g., *Ladies' Companion*) but are comparatively reluctant to perceive similar trends in magazines that published the now canonical works of male writers such as Poe (56).

13. The term "Arnoldian" pertains to the writings of Victorian poet and literary critic Matthew Arnold, who, in *Culture and Anarchy* (1869), associated culture with perfection—including Victorian standards of moral perfection.

14. Twain and Warner's novel satirizes corruption, graft, and the interdependence of political and commercial interests in 1870s U.S. society. The narrative follows the rise and fall of a Tennessee family, the Hawkins, as its members—including its exotic and seductive adoptive member, Laura—move to Washington, D.C., to bank on their modest land holdings. The title of the novel suggests that the late nineteenth century was less a "golden age" than one "gilded over" by superficial and hypocritical special interests.

15. For a concise history of the Gilded Age, see Cashman.

16. Here, in something of a surprising reversal, it is Blair—and not Serena—who plays the role of Olenska. One might be tempted to read this reversal as a self-conscious "in-joke": it depends, that is, on the audience's recognition that it is Serena who has played the part all along.

17. Boym also cites another form of nostalgia, "reflective nostalgia," which "thrives in *algia*, the longing itself, and delays the homecoming—wistfully, ironically, desperately" and which "dwells on the ambivalences of human longing and belonging and does not shy away from the contradictions of modernity" (xviii). Such nostalgia, although it is profoundly engaged with affect, is nevertheless critical, and it not only admits but desires transformation within the future. Boym cites such intellectuals as Vladimir Nabokov and Walter Benjamin as practitioners of such reflective nostalgia. Certainly, *Gossip Girl* and its adaptations are examples of restorative, rather than reflective, nostalgia.

WORKS CITED

"The Age of Dissonance." *Gossip Girl*. The CW network, March 16, 2009. Television.

The Age of Innocence. Directed by Martin Scorsese. Performed by Daniel Day-Lewis, Michelle Pfeiffer, Winona Ryder. Columbia Pictures, 1993. Film.

Alcott, Louisa May. *Little Women*. 1868. New York: Bantam, 1983.

Alloy homepage. Alloy.com. Accessed November 17, 2011. Website.

Arnold, Matthew. *Culture and Anarchy*. 1869. Edited by J. Dover Wilson. Cambridge: Cambridge University Press, 1966. Print.

Beatty, Sally. "You're Reading . . . What?" *Wall Street Journal*, June 24, 2004; ProQuest National Newspapers. Accessed December 8, 2010. Website.

Bellafante, Ginia. "Poor Little Rich Girls, Throbbing to Shop." *New York Times*, August 17, 2003; ProQuest National Newspapers. Accessed December 8, 2010. Website.

Boym, Svetlana. *The Future of Nostalgia*. New York: Basic Books, 2001. Print.

Camfield, Gregg. Afterword to *The Gilded Age*, by Mark Twain and Charles Dudley Warner, 13–34. New York: Oxford University Press, 1996. Print.

Cashman, Sean Dennis. *America in the Gilded Age: From the Death of Lincoln to the Rise of Roosevelt*. New York: New York University Press, 1984. Print.

Clueless. Directed by Amy Heckerling. Performed by Alicia Silverstone, Brittany Murphy. Paramount Pictures, 1995. Film.

Dean, Zoey. *The A-List*. New York: Little, Brown, 2009. Print.

De la Cruz, Melissa. *The Au Pairs*. New York: Simon & Schuster, 2005. Print.

Gossip Girl homepage. Gossipgirl.alloyentertainment.com. Accessed November 30, 2012. Website.

Harrington, C. Lee, and Denise D. Bielby. *Soap Fans: Pursuing Pleasure and Making Meaning of Everyday Life*. Philadelphia: Temple University Press, 1995. Print.

Harrison, Lisi. *The Clique*. New York: Little, Brown, 2004. Print.

"Hi, Society." *Gossip Girl*. The CW network, December 5, 2007. Television.

Mead, Rebecca. "The Gossip Mill: Alloy, the Teen Entertainment Factory." *New Yorker*, October 19, 2009, 62–71. Print.

Mechling, Lauren. "A Nice Girl's Guide to Misbehaving: Cecily von Ziegesar's Books about the Antics of Privileged Manhattan Teenagers Have Parents in a Tizzy." *Telegraph* (London), October 17, 2002. Accessed November 30, 2012. Website.

Milliot, Jim. "Internet Company Buys 17th Street Productions." *Publishers Weekly*, January 17, 2001. Accessed November 17, 2011. Website

Okker, Patricia. *Social Stories: The Magazine Novel in Nineteenth-Century America*. Charlottesville: University of Virginia Press, 2003. Print.

Pattee, Amy. "Commodities in Literature, Literature as Commodity: A Close Look at the *Gossip Girl* Series." *Children's Literature Association Quarterly* 31:2 (2006): 154–175. Print.

Quart, Alissa. *Branded: The Buying and Selling of Teenagers*. Cambridge, Mass.: Perseus Books, 2003. Print.

Reynolds, David S. *Beneath the American Renaissance: The Subversive Imagination in the Age of Emerson and Melville*. New York: Alfred A. Knopf, 1988. Print.

Reynolds, Larry John. *A Historical Guide to Nathaniel Hawthorne*. New York: Oxford University Press, 2001. Print.

Rich, Motoko, and Dinitia Smith. "First, Plot and Character. Then, Find an Author." *New York Times*, April 27, 2006. Accessed October 7, 2013. Website.

Riis, Jacob A. *How the Other Half Lives: Studies among the Tenements of New York*. 1890. New York: Scribner, 1912. Print.

Schor, Juliet. *Born to Buy*. New York: Scribner, 2004. Print.

Sekeres, Diane Carver. "The Market Child and Branded Fiction: A Synergism of Children's Literature, Consumer Culture, and New Literacies." *Reading Research Quarterly* 44:4 (2009): 399–414. Print.

Shepard, Sara. *Pretty Little Liars*. New York: Harperteen, 2007. Print.

Sontag, Susan. *On Photography*. New York: Anchor Books, 1977. Print.

Stanley, Alessandra. "Reading, Writing, and Raunch: Mean Girls Rule Prep School." *New York Times*, September 19, 2007; ProQuest National Newspapers. Accessed December 8, 2010. Website.

Stein, Louisa. "Playing Dress-Up: Digital Fashion and Gamic Extensions of Televisual Experience in Gossip Girl's Second Life." *Cinema Journal* 48:3 (2009): 116–122. Print.

Stern, Madeleine, ed. *Louisa May Alcott Unmasked: Collected Thrillers*. Boston: Northeastern University Press, 1995. Print.

Stowe, Harriet Beecher. *Uncle Tom's Cabin*. 1852. New York: Modern Library, 1996. Print.

Streeby, Shelley. *American Sensations: Class, Empire, and the Production of Popular Culture*. Berkeley: University of California Press, 2002. Print.

10 Things I Hate About You. Directed by Gil Junger. Performed by Heath Ledger, Julia Stiles. Touchstone Pictures, 1999. Film.

Terzis, Melissa. "In Which My Brother Finds Someone Else's Christmas List." *Huffington Post*, December 21, 2010. Accessed December 26, 2010. Website.

Trachtenberg, Alan. *The Incorporation of America: Culture and Society in the Gilded Age*. New York: Hill & Wang, 1982. Print.

Twain, Mark, and Charles Dudley Warner. *The Gilded Age*. 1873. New York: Oxford University Press, 1996. Print.

Von Ziegesar, Cecily. *Gossip Girl*. New York: Warner Books, 2002. Print.

Wallace, David Foster. "E Unibus Pluram: Television and U.S. Fiction." *Review of Contemporary Fiction* 13:2 (1993): 151–194. Print.

Wharton, Edith. *The Age of Innocence*. 1920. New York: Penguin, 1996. Print.

Wolf, Naomi. "Wild Things." *New York Times Book Review*, March 12, 2006, 22–23; ProQuest National Newspapers. Accessed December 8, 2010. Website.

Precious Medals

The Newbery Medal, the YRCA,
and the Gold Standard of Children's Book Awards

CARL F. MILLER

In January 2004, Kate DiCamillo's *The Tale of Despereaux* was awarded the Newbery Medal, the oldest and most prestigious prize in children's literature. The selection of *The Tale of Despereaux* as the finest children's book of 2004 was not surprising; DiCamillo's book garnered almost universal critical approbation, was named a Junior Library Guild Selection, and would eventually be made into a major motion picture by Universal Pictures in 2008. What was surprising was that a little over two years later *The Tale of Despereaux* was also selected as the winner of the Young Reader's Choice Award (YRCA) Junior Division, the oldest literary children's choice award in America and a prize whose selections rarely align with those of the Newbery. By becoming only the eighth book to win both awards,[1] *The Tale of Despereaux* complexly fits the mold of both the Newbery Medal and the YRCA, two children's literary prizes with historically different missions and methods as well as historically different impacts on book sales. In doing so, it raises a series of questions about the relative lack of works able to reconcile the criteria of both awards, and the overall impact—both critical and material—of contemporary children's literary prizes.

Kenneth Kidd's groundbreaking 2007 article, "Prizing Children's Literature: The Case of Newbery Gold," provides an effective foundation for considering the complexities inherent to children's book awards, which offer a material expression of the critical-popular dialectic with legitimate cultural and economic consequences. Kidd's argument is grounded in the work of both John Guillory, who explains that "the hierarchy of cultural capital is reconfirmed most especially when popular or mass art is consumed according to the High mode of consumption" (332), and James English, who stresses that such "prizes . . . are the single best instrument for negotiating transactions between cultural and economic, cultural and social, or cultural and political capital—which is to say they are our most effective institutional agents of capital intraconversion" (10). While the Newbery presents the single most obvious institution of such capital intraconversion within children's literature, it by no means offers an exhaustive example of the role and potential of such prizes. On the heels of his own work, Kidd encourages "a broader focus on children's book awards, one testing and contextualizing the[se] arguments . . . through examination of multiple prizes" ("Prizing" 168), and the contrast between the Newbery Medal and the YRCA provides just such an ideal test case.

"Eminence and Distinction"

One of the primary reasons for the general divergence between the two awards is the difference in the history of each. The Newbery Medal is, as mentioned, the foremost children's literary award, as it has been since the medal's establishment in 1922, when Frederic Melcher campaigned to the American Library Association (ALA) for the establishment of the first children's book award in the world.[2] The Newbery's mission statement stressed that the award's purpose was to "emphasize to the public that contributions to literature for children deserve similar recognition to poetry, plays, or novels"; this criteria evolved over time to stipulate literature "for which children are a potential audience"—with children being defined as persons of ages up to and including fourteen—with an emphasis on literary "eminence and distinction." From its inception, the Newbery Medal was intended to act as a guide for librarians, teachers, parents, and children alike for selecting quality literature for and about young people.

The process of nominating Newbery titles has always been open to the masses, and Irene Smith explains that this was an exercise in both marketing and public relations designed "to create interest and induce good feeling" (40). However, Clara Hunt, cochair of the inaugural Newbery committee, considered it essential to limit committee membership to "a few people of recognized high standards and experience," because "if a majority vote of all so-called children's librarians determines the award it is entirely possible for a mediocre book to get the medal"[3] (Smith 40). While the original selection was left to popular vote,[4] by 1928 the final decision had been fully vested to a concentrated committee of ALA members. This has remained the critical hierarchy to this day, with the current panel of fifteen librarians and educators representing various regions across America.[5] Kidd consequently (and rightly) terms librarians "the mainstay of the medal" ("Prizing" 168), and this is in accordance with Melcher's initial proposal for the award, which stated that its intention was to "give those librarians, who make it their life work to serve children's reading interests, an opportunity to encourage good writing in this field" through their wielding of critical power.

Melcher—a native of Great Britain himself—did not stipulate that the winning author be a native-born American. As such, a number of foreign-born writers have won the award, including the first two winners of the Newbery Medal, Hendrik Willem van Loon (Holland) and Hugh Lofting (Great Britain). The award regulations do state, however, that consideration for the award be limited to citizens or residents of the United States. Potential nominees are thereby required to live in America and produce work that can be added to the canon of American children's literature.

In such a way, the Newbery Medal was designed every bit as much for writers as it was for readers. Melcher believed that the award "could encourage the writing of more worthwhile books for children by really able authors" (Viguers 431), emphasizing that "by creating a greater audience, we are also creating literature itself" (Smith 47). Whether a result of the award or simply an inevitable product of the times—such as the establishment of the first children's publishing house at Macmillan in 1918—the Newbery's material objective was quickly achieved. The number of new books produced for children increased from 433 in 1919 to 931 in 1929 (Viguers 431), by which time eight other publishing houses devoted to children's books had been established. As a result, the total number of children's books printed in the United States rose from twelve million copies in 1919 to more than thirty-one million by 1927 (Viguers 431).

This material expansion of the children's book industry created an unprecedented opportunity for marketing the quality titles that had been recognized by the Newbery committee. Although not stated explicitly anywhere in its mission statement, the Newbery Medal's ability to drive children's book sales has been arguably the most notable achievement of the award. The award was founded by a bookseller—Melcher—who worked for *Publishers Weekly* and had previously been a founding force behind such literary promotions as Children's Book Week. The award was furthermore named after eighteenth-century British book publisher John Newbery, who, according to Smith, "was not an educator. He was a benevolent bookseller.

He saw that children's books could be important in his business, and he developed them with taste and enthusiasm" (23).[6]

This is not to say that there is an overt materialist agenda to the Newbery's selection; to its credit, the ALA sought from the start to downplay the economic emphasis of its award by refraining from giving a cash prize to the winner. (In comparison, the Pulitzer Prize—the oldest literary award in America—offered a $500 award to its inaugural winners in 1917, a prize that has risen over the years to the current figure of $10,000; the Nobel Prize— the oldest literary prize in the world—awarded over $20,000 to its initial winners in 1901, a figure that has since escalated to well over $1 million). In spite of this, the prestige and reward of the Newbery Medal has often come to be measured by both immediate and long-term sales. It has traditionally been seen, in the words of Anita Silvey, as "the one literary prize that can dramatically boost book sales," beyond even the Nobel and Pulitzer Prizes.

As such, the Newbery Medal occupies a prominent spot on the front covers of its winners, and Newbery titles past and present are given featured positions in contemporary children's bookselling catalogs such as *Scholastic* and on websites such as Amazon.com. Many bookstores—particularly larger chain stores like Barnes & Noble—even feature a separate Newbery shelf in their children's book sections; in such a way, English observes, "these instant classics may be perused as a set—more or less as though they were titles bearing a common authorial signature or products manufactured under the same brand name" (361). The Newbery Medal has consequently developed into an award that not only recognizes outstanding works of children's literature but sells them, too, having earned widespread fame for both these activities in its nine decades of existence.

The (Young) People's Choice

While lacking the brand-name recognition of the Newbery Medal, the Young Reader's Choice Award—the oldest children's choice award in North America—has a distinguished history and a selection process of its own. The YRCA was founded almost two decades after the Newbery Medal in 1940 by Seattle native Harry Hartman, who was—like Melcher—a bookseller who insisted that his name not be present on the actual award. Like the Newbery, the YRCA offers no cash prize to its winners, with the only material reward being a silver medal (valued, for the record, at approximately $400), and its committee in charge of administration comprises experienced librarians and educators rather than publishers and members of the media.

In contrast with the national range of the Newbery, however, the YRCA was established as a regional contest conducted by the Pacific Northwest Library Association (PNLA), which serves the American states of Washington, Oregon, Idaho, Montana, and Alaska, and the Canadian provinces of British Columbia and Alberta. The award was intended to reflect the interests of a significantly smaller demographic and allow for a uniform representation within its constituency, with the YRCA committee comprising one representative from each state and province in the PNLA.

The PNLA has also chosen to draw more precise boundaries with regard to the intended age ranges of its award. In comparison with the single-division Newbery Medal, the YRCA has evolved over the years into a multidivisional award. A Senior Division was introduced in 1991 and an Intermediate Division added in 2002, in an effort to better ensure that winning titles are indisputably age-appropriate. In spite of this, it is still the YRCA's Junior Division (fourth to sixth grade) that remains the most hotly contested and prestigious of the awards. In 1999, for example, there were 53,318 votes cast in the Junior Division contest, compared with only 3,252 in the Senior Division. Accordingly, the qualifications of the YRCA Junior Division generally mirror those of the Newbery, with respect to both target audience and subject matter. There have been exceptions to this trend, such as Lois Lowry's *The Giver* and Karen Cushman's *The Midwife's Apprentice*, both Newbery Medal winners that also won the Senior Division YRCA.[7] On the whole, though, the overwhelming majority of YRCA titles that were also considered for the Newbery Medal—including the aforementioned *The Tale of Despereaux*—tend to fall into its Junior Division.

Beyond the subtle differences between the two awards, what makes the YRCA truly distinct from the Newbery Medal is the fact that children themselves are the voters, as the YRCA passes the final selection of the award from librarian to child.[8] The YRCA award description has long stated that Hartman's initial goal was that "every student have the opportunity to select a book that gives him or her pleasure." In giving children responsibility for both the nomination and election process, the YRCA downplays the Newbery's belief in the necessity of experience. To be eligible to vote, a child need simply have read (or have been read) two of the titles on the ballot and be in a grade level represented by that particular YRCA division.

To be fair, this notion of schoolchild autonomy is not absolute: teachers, parents, and librarians—as well as students—from the PNLA's constituent states are all eligible to nominate titles, and the actual nomination list is finalized by the YRCA committee, with consideration to the number of nominations received, reading enjoyment, reading level, genre, diversity, and availability. The committee then submits the nominees—generally a list of eight to ten books—to selection by popular vote by schoolchildren. This sort of subjectivity is required, for example, in the event that a title is nominated in multiple divisions, as has happened on a regular basis. With that exception, though, children are responsible for democratically determining the YRCA recipient, as the award allows them, per the YRCA mission statement, "an opportunity to flex their reading muscles and, at the same time, develop standards of taste."

The YRCA also represents a trend away from the sales influence so often associated with the Newbery Medal. Hartman's rationale in establishing the YRCA was simply to promote reading enjoyment, and he accordingly structured the award's bureaucracy and selection process in a manner that privileged entertainment over economics. While it would be incorrect to call its agenda anticapitalist, it is fair to say that the YRCA carries a low marketing profile in relation to that of the Newbery Medal. The YRCA has remained a regional award, and as such its economic influence in other regions of the United States is generally nonexistent. Its insignia and medal do not appear on book covers and rarely merit mention on websites or in catalogs. For example, the 2011 YRCA winner, Kazu Kibuishi's *Amulet: The Stonekeeper*, carries no mention of the YRCA on its sales pages at Barnesandnoble.com and Amazon.com, and Kibuishi even fails to make mention of it on his *personal* website for Bolt City Productions.[9]

While such lack of mention on corporate websites is evidence of the award's marginalization and lack of immediate sales influence, such omission of the YRCA in the winning books themselves is often the result of a work having yet to win the award at the time of mass printing. The YRCA does not allow titles to be nominated until three years after their initial publication date—as opposed to the Newbery's mandate of one year—with the rationale being that paperback editions will be available by that time and make the titles accessible to all children. This two-year lag is crucial to keep in mind when discerning overlap winners of the two awards. (For example, the 1999 Newbery Medal aligns with the 2001 YRCA, which were both won by Louis Sachar's *Holes*.)

As a result, whereas the Newbery Medal ensures that a large number of children will read the book, the YRCA is awarded because a large number of children have *already* read the book. This has significant implications with respect to critical distinction, given that the Newbery committee must take more risks with their (relatively unknown) selections, a fact that makes its sales reputation all the more impressive. Meanwhile, the YRCA acknowledges that its nominees are titles that "are already favorites with readers," and it is consequently an award that lacks marquee status. By the time the YRCA is awarded to dual winners like *The Tale of Despereaux*, the Newbery Medal has already guaranteed that book's material success. On the other hand, for works that did not win the Newbery, the YRCA is simply the recognition that the book has already achieved reasonable sales and found its way into the homes and school systems of child readers without the YRCA's influence.

A World Apart

Perhaps because of this, the YRCA has steered clear of becoming a vehicle for promoting new writers to children, in stark contrast to the track record of the Newbery Medal. While the Newbery carries no stipulation against multiple winners—indeed, its rules read that "the committee is not to consider the entire body of the work by an author or whether the author has previously won the award"—the rarity of such an occurrence (five times in ninety-two years) suggests a discrimination against past winners, or at least a preference for writers who have not won the award before.

Guillory observes that "the critique of the canon has proceeded as though it were . . . like the Academy Awards" (8), and Kidd agrees that prominent literary prizes "encourage both the making and unmaking of canons" ("Prizing" 166). However, in the case of the Newbery, such canonization often extends beyond the book itself to the writer in general. An author who has won a Newbery Medal will always be considered a Newbery Medal winner, as this recognition appears on subsequent books and fuels sales of both past and future works by that author. Thus, while the impact of an initial Newbery is enormous, the benefit of a second is much less critically and materially significant.

The YRCA, on the other hand, has not been shy about bestowing writers with multiple awards, and it is revealing that these writers are most often individuals who have not won the Newbery Medal, including Cornelia Funke, Judy Blume, Ann M. Martin, John D. Fitzgerald, Jay Williams, William Corbin, and Walter Farley. Perhaps just as tellingly, none of the five authors who have won the Newbery Medal on multiple occasions[10] have won the YRCA Junior Division (the closest being Lois Lowry, who won the 1996 Senior Division YRCA for *The Giver*).

The rationale for this trend is most likely tied to the Newbery's comparatively liberal-pluralist agenda, which strives for an even representation of all identities whether contemporary, historical, domestic, or foreign. Despite its aforementioned emphasis on producing an American canon of children's literature, from its first selection in 1922—Hendrik Willem van Loon's *The Story of Mankind*—the Newbery set a precedent of looking beyond American borders for its winners' settings. Guillory suggests that "the socially progressive agenda of liberal pluralism could be effected in a particular institution . . . by transforming the literary syllabus into an inclusive or 'representative' set of texts" (7), and, in its first decade alone, the Newbery Medal was awarded to books set in Japan, Poland, India, China, and South America.

The potential pitfalls of this trend toward pluralism and foreign settings are pointed out by Anita Silvey, who argues that "valuing uniqueness over universality has often led judges down the wrong road." Those titles set in contemporary America have often found themselves at a distinct disadvantage to their more exotically located competitors. In the most infamous example, E. B. White's *Charlotte's Web*, despite consequently enjoying almost unparalleled critical and commercial appeal across multiple generations, lost out on the 1953 Newbery Medal to the now largely forgotten *Secret of the Andes* by Ann Nolan Clark[11] (with a committee member confessing that she preferred the latter "because she hadn't seen any good books about South America" [Silvey]). While this is a glaring exception amid a solid body of selections, the fact remains that—despite going to great lengths to consider and award titles from as wide a range of settings and experiences as possible—the time and place most often neglected has been that of the Newbery's own contemporary domestic scene.

In contrast, this void has historically constituted the foundation of the YRCA, which has remained firmly entrenched in the domestic sphere. The YRCA was founded at a time when a distinct emphasis on American setting was developing; as Ruth Viguers explains, "the 1940s were not good years for foreign travel and . . . the realistic family story, which is so important to children, regardless of its setting, had, quite naturally in this decade, found American soil most congenial for its home" (444). This trend within the YRCA would continue for the next few generations. In fact, out of the first sixty YRCA winners, only *one* was explicitly set outside the United States and Canada—Marie McSwigan's Norwegian-based *Snow Treasure* (1945). It is worth noting that this tradition has been in transition over the past decade, given that recent YRCA winners have included a trio of foreign-based fantasies: Cornelia Funke's *The Thief Lord* (2005) and *Dragon Rider* (2007) and DiCamillo's *The Tale of Despereaux* (2006), with the caveat being that these books are extensively focused on fanciful worlds of magic and animals that transcend the foreign settings of their titles.

This insistence on American values and settings may come as a surprise, given that—unlike the Newbery Medal—the YRCA has no requirements regarding authorial citizenship or residence (the only such requirement being that the book be published in paperback in the United States or Canada). The written procedures for the YRCA ballot state that the award "is committed to intellectual freedom and diversity of ideas," and have in the past gone out of their way to encourage the inclusion of foreign/pluralist material, stating that even titles deemed to be "controversial or offensive" are acceptable "if their inclusion contributes to the diversity of the ballot." The YRCA guidelines currently conclude by emphasizing that "no title will be excluded because of the race, nationality, religion, gender, sexual orientation, political or social view of either the author or the material."

These aims, however, seem to have little effect on the voting habits of children, who display a proclivity to times and settings that offer a direct reflection of themselves. In the spirit of most large-scale political elections, when democratic power is given to a diverse constituency with a distinct majority, its voting results tend to be strikingly homogeneous. Consequently, in spite of the fact that its Newbery counterpart was consciously designed as an American institution, it is the multinational YRCA that clings tightest to American themes and settings.

Criticism and Materialism

While Kidd's analysis of the Newbery Medal builds usefully on Guillory's influential *Cultural Capital* (1993), it is equally indebted to James English's *The Economy of Prestige* (2005). English's book represents the most comprehensive academic assessment of the institution and industry of cultural prizing, and directly confronts the cultural and material reality of awards from the Oscars to the Razzies. In spite of this, very little of English's book mentions the Newbery Medal, and that which does compares children's literature to pornography in that "there are very few fields of cultural consumption . . . in which prizes have a more direct and powerful effect on sales" (97). While such categorization further implies that adults view both fields as utilitarian in nature, it ignores the fact that children do read children's books with a critical/cultural eye, as opposed to the adults who potentially view them as essential and mundane building blocks to basic education in the same respect as a standard math textbook.

Not surprisingly, the quest for critical legitimacy is a central concern of the Newbery's mission, which seeks to elevate exceptional children's literature above the milieu that fuels such formulaic and utilitarian perceptions. The final note of the current Newbery criteria reads that "the committee should keep in mind that the award is for literary quality and quality presentation for children. The award is not . . . for popularity." Kidd explains that, "if not exactly a canon, the [Newbery] Medal is part of the canonical architecture of children's literature" ("Prizing" 169). The popularity of Newbery books in the economic marketplace is balanced by the Newbery committee's selection of works that are relatively complex and morally meaningful, even at the occasional expense of accessibility to all child readers.

Much like English, cultural theorists such as Pierre Bourdieu have largely omitted children's books in their studies of literature, and the economic complications raised by the Newbery Medal might help to explain why. Bourdieu notably argues that "there is an economy of cultural goods [that] has a specific logic" (*Distinction* 1), characterized by the "incommensurability of the specifically cultural value and economic value in a work" (*Field* 22). In such a way, Bourdieu claims, "the economy of practices is based, as in a generalized game of 'loser wins', on a systematic inversion of the fundamental principles of all ordinary economies" (*Field* 39), with those titles that enjoy the greatest popularity and profitability being those that gravitate away from critical approbation and highbrow culture.

The Newbery Medal and the YRCA, meanwhile, offer a veritable inversion of Bourdieu's theory. While Newbery Medal titles tend to enjoy steady sales, it is not uncommon for YRCA winners to go out of print over time (or in a little over a decade, as is the case with the 1991 YRCA winner, Ann M. Martin's *Ten Kids, No Pets*). Often it can be difficult to surmise why a Newbery Medal winner like *Johnny Tremain* (1944) stays in print while a similar YRCA winner like *The Swamp Fox* (1962) does not. English notes that while winning the Newbery Medal is said to guarantee 100,000 units in hardcover sales in the first year, "more significant is the high likelihood of a Newbery Book maintaining strong sales for years or decades afterward, as parents of each rapidly emerging reader-generation purchase the book for their children" (360–361). Whether the ubiquitous presence of the Newbery

Medal exerts an influence on keeping titles in print or whether the Newbery committee simply does a better job of selecting commercially viable titles might be a matter for debate. The fact remains, however, that Newbery titles have proven astoundingly stable in a traditionally fickle printing market, while YRCA winners have not been immune to market variables.[12]

The Newbery Medal has thereby inverted Bourdieu's argument by repeatedly demonstrating that the highest culture within children's literature *is* the best business. While the reputation of the award has often been focused on its sales clout, the Newbery Medal has also come to represent the pinnacle of culture and aesthetics within children's literature, a distinction achieved by the award's insistence on high standards of theme, clarity, and style. Polly Horvath's *The Canning Season,* one of the finalists for the 2004 Newbery Medal along with *The Tale of Despereaux,* saw its candidacy seriously handicapped by its multiple usage of the f–word; indeed, the customer reviews on Amazon.com almost universally protest Horvath's use of this taboo language. Meanwhile, Susan Patron's *The Higher Power of Lucky,* which won the 2007 Newbery Medal despite using the word "scrotum" on the first page, faced no real scrutiny from adults until it won the highest award in children's literature, at which point it was subject to protests from parents, teachers, and librarians.

Such controversy is in part grounded in the Newbery's status as the standard bearer for the children's literature industry, but equally significant is the understanding that such controversy is not simply a temporary issue. Because of the award's material influence, a Newbery title is virtually guaranteed perpetual circulation, necessitating that the work remain relevant and politically acceptable well into the future. As Kidd explains, "Medal books are instant classics, [and] the selection process an ostensible simulation of the test of time" ("Prizing" 169).[13]

Whether by coincidence or not, Newbery-winning titles have achieved instant canonical credibility by relying on time-tested, already significant moments in time—as opposed to the tenuous concerns of the present day—as the subjects of its winning titles.[14] There has been a significant emphasis on historical fiction by the Newbery Medal from its first winner (Van Loon's *The Story of Mankind*) to the 2012 recipient (Jack Gantos's *Dead End in Norvelt*), and these works appear timeless precisely because readers are granted instant historical perspective with respect to their content. For example, the 2010 Newbery Medal winner, Rebecca Stead's *When You Reach Me,* offers a safe and nostalgic choice for adult critics in that its narrative is set in 1979 and based around episodes of *The $20,000 Pyramid* hosted by Dick Clark.[15]

Had the book actually been published in 1979, it likely would have merited scant consideration for the Newbery on the assumption that its pop cultural foundation would prove short lived. There is thus an inherent irony when critics such as Sophia Goldsmith have implored the Newbery to select winners "against the background of their own day" (316), when this is precisely what committee members are doing with the selection of winners set twenty to fifty years in the past.

The YRCA, on the other hand, has not demonstrated an insistence on aesthetic high-mindedness and literary immortality for its winners. In contrast with the Newbery tendency toward historical fiction, the YRCA has traditionally prioritized works set in the present that offer direct reflections of contemporary childhood. As children are responsible for the YRCA election, accessibility to child readers is paramount for prospective titles. In contrast to adult critics, children, in the words of Sophia Goldsmith, will "demand the stimulus of their own time, or at least of periods not invariably long before their own time" (315). Accordingly, while the Newbery committee has more often than not selected reflections of other times and cultures, the YRCA constituency almost invariably seeks a reflection of themselves. Selections involving some combination of school (Jamie Gilson's *Thirteen Ways to Sink a Sub* [1985]), animals (Deborah and James Howe's *Bunnicula* [1982]), and conventional family life (Judy Blume's *Superfudge* [1983]) have long been the YRCA norm.

The fact that a book is appealing to child voters, however, does not necessarily render it a work of timeless appeal and aesthetic unity; Kidd emphasizes that "prizing . . . underwrites but also undercuts faith in popularity" ("Prizing" 166). The current YRCA guidelines stipulate that books under consideration "will be judged on popularity with readers," with no specific codification of quality, style, or subject matter. Until the YRCA handbook was altered in 2008, it made the veiled concession that its winners "*usually* reflect quality children's literature." This qualification is important, because a number of YRCA titles would be practically impossible to include in any canon of high-culture children's literature, including Eve Bunting's *Nasty, Stinky Sneakers* (1997), Keith Robertson's *Henry Reed's Babysitting Service* (1969), and Jay Williams's *Danny Dunn and the Homework Machine* (1961).

In such a way, the dialectical relationship between Newbery Medal and YRCA selections seems to mirror Guillory's claim—in agreement with Bourdieu—that the two forms of aesthetic judgment are "an elite aesthetic of the dominant classes . . . and a 'popular' aesthetic of the dominated" (332). The aforementioned fears of a "mediocre" book winning the award, so critical in shaping the Newbery selection procedure, bear little upon the YRCA selection process. The YRCA is, admittedly and unashamedly, a popularity contest among children, and there have consequently been a number of YRCA winners that would never have made it past preliminary consideration for the Newbery Medal.

The Medal Platform

This is not to say, though, that YRCA titles can be generally categorized as mediocre books, even by the Newbery committee itself. *The Tale of Despereaux* stands as testament that the two awards can reach a consensus selection. While such agreement is rare (it has happened eight times in sixty-eight years), YRCA-winning titles that did not win the Newbery Medal have regularly made it into the final stages of the Newbery competition. A quick review of the list of Newbery Honor Books—the consolation prize(s) for the runner-up title(s)—reveals a less striking discrepancy between the two awards.[16] Sometimes the difference between awards speaks more to qualification than it does to quality; for example, the 1950 YRCA winner, Dr. Seuss's *McElligot's Pool*, was an Honor Book for the ALA's Caldecott Medal.[17] And there have also been occasions when YRCA-winning writers have won the Newbery Medal with a different title—as is the case with Beverly Clearly, whose lone Newbery winner, *Dear Mr. Henshaw* (1984), was not among her record five YRCA winners.

Furthermore, in spite of its unparalleled critical and material reputation, Kidd contends that "the value of Newbery gold isn't what it used to be" ("Prizing" 181), and he is one of a number of recent critics who have questioned whether the Newbery has gravitated away from enjoyable texts and toward a particular standard of elevated taste that adults applaud and children tend to shun. Silvey reports that, out of the Newbery titles from the first decade of the twenty-first century, "the only recent winners [that teachers] enjoy teaching are *Bud, Not Buddy, A Single Shard,* and *The Tale of Despereaux*." Perhaps more significant, among this century's first decade of Newbery winners, only *Bud, Not Buddy* and *The Tale of Despereaux* have demonstrated consistent sales since their selection (Silvey)—and it is likely little coincidence that these titles are the only dual winners of the Newbery Medal and the YRCA over this time. This raises the question of whether the Newbery's cultural aims have actually come to diminish its material influence on children's literary sales, and whether such a trend is indicative of the increasing significance of children's choice awards on the literary marketplace.

While the Newbery Medal is clearly opposed to censorship, it nevertheless represents a related process; rather than material suppression, it is grounded in material production. It does not ensure that works that do not fit its standards will not be published, but it does ensure that its valued titles will remain in print, which presumably shifts the print marketplace in favor of like-minded works. As Kidd suggests, "literary prizing has been a remarkably effective mechanism for publicity, sales, and scandal, if not always for the production of literature" ("Prizing" 166). Hence, in spite of Melcher's original objective, it is possible that the Newbery Medal—by holding to a relatively conservative model of critical value—is in fact reducing the contemporary production of original works for children.

All of this emphasizes the need to look beyond any single award—even one as distinguished and multiculturalist as the Newbery—in considering the literary marketplace, the academic curriculum, and the literary canon. Guillory explains that while "the politics of canon formation has been understood as a politics of representation" (5), it "is only *as* noncanonical texts that certain other texts can truly represent socially subordinated groups" (9). While this has generally been understood as applicable to underrepresented social minorities,[18] it holds true even if the socially subordinated group in question is the average majority of American schoolchildren. While the front of the Newbery Medal states that the award is "For the Most Distinguished Contribution to American Literature for Children," the back depicts an adult offering a book to a pair of children, with the understanding that it is his duty to shepherd their reading interests. Kidd's impassioned conclusion to his analysis of prizing openly questions many of the assumptions that underlie this image: "We operate *as if* we are a democracy, *as if* we know our best books, *as if* those books are by and for the people—*as if* our scholarship matters. Are we fooling ourselves?" ("Prizing" 184).

With this in mind, there have been a number of instances over the years in which the selections of the YRCA have proven nothing short of independent and insightful. The selection of a graphic novel as the 2011 winner—Kibuishi's aforementioned *Amulet: The Stonekeeper*—stands as a formally progressive selection, as no such work in this often marginalized genre has ever won the Newbery Medal. On the heels of the Newbery committee selecting Madeleine L'Engle's indelibly popular *A Wrinkle in Time* in 1963, the child voters of the YRCA selected Richard Tregakis's biographical *John F. Kennedy and PT-109*, a direct homage to America's fallen president of two years prior.[19] Most strikingly, in 1945, the YRCA was given to Marie McSwigan's *Snow Treasure*, a tale of Norwegian children in the midst of Nazi Germany's occupation of their homeland—and a book that had been passed over as an Honor Book by the 1943 Newbery committee in favor of Mabel Leigh Hunt's *Have You Seen Tom Thumb?*

It is, of course, both attractive and easy to be the Party of No within children's literature (something Kidd is distinctly aware of) and to merely highlight the flaws inherent to any system of prizing. The point is not to question the aims of the Newbery Medal—which have been unfailingly noble—or to diminish its significance, as it remains the single most important institution within children's literature. Rather, it is worth considering whether the *finest* selections of the Newbery committee are also those that align themselves with the critical expectations of the YRCA (and vice versa). The dual selection of titles such as *The Tale of Despereaux* speaks to the awards' concurrent viability and intent to identify and reward outstanding works of children's literature, and the popular and critical acclaim garnered by these crossover winners indicates that, when the bronze medal of the Newbery is combined with the silver medallion of the YRCA, the result is children's literary gold.

NOTES

1. The other dual winners of the Newbery Medal and the YRCA are *King of the Wind* by Marguerite Henry, *Mrs. Frisby and the Rats of NIMH* by Robert C. O'Brien, *Roll of Thunder, Hear My Cry* by Mildred D. Taylor, *Maniac Magee* by Jerry Spinelli, *Shiloh* by Phillis Reynolds Naylor, *Holes* by Louis Sachar, and *Bud, Not Buddy* by Christopher Paul Curtis.

2. Since 1922, the ALA has grown to an organization of more than sixty thousand members that presides over twenty book and media awards annually, including a number of children's literary prizes. As Kidd contends, "While the ALA does not have a monopoly on either prizing or anticensorship programs, the organization does function as a central and centralizing body of literary vetting, especially when it comes to children's books" ("Not Censorship" 202).

3. Hunt was not alone in advocating this change: by 1924, the ALA's Book Evaluation Committee voiced its concern that "the method of the Newbery Medal does not seem satisfactory. We do not believe that a popular vote of the section can be depended upon to select the most distinguished contribution for the year and think another method should be devised" (Smith 52).

4. In this initial election, Hendrik Willem van Loon's *The Story of Mankind* won in a landslide, with 163 out of the 212 votes cast going to Van Loon's book.

5. Of the fifteen members of the Newbery selection committee, eight are elected by the ALA's general membership, including the chair, who is then responsible for appointing the other seven members.

6. Such dual interests should come as no surprise; as Joel Taxel sensibly explains, "The publishing industry always has been a business designed to make a profit" (146). This is, however, a trend that has significantly intensified in the past quarter century, to the point that Taxel warns against "the domination of the industry by huge multimedia conglomerates seeking to maximize the synergistic interplay of their holdings" (182). Newbery titles accordingly offer an attractive commodity for corporations given both their proven sales record and the ability to package individual works by separate authors together as part of a series.

7. With this in mind, an additional study that more closely considers the specifics and qualifications of age-tiered categories could be useful in the context of this larger discussion of children's literary awards.

8. Deborah Cogan Thacker and Jean Webb emphasize that children's literature "includes an implicit power relationship between adults and children in its reason for existence" (112). "The function of literature," they continue, "to offer a comforting vision of the world, as well as to entertain, becomes more difficult as the social spheres of children and adults become more separate" (112). Fully transcending this divide is an obvious impossibility, given that, as Juliet Dusinberre emphasizes, "children do not write their own books" (33). Instead, it is children's critical receptions that most immediately offer a potential bridge between this division.

9. This raises the question of whether mention of the YRCA might be intentionally omitted by certain works wishing to emphasize their critical sophistication, but this is unlikely. One could speculate that this might be the case with such prizes as the Stonewall Book Awards—established in 1971—which distinguish works in the polarizing genre of gay and lesbian children's literature and which might be seen as a potential sales deterrent for books in exceedingly conservative marketplaces. On the other hand, in spite of its status as a children's choice award, there are likely few cases in which the YRCA would be viewed as anathema; instead, it is simply insignificant from a sales perspective.

10. These writers are E. L. Konigsburg, Joseph Krumgold, Lois Lowry, Katherine Paterson, and Elizabeth George Speare.

11. Unfortunately, while one might assume that the YRCA would not have made the same mistake, this must remain a matter of speculation: no YRCA winner was named in 1955, as the award was in the midst of a three-year restructuring from 1953 to 1955.

12. YRCA titles are still more likely to stay in print much longer than the typical children's book, which has an average shelf life of eighteen months.

13. This offers an interesting interplay with Guillory's assessment that "the word 'canon' displaces the expressly honorific term 'classic' precisely in order to isolate the 'classics' as an object of critique" (6). Regardless of the semantics used to describe these books, the canon debate within post-1922 American children's literature has often resorted to a discussion of Newbery-winning titles.

14. While the Newbery's exceeding preference for foreign settings has diminished over time, this adjustment is tempered by the award's continued preference for historical fiction—a genre that offers children a foreign viewpoint of a native setting.

15. Another nostalgic and critical advantage for Stead's book is that it is a thinly veiled homage to Madeleine L'Engle's *A Wrinkle in Time*, the 1963 Newbery Medal winner, as it uses both L'Engle's concept of time travel and her book itself as narrative devices.

16. Kidd concurs that, "to some extent, the Honor Books offset the relative conservatism of the Medal books" ("Prizing" 177).

17. Established in 1938—and also administered by the ALA—the Caldecott Medal is the equivalent of the Newbery Medal within the children's picture book genre.

18. For a more comprehensive assessment of this trend beyond the Newbery, see Bonnie J. F. Miller's "What Color Is Gold?"

19. This YRCA comparison with the Newbery must be qualified with the fact that the selection of these two awards came on opposite sides of the assassination of President Kennedy, with the former following and the latter preceding that event. However, it does speak volumes that children decided to bypass such a universally popular work as L'Engle's *A Wrinkle in Time* for a straightforward historical biography, regardless of that biography's subject.

WORKS CITED

Bourdieu, Pierre. *Distinction: A Social Critique of the Judgement of Taste*. Translated by Richard Nice. Cambridge: Harvard University Press, 1998. Print.

――――. *The Field of Cultural Production*. Edited by Randal Johnson. New York: Columbia University Press, 1993. Print.

Dusinberre, Juliet. *Alice to the Lighthouse: Children's Books and Radical Experiments in Art*. New York: St. Martin's Press, 1987. Print.

English, James. *The Economy of Prestige: Prizes, Awards, and the Circulation of Cultural Value*. Cambridge: Harvard University Press, 2005. Print.

Goldsmith, Sophia. "Ten Years of the Newbery Medal." *The Bookman*, November 1931, 308–316. Print.

Guillory, John. *Cultural Capital: The Problem of Literary Canon Formation*. Chicago: University of Chicago Press, 1993. Print.

Habermas, Jürgen. *The Structural Transformation of the Public Sphere*. Translated by Thomas Burger. Cambridge: MIT Press, 2001. Print.

Kidd, Kenneth. "'Not Censorship but Selection': Censorship and/as Prizing." *Children's Literature in Education* 40 (2009): 197–216. Print.

――――. "Prizing Children's Literature: The Case of Newbery Gold." *Children's Literature* 35 (2007): 166–190. Print.

Miller, Bonnie J. F. "What Color Is Gold? Twenty-One Years of Same-Race Authors and Protagonists in the Newbery Medal." *Joys*, Fall 1998, 34–39.

Newbery Medal homepage. American Library Association. Accessed December 15, 2011. Website.

Silvey, Anita. "Has the Newbery Lost Its Way?" *School Library Journal*, October 1, 2008. Accessed December 15, 2011. Website.

Smith, Irene. "A Challenging Proposition." In *A History of the Newbery and Caldecott Medals*, 35–41. New York: Viking, 1957. Print.

Taxel, Joel. "Children's Literature at the Turn of the Century: Toward a Political Economy of the Publishing Industry." *Research in the Teaching of English* 37:2 (2002): 145–197. Print.

Thacker, Deborah Cogan, and Jean Webb. "Introducing Children's Literature: From Romanticism to Postmodernism." *The Lion and the Unicorn* 27:3 (2002): 437–443. Print.

Viguers, Ruth Hill. "Childhood's Golden Era." In *A Critical History of Children's Literature*, edited by Cornelia Meigs et al., 427–447. New York: Macmillan, 1953. Print.

"Young Reader's Choice Award." Pacific Northwest Library Association. Accessed December 15, 2011. Website.

"We Are All One"

Money, Magic, and Mysticism in Mary Poppins

SHARON SMULDERS

About the origins of the fairy tale, P. L. Travers said: "[T]he tracks lead eastwards. The sun of wisdom, like the sun of light, has its rising there" ("Fairy-Tale as Teacher" 205). *Mary Poppins*, too, has its origins in the East. Visiting Ireland in 1925, Travers first met Æ (George William Russell), editor of the *Irish Statesman*, who later exercised a profound influence on her intellectual, aesthetic, and spiritual development.[1] "Listening to his reiterated chantings of the *Bhagavad Gita* and snatches from the old Celtic legends" (Travers, "Death of Æ" 244), she came to appreciate that these ancient stories were meant "to instruct the generations in the inner meanings of things" ("Fairy-Tale as Teacher" 202). Under Æ's tutelage and at his prompting, she began work on *Mary Poppins*. Then, in 1933, the year before she published the novel, she met A. R. Orage, editor of the *New Age* and disciple of George Ivanovitch Gurdjieff. Travers, accustomed to Æ's blend of theosophical esoterica, Eastern scripture, and Irish folklore, discovered in Gurdjieff's work "parallels in various traditions—Tantric Buddhism, Hinduism, Sufism, Greek Orthodoxy" (Travers, *George Ivanovitch Gurdjieff*)—confirming for her the truth of Æ's "Law of Spiritual Gravitation": "Your own will come to you" (Travers, "Death of Æ" 244–245). In light of the author's attraction to Eastern myth and mysticism, *Mary Poppins* emerges as much less an entertainment for children than a vehicle to enlightenment for those who, at whatever age, seek after truth by perceiving connections between "separate and fragmentary" things (Travers, "Only Connect" 301). For Travers, "this form of thinking, which perhaps should properly be called linking, is the essence of fairy tale" (*About the Sleeping Beauty* 50).[2] Travers's yogic approach to thought as syncretic rather than analytic finds its image in "the

Chinese symbol of the Great Ultimate, black fish with white eye, white fish with black, the opposites reconciled to themselves and each other within the encompassing circle" (Travers, "Black Sheep" 230). Infused with Eastern wisdom, *Mary Poppins* thus invites a holistic awareness to understand how Travers, "a born classicist" (qtd. in Guppy 139), uses the material culture of depression-era Britain to engage in what Patricia Demers has called "subversive activity" (11).[3] Yet such philosophical radicalism, grounded in antimaterialist belief, is consistent with and supportive of conservative ideology. Indeed, in *Mary Poppins*, Travers's humanism possesses a homogenizing quality that ultimately deflects attention from contemporary social anxieties related to class, gender, and race.

On a blustery fall day, the East Wind delivers Travers's corporealization of oriental philosophy, Mary Poppins, to 17 Cherry-Tree Lane.[4] Descending from the sky, she is a goddess figure who embodies aspects of the divine and the human, "but, this being Kali Yuga, as the Hindus call it—in our terms, the Iron Age—she comes," said Æ, "in the habiliments most suited to it" (qtd. in Travers, "Only Connect" 294).[5] Mistaken by Michael for Mr. Banks, Mary Poppins immediately establishes herself as the real authority of the household by usurping the power of her employers and reversing the hierarchies of British existence in the 1930s. Although Travers later described *Mary Poppins* as a "timeless" product of imagination rather than "a contemporary book" reflecting "the sociology of the time" (Schwartz 29), the novel addresses the exigencies of depression-era England by locating the Banks family in a "dilapidated" house, "the smallest" on Cherry-Tree Lane, in suburban London (Travers, *Mary Poppins* 1). In fact, Mr. Banks's financial situation is such that his wife "could have either a nice, clean, comfortable house or four children. But not both, for he couldn't afford it" (2). Financial difficulties notwithstanding, the Bankses possess as surety of their middle-class status four servants: the cook, the maid, the gardener, and the nanny. Domestic service, which, in 1931, employed some 2.6 million people in Great Britain (More 99), was one sector of the British labor market resistant to economic recession. Accordingly, the disappearance of Katie Nanna precipitates the crisis that brings a new nanny to the Banks household. Further destabilizing class relationships in the initial exchange with her new employer, Mary Poppins consolidates her power when she says, "Oh, I make it a rule never to give references" (8). Indeed, the physical image of Mary "slid[ing] gracefully *up* the banisters" (9) suggests how Travers elevates the lowly nanny to subvert the hierarchies of dominance in 1930s Britain.

Characterized by fiscal restraint, suburban affluence, and class consciousness, the Banks household is a microcosm of the British state during the Great Slump. Because of the size and stability of its banking system, Britain was relatively immune to the solvency and liquidity crisis that affected Europe following the stock market collapse of 1929, but late in 1931 the nation suffered a political crisis when financial contagion spread from the continent and, together with low export trade and high interest rates, forced the overvalued pound off the gold standard. To restore confidence and balance the budget, the National Government, an all-party coalition formed in the aftermath of the exchange-rate debacle, slashed public spending, reduced unemployment benefits, and introduced household means tests. This climate of financial and political anxiety infects *Mary Poppins*. Yet, even as Mr. Banks's hyperbolic refrain, "[t]he Bank is broken" (5), emphasizes the threat that economic recession posed to bourgeois complacency and masculine assurance, the Great Slump had little effect on suburban London. Between 1905 and 1935, Greater London grew roughly six miles in all directions so that, by 1939, the metropolis housed some 9.5 million people, "about one fifth of the total population of Great Britain," within "a circle of about 25 miles radius from Charing Cross" (Bressey 354–355). Paradoxically, while much of Britain suffered privation and want, bourgeois prosperity, including a higher standard of living and greater degree of consumption, characterized the southeast.[6] Nevertheless, much as J. M. Barrie uses Mr. Darling to explode the paternal myth of rational authority in *Peter Pan*, Travers satirizes capitalist endeavor in the charmingly naïve description of Mr. Banks at work in the City—the Square Mile that includes London's financial district—"[w]here he sat on a large chair in front of a large desk and made money. All day long he worked, cutting out pennies and shillings and half-crowns and threepenny-bits" (4). That the British monetary system underwent cataclysmic change during the early 1930s heightens the absurdity of Mr. Banks's efforts at wealth creation.

While her "first allegiance . . . is not to the mundanities of household finances, but to a heightened reality" (Demers 75), Travers sets her concern for essential truths within a materialist framework. For her, the extraordinary and the ordinary, the supernatural and the natural, are coextant. "In order to fly, you need something solid to take off from," she explained: "It's not the sky that interests me but the ground" (qtd. in Lawson 161). An avatar of "everyday life, which is composed of the concrete and the magic" (qtd. in Lawson 161), Mary Poppins mediates between two opposing realities, one inner and one outer. Travers best demonstrates this function when Mary, first settling down in the nursery, takes an apron from an apparently empty carpet bag. Then, in addition to "a large cake of Sunlight Soap, a toothbrush, a packet of hairpins, a bottle of scent, a small folding armchair and a box of throat lozenges" (11), she conjures from the bag "seven flannel nightgowns, four cotton ones, a pair of boots, a set of dominoes, two bathing-caps and a postcard album" as well as "a folding camp-bedstead with blankets and eiderdown complete" (13). Disgorged, the carpet bag fulfills the children in a way that Mr. Banks's "little black bag" (4), the repository of middle-class power, cannot, since it contains, apart from such small coin as may be given to the children for their money boxes, only "Income Tax papers" (197). While the magic carpet bag yields the most mundane compendium of domestic items, its hyperbolic emptying is nonetheless an imaginative spectacle "performed" before the children who "s[i]t hugging themselves and watching" (13). Admitting to Laurens van der Post that the carpet bag was a magic carpet "disguised," Travers seeks to transport her readers to the paradoxical realization that "emptiness is fullness" ("Where Will All the Stories Go?" 104). For the Banks children, Mary Poppins thus represents perpetual fulfillment.

Offering such fulfillment outside as well as inside the domestic sphere, Mary Poppins allows Jane and Michael Banks the freedom to move (often aboard a London bus) beyond the confines of the suburban household. This freedom in *Mary Poppins* possesses a transgressive quality that undercuts conventions of both class and gender. Having demanded from Mrs. Banks a day out every second rather than every third Thursday, Mary does a disappearing act with Bert, who is "turn-about according to the weather" a match seller and a pavement artist: "If it was wet, he sold matches because the rain would have washed away his pictures if he had painted them. If it was fine, he was on his knees all day, making pictures in coloured chalks on the side-walks" (17–18).[7] Surviving extemporaneously from day to day, he has only tuppence in his cap when Mary, expecting "the raspberry-jam-cakes they always had on her Day Out," arrives (19). The fantastic nature of the adventure that follows, indeed "a fair treat" (20), overrides the historical reality of the jobless—many of them ex-servicemen who "resisted their plight" by "busking for money"—during the Great Slump (Alexander 417).[8] Never under one million after 1920, unemployment swelled to nearly three million after the stock market crash of 1929 and had an exceptionally deleterious impact on the "men's trades" in the coal, iron, and steel industries (Alexander 406). Whereas contemporary works such as E. Wight Bakke's study of Greenwich, *Unemployed Man* (1932), or H. L. Beales and R. S.

Lambert's *Memoirs of the Unemployed* (1934) focused on the mental debili-
tation of men subject to long-term unemployment, Travers instead created
in Bert a street performer who gets the "real *idea*" of leaving the temporal
world and going "into the picture" that he has drawn (*Mary Poppins* 21).
The act of moving "out of the street, away from the iron railings and the
lamp-posts, into the very middle of the picture," is accomplished magically:
"Pff!" (21). Insofar as this escapist retreat involves a realization of ideation,
it functions as an act of imagination and so resembles the "Real Supernatural Phenomena" that Gurdjieff's pupils studied in the 1920s (Travers,
George Ivanovitch Gurdjieff). As Mary explains to the children later, she and
Bert have been "in Fairyland" (28). Moving from the material reality of an
iron-barred streetside into the middle of an idyllic green world, this action
demonstrates how artistic production frees individuals from the marginalized confines of mundane existence. In keeping with this pastoral fantasy,
Bert and Mary are transformed, both wearing fine, new clothes. The fantasy
reaches its orgiastic climax not with the much-anticipated afternoon tea, "a
Pleasure" that requires no payment (25), but with the unanticipated merry-
go-round. The tea and the carousel, both childlike pleasures, consummate
the experience and sublimate the sexual tension between Bert and Mary,
whose "cool green core of sex" so "enthralled" Irish landowner, poet, and
hotelier Francis Macnamara (qtd. in Lawson 165). Thus, the imagination
allows the gratification of desire without financial or emotional cost. Both
free and freeing, such extravagance permits a compensatory escape from
real, adult, depression-era concerns of money and morality, but as fantasy,
it retreats from the need for political and social reform.

Like Bert, the Bird Woman, whom the children meet on one of their
days out, not only lives on close terms with magic in spite of her social
exclusion but also belongs to that urban underclass, homeless and unskilled,
that Henry Mayhew, writing in the mid-nineteenth century, described as
"London Street Folk." Engaged in petty trade, the Match-Man and the Bird
Woman are, in fact, virtual beggars.[9] After World War I, economic depression fed the growth of the British underclass until, by 1935, one year after
the publication of *Mary Poppins* and one year before the Jarrow Crusade,
chronic unemployment "had existed for so long and had proved to be so
irremediable that it came to be regarded as a normality" (Blythe 155). As
Ronald Blythe observes, not only had the jobless "learned to make a pattern of idleness" (155), but the proletariat came to be seen "as something not
quite human, and therefore not subject to an entirely human reaction to
its wretched condition" (20). In the actuality of the 1930s, such people, like

ᴜ̆ᴜ̆the pigeons and doves that congregate at Saint Paul's Cathedral, were seen as pestilential. In the fantasy of *Mary Poppins*, however, the children view the Bird Woman, her penury notwithstanding, as "the best of all Treats" (105) as she repeats, "over and over again, the same thing, in a high chanting voice that made the words seem like a song" (107). An "almost biblical figure" (Demers 78), she possesses an oracular quality, resembling thereby one of "the first legendary Fools," Iambe, who enlivened a grief-stricken Demeter's search for her lost daughter with "stories and poems and ballads to charm the time away" (Travers, qtd. in Guppy 139). Just as her words enchant the children, the bread crumbs that she sells summon the birds that "r[i]se with one grand, fluttering movement and fl[y] round the Bird Woman's head, copying in their own language the words she said" (109). In contrast to contemporary evidence of malnutrition among the poor, she functions as a source of nourishment.[10] Yet, that Michael readily buys a bag of bread crumbs for "four halfpennies" (108)—the same amount that Bert earns sidewalk painting—emphasizes both the affluence of the Banks children and the poverty of the Londoners whom they encounter. To the degree that Travers constructs the Bird Woman as an object of wonder, not pity nor outrage, she elicits an imaginative rather than a moral or political response to her situation. This creative response, which Jane provides in her story of Saint Paul's after dark, magically occludes the misery of homelessness in contemporary London.[11]

To a large extent, Mary's day out with Bert provides the model for all succeeding adventures with the children. Central to most of these episodes are strong female characters—the Dancing Cow, Mrs. Corry, the Bird Woman, Maia, and Mary Poppins herself—who, notwithstanding their material impoverishment, provide imaginative fulfillment. The children's pleasures, both innocent and inexpensive, thus tend to involve a trip, a treat, and a trick. Having witnessed conjuring and vanishing acts in the first two chapters, the children accompany Mary Poppins to Uncle Albert's, where they experience levitation. Although the old-age pension, begun in 1908, was insufficient to maintain the elderly above the poverty line unless they lived rent free (Stevenson and Cook 44), Uncle Albert "laugh[s] at pretty nearly everything" (33)—including the indignities of old age. While this episode, "Laughing Gas," locates mirth and magic in the mundanity of bed-sitter-land, others resemble "The Day Out" in involving imaginative excursions to fairyland. When Jane, suffering from ill health, is bedridden, Mary transports the children mentally to the world of nursery rhyme and folktale by telling them the story of a dancing cow. Using "a brooding, story-telling voice," she mesmerizes the children, speaking "dreamily, still gazing into the middle of the room, but without seeing anything" (66). By contrast, when Michael, having awoken on the wrong side of the bed, suffers from ill temper in "Bad Tuesday," she uses the compass to transport them physically to the ends of the earth. Escorted to the heart of London in the next two chapters, the children again find enchantment in everyday existence, marveling at the Bird Woman, who conjures doves from the air, and Mrs. Corry, the creepy confectioner, who, through sleight of hand, exchanges fingers for barley sugar and gingerbread paper for stars in the sky. Turning to look at the confectionery after leaving it, Jane and Michael are amazed to discover that "the shop *was* not there. It had entirely disappeared" (128). Both a reinvention of the witch in "Hansel and Gretel" and an uncanny casualty of the "retailing revolution" that saw small shops lose to corporate chains during the 1930s (Stevenson and Cook 23), Mrs. Corry anticipates the appearance of Maia, the second of the Pleiades, in the penultimate chapter of the novel. In classical mythology, Maia, whose name comes from ancient Greek for *(foster) mother* or *midwife* (*Oxford English Dictionary*), is a fertility goddess, but in *Mary Poppins* she is a penniless child who, in an uncomfortable parody of burlesque, spins nearly naked through the revolving doors of "the Largest Shop in the World" (179), no doubt Harrods, Knightsbridge, renowned for its dress code for visitors and its seasonal toy fair.[12] Maia's unclothed state tacitly rebukes the hordes of holiday shoppers, among them Mary Poppins, who uses any available reflective surface—a car windshield or a shop window—to admire herself in a "new hat" (105), "new shoes" (114), or "new gloves" (180), and who thereby emerges as a spectacle of self-indulgent consumerism. From this perspective, her decision to make a gift of her fur-topped gloves is no less miraculous than Maia's heavenly ascent. Finally, the climax of the novel occurs when Mary, in "Full Moon," allows Jane and Michael to travel independently to the London Zoo, where she emerges as a dancing snake charmer. Drawn from various mythologies, these female characters "are all really one person rolled into one" (Travers, qtd. in Lawson 145), and in "the triple role of maiden, mother, and crone" (Travers, "Only Connect" 298), they suggest a maternal sky deity not unlike the Egyptian Nut.[13] Liberated by imaginative power from social disadvantage, these characters are not necessarily indicative of a feminist polemic in *Mary Poppins*, for as Travers reiterated in interview after interview, "women belong in myth," not on the executive boards of large corporations (Guppy 139).[14]

While Travers offers a qualified rejection of inherited gender and class structures in *Mary Poppins*, ethnocentric bias corrodes her examination of race in "Bad Tuesday." Described as "a very bad heathen boy" (83), Michael suffers from a "hot, heavy feeling inside him [that] made him do the most awful things" (83). This mood persists on the walk in the park that involves the discovery of the magical compass, which, "spinning round," resembles "a Merry-go-Round" (*Mary Poppins*, 1934 ed., 90) and so recalls the ecstatic fulfillment of "The Day Out," but "Bad Tuesday" works as a counteractive to the former chapter insofar as it shows how emotional distemper, reified as primitive or "heathen" passion, invites punishment rather than pleasure. Originally, in the first edition of *Mary Poppins* (1934), the trip round the world involved encounters with the aboriginal peoples of the regions visited and so contrasted the "relative uniformity in language, confession, and ethnicity" that historian Charles More argues characterized Britain before World War II (89). Representing the four points of the compass, Travers sought perhaps to evoke the "spiritual clan . . . scattered all over the world" with whom Æ, disavowing any "interest in nations," claimed kinship (Travers, "Death of Æ" 245). Yet the language used by and for the black couple, who invite "dem chillun dere" to eat "a slice of watermelon" (*Mary Poppins*, 1934 ed., 92), is far from the only place where the chapter, as initially conceived, enables damaging stereotypes.[15] In addition to the unutterably offensive description of their child as "a tiny black piccaninny" (1934 ed., 92), the couple's dress, involving "a great many beads" though "few clothes" (1934 ed., 92), and behavior, acting "as though the whole of life were one huge joke" (1934 ed., 93), reinforce the crassest of stereotypes. Moreover, in imagining South on the compass, Travers conflates assumptions about black experience in Australia, Africa, and North America.[16] The other three portraits of foreign peoples are hardly less problematic in their depiction. Indeed, living in "a clearing where several tents were pitched round a huge fire," Chief Sun-at-Noonday yet says to Mary and the children, "My wigwam awaits you" (1934 ed., 96). Just as the speech of indigenous Americans is stylized, so too is that of the elaborately courteous Mandarin. Stepping out of a "curiously shaped" house that fuses quite different Asian architectural traditions, including paper screens and "curved roofs" (1934 ed., 93), the Mandarin is rather incongruously dressed in a Japanese robe, "a stiff brocade kimono of gold" (1934 ed., 94). Similarly, Travers's description of the Eskimo's "long white fur coat," with its "bonnet of white fur" (1934 ed., 89), suggests an ignorance of traditional arctic fashion, since the Inuit preferred caribou for fur-lined parkas, sealskin for waterproof boots, and polar bear for pants. Notwithstanding her respect for indigenous wisdom, Travers's depictions of the peoples of the four points of the compass fail to transcend the prejudices of the time and place they were conceived.

Even more problematic than these four portraits, however, is Travers's original depiction of the four revenants whom Michael summons to the night-nursery. Indeed, Michael, as punishment for his theft of the compass, finds himself in the grip of a potently "racist nightmare" (Schwartz 32): "Four gigantic figures b[ore] down towards him—the Eskimo with a spear, the Negro Lady with her husband's huge club, the Mandarin with a great curved sword, and the Red Indian with a tomahawk. They were rushing upon him from all four quarters of the room with their weapons raised above their heads, and, instead of looking kind and friendly as they had done that afternoon, they now seemed threatening and full of revenge" (1934 ed., 99–100.) On some level, the four angry figures represent British colonial subjects or "Third World people" (Schwartz 32), who threaten imperial complacency by rising in violent revolt against the mother country. In Michael's imagination, they are armed, they are magnified, they are incensed, and they are united in their convergence on the center of British domesticity: the nursery. For Travers, the fearsome specters of fairy tale had a healing purpose: "Children, beneath their conforming skins, have aboriginal hearts, savage, untutored, magic-ridden. . . . It can be frightening, even appalling, to a child to meet in himself the ancestral ghosts. 'Who am I,' he will ask, 'in this situation—caught between the world of the sun and the dark corroboree?'" ("Black Sheep" 231). That Michael's nightmare vision functions as just such a cathartic self-encounter only emphasizes the problematic association of the infantile and the primitive in *Mary Poppins*. Yet, "even reading the chapter again, and very carefully," Travers expressed amazement "that anyone could take exception to it" and attempted to justify her descriptions as factually correct (Moore and Travers 216). In the face of growing criticism, she finally acceded to revise "Bad Tuesday," altering the language in 1972 and substituting animals—a polar bear, a hyacinth macaw, a panda, and a dolphin—for people in 1981.[17] Toning down the description of the revenants, she told Edwina Burness and Jerry Griswold that she had made the changes "not as an apology for anything [she had] written," but because she did "not wish to see Mary Poppins tucked away in the closet." Aghast at the charges of racism, she asserted, "*Minorities* is not a word in my vocabulary" (Burness and Griswold).[18] But even as she failed abysmally in her effort to celebrate cultural diversity in *Mary Poppins*, Travers used the opportunity of revision to augment her exploration of species within the so-called natural order. In this respect, "Bad Tuesday," as revised, looks forward to the climactic chapter, "Full Moon," which adds respect for animals to the wisdom that Travers promulgates in *Mary Poppins*.

From the beginning, "Full Moon" works to overthrow the Western orthodoxy that holds humans to be superior to animals. Indeed, so striking is the resultant assault on traditional values that Catherine Elick, examining the role of the carnivalesque in *Mary Poppins*, tentatively positions Travers as an advocate for animal rights (466). Similarly, in her discussion of Travers's debt to modernism, Jean Webb argues that "Full Moon" draws on Eastern mysticism so as to expose the "inadequate and destructive" nature of "hierarchical power structures," thereby to offer a "politically charged" critique of Western materialism (120). Fittingly, the chapter opens with the children counting coins, and when Mary Poppins tells Michael to contribute his to the poor-box, he explains that he is saving "for an elephant—a private one for myself, like Lizzie at the Zoo" (152). In so saying, he unwittingly articulates the notion that, under capitalism, money is power. As fetishized colonial possessions, Lizzie and the other animals in Regent's Park suggest how capitalism converts things, including living beings, into commodities for private consumption.[19] Yet Mary's birthday, falling on the full moon, results in a suspension of conventional order, so that everything is "all upside down" (156) and "topsy-turvy" (158). Like Halloween, it represents "a propitious moment, a ritual moment, . . . a kind of crack through which some element of the unknown can be brought into the known" (Travers, "Only Connect" 303). At this moment, "the small are free from the great and the great protect the small" (*Mary Poppins* 174). For Travers, "to stand in the presence of a paradox, to be spiked on the horns of dilemma, between what is small and what is great, microcosm and macrocosm, or, if you like, the two ends of the stick, is the only posture we can assume in front of . . . ancient knowledge" ("What the Bee Knows" 80–81). This "ancient knowledge" informs the words of the Hamadryad: "To eat and be eaten are the same thing in the end. My wisdom tells me that this is probably so. We are all made of the same stuff, remember, we of the Jungle, you of the City. The same substance composes us—the tree overhead, the stone beneath us, the bird, the beast, the star—we are all one, all moving to the same end. . . . Bird and beast and stone and star—we are all one, all one. . . . Child and serpent, star and stone—all one" (*Mary Poppins* 174–175). The language here looks forward to the truth that Travers discovered in Gurdjieff's *All and Everything* with its focus on "the reciprocal feeding of all created things": "Everything at every moment partakes of something else" (Travers, "Fairy-Tale as Teacher" 207). This knowledge is similar, too, to what, according to

Travers, the Aborigines of Australia taught amateur anthropologist Daisy Bates: "Eater and eaten, all was one" (Travers, "Legacy of the Ancestors" 33). In *Mary Poppins*, however, the children, Michael especially, resist this existential paradox, because it threatens the boundaries defining the material self. "A bird is not me," he states: "Jane is not a tiger" (175). Indeed, Michael's assertions self-consciously defend the individual ego against its transcendent consumption within a collective whole. Nonetheless, Travers clearly seeks to show that "we are meant to be something more than our own personal history" ("What the Bee Knows" 86).

The children first see the Hamadryad when he salutes Mary, and "rais[ing] the front half of his long golden body, and, thrusting upwards his scaly golden hood, daintily kisse[s] her, first on one cheek and then on the other" (167). Better known as the king cobra, the Hamadryad is, in fact, the largest venomous snake in existence, growing up to six yards in length and feeding on other serpents. It is, moreover, indigenous to the forests of Southeast Asia, whence it derives its name, meaning *together with* (ἅμα) *tree* (δρῦς) (*Oxford English Dictionary*). Documenting the history of the term, the *Oxford English Dictionary* cites the *Daily News* (London) for 1894: "When the Zoological Gardens were first opened, a hamadryad, imported with a selection of cobras, ate up fifty pounds' worth of the latter before its nature was discovered." Ironically, the word *hamadryad* refers not only zoologically to the snake-eating cobra but also mythologically to the wood nymph. This second meaning unsettles the gender identity of the cobra, referred to throughout the chapter as "he," not "it." From this perspective, his name, like Mary Poppins's, "evokes the fundamental androgyny of the mother goddess, who as creator of all must provide the seed as well as the matrix" (DeForest 141).[20] Insofar as Æ had once described Travers as a dryad (Travers, "Death of Æ" 248), the author perhaps intended a punning self-reference in the Hamadryad, who is Mary Poppins's "first cousin once removed—on the mother's side" (*Mary Poppins* 169). Tellingly, Jane and Michael cannot distinguish between the Hamadryad's sibilant speech and "their Mother's voice as she tucked them in" (176). These elisions, by feminizing the phallicism inherent in the image of the snake, offer insight into Travers's yogic reconciliation of opposites within an existential totality.

Characterized by sibilant susurration, Travers's prose style in "Full Moon" intensifies the ritualized speech and action at the philosophic heart of *Mary Poppins*. Possessed of a "soft, terrifying voice," the Hamadryad features a "gaze" so "compelling" that the children "with difficulty drew their eyes from" him (168). As such, he is the hypnotist par excellence, representative of "enchantment" and "danger," both "opposites and instruments of fate" ("Endless Story" 226). Using his "small, delicate, hissing voice" (*Mary Poppins* 167), the Hamadryad mesmerizes the object of his gaze. Looking into his face, Michael and Jane "took a step forward, for his curious deep eyes seemed to draw them towards him. Long and narrow they were, with a dark sleepy look in them, and in the middle of that dark sleepiness a wakeful light glittered like a jewel" (167–168). Revered in the East and reviled in the West, the snake emerges in *Mary Poppins* as "the Lord of the Jungle" (169), "the wisest and most terrible of . . . all" (168). As Travers well knew, snakes, or *nāgas*, feature prominently in Hindu and Buddhist lore. Not only do they appear often in the *Mahabharata*, a Sanskrit epic that dates to no later than the fourth century BCE, but Nāg Panchami, the Festival of the Snakes, remains a popular Hindu holiday. Shiva, the transformer, frequently appears with a snake around his neck or waist, and as Nataraja, or the God of Dance, he performs the cosmic dance of tandava, a dance of destruction and creation. Snake worship, no doubt developed to deal with the threat of snakebite, positions the snake as a divinity representing immortality, energy, and prosperity. By contrast, Judeo-Christian tradition associates the snake with evil. Accordingly, in the Great Chain of Being, it is the lowest of the beasts. In Genesis 3:1–4, the serpent tempts woman to partake of the fruit of the tree of knowledge, leading to the expulsion of Adam and Eve from Eden. For its perfidy, the Lord curses the serpent, condemning it to crawl on its belly and eat dust: "I will put enmity between thee and the woman, and between thy seed and her seed; it shall bruise thy head, and thou shalt bruise his heel" (Gen. 3:15). Deliberately reworking the story of Genesis, Travers substitutes the Grand Chain for the Great Chain to revolutionize awareness, for "to understand is to stand under" (Travers, "World of the Hero" 15).

A figure of rebirth and renewal, the Hamadryad throws his skin, fashioning "the golden sheath into a circle, and diving his head through this as though it were a crown," to present to Mary (170). The snakeskin, fashioned into a belt, not only suggests the iconography associated "with the Cretan earth goddess and the Indian goddess Kali" but also "allud[es] to the notion of the oroboros, the image of time in which the snake eats its tail" (DeForest 144, 145 n18). In a Wordsworthian moment, Travers writes elsewhere: "the snake takes its tail in its mouth and you and I, linnet and hare, parts of one single whole that sometime will reveal all names, are rolled round in our eternal course with rocks and stones and trees" ("Name and No Name" 128). Like the Grand Chain, the snakeskin belt is another image for the Great Ultimate: yin and yang together within the reconciling

circle. The Grand Chain, a dance figure involving the animals "all forming themselves into a ring round Mary Poppins . . . and exchanging hand
and wing," doubles upon the circular motifs of carousel and compass and
celebrates the kinship that constitutes the heart of the mantra, "we are all
one." Dance, "both a symptom of modern alienation and its potential cure,
an evanescent yet visceral form of collectivity that offered a vision of community as well as a sign of its elusiveness" (Zimring 708), was an important
concept for Travers, who, as a young woman, had worked as a professional
dancer. Quoting Irish writer James Stephens, she maintained that "the first
and last duty of man is to dance" ("Endless Story" 223). Later, with respect
to Gurdjieff, she observed that "sacred dances, or 'Movements' . . . were
an integral part of the teaching" (*George Ivanovitch Gurdjieff*), and in conversation with archaeologist Michael Dames, she ascribed to such ritualized movements a religious function, so that "all dance, however profane,
is even if unconsciously, done before the Lord" ("If She's Not Gone" 48). In
response, Dames defined dance as "the kinetic involvement of the individuals in a thing greater than themselves, a pattern which can turn from solar
orb into serpentine riverflow with an ordered measure to it, the bringing
of order into the random chaos of overwhelming experience" ("If She's Not
Gone" 48). From this perspective, the Grand Chain, as choreographed by
the Hamadryad, recalls only to subvert the classical Western notion of the
Great Chain of Being, which immutably and hierarchically orders the universe. In response to the capitalist fantasy of private ownership that opens
the chapter, Travers thus offers in the reconciling circle of dance a symbol
for transcendent unity.

The oneness of all is the existential paradox at the center of *Mary Poppins*.
But even as the novel exposes the deficits of materialist logic, the financial
security of the Banks family blunts any significant criticism of bourgeois
capitalism. Naïve witnesses to the hardships of depression-era London,
Michael and Jane interact with unemployed men and homeless women,
street hawkers and small shopkeepers, old-age pensioners and juvenile
vagrants, but these encounters with the urban poor inspire no awareness
of their own privilege, becoming instead occasions for imaginative flight
or for eating things—like raspberry-jam-cakes, whelks, bread and butter,
crumpets, coconut cakes, plum cake, shortbread fingers, gingerbread, and
barley sugar—or buying things. Such curiously detailed spectacles of middle-class consumption travesty the ideal of self-transcendence at the climax
of the novel. Indeed, the resultant tension is particularly observable in the
chapter that follows "Full Moon" wherein Maia's shopping spree perversely

demonstrates "the whole point of Christmas": "that things should be *given away*" (190). Consequently, the real paradox of *Mary Poppins* has less to do with the essential oneness of all than with the reconciliation of anti-materialist belief to bourgeois consumerism. Even as Travers revised "Bad Tuesday" to anticipate the wisdom that the children receive in "Full Moon," her criticisms of Western materialism adumbrate a liberationist philosophy without necessarily bespeaking either a feminist awareness or a postcolonial consciousness. Certainly, Travers based her apprehension of "the selfsame themes" reappearing "as though something in the psyche of a race had ripened and produced a fruit that corresponded, not in its form but in its substance, with the fruit of all other races" ("World of the Hero" 13), on a close study of the myth and folklore of many peoples. But insofar as her humanism was unable to acknowledge and incorporate contemporary racial, ethnic, or national differences, her vision in *Mary Poppins* is one in which the relative homogeneity of 1930s Britain pretends to timeless universality.

NOTES

1. Æ bequeathed his copy of the *Bhagavad Gita* to Travers (Travers, "Death of Æ" 255).

2. Travers's most famous articulation of this notion of thinking as linking appears in the much-anthologized "Only Connect" (285).

3. That Travers drew on her own childhood in writing the novel and authorized an Edwardian setting for the film obfuscates the novel's mediation of British experience between the world wars. Brian Szumsky, for example, alleges that "the materials that the Disney screenwriters appropriated from the novels of P. L. Travers have the characteristic spirit of late-Victorian and Edwardian critiques or reassessments of various preconceptions of status-quo Victorian society" (98). Equating the "anti-materialist tone of Travers's original materials" (100) with "a chiding, Horatian (gentle) satire of imperialist Britain" (101), Szumsky somewhat oversimplifies the novel's politics.

4. Mary Poppins's origins have received much critical attention. Jonathan Cott traces the ancestry of the "cosmic nanny" to the "Ecstatic Mother" embodied in Artemis and Sophia (qtd. in Demers 76, 83). Mary DeForest argues that Travers's hero is modeled after the Great Goddess (139). Feenie Ziner calls her an "embodiment of Zen" (145). Although Travers did not study Zen until later in life, she endorsed Ziner's assessment, noting that her Zen master had decreed the novel to be "full of Zen" (qtd. in Ziner 146). Catherine Elick describes Mary Poppins as a "hybrid central character," both "semi-divine being" and "working-class woman of 1930s England" (465). Similarly, Lois Rauch Gibson claims that she "mediates between myth and reality, literature and life," to emerge as "a fully-developed person" (179). Dubbing her "the quintessential shapeshifter," Patricia Demers notes that she is "at home in both a domestic reality and a mythic universe" (68). "She does not," says Demers, "correspond to other nannies in either literature or life" (73). Most recently,

Cristina Pérez Valverde has said that Travers drew "the Great Mother archetype, which may be both creative and destructive," from the collective unconscious and thus created a "wizard woman" whose function was to question, if not change, the constituents of the patriarchal order (264).

5. Like Æ, Travers held myth to be present within contemporary life. Indeed, "if man does not, of intention, enact it, keep alive its rituals, preserve unbroken the chain of its being, myth will enact itself through man." Thus, she cited women's liberation as an embodiment of "the Great Goddess rising in wrath, dressing up as female priest or terrorist; she who *is* terror as well as beauty" ("What the Bee Knows" 88). Politically conservative, Travers dismissed feminism while venerating the feminine principle in myth. Speaking of herself, she said: "I was lucky not to be in a profession where women are paid less than men. So, I never had to go and nobble the Government about Women's Rights. Perhaps as a result I have been perfectly happy to be a woman. Yin does not resent but receives" (Guppy 139).

6. John Stevenson and Chris Cook make "the paradox which lay at the heart of Britain in the thirties" central to their examination of depression-era experience (12).

7. The second chapter of *Mary Poppins*, "The Day Out," is based on a story that Travers first published in the Christchurch *Sun* in 1926 (Lawson 100). Travers vociferously objected to Walt Disney Studios' amplification of Bert's role for the 1964 film. Denying that Bert was Mary's lover, she described him as "a supernumerary character, and there to point up aspects of Mary Poppins, not at all to aspire to her hand" (Cott 165).

8. During the 1920s, buskers frequently cross-dressed to protest "the violation of the sexual division of labour" that rendered them unemployed (Alexander 417).

9. See Henry Mayhew, "Of the Street-Sellers of Lucifer-Matches," *London Labour and the London Poor* (1:431–433). Mayhew emphasizes that this particular trade employed those who, because of age or infirmity, were unemployable: "The real sellers," says one informant, are "old men and women out of employ, or past work, and to beg they are ashamed. . . . Yes, and depending a good deal upon them, for they're an easy carriage for an infirm body, and as ready a sale as most things" (1:433). Mayhew treats "Street Exhibitors" in the third volume (3:51–168) and "Petty Trading Beggars" in the fourth volume (4:438–441) of *London Labour and the London Poor*. The commodities sold by such traders, grouped with the insane and the illicit, were so cheap that customers were merely being charitable.

10. Published in 1936, John Boyd Orr's study *Food, Health and Income* "showed that a tenth of the [British] population, including a fifth of all children, were chronically ill-nourished, while a half of the population suffered from some sort of deficiency" (Stevenson and Cook 47).

11. The Bird Woman of the novel is far different from the Bird Woman of the Disney film. As Brian Szumsky suggests, Disney's Bird Woman functions as a "manifest victim of bourgeois oppression" (100) and offers an object lesson on the need for compassion (104).

12. Until recently, Harrods "d[id] not permit any person [to enter] the store . . . wearing high cut, sports or beach shorts, swimwear, bare midriffs, athletic singlets, cycling shorts or general sporting attire, bare feet or any extremes of personal presentation" ("Harrods Store FAQs"). Company policy has since changed. In 2011, the resignation of sales assistant Melanie Stark, who refused to wear cosmetics as mandated for female employees, brought unfavorable publicity to the dress code as a whole.

13. Talking about fairy tale, myth, and symbol, Travers returns often to woman as goddess. In "Grimm's Women," she states: "Grimm's—or any other collection of traditional tales or myths—is a mine of feminine lore. Every woman—maiden, mother or crone, Kore, Demeter or Hecate—can find there her prototype, a model for her role in life" (257). In "The Black Sheep," she says: "The 13 wise women were nymph, mother, crone, goddess; Kore, Demeter and Astarte, the Witches, the Fates and the Furies" (233). According to Travers, such manifestations of the Great Goddess pervade folklore: "You can't take a step without her! In my field, which I think of as the fairy tale, you can always tells the antiquity of a tale when it has, as its chief character, a woman. She always refers to the Great Mother" ("If She's Not Gone" 47). Likewise, in *About the Sleeping Beauty*, she argues that the wise woman or fairy "is, in fact, an aspect of the Hindu goddess, Kali, who carries in her multiple hands the powers of good and evil" (56). "All women, in or out of fairy tales, are born princesses, being descended from the Goddesses who, by the very nature of things, had to precede the gods," she says in "The Unsleeping Eye"; "Inanna of Sumeria was the first to be known to us historically but there can be no doubt that she herself was merely a descendant, the latest comer, as it were, to the hidden genealogies of those who belong to the north side of the mountain and the south side of the river. Thus, with such a lineage, sovereignty was and still is the prerogative of woman" (189).

14. See also the end of Travers's interview with Edwina Burness and Jerry Griswold.

15. After she had made the changes, Travers described the "pickaninny language" or "dialect" as if it were an objective linguistic fact rather than a racist cultural convention (Burness and Griswold). Travers "didn't know where she had picked up the 'piccaninny' language since, she said, she had known no Black people at the time she wrote *Mary Poppins*. However, she had read *Uncle Remus* and still knows *Little Black Sambo* by heart" (Schwartz 28).

16. Travers meant "South as regards the compass, . . . not the Southern states of the U.S.A." (Moore and Travers 215). She "had thought of the people of the South as, roughly, coming from Australia, where I was born, or from the South Sea Islands" (Moore and Travers 216).

17. Travers "refuse[d] to be arraigned" on the charge of racism, and she gradually came round to the need to do more than simply substitute "formal English, grave and formal," for the "piccaninny" of the original (Schwartz 28). The final version of the text still contains some racist slurs. Although Schwartz had questioned the use of the term *street arabs* in "Miss Lark's Andrew," Travers did not remove the phrase when she made the revisions for the 1981 edition (*Mary Poppins* 52). Similarly, the language used to chasten a tearful Michael remains problematic: "You will *not* behave like a Red Indian" (205).

18. See also Moore and Travers (216). During World War II, Travers lived briefly among the Navajo, Hopi, and Pueblo peoples. Recognizing them as members of her "spiritual clan," she was flattered to receive "an Indian name": "Every Indian has a secret name as well as his public name. This moved me very much because I have such a strong feeling about names, that names are a part of a person, a very private thing to each one" (Burness and Griswold). Despite her deep gratitude to the "ancient people" who made her feel so welcome, she saw them as Other. Invited to give a speech, she "told them about England: "I said that for me England was the place 'Where the Sun Rises' because, you see, England

is east of where I was. I said, 'Over large water.' . . . I put it as mythologically as I could, just very simple sayings" (Burness and Griswold).

19. I am grateful to Althea Tait, Old Dominion University, for identifying the elephant as a token of empire.

20. Attuned to questions of gender identity, Travers said: "I signed my name P. L. Travers originally because it seemed to me at the time that all children's books were written by women and I didn't want to feel that there was a woman or a man behind [the novel], but a human being" (qtd. in Lawson 162).

WORKS CITED

Alexander, Sally. "Men's Fears and Women's Work: Responses to Unemployment in London between the Wars." *Gender and History* 12:2 (2000): 401–425. Academic Search Complete. Accessed October 26, 2012. Website.

The Bible. Authorized King James Version. Bible Gateway, 1995–2010. Accessed October 26, 2012. Website.

Blythe, Ronald. *Age of Illusion: England in the Twenties and Thirties, 1919–1940.* 1963. London: Phoenix, 2001. Print.

Bressey, Charles. "Greater London Highway Development Survey." *Geographical Journal* 94:5 (November 1939): 353–360. JSTOR. Accessed October 26, 2012. Website.

Burness, Edwina, and Jerry Griswold. "The Art of Fiction, no. 63: P. L. Travers." *Paris Review* 86 (1982): n.p. *Paris Review.* Accessed October 26, 2012. Website.

Cott, Jonathan. "No Forgetting." In *A Lively Oracle: A Centennial Celebration of P. L. Travers,* edited by Ellen Dooling Draper and Jenny Koralek, 157–167. New York: Larson, 1999. Print.

DeForest, Mary. "Mary Poppins and the Great Mother." *Classical and Modern Literature: A Quarterly* 11:2 (1991): 139–154. Print.

Demers, Patricia. *P. L. Travers.* Boston: Twayne Publishers, 1991. Print.

Elick, Catherine L. "Animal Carnivals: A Bakhtinian Reading of C. S. Lewis's *The Magician's Nephew* and P. L. Travers's *Mary Poppins.*" *Style* 35:3 (2001): 454–471. Academic Search Complete. Accessed October 26, 2012. Website.

Gibson, Lois Rauch. "Beyond the Apron: Archetypes, Stereotypes, and Alternative Portrayals of Mothers in Children's Literature." *Children's Literature Association Quarterly* 13:4 (1988): 177–181. Project Muse. Accessed October 26, 2012. Website.

Guppy, Shusha. "P. L. Travers." *Looking Back: A Panoramic View of a Literary Age by the Grandes Dames of European Letters.* New York: British American Publishing, 1991. Reprinted in *Children's Literature Review* 93, edited by Allison Marion, 132–141. Detroit: Gale Research, 2003. Print.

"Harrods Store FAQs." Harrods.com. Accessed June 25, 2011. Website.

Lawson, Valerie. *Mary Poppins, She Wrote: The Life of P. L. Travers.* New York: Simon & Schuster, 1999. Print.

Mayhew, Henry. *London Labour and the London Poor.* 4 vols. 1851. London: Griffin, Bohn, 1861. Tufts Digital Library. Accessed October 26, 2012. Website.

Moore, Robert B., and P. L. Travers. "*Mary Poppins*: Two Points of View." *Children's Literature* 10 (1982): 210–217. Print.

More, Charles. *Britain in the Twentieth Century*. Harlow, England: Pearson Longman, 2007. Print.

Oxford English Dictionary Online. Oxford University Press. Accessed October 26, 2012. Website.

Pérez Valverde, Cristina. "Magic Women on the Margins: Ec-centric Models in *Mary Poppins* and *Ms Wiz*." *Children's Literature in Education* 40 (2009): 263–274. Wilson OmniFile. Accessed October 26, 2012. Website.

Schwartz, Albert V. "Mary Poppins Revised: An Interview with P. L. Travers." *Interracial Books for Children Bulletin* 5:3 (1974): 1–5. Reprinted in *Racism and Sexism in Children's Books*, edited by Judith Stinson, 27–34. London: Writers and Readers Publishing Cooperative, 1979. Print.

Stevenson, John, and Chris Cook. *The Slump: Britain in the Great Depression*. 3rd ed. Harlow, England: Pearson Education, 2010. Print.

Szumsky, Brian E. "'All That Is Solid Melts into the Air': The Winds of Change and Other Analogues of Colonialism in Disney's *Mary Poppins*." *The Lion and the Unicorn* 24 (2000): 97–109. Project Muse. Accessed October 26, 2012. Website.

Travers, P. L. *About the Sleeping Beauty*. Illustrated by Charles Keeping. New York: McGraw-Hill, 1975. Print.

———. "The Black Sheep." *New York Times Book Review*, November 7, 1965. Reprinted in Travers, *What the Bee Knows*, 229–234. Print.

———. "The Death of Æ: Irish Hero and Mystic." In *The Celtic Consciousness*, edited by Robert O'Driscoll. New York: George Braziller, 1981. Reprinted in Travers, *What the Bee Knows*, 242–256. Print.

———. "The Endless Story." *Parabola* (1988). Reprinted in Travers, *What the Bee Knows*, 219–228. Print.

———. "The Fairy-Tale as Teacher." *World Review*, 1950. Reprinted in *A Lively Oracle: A Centennial Celebration of P. L. Travers*, edited by Ellen Dooling Draper and Jenny Koralek, 200–209. New York: Larson. Print.

———. *George Ivanovitch Gurdjieff*. Toronto: Traditional Studies, 1973. Print.

———. "Grimm's Women." *New York Times Book Review*, November 16, 1965. Reprinted in Travers, *What the Bee Knows*, 257–259. Print.

———. "If She's Not Gone, She Lives There Still: A Conversation between Michael Dames and P. L. Travers." *Parabola* 3:1 (1978). Reprinted in Travers, *What the Bee Knows*, 36–49. Print.

———. "The Legacy of the Ancestors." *Parabola* 2:2 (1977). Reprinted in Travers, *What the Bee Knows*, 30–35. Print.

———. *Mary Poppins*. New York: Reynal and Hitchcock, 1934. Reprinted, Orlando: Harcourt Brace, 1997. Print. Page references are to the 1997 edition unless otherwise indicated.

———. "Name and No Name." *Parabola* 7:3 (1982). Reprinted in Travers, *What the Bee Knows*, 117–128. Print.

———. "Only Connect." *Quarterly Journal*, 1967. Reprinted in Travers, *What the Bee Knows*, 285–303. Print.

―――. "The Unsleeping Eye: A Fairy Tale." *Parabola* 11:1 (1986). Reprinted in Travers, *What the Bee Knows*, 189–194. Print.

―――. *What the Bee Knows: Critical Reflections on Myth, Symbol and Story*. 1989. Harmondsworth, England: Penguin, 1993. Print.

―――. "What the Bee Knows." *Parabola* 6:1 (1981). Reprinted in Travers, *What the Bee Knows*, 80–90. Print.

―――. "Where Will All the Stories Go? A Conversation between Laurens van der Post and P. L. Travers." *Parabola* 7:2 (1982). Reprinted in Travers, *What the Bee Knows*, 95–106. Print.

―――. "The World of the Hero." *Parabola* 1:1 (1976). Reprinted in Travers, *What the Bee Knows*, 11–18. Print.

Webb, Jean. "Connecting with Mary Poppins." In *Introducing Children's Literature: From Romanticism to Postmodernism*, edited by Deborah Cogan Thacker and Jean Webb, 114–121. London: Routledge, 2002. Print.

Zimring, Rishona. "'The Dangerous Art Where One Slip Means Death': Dance and the Literary Imagination in Interwar Britain." *Modernism/modernity* 14:4 (2007): 707–727. Project Muse. Accessed October 26, 2012. Website.

Ziner, Feenie. "Mary Poppins as a Zen Monk." *New York Times Book Review*, May 7, 1972. Reprinted in *A Lively Oracle: A Centennial Celebration of P. L. Travers*, edited by Ellen Dooling Draper and Jenny Koralek, 144–148. New York: Larson, 1999. Print.

Solidarity of Times Past

Historicizing the Labor Movement in American Children's Novels

CYNTHIA ANNE MCLEOD

In the mid-nineteenth century, a young New England textile worker fears that supporting her coworkers' petition for shorter work days will cause her to lose her job. Garment workers in New York City, many of them teenage girls, walk away from their sewing machines in protest of poor working conditions and low wages; their concerns are validated months later when the Triangle fire kills 146 workers. Agricultural workers attempt to form a union that will bridge the racial divide in Mississippi during the Great Depression. Employees of a poultry processing plant in Georgia in the early 1960s unionize after being forced to work long hours with no breaks and few benefits. A community college student in Fresno, California, joins United Farm Workers' protests in 1970 and incorporates labor themes into his art.

Lyddie by Katherine Paterson, *Uprising* by Margaret Haddix, *Let the Circle Be Unbroken* by Mildred Taylor, *Kira-Kira* by Cynthia Kadohata, and *Jesse* by Gary Soto are among novels for young readers in which labor unions appear. While race and gender issues in books for children have for many years inspired substantive studies, comparable research in the area of social class, particularly in the United States, is lacking. This gap in scholarship regarding social class and children's books may be due in part to the paradoxical way in which many Americans traditionally think about class, viewing it as something simultaneously nonexistent and yet possible to overcome with sufficient ingenuity.[1] The fifty-three novels in this study's sample provide opportunities to explore the neglected issue of social class in American children's literature, as the conflicts that drive the narratives are most often between workers and their employers, and the books take up issues that have reemerged after decades in which the political power of unions declined, along with their membership numbers.[2]

This essay is concerned with how the topic of labor is historicized, or conceptualized as history, in the novels of this study. Specifically, children's novels about unions often historicize labor issues in ways that make it difficult for young readers to find links between the conflicts of the past and present. This study describes distinct differences between representations of unions in historical and contemporary fiction, with union members in the present more often portrayed as instigators of violence or intimidation. In contrast, union members in historical novels are much more likely to be cast as victims of repression. Occasionally this unfavorable comparison between labor activists past and present is explicitly made through recollections of older characters in the story. Finally, certain historical periods and industries appear over and over, while others that might have been included in children's literature are underrepresented or missing. An exploration of these representations of labor requires examining a process that ensures that these particular stories are told, rather than ones that focus attention on aspects of the movement that resist industrial capitalism itself or that are more relevant to the present day.

Historicizing labor in this way can be seen as an example of what Raymond Williams termed "a selective tradition" whereby "certain meanings and values are selected for emphasis and certain other meanings and values are neglected or excluded" (115). The traditional conception of the past is then used to "connect with and ratify the present. What it offers in practice is a sense of *predisposed continuity*" (116, italics in original). In this process, people make sense of the present through very specific notions of a past, identifying with the values that tradition espouses.[3] Identifying ideas and images missing from popular culture can offer as much insight as exploring those that are included. In a study of fiction about the American Revolution published over a period of eighty-seven years, Joel Taxel found that only one of his sample of thirty-two novels dealt with the paradox of a war fought for the ideal of liberty that extended that liberty only to the nation's white citizens. Political leaders of the period openly debated the issue of slavery, yet those arguments were incorporated into just one novel about the Revolution, an omission that validated the segregationist beliefs of the periods in which the books were published. Violet Harris, examining representations of African Americans in children's books, described how stereotypical characters such as Little Brown Koko and Epaminondas were prevalent in books intended for white children in the mid-twentieth century, while positive and authentic depictions of African Americans were rare: "Those who desired to offer alternative images had to battle against the institutions and processes involved in the development of popular culture" (170).

As the present study will demonstrate, this selective tradition can be seen in representations of labor in novels for young readers. These texts offer opportunities to explore how unionism past and present is constructed and explained, even as critical examination suggests alternative constructions and depictions. In these novels, labor is historicized in the most literal sense of the word, set in history and removed from discussions of workers' rights in the present day, even though most of the books have publication dates of 2000 or later.

The Rise of the Labor Novel: 1976–Present

Social activists and scholars have long advocated children's literature that focuses on less powerful groups in society in order to advance their positions. Herbert Kohl notes that George Orwell in 1939 "wondered why the most effective writing for young people was infused with the mythology of elitism, individualism, and capitalism" (60–61) as he echoed Orwell's call for children's books that depicted the struggles of the poor and working classes and proposed collective action to remedy social ills. In 1988 Betty Bacon identified only two works of historical fiction in which labor unions appear, *Call Me Ruth* by Marilyn Sachs and *A Spirit to Ride the Whirlwind* by Athena Lord, and just one example of contemporary fiction, Barbara Corcoran's *Strike!* As Bacon observed, this lack of representation of labor ignored the fact that many young readers' families were involved in labor organizations and that the children themselves would also be part of the workforce in the near future.

Just thirteen years later, Deborah Overstreet expressed surprise that so many books about the labor movement were available when she set out to analyze twelve historical children's novels set in the textile and garment or mining industries in the late nineteenth and early twentieth centuries. Instead of critiquing a capitalist system that encouraged industrialists to maximize profit by ignoring worker safety and keeping wages as low as possible, the novels focused on conflicts between individual workers and their unfeeling employers, without connecting them to a broader social movement.

The fifty-three novels that make up the sample of the present study were published between 1976 and 2009. All depict involvement in a union by at least one character in the book, and in most (but not all) it is labor conflict that drives the narrative. The roots of these novels can be found in a shift in historians' approaches to labor history that occurred almost fifty years ago. Labor historians in the 1960s, influenced by E. P. Thompson and Herbert Gutman, changed the focus of their analyses from institutional histories of unions and industries to explorations of the lives of workers themselves. At the same time, civil rights and women's issues moved to the forefront, further expanding the scope of historiography. Katherine Paterson acknowledges Hannah Josephson's and Thomas Dublin's histories of female textile workers in New England in her author's note for *Lyddie*. Cultural histories of workers on New York's Lower East Side in the early twentieth century informed Margaret Haddix's portrayal of young shirtwaist workers in *Uprising*. Other books reflect personal experiences of the author or members of the author's family. Pamela Muñoz Ryan based *Esperanza Rising* on her grandmother's experiences, and Mildred Taylor's *Let the Circle Be Unbroken* is part of her chronicle of the Logan family of Mississippi, drawn from stories shared by her father and other family members. When labor history made the cultural turn, children's literature was a beneficiary.

The mere presence of working-class characters cannot guarantee engagement with larger issues of class, any more than the inclusion of African American characters in books ensures authentic representation of racism embedded within society, but class analysis is rare within American scholarship on children's literature. In the introduction to a themed issue of *The Lion and the Unicorn* in 1993 that focused on social class and children's literature, Ian Wojcik-Andrews reflected on this gap in scholarship about books and films for young people: "The absence of class analysis has nothing to do with class being a settled issue. Quite the contrary. Perhaps it is *too* unsettling. Class, I think, is endlessly discussed, but never addressed" (117). The present study offers hints of some unsettling aspects of class conflict, not least of which is how often intimidation and outright violence accompany such disputes and which side is depicted as engaging in negative behavior.

From Victims to Perpetrators: Union Members
and Violence

Only six books in the sample are contemporary fiction; the remaining forty-seven are historical.[4] In most of the historical novels, union members are portrayed as victims of violence and intimidation from company owners and police. A union activist in *Ashes of Roses* by Mary Jane Auch explains to Rose Nolan that her participation in the 1909 garment workers' strike resulted in an arrest. In Christopher Paul Curtis's *Bud, Not Buddy*, a union organizer who has given Bud a ride prevails on him to quickly hide the union flyers in the back seat when they are stopped by the police. Police or hired security guards attack strikers in *The Breaker Boys*; *Bread and Roses, Too*; *Jesse*; and *Uprising*, among others. While some authors attempt to balance their portrayals of labor by showing union members engaging in violent or threatening behavior, as in *Esperanza Rising* and *On Fire*, in most of the historical fiction, union members are the victims.[5]

In contrast, unions in the contemporary novels set in the late twentieth and early twenty-first centuries are more often portrayed as angry mobs, instigating violence and intimidating those who oppose them. *Dream Factory* by Brad Barkley and Heather Hepler opens with striking Disney characters hurling eggs and shouting epithets at their replacements. A striking teacher in *Time to Take Sides* by Sharlya Gold lies to parents with limited understanding of English, telling them that their child should not come to school because students are out for "vacation." The striking teachers also threaten to have the protagonist's mother, a single parent who works in the school cafeteria, fired because she does not join them on the picket line. Talk of a coming strike at the factory in *The Winchesters* by James Lincoln Collier is enough to trigger threats from workers against the protagonist, Chris, whose uncle and grandfather own the plant. There are repeated references to violence associated with strikes, as Chris's uncle explains that "once you get a strike, you get violence" (20).

Amy Goldman Koss in *Strike Two* makes a connection between the relative powerlessness of the working class and violence by striking union members. Strikers attack an employee in her car, and a manager receives a threatening note. The protagonist's father offers an explanation after his daughter questions him about vandalism at a local car dealership that continues its newspaper advertising during the strike. "'Gwen, these are the tools of the powerless,' Dad said. 'Management has all the big guns: They've got the building, the presses, the fancy lawyers. . . . On the other hand, we've got nothing—and no choice but to fight back like cavemen, like terrorists.' Dad glanced at me, then quickly added, 'That is, some strikers think violence and vandalism are our only options. They're wrong, of course'" (37).

In only one of the six contemporary novels are members of the union portrayed as victims of violence or intimidation. (An organizer of the teachers' walkout in *Strike!* is severely beaten by a member of the Committee for a Balanced Curriculum, which is opposed to the strike.) This shift may be due in part to the perspective from which the stories are told: Just one of the six contemporary novels, *Time to Take Sides*, has a protagonist whose family is working class. The remaining books' protagonists are members of the middle or upper classes, torn between sympathy for the union cause and loyalty to family members and friends opposed to the strike. For example, Mary Casanova's *Riot*, based on actual events in International Falls, Minnesota, in 1989, tells the story of Bryan Grant, whose crush on the daughter of a nonunion worker is complicated by his own father's participation in a wildcat strike against a local paper mill. Bryan's father, Stan, engages in repeated vandalism against employees of the nonunion company hired for a major construction project. His wife is a teacher and herself a union member, but her higher level of education distances her from her husband's brand of roughneck radicalism. The family's lifestyle is middle class, with the mother shuttling between her aerobics classes and the children's music lessons in a red minivan. Bryan notices the contrast between their own home in a neighborhood "where new two-story houses, complete with decks and two-stall garages sprouted up as quickly as dandelions after a rain" with the rundown houses rented by employees of Badgett, the nonunion company, and wonders, "Is this what it meant to work for Badgett— to live on a lot less money? If unions helped people to earn better wages so they could live better, then unions were a good thing" (34). His question remains unanswered by the novel's conclusion, as the story focuses on how the father's unbridled anger affects Bryan and the rest of the family rather than exploring the economic implications of unionism.

The middle-class perspective seen in most of the contemporary novels in this survey offers an accurate depiction of many union members in the present day. Unions represent more white-collar professionals than they once did, but more importantly, unions in the twentieth century succeeded in raising blue-collar wages to levels that permitted a middle-class standard of living. In 2011, workers represented by unions earned a median of just over $200 more per week than their counterparts not represented by unions, according to the Bureau of Labor Statistics. For working families, that higher wage can make a tremendous difference in paying monthly bills and affording extras like the piano lessons Bryan Grant enjoyed.

The notion of workers having financial or other unmet needs as a result of their working conditions or their decision to strike is downplayed in the contemporary novels. Barry, the protagonist of *Strike!*, is the son of an attorney who serves on the school board, but he views his teachers' walkout sympathetically because of his personal relationships with them. The teachers' material conditions in *Strike!* are minimized by the narrative, as a teacher explains to Barry that "It's not so much the money, though that's an issue. . . . The main thing is all the interference we've been getting lately, people wanting to tell us how and what we should teach" (6). The strike is directed by a "committee" with little mention of a teachers' union. When Barry first arrives at the picket line, he finds it odd: "It was strange to see them out on the sidewalk with signs, like a bunch of carpenters or supermarket clerks or something. It had never occurred to him before to think of them as workers" (30).

In this small number of contemporary novels, union members are portrayed as fighting, often literally, to hold onto what they have, yet none of the novels explain how union membership can itself result in higher wages and an improved standard of living. In contrast, the labor movement of the past is represented as standing up for workers' rights against employers willing to exact retribution against union members in the form of their livelihood or even their lives. Each of the six contemporary novels depicts a strike, while the historical fiction also portrays union members engaged in common union activities such as organizing, attending meetings, and lobbying. When more than one out of ten workers in the United States remains a union member, the lack of representation of present-day workers engaged in these activities associated with labor organization, as opposed to the direct action of a labor stoppage, skews representations of unions in ways that are both negative and inauthentic.

Back in the Day: Recalling Labor's Glorious Past

Occasionally, historicizing the labor movement as worthwhile in the past but irrelevant to contemporary America is explicit. In a few novels, both historical and contemporary, a character reminisces about American labor history, unfavorably comparing the present with the more noble efforts of unions in years past. In *Strike Two*, the grandmother expresses concern about the strike in which her twin sons have chosen opposite sides, and Gwen's father assures her, "[a] *little* picketing builds character." She replies, "but more than that destroys it.... Strikes were more dramatic and romantic in the old days ... about workers' rights and decent conditions. Now it's all about money" (15–16).

Similarly, the great-grandparents in *Riot* recall the strike of 1934 as "part of Teamster history" (37). Grandpa Howie is the embodiment of the need for worker safety regulations, having long ago lost his right arm in an accident that inspired a drive by the union for safer working conditions. In 1934, Bryan's great-grandmother worked in soup kitchens organized by the labor union to feed striking workers: "Oh, and it was a long strike. Not like today. Things are easy today.... [M]en were fighting to earn enough money to feed their families. Some starved right in the streets" (37). These recollections, served up on a Labor Day family visit, cast her grandson's involvement in the construction workers' wildcat strike as pointless and nihilistic by comparison. Although the aim of the strike is to protest the paper mill's hiring of a nonunion company for a project, the strikers' sole target appears to be the underpaid nonunion workers. The mill itself is excused from any responsibility beyond profit, its stench dismissed with comments such as "That's what money smells like" (26).

Some historical novels also feature older characters who suggest that current labor protests are less worthy than those of the past. *Up Molasses Mountain* by Julie Baker is set in West Virginia in 1956 and tells the story of a father and son divided by their views of the United Mine Workers (UMW). Their daughter and sister Elizabeth is surprised to find that her own grandfather had belonged to the union. Her grandmother recalls a time when "the mines were even more hateful than they are today. They'd kill dozens at a time, men with babies and wives, leaving them with nothing. And little children would be down there all day, crawling in the black, digging all day, just to eat" (44). Labor activist Mother Jones had come to the small mining community to help organize the union. Ultimately, Elizabeth's grandmother tells her, the union "milked the cow dry, so the farmers had to go somewhere else. After a time, the union bosses started looking an awful lot like the mine owners." Later Elizabeth asks her father why he and her brother Sterling hold such different views of the union. "I know it must be hard to understand.... Long ago, unions did a lot of good" (89). Now, he explains that he opposes the UMW because "the union makes men think they can't change anything without them. I know men have more power together, but I don't want to stand with a bunch of thugs" (89).

Minimizing the struggles of the present day by characterizing contemporary strikes as "all about the money" ignores real problems that persist in terms of worker safety. A 2011 report by the American Federation of Labor–Congress of Industrial Organizations (AFL-CIO) explained that while progress has been made in the years since the Occupational Health and Safety Administration (OSHA) was created in 1970, more needed to be done to improve working conditions. The report cited the explosion in 2010 at Massey Energy's Upper Big Branch coal mine in West Virginia that cost twenty-nine miners their lives, as well as the BP/Transocean Gulf Coast oil spill caused by an explosion that killed eleven oil rig workers. Their recommendations called for stiffer penalties, more OSHA inspectors, and stronger laws to protect workers, including strengthening the Mine Health and Safety Act. Suggesting that labor organizations may once have done some good but are now irrelevant to present workers' concerns is akin to implying that racism and sexism are no longer the problems they once were.

Historical Settings and Industries Represented in the Sample

The historical settings of the novels range from 1836 to the early 2000s, but their distribution over these years is uneven. The majority of books in the sample, thirty-seven out of fifty-three, are set in the twentieth century, with twenty-one taking place from 1900 through 1920. Forty-three are set between 1836 and 1936, while only ten, including the six contemporary novels, are set in the years since 1936. Thus, the novels mainly depict events that young readers and their families, and even their grandparents, have no personal memories or knowledge of. It is in these gaps in the timeline and in the identification of stories that are "are neglected or excluded," as Raymond Williams (115) described, that one can find other, alternative versions of history that, by their absence, suggest the power of a selective tradition to shape how a society views its past and present. In these gaps lie stories that could cast labor conflicts in ways that make clearer their connections to issues of the present, particularly in regard to social class.

Three novels have a pre–Civil War setting: *A Spirit to Ride the Whirlwind* by Athena Lord; *Lyddie*; and *So Far from Home: The Diary of Mary Driscoll, an Irish Mill Girl, Lowell, Massachusetts, 1847*, by Barry Denenberg, the latter title part of Scholastic Press's Dear America series. All are set in Lowell, Massachusetts, the scene of labor unrest among the town's young, mainly female textile workers. During the first half of the nineteenth century, many workers found themselves locked into an economy based on wage labor rather than on participation in networks of independent producers. The teenage textile mill worker in *Lyddie* touches on this in her journey from the farm to the textile mill, but the implications for female workers leaving rural farms for urban areas like Lowell were far different than those for their male counterparts, particularly those working in urban centers. Sean Wilentz, in *Chants Democratic*, argues that those in the past and present reflecting on the coming of industrialization to North America tend to focus on what he termed "a mechanized contrivance like Lowell" (107) and to ignore the growth of industry in New York, the city that would dominate commerce over the next two centuries. Although the novels set in Lowell tell important stories particularly about women's history, others set in this pivotal period in more urbanized areas and about other industries would offer broader perspectives on the faltering republican ideal of economic independence.[6]

Immigration and ethnicity are key elements in the eleven novels set between 1867 and 1899 as well as in the twenty books set in the first two decades of the twentieth century, reflecting the waves of immigration to the United States during the period.[7] Most depict workers and their families arriving from areas other than northern Europe. Chinese, Italian, Russian, Polish, Finnish, Slovakian, and Greek workers are among those portrayed. A focus on miners predominates in novels set in the late nineteenth and early twentieth century (*Chase; A Real American; A Coal Miner's Bride: The Story of Anetka Kaminska; Trouble at the Mine; The Breaker Boys;* and *Fire in the Hole!*), eclipsed only by books set in the textile or garment industries. The plight of New York garment workers in the wake of the 1909 strike and the fire at the Triangle Waist Factory in 1911 has been the focus for a number of novels in recent years (*Ashes of Roses; Changes for Rebecca; Factory Girl; Uprising; Hear My Sorrow: The Diary of Angela Denoto, a Shirtwaist Worker; The Locket: Surviving the Triangle Shirtwaist Fire;* and *Rosie in New York City: Gotcha!*) Many include female characters, not necessarily the protagonists, who speak out in defiance of class and gender expectations in ways that mark them as self-consciously modern women. The moral ambiguity that appears in some of the other novels is not a part of the story of the Triangle. Working conditions that led to the tragedy were so unsafe and the factory's owners so unconcerned about the safety of their employees that workers could be portrayed as innocent victims of their greedy employers.

The first significant gap in the settings of novels depicting the labor movement is the immediate post–World War I period. Despite the fact that the years following the war saw record numbers of strikes by American workers, the years 1919 through 1928 provide settings for only two novels: *The Ornament Tree* by Jean Thesman and *A Test of Loyalty* by S. D. Jones. *The Ornament Tree*, set in Seattle and based on historical events, is the only novel of the sample to portray a general strike. The dearth of books portraying strikes that take place during the decade may be due in part to the extraordinary success with which the unrest that followed the war was put down. According to Robert H. Zeiger, approximately one-fifth of American workers were involved in the strikes of 1919, but by 1929 this wave of labor unrest had largely been quelled. The Boston police strike of 1919, streetcar strikes in Chicago and other cities, struggles within organized labor regarding the inclusion of African American workers: none of these aspects of labor history appear in the novels. The proximity of this period of labor militancy to the 1917 Russian Revolution meant that when union organizers were called "reds" or "communists," the association with the Soviet Union was immediate. The roots of the McCarthy era and the blacklist can be found in the historical memory of those for whom even the conservative trade unionism of the American Federation of Labor meant a dangerous step toward revolution.

The next novels are the seven set during the Great Depression; their small number belies the breadth, if not the depth, of their coverage of events of the 1930s, as their authors touch on a wide range of labor topics.[8] In *El Lector*, the primary event is the cigar factory workers' strike in Ybor City, Florida, but the author includes references to the coal miners' strike in Harlan, Kentucky, as well. James Lincoln Collier's *The Worst of Times* features a fictional strike in a Chicago factory that manufactures chrome-plated automobile parts. Throughout the book, the main character, Petey, his father, and his uncle discuss economic issues in a didactic fashion reminiscent of the discussions in Collier's other book in the sample, the contemporary novel *The Winchesters* (1988). Petey's cousin Steve, the son of the owner of Rayfield Chrome, outrages his father by leaving college to work as a union organizer. Through his letters to his family, the reader hears of the 1934 longshoremen's strike in San Francisco, the Goodyear strike in Akron, Ohio, and a sit-down strike at General Motors in Detroit. The Detroit strike is mentioned briefly in *Bud, Not Buddy* in the scene in which Bud and union organizer Lefty Lewis are pulled over by the police. The policeman explains, "I don't know if you've heard, but we're having a lot of trouble in the factories here. We've been stopping all cars we don't recognize. There've been reports that some of those stinking labor organizers might be sneaking up here from Detroit" (135). The union Lefty is helping organize is the Brotherhood of Pullman Porters, or the Brotherhood of Sleeping Car Porters, established in 1925 by A. Philip Randolph. In 1936, when *Bud, Not Buddy* takes place, the union had only recently received its charter from the American Federation of Labor, the first African American union to do so. Thus, Christopher Paul Curtis, in a book that has nothing to do with the labor movement, manages to deftly reference two historic events in labor history.

What is remarkable is that the period immediately following the years of the Great Depression, the 1940s through the mid-1950s, is the point at which the largest gap in the timeline of the sample novels occurs. After *Bud, Not Buddy*, which takes place in 1936, the next setting is 1956 (*Up Molasses Mountain*). It is this gap in representation that is most fascinating, as the years after World War II saw an unprecedented volume of strikes and union activity, none of which appears in any children's novels I was able to locate, although one, *Strings Attached* by Judy Blundell set in 1950, was published in 2011, after the study was completed. Senator Joseph McCarthy's anticommunist crusade began in the late 1940s, and unions themselves embarked on serious efforts to purge communists from their membership. African American unionists gained ground in the United Automobile Workers and the United Mine Workers, but these stories, which provide context for much of the political activism of the civil rights movement, are not yet part of children's literature.

Just four historical novels in the sample depict labor unions from the late 1950s through 1970: *Up Molasses Mountain* set in 1956; *Kira-Kira*, which follows a Japanese American family's story from the late 1950s through the early 1960s; *Fight in the Fields: César Chávez*, a time-slip novel by Margo Sorenson in which two children are transported back to 1966; and Gary Soto's *Jesse*, set in 1970. *Up Molasses Mountain* takes place in the coal mines of West Virginia, while the remaining three portray agriculture workers; thus, labor unions in these novels set in the relatively recent past are represented only as advocates for manual labor, even as the movement's leaders began recruiting white-collar workers to their ranks.

The disconnect with the contemporary labor movement in the United States is stark. The typical union member portrayed in the novels of the sample is a garment worker living a hundred years ago. Workers employed in textile or garment manufacturing and mining, the two occupations most

often represented in the novels, make up only a small fraction of union-
ized workers today compared to groups like teachers, police, and firefight-
ers. The automobile industry is represented in only two novels: *The Worst
of Times* and *Bud, Not Buddy*, and the United Automobile, Aerospace and
Agricultural Implement Workers of America (UAW), a union that played
a prominent role in mid-twentieth-century politics particularly under its
president Walter Reuther, is never mentioned by name. It is unlikely today
that many young people have even heard of Reuther, much less realize that
the president of the UAW, along with the aforementioned A. Philip Randolph, shared the stage in 1963 at the March on Washington for Jobs and
Freedom. Another industry that might well appear in the novels but that
has not yet been represented is the service industry, which includes custo-
dians, maids, and healthcare workers.[9] Students know about Martin Luther
King's leadership of the Montgomery bus boycott, but few understand that
he was in Memphis to support a sanitation workers' strike when he was assassinated in 1968.

Critics may only speculate about why authors of the novels in the sample
tend to focus on particular industries and historical periods while ignoring
others. Perhaps they hope to provide young readers with some understanding of the foundations of the labor movement, but they fail to include its actual origins in the trade guilds of the growing metropolitan centers of New
York and Philadelphia early in the nineteenth century. Certainly the historical periods most often depicted, the late nineteenth and early twentieth
centuries, were pivotal periods in American labor history, with the growth
of the Eight-Hour Day movement and numerous labor actions including
the 1909 garment workers' strike, but the images of labor that emerge even
from that period are oddly incomplete. The Knights of Labor in the 1880s
put forward a version of unionism that was less exclusive of women and
African American workers than the American Federation of Labor, yet this
early national organization appears in only one book, Harriette Robinet's
Missing from Haymarket Square. Although the Industrial Workers of the
World (IWW, or "Wobblies" as they came to be known) are mentioned in
several novels (*Bread and Roses, Too*; *The Ornament Tree*; *Rockbuster*), Eugene Debs, who helped found the organization, appears in only one book
of the sample, *Gilded Delirium*.[10] Debs ran for president five times as the
Socialist candidate and received almost a million votes in the 1920 election,
despite the fact that he was serving a prison sentence for his outspoken
opposition to the Great War at the time. Labor's more radical roots, those
parts of its history that might present fundamental challenges to capitalism,

rarely appear in the novels, permitting more conservative perspectives to dominate.

Possibilities of the Past and Present

In 1987, Roy Rosenzweig mused as to whether a "conspiracy of silence" (51) was to blame for omissions and misrepresentations of labor history within American popular culture, even as labor historians achieved acclaim for recent outstanding works on the topic. Those award-winning labor histories, as described earlier, provided detailed descriptions of working-class life that children's authors have put to good use in stories about certain occupations and in particular periods of American history, yielding many strong individual novels; yet the cumulative effect of the sample as a whole is to offer up a version of labor that is historicized as more relevant to the past than to the present. Rosenzweig found this troubling within the larger popular culture: "It is the sort of attitude that allows us to celebrate the lives of leaders of important social and political movements while allowing the gains achieved by those lives to be eroded. It is also the sort of attitude I see in my students, who are perfectly willing to sympathize with the sufferings of workers in the late nineteenth century while denouncing labor unions in the present" (52).

The attenuation of labor, this weakening of unionism by removing it from more authentic historical contexts and ignoring its connection with the present, sets forth a very specific version of labor history. Just as a weakened virus may serve as a vaccination against full-blown versions of specific dangerous diseases, might the novels offer a sort of "vaccination" against infection by radical ideas, limiting their potential to challenge students to take a more critical stance of economic relations in the present-day workplace? Awareness of the ability of the selective tradition to shape past and present into versions that can best serve powerful interests in a society is the first step in considering how to subvert that process. The task of identifying the silences that persist in stories about labor requires familiarity with the history of unions in the United States as well as awareness of the role labor plays in contemporary society.

Although historical fiction is overrepresented within the sample, I do not mean to suggest that the genre precludes possibilities of engagement with the present. Raymond Williams stresses that "cultural formations" (118–119), including literature, can indeed offer alternative or oppositional versions of the past and present, along with those of the more hegemonic tradition. Such cultural formations have the potential to reclaim the past in ways that cast the present in a different light. According to Williams, historical work that presents alternative or oppositional formations is an effective way to resist the dominant selective tradition.

Historical fiction that attempts to portray such oppositional formations has sometimes been accused of presentism, unrealistically imposing the values of the present day on characters in the past. Chandra Power challenges such critics' accusations that historical fiction for young adults is presentist by documenting the existence of the contested values and attitudes using historical research. One example is *The True Confessions of Charlotte Doyle* by Avi, in which an upper-middle-class girl forms an alliance with sailors staging a mutiny on their voyage across the Atlantic in the nineteenth century. Power's historical research demonstrated that while Charlotte's feminist beliefs may have been held by a small minority of women at that time, they did in fact exist and were not the complete anachronisms critics charged. Authors of historical fiction offering such perspectives provide more complete and complex representations of history. A simple conception of the past as a less enlightened time than our own implies that issues of classism, sexism, and racism belong solely to the past. Historical fiction that aims to recover voices that would otherwise be lost can be faithful to the historical record while offering fresh perspectives on past and present.

Critiques of the capitalist economic system in historical fiction can demonstrate how minority voices of the past achieved some progress, even in the face of overwhelming opposition. One book that does this is *Uprising*, a novel that weaves together the stories of three young women and the Triangle Waist Factory fire. Throughout the novel, Margaret Haddix provides a critique not just of the owners of the factory but of capitalism itself, as Jane, the daughter of a wealthy businessman, wonders: "Was the speaker right, the one who claimed there was enough wealth in America that *no one* should have to live in poverty?" (64). On the picket line, Yetta, a striking garment worker, is shocked when a prostitute punches her in the face. She asks, "Why do you care about our strike?" and the woman replies, "Money, of course. . . . Don't you know anything? In America, money is God" (86). Jane eventually runs away from home to join Yetta and her roommate Bella in their Lower East Side tenement. The three friends fashion their own pact of social action, aspiring to overcome the limitations of gender and class: "'So we will not be stupid girls,' Bella said. 'And we will not be useless girls,' Jane added. 'And we will not be powerless girls,' Yetta finished" (233).

Haddix provides a detailed author's note that describes immigration in the early twentieth century, events leading up to the garment workers' strike, and the disastrous fire and its aftermath. She describes the involvement of future labor secretary Frances Perkins in the Triangle fire investigation, quoting her as saying: "The Triangle Fire was the first day of the New Deal" (342). (Perkins is not mentioned in any of the other novels of the sample.) She explains that industrial disasters are not just a thing of the past, citing a 1991 fire at a chicken-processing plant in North Carolina and, as an example of the effects of globalization and lack of concern with worker safety, a 1993 fire at a toy factory in Thailand. The death tolls for the two fires together numbered over two hundred: "Like the shirtwaist-wearing college girls in 1909, we have to ask ourselves what responsibility we bear for the people who make our clothes and other possessions" (343). Throughout the narrative and beyond, Haddix focuses on this responsibility so that the connection between past and present is clear.

Providing extensive historical detail while remaining mindful of links to the present is one way to portray labor in a way that maintains its relevance to the lives of young readers. Another is a paradoxically "less is more" approach, treating union membership as an incidental and normal part of a character's life, so that it is not the focus of the novel. Almost no authors take this approach. Union membership is seemingly like Chekhov's gun; once introduced, it must be employed in the interest of plot. As noted earlier, one novel in which union membership is handled in this manner is Christopher Paul Curtis's *Bud, Not Buddy*. Curtis first planned to write a book about the 1937 UAW strike in Flint, Michigan (Lamb 399), but the project turned instead into the story of Bud, a runaway child in search of the musician he believes to be his long-lost father. Soon after he encounters Pullman Porter organizer Lefty Lewis, the two part ways, and the union is not mentioned again. Making this involvement with the union simply one more fact about the character, as natural as any other descriptor, Curtis normalizes labor and casts it as something unremarkable rather than exceptional.

Stories like *Uprising* and *Bud, Not Buddy* have the potential to offer sites of resistance to the powerful forces of postindustrial capitalism, addressing social class as well as other issues. These two novels as well as others speak to racial division and the denigration of the poor. *Let the Circle Be Unbroken* includes an unforgettable scene in which powerful segregationists in the community use race as a wedge to drive apart a potential integrated alliance of farm workers. *Jesse* by Gary Soto shows the relentless inconveniences of a life of poverty but also the strong bonds of friendship and family that struggling workers must maintain to withstand the challenges. Such stories also provide images of characters engaging in collective action to improve their circumstances, images that are oddly missing from most children's books, according to Wendy Saul, who argues that texts that depict collectivism would provide young readers with "some realistic sense of how power is distributed and how decisions are made. Causes as diverse as the nuclear freeze movement, feminism and creationism have all been furthered by widespread grass-roots collective action" (30).

Global economic crises that have arisen in the new century, as well as continued struggles for racial and gender equality, give fresh urgency to the need to reexamine and better understand how social and economic issues are represented in popular media, including children's literature. Understanding how the selective tradition functions allows the framing of questions aimed at the vulnerabilities of the process. Whose interests are served by representations of American labor as noble in the past but selfish and violent in the present? Why do so few novels include aspects of labor history in which the capitalist system itself faced actual opposition? And why are there so few contemporary novels for young people that include characters like Lefty Lewis in *Bud, Not Buddy*, decent, caring individuals who happen to also be a part of a labor union? Stories of the journeys and struggles of organized workers in the present day have the potential to produce fascinating narratives about social class, race, and gender, for young people and adults as well. Such books that tell the stories of workers in the twenty-first century may one day offer children more authentic and complete representations of the American labor movement.

NOTES

1. In fact, the American dream of upward social mobility can be described more accurately as the American myth: upward mobility in American families is roughly the same as for families in Great Britain and less than that for Scandinavian families, according to *Economic Mobility: Is the American Dream Alive and Well?*, a 2008 report issued by the Economic Mobility Project of the Pew Charitable Trusts.

2. The Bureau of Labor Statistics reports that American workers' membership in labor unions decreased from 20.1 percent in 1983 to 11.8 percent in 2011, a slide halted by small gains in 2008 and 2009 before falling again the following year.

The popular media had deemed the political obituary for the American labor movement old news when battles reminiscent of those of a half century earlier broke out after midterm elections in 2010. A new class of deeply conservative governors and legislators who had campaigned on promises to cut government spending translated their pledges into initiatives that included eliminating public employees' rights to engage in collective bargaining. In early 2011, state workers, including teachers and police, occupied the state capitol in Madison, Wisconsin, for weeks, reviving debate about workers' rights in the twenty-first century. Union members' political power, although far from what it had once been, remained sufficient to make them the target of similar legislation in Ohio, Tennessee, Idaho, and Indiana. Just months later, labor unions were among the first organizations to offer support to Occupy Wall Street protesters in demonstrations that began in New York but quickly spread around the country. Union membership for the tumultuous year 2011 remained steady, slipping only 0.1 percent from 2010.

3. An example of the process can be seen in Jean Anyon's study of high school social studies textbooks in which she found that the perspectives of dominant groups persisted, even as curriculum content was updated and textbooks were revised. Textbooks devoted an average of six pages to labor history and usually focused on three of more than thirty thousand strikes that took place during the period between the Civil War and World War I. Anyon notes that these strikes—the railroad strike of 1877, the Homestead strike of 1892, and the Pullman strike of 1894—were violent and represented setbacks to the labor movement. Furthermore, she observed that textbooks emphasized the divisions that existed between workers of various ethnic groups while ignoring the promotion of such divisions by management as a way to discourage labor organization. Focusing on certain strikes allowed the texts to portray unions as violent mobs while ignoring the repression they experienced by government and business interests, and makes their relatively diminished political profile today appear to be a natural outcome of these past actions. Were the textbooks to showcase other strikes instead and focus on the real gains that labor achieved such as the eight-hour workday and weekends, students might well wonder why so few workers are now union members.

4. One question that arose was, at what point can a book be considered historical rather than contemporary fiction? Specifically, was Gary Soto's *Jesse*, set in 1970 and published in 1994, historical fiction? Children's literature textbooks have attempted to establish guidelines as to how much time between the book's setting and its production must elapse before the author is writing historically. A staple of children's literature courses, *Literature and the Child* by Lee Galda and Bernice Cullinan, lists various periods in which historical fiction might be set, with the most recent being "[t]he 1950s through the 1980s: Political and Social Turmoil" (228).

This confirmed my sense that *Jesse* was historical; in 1970, Richard Nixon was president and the war in Vietnam was a major issue. The 1990s, when the book was written, seemed far removed from 1970. It did mean that only six years separated this, the most recent setting of books classified as historical fiction, and 1976, the year in which the first of the contemporary novels, *Time to Take Sides*, was set.

5. There is ample historical evidence to support these representations. Sean Wilentz's essay "Against Exceptionalism: Class Consciousness and the American Labor Movement, 1790–1920" describes how "extraordinary repression [was] visited upon organized workers by employers' associations, with the cooperation of the courts, state legislatures, and increasingly, the federal government" (15) in the late nineteenth century.

6. Wilentz's *Chants Democratic: New York City and the Rise of the American Working Class, 1788–1850* offers rich detail about how workers' expectations shifted in the decades following the American Revolution. The notion of wages has become so much a part of American economic culture in the years since the early nineteenth century that it may be difficult, especially for young readers, to grasp the implications of accepting permanent employment for wages. For males, the apprentice system, memorably described in Esther Forbes's 1943 novel, *Johnny Tremain,* represented a career path that, ideally, culminated with the trained craftsman establishing his own business. The years in which men accepted wages were stigmatized as dependence on another for one's living. Under the system by which men learned their trade, working for wages was supposed to be a temporary situation, not a permanent one. By 1850, New York's working class had seen relations with their employers deteriorate markedly, even as workers realized that they themselves were unlikely to ever realize the economic independence they had once aspired to. Stories that trace these shifting expectations and the rise of labor organizations might well resonate with young people who see their own families' financial challenges and diminished expectations in the present day.

7. Novels set in the period from 1867 through 1900 are *The Iron Dragon Never Sleeps; Forbidden Friendship; Chase; Missing from Haymarket Square; The Streetcar Riots; A Real American; Gilded Delirium; A Coal Miner's Bride: The Story of Anetka Kaminska; Trouble at the Mines; The Breaker Boys;* and *Fire in the Hole!* Those set between 1901 and 1920 are *Theodore Roosevelt: Letters from a Young Coal Miner; The Candle and the Mirror; Breaker; The Journal of Otto Peltonen: A Finnish Immigrant; Billy Creekmore; Rockbuster; East Side Story; Rosie in New York City: Gotcha!; Hear My Sorrow: The Diary of Angela Denoto, a Shirtwaist Worker; Uprising; Call Me Ruth; On Fire; Ashes of Roses; Fire! The Beginnings of the Labor Movement; The Locket: Surviving the Triangle Shirtwaist Fire; Making Waves; Bread and Roses, Too; Factory Girl; Frankie;* and *Changes for Rebecca.*

8. The novels set during the Great Depression include *Let the Circle Be Unbroken; Esperanza Rising; Bud, Not Buddy; The Stunt; El Lector; The Worst of Times;* and *Franklin Roosevelt: Letters from a Mill Town Girl.*

9. A picture book, *¡Sí, Se puede! / Yes, We Can! Janitor Strike in L.A.,* by Diana Cohn does offer younger children a positive image of collective action on the part of janitors in Los Angeles.

10. This time-travel novel by Jordan Stokes and Matthew Belinkie, published by SparkNotes, is a decidedly odd study guide to American history. Published in 2007, it demonstrates that Jean Anyon's observations almost thirty years earlier about the three strikes likely to be included in history textbooks remain valid. Interspersed in the novel are sections of historical information, one of which includes the fact that "[s]ome of the most infamous Gilded Age strikes, meanwhile, were the Great Railroad Strike of 1877, the Homestead Strike of 1892, and the Pullman Strike of 1894" (10).

BOOKS OF THE SAMPLE

Armstrong, Jennifer. *Theodore Roosevelt: Letters from a Young Coal Miner.* New York: Winslow Press, 2000.

Auch, Mary Jane. *Ashes of Roses*. New York: Dell, 2002.

Bader, Bonnie. *East Side Story*. New York: Silver Moon, 1993.

Baker, Julie. *Up Molasses Mountain*. New York: Dell, 2002.

Barkley, Brad, and Heather Hepler. *Dream Factory*. New York: Dutton, 2007.

Bartoletti, Susan. *A Coal Miner's Bride: The Diary of Anetka Kaminska, Lattimer, Pennsylvania, 1896*. New York: Scholastic Press, 2000.

Casanova, Mary. *Riot*. New York: Hyperion, 1996.

Collier, James Lincoln. *The Winchesters*. New York: Avon, 1988.

———. *The Worst of Times*. Columbus, Ohio: School Specialty Publishing, 2000.

Corcoran, Barbara. *Strike!* New York: Atheneum, 1983.

Curtis, Christopher Paul. *Bud, Not Buddy*. New York: Dell, 1999.

Denenberg, Barry. *So Far from Home: The Diary of Mary Driscoll, an Irish Mill Girl, Lowell, Massachusetts, 1847*. New York: Scholastic Press, 1997.

Durbin, William. *The Journal of Otto Peltonen: A Finnish Immigrant*. New York: Scholastic Press, 2001.

———. *El Lector*. New York: Yearling, 2007.

Easton, Richard. *A Real American*. New York: Clarion Books, 2002.

Farrell, Mary Cronk. *Fire in the Hole!* New York: Clarion Books, 2004.

Gold, Sharlya. *Time to Take Sides*. New York: Clarion Books, 1976.

Goldin, Barbara Diamond. *Fire! The Beginnings of the Labor Movement*. New York: Viking, 1992.

Greene, Jacqueline Dembar. *Changes for Rebecca*. Middleton, Wis.: American Girl, 2009.

Greenwood, Barbara. *Factory Girl*. Tonawanda, N.Y.: Kids Can, 2007.

Haas, Jesse. *Chase*. New York: Greenwillow, 2007.

Haddix, Margaret P. *Uprising*. New York: Simon & Schuster, 2007.

Hopkinson, Deborah. *Hear My Sorrow: The Diary of Angela Denoto, a Shirtwaist Worker*. New York: Scholastic Press, 2004.

Hughes, Pat. *The Breaker Boys*. New York: Farrar, Straus and Giroux, 2004.

Jones, J. Sydney. *Frankie*. New York: Dutton, 1997.

Jones, S. D. *A Test of Loyalty*. Belmont, Calif.: Fearon, 1989.

Kadohata, Cynthia. *Kira-Kira*. New York: Scholastic Press, 2004.

Koss, Amy Goldman. *Strike Two*. New York: Dial, 2001.

Krensky, Stephen. *The Iron Dragon Never Sleeps*. New York: Delacorte, 1994.

Lieurance, Suzanne. *The Locket: Surviving the Triangle Shirtwaist Fire*. Berkeley Heights, N.J.: Enslow, 2008.

Lord, Athena V. *A Spirit to Ride the Whirlwind*. New York: Macmillan, 1982.

Matas, Carol. *Rosie in New York City: Gotcha!* New York: Aladdin, 2003.

Mays, Lucinda. *The Candle and the Mirror*. New York: Atheneum, 1982.

Miller, Susan Martins. *The Streetcar Riots*. Uhrichsville, Ohio: Barbour, 1998.

Paterson, Katherine. *Bread and Roses, Too*. New York: Clarion Books, 2006.

———. *Lyddie*. New York: Penguin, 1991.

Perez, Norah A. *Breaker*. Boston: Houghton Mifflin, 1988.

Porter, Tracy. *Billy Creekmore*. New York: HarperCollins, 2007.

Rappaport, Doreen. *Trouble at the Mines*. New York: Crowell, 1986.

Robinet, Harriette Gillem. *Missing from Haymarket Square*. New York: Atheneum, 2001.

Rue, Nancy. *The Stunt*. Minneapolis: Bethany House, 1999.

Ryan, Pamela Muñoz. *Esperanza Rising*. New York: Scholastic Press, 2000.

Sachs, Marilyn. *Call Me Ruth*. New York: Doubleday, 1982.

Sebestyen, Ouida. *On Fire*. Boston: Atlantic Monthly Press, 1985.

Skurzynski, Gloria. *Rockbuster*. New York: Atheneum, 2001.

Sorenson, Margo. *Fight in the Fields: César Chávez*. Logan, Iowa: Perfection Learning, 1998.

Soto, Gary. *Jesse*. New York: Scholastic Press, 1994.

Stokes, Jordan, and Matthew Belinkie. *Gilded Delirium*. New York: SparkNotes, 2007.

Taylor, Mildred. *Let the Circle Be Unbroken*. New York: Puffin, 1981.

Thesman, Jean. *The Ornament Tree*. Boston: Houghton Mifflin, 1996.

Weber, Judith Eichler. *Forbidden Friendship*. New York: Silver Moon, 2004.

Williams, Barbara. *Making Waves*. New York: Dial, 2000.

Winthrop, Elizabeth. *Franklin Roosevelt: Letters from a Mill Town Girl*. New York: Winslow Press, 2001.

WORKS CITED

American Federation of Labor–Congress of Industrial Organizations, Safety and Health Department. "Death on the Job: The Toll of Neglect." April 2011. Accessed February 4, 2012. Website.

Anyon, Jean. "Ideology and United States History Textbooks." *Harvard Educational Review* 49 (1979): 361–386. Print.

Avi. *The True Confessions of Charlotte Doyle*. New York: Orchard Books, 1990.

Bacon, Betty, ed. *How Much Truth Do We Tell the Children? The Politics of Children's Literature*. Minneapolis: Marxist Educational Press, 1988. Print.

Blundell, Judy. *Strings Attached*. New York: Scholastic Press, 2011. Print.

Bureau of Labor Statistics. "Union Membership (Annual) News Release." United States Department of Labor, January 28, 2009. Accessed April 4, 2009. Website

———. "Union Members Summary." United States Department of Labor, January 27, 2012. Accessed February 2, 2012. Website.

Center on Budget and Policy Priorities. "Income Inequality Grew in Most States over the Last Two Decades." April 9, 2008. Accessed April 15, 2008. Website.

Cohn, Diana. *¡Sí, Se puede! / Yes, We Can! Janitor Strike in L.A.* El Paso: Cinco Puntos, 2002. Print.

Galda, Lee, and Bernice E. Cullinan. *Literature and the Child*. 5th ed. Belmont, Calif.: Wadsworth / Thomson Learning, 2002. Print.

Harris, Violet. "African American Children's Literature: The First One Hundred Years." In *Freedom's Plow: Teaching in the Multicultural Classroom*, edited by Jim Fraser and Theresa Perry, 167–181. New York: Routledge, 1993. Print.

Kohl, Herbert. *Should We Burn Babar? Essays on Children's Literature and the Power of Stories*. New York: New Press, 1995. Print.

Lamb, Wendy. "Christopher Paul Curtis." *Horn Book* 76:4 (2000): 397–401. Print.

Overstreet, Deborah. "Organize! A Look at Labor History in Young Adult Books." *ALAN Review* 8:4 (2001): 60–66. Print.

Power, Chandra. "Challenging the Pluralism of Our Past: Presentism and the Selective Tradition in Historical Fiction Written for Young People." *Research in the Teaching of English* 37 (2003): 425–466. Print.

Rosenzweig, Roy. "American Labor History: A Conspiracy of Silence? *Monthly Labor Review* 110:8 (1987): 51–53. Print.

Saul, Wendy. "We Gather Together: Collectivism in Children's Books." *School Library Journal* 29:8 (1983): 30–31. Print.

Sawhill, Isabel, and John E. Morton. *Economic Mobility: Is the American Dream Alive and Well?* The Pew Charitable Trusts, Economic Mobility Project, February 2008. Accessed October 28, 2011. Website.

Schmitt, John, and Kris Warner. *The Changing Face of Labor, 1983–2008.* Center for Economic and Policy Research, November 2009. Accessed August 7, 2011. Website.

Taxel, Joel. "Outsiders of the American Revolution: The Selective Tradition in Children's Fiction." *Interchange* 12:2–3 (1981): 206–228. Print.

Wilentz, Sean. "Against Exceptionalism: Class Consciousness and the American Labor Movement, 1790–1920." *International Labor and Working Class History* 26 (1984): 1–24. Print.

———. *Chants Democratic: New York City and the Rise of the American Working Class, 1788–1850.* New York: Oxford University Press, 1984. Print.

Williams, Raymond. *Marxism and Literature.* Oxford: Oxford University Press 1977. Print.

Wojcik-Andrews, Ian. "Introduction: Notes toward a Theory of Class in Children's Literature." *The Lion and the Unicorn* 17 (1993): 113–123. Print.

Zieger, Robert H. *The CIO, 1935–1955.* Chapel Hill: University of North Carolina Press, 1995. NetLibrary.com. Accessed January 4, 2010. Website.

"The Disorders of Its Own Identity"

Poverty as Aesthetic Symbol in Eve Bunting's Picture Books

DANIEL D. HADE AND HEIDI M. BRUSH

Introduction

" Children's literature is an artistically mediated form of communication—a conversation—that a society has with its young. It is shaped by the concerns of the many stakeholders that are part of the 'world that creates the text' (Bakhtin, *Dialogic Imagination* 253)" (Johnston 303). Among these stakeholders would necessarily be those adults who are the owners of the publishing houses who control the means of production of children's books. Also included would be a collection of petit bourgeois workers: writers, editors, illustrators, marketing directors, booksellers, and, in some cases, teachers and librarians who exercise day-to-day management over the production, distribution, and exchange of the books. In classic Marxist theory, although these workers earn wages and royalties, they do not share a working-class or poor consciousness. They are separated from the lower classes.

Although it has been accepted since the publication of Jacqueline Rose's *The Case for Peter Pan; or, The Impossibility of Children's Fiction* that it is important to understand the roles of adults in producing children's literature, that understanding has mostly revolved around how the child is constructed as an implied audience. But the production of children's books is also an enterprise conducted by adults for children in order to make a profit (Hade 298). In other words, the children's book is a commodity, an object to be purchased and sold, whose continued production is determined by the existence of a substantial market to create profits for the producers. This means

that children's books cannot exist without a middle and upper class willing to buy them. Scholars rarely consider this aspect of children's literature,
although the implications are profound, especially when it comes to the
portrayal of children from disadvantaged, nonmainstream backgrounds.

It's no coincidence that children's literature rarely exists absent a bourgeoisie and petit bourgeoisie. Children's books and children's book publishers began to emerge in the eighteenth century just as a merchant class was
expanding in Great Britain and North America. Children's book pioneer
John Newbery recognized the dual nature of children's books as entertainment and as commodity with his motto, "Trade and Plum Cake Forever!
Huzzah!" The books produced by Newbery and his peers were filled with
bourgeois assumptions and morality. If poor children appeared in those
books, they were seen through bourgeois eyes. The place of poor children
in the production of children's books wasn't as readers but rather as rag
pickers procuring cloth that was used in the production of paper and as
sweatshop workers painting watercolor wash on illustrations. Flash forward to the beginning of the twentieth century when Franklin Mathiews,
in his 1914 essay "Blowing Out the Boy's Brains," admonished parents not
to purchase cheap dime novels, which he felt overstimulated young readers,
but rather to purchase the much more expensive books from "reputable"
publishers. Mathiews, like his contemporaries who were so instrumental in
developing and promoting children's books, Frederic Melcher, Anne Carroll Moore, Louise Bechtel, and Bertha Mahoney, ignored the economic
realities of the majority of children in the United States: most children were
poor and working on farms, in factories, mines, and sweatshops, helping
their families to survive.

These class issues aren't recognized in the classic histories of children's
literature such as those by F. J. Harvey Darton and John Rowe Townsend
or in the comprehensive textbooks by May Hill Arbuthnot and Charlotte
Huck. Public and school libraries, which offer the possibility of including
poor and working poor children in the marketplace of children's book readers, have historically been underfunded and in recent times have seen their
budgets slashed, while the elementary school curriculum, which school
libraries support, has seen children's literature squeezed out of literacy programs. The market has been left to the private sector, in other words those
families with money. With the bourgeoisie and petit bourgeoisie as both
producer and consumer of children's books, poor children, if they appear in
children's books at all, are left to the gazes of those above them in the social
and economic worlds. As Pierre Bourdieu has argued, the gaze of the artist

and of the reader on the book or other aesthetic object is one that creates social distance. We find that the work of author Eve Bunting demonstrates this social distance between upper classes and poor and working classes in children's books.

The Poor as Art Objects

Eve Bunting was born and raised in Northern Ireland. She emigrated to the United States at the age of thirty with her business executive husband and three children in 1958 and settled in Pasadena, California. She came late to the career of writing, publishing her first book in 1971, but has been prolific since, producing more than 250 books, nearly all written for a child audience. Although her work includes novels, critically acclaimed and award-winning mysteries, and folktales, she is best known for her picture-book stories, which deal with social issues and historical events such as the Holocaust, immigration, religious intolerance, migrant workers, urban gangs, Japanese internment, American Indian boarding schools, orphan trains, Middle East conflict, and homelessness; and personal issues such as divorce, adoption, death of a parent, and remarriage of a parent. Her books appear at the top of many children's reading lists devoted to issues of social justice and diversity.

Bunting confesses her purpose in these books to Stefanie Weiss of *NEA Today*: "I don't ever start off to give a message in my books, although often it must seem as though I do. I like to write about loving and caring and how both can ease everyone's way through life. Maybe that sounds Pollyanish, maybe it's optimism carded to the nth degree, but that's what I want to do." We will argue that this view isn't just "Pollyanish," it's an erasure of the poor via upper/middle class moralizing.

Our focus will be on three of Bunting's most acclaimed books, *Fly Away Home, Smoky Night,* and *A Day's Work.* We consider the tendency of Bunting's books to echo the sentimentality of social reform literature of the nineteenth century, filled with piteous waifs and urchins with hearts of gold. Using picture books and illustrated pamphlets, the middle classes gaze into the slums with sentimental fascination and horror from the comfort of their drawing rooms. Likewise, Bunting's implied readers are given the opportunity to peek from a middle-class vantage point into plights such as homelessness, urban violence, and migrant labor. Bunting manages this simulated veneer of voyeuristic authenticity through her use of child focalizers.

"Once the poor become aestheticized, poverty itself moves out of our field of social vision except as a passive depiction of otherness, alienation, and contingency with the human conditions" (Harvey 336–337). We argue that the aestheticization and sentimentalization of poverty and the carnivalesque inversion of high and low lie at the heart of Bunting's work. Using examples from Bunting's picture books, nineteenth-century pamphlets, and contemporary consumer products such as the "homeless American Girl" doll, we show the ways in which poverty is used as an aesthetic object to subvert real change. Because of the underlying passivity of Bunting's messages, we decidedly reject the inclusion of her works on readings lists devoted to social justice issues for children. Overall, we argue that Bunting's message is inherently conservative: relying on passive techniques such as hope and a belief in providence as a means of escaping poverty or oppressive regimes quite often reinforces oppression while discouraging rebellion and social direct action.

Bunting's books offer a middle-class vantage point into social justice issues while simulating the veneer of authenticity by employing first-person narration. This narration results in an improbably naïve point of view. Her picture books offer a glimpse into the world of poverty, homelessness, and urban riots, but from the point of view of the middle-class backgrounds of children's book stakeholders, not necessarily from that of actual poor children. In *Fly Away Home*, she speaks through the voice of a young homeless boy who's making the best of living in an airport with his father. While the narrator purportedly is a young homeless boy, the tone sounds particularly middle class and distant from the actualities of homelessness. For example, consider the following passage in which the boy describes himself and his father: "He and I wear blue jeans and blue T-shirts and blue jackets. . . . Not to be noticed is to look like nobody at all." Similarly, in *Smoky Night*, Bunting employs first-person narration to share the point of view of a young boy impacted by the swirling chaos of the Los Angeles riots. The reader learns about riots through a calm lesson conveyed by the boy's mother in the midst of looting and violence: "Mama explains about rioting. 'It can happen when people get angry. They want to smash and destroy. They don't care anymore what's right and what's wrong.'" In both of these cases, Bunting isolates the problems to the confines of the airport or South Central Los Angeles. The solution lies outside, in the loving embrace of the middle class. In each case, Bunting ends the book with the sentiment that optimism and an upbeat attitude will deliver these characters out of their predicaments.

Homelessness in a Home-Centered Culture: *Fly Away Home*

Fly Away Home is the story of a nameless homeless boy who lives in an airport terminal with his father, moving from terminal to terminal to avoid being noticed. Published in 1991, it was well received by critics and reviewers. It earned starred reviews from the prestigious reviewing journals *Booklist*, *Kirkus Reviews*, and *School Library Journal*. It also was recognized as one of the best children's books of the year by the American Library Association, the International Reading Association, and the National Council for the Social Studies. The book was recommended by the California Department of Education and included in the *Children's Catalog*, a reference book that lists the books considered to be core to a public library's children's department.

In the *New York Times* review of the book, Dinitia Smith writes:

> "Fly Away Home" is about a homeless boy, Andrew, about 6 years old, who is living in an airport with his father. But the author, Eve Bunting, makes homelessness seem almost like fun. The airport is clean, and there seems to be enough to eat—a lot of it sugar. Andrew says he doesn't mind having to walk all the time. Judging from Ronald Himler's watercolor illustrations, Andrew and his father even have reasonably nice clothes.
>
> Although we're told—sketchily—that Andrew's mother has died and his father has only a part-time job, that's not enough explanation. There's needless stereotyping: Andrew's father says school is "important. We'll work it out," while Mrs. Medina, the mother of Andrew's Hispanic friend, says her son "can wait for a while" to go to school. There is something lazy about this storybook, which is intended for 5- to 9-year-olds.

By housing the boy and his father in the terminal space of an airport, Bunting creates a heavy-handed parallel between homelessness and the migrancy of modern life. While the passengers at the airport may very well be flying away toward home, the boy and his father make their residence or non-home in the space that allows arrivals and departures. Bunting employs the mobile space of the airport as a symbol of a temporary space that encourages departures—but to where?

As David Morley argues, "in this era people are both always and never 'at home', in the traditional sense" (174). Bunting picks up on the trope of rootlessness and modernity in her choice of the airport as the way station for the boy and his father. "Images abound of our supposedly de-territorialised culture of 'homelessness': images of exile, diaspora, time-space compression, migrancy and 'nomadology'. The concept of home often remains as the uninterrogated anchor or alter ego of all this hyper-mobility" (Morley 3). Home and domesticity indeed serve as the unquestioned destination in Bunting's tale. However, Bunting never quite explains how it happens that some people have homes while others are defined by the lack thereof—homeless. Nor does she explain how the boy might arrive at the destination of home.

Bunting shows a bird that tries to escape the confines of the airport and shows the boy breathlessly rooting for the bird's escape. The reader is strongly nudged to similarly root for the boy's escape—but to where, and by what means? The implication of course is that the bird naturally escapes from the airport, and therefore it's natural and good and expected that the boy (and perhaps his father) will, too. But even the youngest of readers will realize that boys aren't birds. Where would the boy go when he escapes from the airport? Bunting completely ignores the social and economic realities that homeless people and homeless children face.

Bunting offers next to no back story on the reasons behind the boy and his father's homelessness. On one occasion we hear a vague, slipping reference to the time when they used to have a house "before mother died." This simply creates another heavy-handed metaphor, as Bunting links home with mother. In some ways, the disappearance of the mother serves as an explanation for the boy and his father's homelessness. But why? By offering no explanation (Did they depend on the mother's paycheck? Did the father become depressed and start drinking?), Bunting makes homelessness seem random. By glossing over the reasons for poverty and homelessness, Bunting does her young readers a great disservice. Economic and social systems remain a mystery, and the boy is left to the meanderings of fortune.

Domestic space for Bunting silently stands against the crisis space of homelessness. Bunting creates a dichotomy between domestic space and transitory spaces such as the airport (and, in other books, orphan trains, etc.). By creating this dichotomy, Bunting creates an inside and outside for her readers. For the most part, her implied readers are middle-class, inside-the-fold children. Quite distinctly outside the fold lie Bunting's characters: kids in LA ghettos, homeless, orphan-train-riding waifs straight out of Victor Hugo's central casting for *Les Misérables*.

It is nothing new to create a settled and domestic us and an unsettled them. Jews and gypsies were routinely persecuted for their rootlessness, ultimately culminating in the Jewish and Romani holocausts. James Clifford challenges us to "think comparatively about the distinct routes/roots of tribes, barrios, favelas, immigrant neighborhoods—embattled histories with crucial community insiders and regulated traveling outsiders" (24–36). Of course, Bunting wants to show the inherent goodness in all children and the importance of positivity and faith. However, the logic of rootedness versus rootlessness nonetheless creates an us-them situation whereby the middle-class consumers of Bunting's picture books can gaze freely on the other, the children they don't go to school with, they don't have playdates with. Indeed, Bunting's inside-outside logic invites the reader into voyeurism and vicarious experiences of poverty—all from the safety of home or a well-equipped classroom.

In the end, the problem of homelessness exists within the airport terminal and with the boy and his father. What events uprooted the boy and his father and forced them to seek shelter surreptitiously is not discussed. It just happened. Likewise, the solution resides with the boy and his father. Be patient. Don't give up hope. Could there be a more convenient message for the middle and upper classes? They have no responsibility toward the homeless save preaching patience. What comfort may come from that message is not for the homeless, but for the elite. They are absolved of action. What shared humanity they may have with the homeless remains as distant as their gaze.

Urban Space, *Smoky Night*, and the Space of Literature

At a session at the National Council of Teachers annual conference in 1995, Bunting said that, as she watched television reports of the riots in South Central Los Angeles that followed the acquittal of the police officers charged in the beating of Rodney King, she tried to imagine what a child living in South Central must be thinking and feeling. The story she created was *Smoky Night*. The book's reception from the critics was euphoric. *Booklist*, *Publisher's Weekly*, *Kirkus Reviews*, and the *Bulletin of the Center for Children's Books* all printed glowing reviews, and the California Department of

Education put it on their recommended literature list. The book was included in the *Children's Catalog* and in the reading list of the National Council of Teachers of English, *Adventuring with Books: A Booklist for PreK–Grade 6*. The book was also included in the highly selective booklists of multicultural children's books produced by the American Library Association and the National Council of Teachers of English, and it won the ultimate prize for a picture book, the Caldecott Medal.

Susie Wilde's review of *Smoky Night* for *Children's Literature* provides a good example of the excitement reviewers had for the book:

This book, the Caldecott Award winner for the year's finest illustrations, is a story of tolerance placed in the violent setting of the LA riots. The illustrations are collages that add intrigue and extend the story. Shattered glass surrounds a picture of looting; spilled multicolored cereal accents items spilled from grocery store thieving; and plastic bags describe the senseless stealing from a dry cleaner. The young hero is confused by the chaos and frightened by fire, smashed glass, and his missing cat. His protective mother calmly explains every part of the night's madness. But it is the boy who is the agent of change when he notices how his cat has made friends with another cat; an enemy cat belonging to the Korean woman who owns the grocery down the street. The Korean woman, who had always seemed different and separate, becomes a friend in the shelter during the smoky night. This book would be incredibly helpful for children who have shared the protagonist's experience. It is a meaningful book to help talk about the violence that surrounds today's children. [Illustrator David] Diaz helps to convey the strong message by placing dramatic insets in his powerful collages.

Again, as with *Fly Away Home*, *Smoky Night* offers a glimpse into the world of urban discord. While the illustrations are brilliantly rendered, it is the text that is problematic. When the boy, Daniel, asks his mother why people are rioting, she replies, "People get angry. They want to smash and destroy. They don't care anymore what's right and wrong. . . . After a while it's like a game." Just as with *Fly Away Home*, no reason is given for the conditions in which the characters live. Chaos just happens because people get angry, apparently for no reason. Apparently, if they would just remember what is right and wrong, the neighborhood would be peaceful. James Loewen, in his study of American history textbooks, *Lies My Teacher Told*

Me, observes that in discussing protests, strikes, demonstrations, and riots by the underclass, rarely do writers or teachers give reasons for why the poor are malcontent. Rather, these uprisings are described as just happening spontaneously for no cause. This erases injustice as a motivation for civil disobedience. The Los Angeles riots happened for a reason, and, unlike Daniel in this story, an African American boy living in South Central Los Angeles would know why people are angry. Daniel and his mother are actually suburbanites costumed as urban African Americans. The words they speak are shallow and devoid of talk of racism, poverty, and injustice. Instead, readers get an admonishment to get along.

Peter Stallybrass and Allon White write of the ways in which fears of difference were articulated through the "body" of the nineteenth-century city (266). Many texts and performances of that time described the city as a "locus of fear, disgust and fascination" (266). The vileness of the nineteenth-century city became an obsession for some. Often, the bourgeoisie "devoured tales of the city's scum" (266).

In many ways, the nineteenth-century city spatialized new boundaries between high and low. In *London Labour and the London Poor* (1851), Henry Mayhew distinguished the "wanderers and the civilized tribes" (qtd. in Stallybrass and White 267). Stallybrass and White compare Mayhew's nomad to Mikhail Bakhtin's concept of the grotesque. For Mayhew, the nomads are "not domestic," as they resist settledness and home (Stallybrass and White 268). These unsettled people posed a problem for Karl Marx as well, forcing him to call on many terms to describe the *Lumpenproletariat* (translated as "riffraff," *la bohème*, etc.). Friedrich Engels notes the ways that city planning made the dirty invisible. This separation between the slums and the suburbs firmly spatializes class distinction within the city (Stallybrass and White 273).

Because the sanitized city kept the filthy at bay, public spaces and pathways threatened pollution for the middle classes. The pathways and public spaces allowed mixing between high and low, clean and unclean: "The tram, the railway station, the ice rink, above all the streets themselves, were shockingly promiscuous" (Stallybrass and White 273). In public spaces and in the streets, the middle class came into contact with "the great unwashed," a term that dates to 1830s England.

While "avoiding and excluding" impure bodies became the goal for many in the middle class, they were nonetheless transfixed by reading about the sordid conditions of the unwashed. Stallybrass and White note the tensions between the gaze/the touch; desire/contamination (274). The middle classes enjoyed reading about these untouchable nomads: "nomad and slum made their way into the bourgeois study and drawing room, to be read as objects of horror, contempt, pity and fascination" (277).

Finding pleasure in the "urban carnival," many flaneurs took to the streets in search of thrilling encounters with the forbidden (prostitutes, gamblers, and the like). Literature of the time reveled in the chaos of the streets. Victor Hugo's *Les Misérables* emerges as a testament to the dictum that "the sincerity of filth pleases us and soothes the spirit" (389). Hugo also spoke of the role of the sewer as the city's "conscience" and "the labyrinth below Babel" (279). Stallybrass and White discuss the sewer as embodying all that's low and grotesque. Furthermore, rats (and sometimes pigs)— the creatures of the sewers—acted as toxic intermediaries between "noble buildings" and "foetid darkness" (283).

Bunting's middle-class audience occupies a similar position, gazing on visions of the abject—of rioting and homelessness. Treated to lavish artwork by David Diaz in *Smoky Night*, the reader can fall into Bunting's spell of the saccharine as we learn that the cats of warring parties can come together despite their differences. If cats can do it, why not people? Bunting reasons. Cats coming together for a shared meal, a bird escaping from the confines of an airport, reveals the mechanism of Bunting's implicit argument: it's simple, it's natural—even animals can do it, why not people too?

Bunting's Pollyannaish treatment of poverty sentimentalizes and aestheticizes poverty without any critique or deeper interrogation of the structural causes of poverty. Through the voyeuristic positioning of inside versus outside, Bunting's readers are treated to a peepshow view of the lives of those less fortunate. Not only is Bunting's world of poverty sanitized, it's also fascinatingly lovely. In "Transnational Trespassings: The Geopolitics of Urban Informality," Ananya Roy defines the aestheticization of poverty as "the gaze that looks toward a squatter settlement and sees in the original lines of beauty, the primitive organicism of the vernacular" (296).

Hazel Rochman emphasizes the aesthetic pleasures of *Smoky Night* while giving little attention to the social issues represented in the book:

> His mother explains that rioting can happen when people get angry: "They want to smash and destroy. They don't care anymore what's right and wrong." The boy says that they look angry, but they look happy, too. He sees them looting Mrs. Kim's grocery store across the street; his mother never shopped there. That night, the apartment building burns, and everyone has to rush out to the shelter. The boy's

cat is gone, and so is Mrs. Kim's cat, but a kind fire fighter finds both animals; they were hiding together. Then Bunting overstates her message: maybe the people, like the cats, need to get to know each other, so the boy's mother and Mrs. Kim agree to visit. . . . In fine contrast, the story is told quietly from the child's point of view, safe with his mother despite the fear, reaching out to the neighborhood community within the chaos. (Review of *Smoky Night*, 1267)

Smoky Night shares many of the same problems as *Fly Away Home*. Bunting provides no context for the riots—they just happen. Her use of a young child as a first-person narrator limits, at least in her conception, what a young boy would know. But Bunting is watching the riots from the safety of her Pasadena home. Residents, even young ones, surely knew why people were rioting; surely even children knew who Rodney King was and why he was beaten by the police. Parents and older siblings teach young children in urban areas such as South Central Los Angeles how to behave around law enforcement so as not to be perceived as threatening. The naïve narrator of this book seems more in keeping with privileged children living in the suburbs than with streetwise South Central children. The problem resides in South Central: it's that the residents do not get along with each other. Another heavy-handed metaphor, this time a pair of cats, provides the clues—get to know each other. If cats, notoriously territorial, can figure out how to get along, so can the urban poor of South Central LA. No need to address poverty. No need to address racism. No need to address abusive law enforcement. Just get along.

The Working Poor: *A Day's Work*

A Day's Work, published in 1994, is the story of Francisco, a young Mexican American boy, who accompanies his *abuelo* (grandfather) to the parking lot, where they compete with other day laborers for temporary work. The grandfather speaks no English, so the boy barters with a landscape contractor for his grandfather's labor. Francisco lies to the contractor, promising that his grandfather is an expert at gardening, when in fact his grandfather, a carpenter, knows nothing of gardening. Set to work weeding, the pair mistakenly remove the ice plant while retaining the chicory weeds. The contractor returns and is furious, but grandfather intuits what has happened and promises to return and replant the ice plant and pull the chicory at no cost. The contractor is impressed with the grandfather's honesty and implies that there will be future work for him.

Critical reception for *A Day's Work* was positive, with favorable reviews from *Booklist*, *Kirkus Reviews*, and the *Bulletin of the Center for Children's Books*. Additionally, the book made "best book" lists from the Consortium of Latin American Studies Programs, the National Council of Teachers of English, and the National Council for the Social Studies. The book is also included in the Accelerated Reader program and Scholastic's Reading Counts! program. Typical of the praise the book received was this comment by Hazel Rochman in *Booklist*: "The family drama captures that universal immigrant experience in which the child must help the adult interpret the new world, while the wise adult still has much to teach the child about enduring values" (Review of *A Day's Work*, 505).

On the surface the book appears to be a sympathetic look at the plight of Mexican American immigrants, the working poor. While even a cursory view beneath the surface shows this book to be a bourgeois fantasy, the surface appears to be all the critics gleaned from the book, judging by their reviews. As Judy Zalazar Drummond argues, the reader is asked to believe without question several unlikely facts in this story. Would a Mexican American mother allow her young son to accompany his grandfather into the rough-and-tumble world of day laborers, where potentially dangerous strangers come and go throughout the day? Would even a young boy and a carpenter grandfather not recognize ice plant, a common landscaping plant in southern California, a succulent with features that would suggest it is a member of the cactus family? Would a day laborer contractor in southern California really not know any Spanish? Why would he hire an old man and a young boy for labor better suited to young men who appear to be plentiful? Would such a contractor really reward incompetence with a promise of future work, or would he seek out someone else from the plentiful supply of cheap and easily exploitable day laborers? Or is Bunting suggesting that it's so difficult and surprising to find an honest Mexican American worker that a contractor wouldn't pass on hiring such a rare individual?

As is the case with *Fly Away Home* and *Smoky Night*, Bunting provides little in way of context. There's no insight into why Francisco and his family would leave Mexico and come to the United States. There's little description of how the family survives on the meager wages of day labor or how contractors exploit this labor force. There's no discussion of whether Francisco's family are legal immigrants and no discussion of the threat of deportation.

The solutions that Bunting offers to day laborers appear to be work hard, be honest, and learn English so you can understand your employer. What more could the bourgeoisie want from immigrant labor?

Aestheticizing Poverty

The aestheticization of poverty acts as a temporary inversion of the high and low, called the carnivalesque by Mikhail Bakhtin. Drawing on his work with humor and popular culture in the Middle Ages (particularly the work of Rabelais), Bakhtin's carnivalesque "invokes laughter, linked to the over-turning of authority" (*Rabelais and His World*, 14). In Bunting's work, the carnivalesque overturning invokes more sentimental pathos than laughter. Peter Stallybrass and Allon White, in *The Politics and Poetics of Transgression*, argue that the middle classes have always defined themselves in opposition to the Low Other. Because the Low Other is so vital to middle-class identity formation, it carries great symbolic weight for the middle class. As Barbara Babcock put it, "what is socially peripheral is so often symbolically central and if we ignore or minimize inversion and other forms of cultural negation, we often fail to understand the dynamics of symbolic processes generally" (32). For example, in the 1960s hippies were prominent in the consciousnesses of North Americans. Although few in number and holding very little if any political and economic power, they nonetheless served as important symbols of that decade. Long hair, the most identifiable characteristic of hippies, became a vital and powerful symbol and was quickly adopted by large numbers of mainstream, middle-class young men as a sign of their own dissatisfaction and rebellion. This kind of signification is an inversion of high and low, and so is an example of the carnivalesque. In the carnivalesque, privileged people play out the dysfunctions and disorders of their identities by putting on as exotic costumes that which is symbolic of the Low Other. In Bunting's works, this plays out with Bunting taking on the voices of the Low Other; in her case, a poor boy living in the airport terminal, a poor boy living in the slums of South Central Los Angeles, and a poor boy accompanying his day-laborer grandfather to work.

Bunting's work takes place alongside a larger movement of the aestheticization of poverty in media, advertising, and fashion. For example, quoting from an article in *Jezebel*:

Vivienne Westwood's menswear show on Sunday featured models in frostbitten makeup carrying bed rolls and pushing shopping carts down the runway. It also made us ponder the evolution of the curious (and strangely recurrent) trend known as "homeless chic." . . . German designer Patrick Mohr had already upstaged her—he showed his last collection on a group of models that included actual homeless people. (One, says an observer, muttered as he walked the runway.) (Sauer)

A 2008 episode of *America's Top Model* challenged the pert young models to leave their chic Fashion Avenue and pose as homeless people. Wearing oversize knits reminiscent of homeless chic icon Mary-Kate Olsen, the models made homelessness look just a little lovelier for the viewing public. "They walked, sometimes less than gracefully, a catwalk covered in cardboard boxes. Sometimes they emerged from boxes and pushed shopping carts or carried sleeping bags or bedrolls" (Sauer).

Within children's literature and toys, the American Girl books and brand made headlines by releasing the "Homeless" doll and book, Gwen Thompson. *Time* magazine reported:

But there's a new kid on the block: Gwen Thompson, who literally lives on the street. Gwen's story starts with a deadbeat dad who walks out on the family, leaving her single mom struggling to get by. Some parents have expressed outrage, calling Gwen's story insensitive and crass. Others, however, say it's a great idea. "The only thing obscene about this American Girl controversy is that it takes a plastic doll and her fictional biography to have everyone up in arms," noted blogger Shannon Moriarty. "Yet the real stories of homeless children crowding shelters and schools are accepted without an ounce of outrage." For just $95, a young girl (or, more likely, her parents) can give Gwen a home.

The homeless American Girl brings homeless chic to the under-ten set. And, yes, it caused a furor on both the Right and the Left. Many felt that the doll helped to "raise awareness" of homeless children. However, Tanya Tull, the president of Beyond Shelter, said that she was "afraid that they're going to pick up the idea that it's OK, that it's an accepted segment of society that some children are homeless and some children are not" (CBS News). In many ways, Bunting's young readers may take away the same feel-good message. Bunting's work easily fits within the logic of the aestheticization of poverty that homeless chic exemplifies. Employing lavish illustration and using first-person narration allows her readers a titillating glimpse into another world that they may have previously feared. In all, Bunting presents a sentimental view of those outside the middle classes that erases the structural causes of poverty.

Conclusion

While Bunting's books appear to honor the poor by using young, poor children as the focalizers of her stories, the narrative voice is actually a bourgeois voice. The implied readers are middle- and upper-class children. Homelessness, racial strife, poverty, and migrant labor have no causes in Bunting's books. Because causes are not explored, the conditions are presented as inevitable. Solutions are about coping with these inevitable conditions. These endings are satisfying if you are not actually poor. The books offer solutions consistent with the American myth of individual hard work and persistence. Those who are afflicted with homelessness, poverty, and insufficient work can only rely on themselves to solve their problems. Such solutions are those that the wealthy desire as they absolve themselves of any responsibility.

"[W]e have argued that [the bourgeoisie] *uses* the whole world as its theatre in a particularly instrumental fashion, the very subject which it politically excludes becoming exotic costumes which it assumes in order to play out the disorders of its own identity" (Stallybrass and White 200).

The poor in these books are costumes of the wealthy. The stories are news to the wealthy, but they are not news to the poor. And, despite using poor children as narrators, the stories aren't the voices of the poor, either.

ACKNOWLEDGMENTS

We wish to thank Beverly Slapin and Judy Zalazar Drummond for sharing their ideas and pointing out features concerning Eve Bunting's work. We found these to be most helpful in shaping our own thinking about the books.

WORKS CITED

Babcock, Barbara. Introduction to *The Reversible World: Symbolic Inversion in Art and Society*, edited by Barbara Babcock, 13–36. Ithaca: Cornell University Press, 1978. Print.

Bakhtin, Mikhail. *The Dialogic Imagination*. Austin: University of Texas Press, 1981. Print.

———. *Rabelais and His World*. Bloomington: Indiana University Press, 2009. Print.

Bourdieu, Pierre. *Distinction: A Social Critique of the Judgement of Taste*. Translated by Richard Nice. Cambridge: Harvard University Press, 1984. Print.

Bunting, Eve, and David Diaz. *Smoky Night*. New York: Clarion Books, 1994. Print.

Bunting, Eve, and Ronald Himler. *A Day's Work*. New York: Clarion Books, 1994. Print.

———. *Fly Away Home.* New York: Clarion Books, 1991. Print.

CBS News. "Flap over 'Homeless' American Girl Doll." CBSnews.com, September 26, 2009. Accessed December 17, 2012. Website.

Clifford, James. *Routes: Travel and Translation in the Late Twentieth Century*. Cambridge: Harvard University Press, 1997. Print.

Darton, F. J. Harvey, and Brian Alderson. *Children's Books in England: Five Centuries of Social Life*. London: British Library, 1988. Print.

Drummond, Judy Zalazar. "A Day's Work: The Exploitation of Mexican Day Laborers as a Cautionary Morality Tale." De Colores: The Raza Experience in Books for Children. Accessed October 9, 2013. Website.

Hade, Daniel. "Publishers and Publishing." In *Encyclopedia of Children's Literature*, edited by Jack Zipes. New York: Oxford University Press, 2006. Print.

Harvey, David. *The Condition of Postmodernity: An Enquiry into the Origins of Cultural Change*. Cambridge: Blackwell, 1990. Print.

Hugo, Victor. *Les Misérables*. Translated by Lee Fahnestock and Norman MacAfee. New York: Signet, 1980. Print.

Johnston, Rosemary Ross. "Children's Literature." In *Literacy: Reading, Writing and Children's Literature*, edited by Gordon Winch, Rosemary Ross Johnston, Marcelle Holliday, Lesley Ljunghahl, and Paul March, 287–437. Melbourne: Oxford University Press, 2001. Print.

Loewen, James. *Lies My Teacher Told Me: Everything Your American History Textbook Got Wrong*. 2nd ed. New York: Simon & Schuster, 2007. Print.

Mathiews, Franklin K. "Blowing Out the Boy's Brains." *Outlook*, November 18, 1914, 652–654. Print.

Mayhew, Henry. *London Labour and the London Poor*. 4 vols. New York: Cosimo, 1851. Print.

Morley, David. *Home Territories: Media, Mobility and Identity*. New York: Routledge, 2000. Print.

Rochman, Hazel. Review of *A Day's Work*, by Eve Bunting. *Booklist* 91:5 (1994): 505. Academic OneFile. Accessed December 17, 2012. Website.

———. Review of *Smoky Night*, by Eve Bunting. *Booklist* 90:13 (1994): 1267. Academic OneFile. Accessed December 17, 2012. Website.

Rose, Jacqueline. *The Case of Peter Pan; or, The Impossibility of Children's Fiction*. Philadelphia: University of Pennsylvania Press, 1992. Print.

Roy, Ananya. "Transnational Trespassings: The Geopolitics of Urban Informality." In *Urban Informality: Transnational Perspectives from the Middle East, Latin America, and South Asia*, edited by Ananya Roy and Nezar Alyayyad, 289–317. Lanham, Md.: Lexington Books, 2004. Print.

Sauer, Jenna. "The Evolution of Homeless Chic." *Jezebel*, January 19, 2010. Accessed December 17, 2012. Website.

Slapin, Beverly. Review of *Smoky Night*, by Eve Bunting. Teaching for Change, Busboys and Poets Bookstore, 2010. Accessed December 17, 2012. Website.

Smith, Dinitia. "No Place to Call Home." *New York Times*, November 10, 1991. Accessed December 17, 2012. Website.

Stallybrass, Peter, and Allon White. *Politics and Poetics of Transgression.* New York: Routledge, 1986. Print.

Time. "Top 10 Dubious Toys." Time.com. Accessed December 17, 2012. Website.

Townsend, John Rowe. *John Newbery and His Books.* Lanham, Md.: Scarecrow Press, 1994. Print.

———. *Written for Children: An Outline of English-Language Children's Literature.* Twenty-fifth anniversary ed. New York: HarperCollins 1992. Print.

Weiss, Stephanie. "Suitable for Children?" *NEA Today* 13:8 (1995): 7. Print.

Wilde, Susie. Review of *Smoky Night*, by Eve Bunting. Children's Literature: Independent Information and Reviews. Accessed December 17, 2012. Website.

The Young Socialist

A Magazine of Justice and Love (1901–1926)

JANE ROSEN

Socialists have always looked for alternative ways of educating children to counter the repressive training of the state education system; specifically, they sought teaching methods that were relevant to the children of the working class and that reflected the aims and ideals of a future socialist society. They also considered the available reading material for their children and concluded that it promoted the class values and morals of the ruling class, which had as its aim the provision of a dutiful and diligent labor force. One response to this was the creation of *The Young Socialist*, established in 1901 as the magazine of the Socialist Sunday School movement. This essay looks at the periodical in depth from its inception to 1926, the year of the General Strike. It examines the editorials, articles, and stories for their coverage of the working-class movement, socialist organizations, and personalities and analyzes the reaction of the journal to important national and international events. It assesses *The Young Socialist*'s attempts to provide an alternative to the accepted values of class chauvinism and imperialism that were prevalent in much of the children's literature produced in Britain at the time.

The end date of 1926 has been chosen for this analysis because it marks a watershed in the British radical movement. The defeat of the General Strike and of the miners that year dealt a blow to the socialist movement from which it never really recovered. The international situation was also worsening with the growth of fascism, and at the same time a new editor was appointed and the editorial style altered to reflect the new requirements of the movement.

As the socialist movement developed at the end of the nineteenth century, many members became concerned with the education of children of the working class. State schools were set up to produce obedient workers and were therefore limited in the education they provided, proving as frustrating for the committed teacher as for the child.

These concerns coincided with a time of great poverty, and the education of working-class children became linked to their physical well-being. Socialist organizations were involved in welfare activities directed at children, perhaps the best known being the Cinderella Clubs initiated by Robert Blatchford and the *Clarion*. Originally based in the textile areas of Lancashire, they spread throughout the country as other organizations such as the Labour Church became involved. The Church's founder, John Trevor, "suggested that Cinderella children might be taught as well as fed" (Reid 21–22).

Fred Reid draws attention to the importance of Keir Hardie, founder of the Independent Labour Party (ILP), in the development of socialist education for children (22). In May 1893, Hardie proposed a crusaders' movement directed at children under the age of sixteen, and one thousand children enrolled. Hardie urged Glasgow comrades to set up schools, and a few "sparkling personalities" (Fleming 2) took up his challenge and began the Socialist Sunday School movement (SSS). These personalities included Alfred Russell, Adam Carnegie, Archie McArthur, Lizzie Glasier, and Tom Anderson.

However, while Glasgow was to become the center of the SSS movement, it was not the location of the first school. In 1892, Mary Gray of the Battersea branch of the Social Democratic Federation (SDF) was motivated by the poverty of the children around her to begin a school for working-class children. She recalled working in an SDF soup kitchen when a child asked for the crumbs from the bread she was cutting for his sister at home. His father was out of work, and he felt that his sister would be glad of the food. She decided that a school was required to teach these children socialism, which would reveal to them the reasons for their families' unemployment and their poverty. Her first pupils were her two daughters and one boy; her school was to continue well into the next century (Blackburn 1).

It was in 1896 that, inspired by Keir Hardie's call, the Central Socialist Sunday School in Glasgow was founded. In an article published in the *Labour Leader* on May 25, 1895, Lizzie Glasier said: "Hitherto hardly any attempt has been made in Scotland to draw children to the Socialist ranks yet it is obvious that if the World is to be led to the pure ideal of Socialism through an educational process of evolution, efforts ought to be made to get at the little ones when their minds and susceptibilities are plastic and

impressionable" (qtd. in *Socialist Sunday Schools Potted History* 2). She en-
visaged socialist classes for children being formed in cooperation with the
ILP and other organizations, and shortly Socialist Sunday Schools began to
appear throughout the country.

One of the most outstanding features of the SSS movement was the
range of ideas and beliefs that came together in the teaching of the children
of the working class. Three main organizations were involved from the be-
ginning: the SDF, the Clarion Fellowship, and the ILP. Ideas ranged from
John and Katharine Bruce Glasier's "religion of Socialism" to those of Tom
Anderson, "an ardent Socialist of the Karl Marx School" (*Young Socialist*
[*YS*], May 1906, 41). Other organizations were also involved, including the
British Socialist Party, the Labour Church, and the Fabian Society.

Related to the desire for an alternative system of education was concern
over the reading material available to the socialist child. Various educators
provided suggestions for suitable books, but as the names of authors included Rudyard Kipling and G. A. Henty, the latter a writer of imperialist
adventure novels for boys, their suitability could be called into question.
There was certainly no acceptable children's periodical, those on the market
being either the *Boys' Own Paper*, published by the Religious Tract Society,
or the various comics issuing from the Northcliffe stable and their like.

In January 1901, Archie McArthur launched the first issue of the *Young
Socialist: A Magazine of Love and Service*. The subtitle was to change to
A Magazine of Justice and Love in its second year. The first issue was four
pages in length, duplicated and published by the Twentieth Century Press,
the publisher of *Justice*, the organ of the SDF. The first issue is in the form of
a letter to the children of the SSS movement: "My Dear Socialist Children,
This surely is the tiniest Magaxine [*sic*] in the world. It is put forth to keep a
place warm for a better thing in days to come, and to place it in the power
of the Socialist children of a hundred years hence to say that they and those
who had gone before them had carried on a Magazine of their own right
through the century" (*YS*, January 1901, 1). The letter ends by describing the
magazine's theme as Love. There are no banners and no illustrations, and
the issue ends as all the issues did under the editorship of McArthur with
the words, "Yours affectionately, Uncle Archie."

The second issue was in the same format, but from March 1901 the journal was in printed form. Throughout the first year of existence it only twice
reached eight pages in length. After the second issue, the quality of the paper and the printing improved drastically and other contributions began to
come in, expanding the content beyond just the words of "Uncle Archie."

7.1. Masthead of *The Young Socialist*, designed by John Bruce Glasier. Courtesy of the Marx Memorial Library, London.

The third issue, although still mostly written by McArthur, did have a call for letters to be sent to the magazine, and the first school reports appear. After this, additional contributors began to submit articles and letters. These included Keir Hardie and Katharine Bruce Glasier as well as the children themselves. Many of the contributions are either reports of activities of classes and picnics or letters from concerned adults on moral and idealistic subjects. Glasier provides an extract from one of her books dealing with the British government and concludes, "All loving congratulations to you on being Socialist children" (*YS*, June 1901, 3).

This does throw up an issue that was to haunt *Young Socialist* throughout this period. Who was the audience; who was expected to read the magazine? The first issues were addressed directly to socialist children, but the magazine was always aimed at two audiences. Some articles clearly suggested an adult audience.

As the journal progressed and increased in size, articles on teaching in Socialist Sunday Schools as well as reports from the National Conferences began to appear.

John Searson, in his editorial of July 1905, addressed both adults and children. After offering advice and quoting from letters received, he wrote, "I have still a very important message to convey. You, children, might just sit quietly while I say a word to your teachers and superintendents" (53). It is pertinent to remember what age these children were and what was expected of them. The vast majority were from working-class families; many of them were required to contribute to the family's income from an early age. Until 1918 the school-leaving age was twelve, and children were likely to be working in some capacity before that age.

Young Socialist's creators constantly discussed this question of the age of their readers and the types of article to be provided for them. The involvement of children in writing for the magazine was addressed from the beginning, as Archie McArthur sent out a request in the February 1902 issue: "This is meant to be a *children's* paper and the children themselves must do some of the writing for it" (4, italics in original).

From the beginning, the magazine faced financial shortages, and in September 1901 it was taken over by the Glasgow Socialist Sunday School Union to prevent its closure. The Glasgow Union agreed to become the owners for a year and to bear any losses, and a guarantee fund was set up to provide a safety net. The magazine began to develop, gaining a banner in January 1903 designed by John Bruce Glasier, chairman of the ILP and an artist in the style of Walter Crane; Glasier's banner was to remain with the journal for many years.

A National Council was set up in 1909, and in 1910 it took over the publication of *Young Socialist* with a £42 debt. A special effort was made, and £180 was raised within two years. By 1911 the magazine's circulation was 3,450, mostly distributed through the various Unions, with a monthly loss of £1-5-0. By 1914, the circulation had increased to 6,360 and the monthly loss was 9s-11d. The magazine gradually increased in size, reaching a standard length of eight pages in 1903, twelve pages in 1906, sixteen and twenty pages in 1907, and its largest size of twenty-four pages in 1912, although this maximum length was not to survive the First World War.

From 1901 to 1926, *Young Socialist* had five editors. In the December 1903 issue, Archie McArthur announced his resignation. Although the journal ran at a loss during his tenure, circulation increased, reflecting the growing popularity of the socialist movement in response to the Boer War. McArthur himself summed up his role accurately, regretting that he had not done more for the very young children and writing: "I think I have striven especially for three things, (1) to place the children's movement on a high level, (2) to work unity in it, and (3) to give it a world-wide outlook" (*YS*, December 1903, 4).

Archie McArthur was a carpenter (a joiner), and his successor, John Searson, a textile worker from Glasgow, was from the same class. Although not as engaging a personality or editor as McArthur, Searson approached the job painstakingly. He was criticized by Lizzie Glasier, writing as Little Goldwing, for not being approachable to the children; Glasier suggested that he use a friendlier name than "Mr. Editor" or "J. S." (YS, December 1904, 92). However, he treated children with respect, and with warmth and affection. During his tenure, the editor's page became the children's page, publishing advice from Searson as well as thoughts and ideas from children themselves.

John Searson retired at the end of 1906, due to ill health. In 1907 Lizzie Glasier replaced him. Her husband, Fred Glasier Foster, who was to be appointed assistant editor and then joint editor during the First World War, stated that after the conference establishing the National Council of the British Socialist Sunday Schools, "the magazine began to fulfil its purpose of becoming 'the winged messenger' and directing spirit of the whole movement" (2). He went on to describe the improvements that the expansion of pages enabled, mentioning the articles and reports from the Young Socialist Citizen Crusaders (the school movement's answer to the militant activities of the Scouts and the Boys' Brigade organizations), the classes on decorative needlework, and the advice given to teachers by the Young Socialist Education Bureau. He made the point that the magazine encouraged the development of imagination in childhood by publishing folklore and fairy tales (4).

At all the SSSU National Conferences there were discussions regarding the Young Socialist. There were usually two reports—one dealing with the administration and finances of the journal, the other with editorial decisions and content. The 1911 National Conference passed a resolution stating that "all articles in [the] Magazine be non-theological in character." It was also agreed that the SSSU's national secretary write to Lizzie Glasier and point out the desirability of including lighter verse and such things "as appeals more to children" (National Conference of Socialist Sunday School Union [NCSSSU] Minutes, Easter 1911, Young Socialist Report, 3). A resolution was passed agreeing to appoint a Literary Committee to be composed of a member from each Union and the editor, and another resolution called for a Business Committee for the magazine. This was to be made up of members from Glasgow, the Union responsible for the publication of the magazine (NCSSSU Minutes, Easter 1911, Young Socialist Report, 4).

In his notes Foster also gives a list of the contributors whom the movement managed to attract to the journal, especially through the efforts of Lizzie Glasier. Glasier's brother and sister-in-law, John and Katharine Bruce

Glasier, were already supporters of the movement, and Katharine, particularly, was a regular contributor. Foster also mentions Keir Hardie, Edward Carpenter, George Lansbury, and Ramsey and Margaret MacDonald. Artists were represented by John Bruce Glasier, George Meggitt, F. J. Bourne, and most significantly Walter Crane: "A personal appeal from the editor for a contribution from their pen seldom failed to bring a response, however engrossed they might be in their own work. It was never easy to refuse an appeal made by Lizzie Glasier!" (Foster 7).

Frederick James Gould was one of the most prolific of the contributors particularly just before the First World War and afterward. He began as a village schoolteacher and then taught in two East End schools, where he was a witness to the 1889 dock strike which drew him to the ideas of socialism. He was a humanist teacher and dedicated his life to secular and moral teaching particularly of the young. Gould was a prolific writer on secularism and ethical and moral education; many of his books were used in the curriculum of the Socialist Sunday Schools. He was appointed to the *Young Socialist* Education Bureau as a much-respected socialist and humanist pedagogue.

From its first issues, the magazine was committed to cooperation with socialist organizations abroad. Letters came from European, American, and Japanese organizations exchanging ideas and opinions. This ideal of internationalism was prevalent in the movement and was particularly propagated by Archie McArthur and Alex Gossip, the latter a founding member of the Glasgow Socialist Sunday School, prominent trade unionist, ardent internationalist, and superintendent of Fulham School. He was the subject of the portrait gallery in the October 1904 issue. This was a regular feature that highlighted stalwarts of the SSS movement and in this case concentrated on Gossip's report of the International Socialist Conference. He ends, "You see, it does not matter in the least to us Socialists what country one belongs to, we are all brothers and sisters" (*YS*, October 1904, 75).

The magazine regularly reported on resolutions made and discussions held at Union and National Conferences. In the report "The Glasgow Anniversary," Alfred Russell records a resolution that was passed: "That this meeting of Glasgow Socialist Sunday Schools' children and grown-ups express regret at the murderous methods of the Russian ruling classes, and sympathises with the Russian people in their righteous endeavour to gain their freedom. We further protest against the cruel action of the troops on shooting down innocent little children" (*YS*, March 1905, 18). The magazine also reported on various school lessons and addresses commemorating

Francisco Ferrer and condemning his assassination (*YS*, November 1909). In the December 1909 issue, Tom Anderson is reported as speaking on the execution of the Chicago Martyrs, singing "Annie Laurie" in memory of Albert Parsons and the others.

The magazine also reported on the situation in Great Britain. This ranged from analysis of economics as well as the actual events in which scholars— as students at the Socialist Sunday Schools were commonly called—were involved. In the December 1905 issue, the prominent socialist Isabella Ford contributed an article on the Hemsworth miners and the makeshift conditions in which they and their families were living. This situation was due to the miners' evictions from the homes they rented from the colliery because of a bitter dispute with the mine owners. Ford reported on the conditions of the families who were living in tents and described the assistance given by the local community and by the Miners' Association. She suggested that a Socialist Sunday School should be set up there so that the children of the striking miners could be taught "that because the mines are owned by a few persons instead of by the whole nation, and therefore by the miners as much as by anyone else, they are used merely as a means of making money for those few owners. We want them to be used for the good and profit of all, so they must be owned by all" (*YS*, December 1905, 91).

Subsequent issues of the journal carried reports of the attempts by various Socialist Sunday Schools to raise funds for the miners' families with messages of support, and stories about the Sunday collection being sent to the Hemsworth miners.

Another topic that concerned the magazine was cruelty to animals. Of course many children's publications then, as now, dealt with this topic, endeavoring to teach children kindness. However, *Young Socialist* and the movement it represented went further. For example, there were reports from the newspapers showing statistics of cases of cruelty coming to court (August 1903), articles and letters regarding vegetarianism and its benefits, and an account of the Halifax Socialist Sunday School collecting three to four hundred signatures for an antivivisection petition issued by the National Canine Defence League (December 1903).

The magazine produced articles on evolution and sex education, contentious subjects that would not generally be covered in more mainstream children's periodicals. The first article on evolution, written by George Knox, was titled "The History of the Earth." It dealt with the geological development of the world, explaining its formation, and ended with the hope that evolution would finally lead to a better world (January–March 1904).

Fairy tales and folklore also had their place in the magazine. John Bruce Glasier wrote a fairy tale for the April 1902 issue titled "How Fairy Stories Are True" in which Wisdom, Love, Kindness, Honesty, and Work appear as good fairies. Bad fairies include Ignorance, Selfishness, Cruelty, Falsehood, and Indolence, and Glasier wrote that these vices are in us all, referencing the men, women, and children being killed in war particularly in South Africa as evidence of this (1–3). Fairy tales in *Young Socialist* at that time were primarily in the form of practical allegories.

It does seem that the change in the magazine's style from the practical and polemical to the more fanciful and polemical occurred when the social class of the editor changed. Allegories and fairy tales, which proliferated under the editorship of Lizzie Glasier, a schoolteacher, were to be even more prevalent under the leadership of May Westoby, the next editor. There are several examples, including the serial by Helen Frazer that ran through the first months of 1908. In the story, the king sends his five sons on a quest, instructing each to return with a casket of treasures that they must discover. The treasures include the trophies of war, complete with dripping blood; the bubbles of pleasure, which are illusory and disappear; a scroll of wisdom, which is withered; and the hair and pearls of the woman that the fourth son loves, which are covered with dust. The fifth son confesses that he has nothing in his casket, because he has been too busy to fill it; but when it is opened, it is full of light radiating from a golden heart—it is Love. In a self-confessed socialist periodical for children, a great deal of fantasy concerning royalty is apparent. This, and a general view that all, including capitalists and landlords, should be treated with the same level of love and equality, was not met with the unanimous approval of the members of the movement.

For example, Tom Anderson contributed to the music page in May 1908, stating: "We can't save the workers by mending the present system. No, we must have 'The Revolution'" (*YS*, May 1908, 238). The June 1908 editorial responded: "the note which appeared on the song page of our last month's issue entitled 'The Revolution,' is in no sense an expression of the sentiment of our general School movement. Nor does it voice the official opinion of our various Unions. Our National Socialist Sunday School Movement stands for the teaching of *Socialism*—not Revolution.... [I]n no sense does the term revolution express our glorious ideal of Socialism. And to teach revolution is not to teach Socialism" (248, italics in original). Although Anderson was to set up his own Proletarian School movement in 1910, this disagreement did not lead to a complete split as members of both school movements participated in each other's classes. However, it signified the difference of opinion in the SSS movement, which had been there from the beginning and which was to grow as the twentieth century progressed.[1]

For instance, Alex Gossip produced a retelling of the Midas story with a revolutionary bent. He described Midas as very rich with no need to pay rent or to worry about food and clothing for his children, pointing out that a few gain gold only at the expense of the many. He concluded: "We, I hope, dear children are working for the day when our country will be full of beautiful, sweet-scented flowers, and the hearts of the grown-ups will be gladdened by the sight of happy, romping boys and girls; and if the King Midases of to-day do not learn their lesson themselves, you and I, dear comrades, will have to teach them" (*YS*, November 1902, 2).

When war was declared in August 1914, *Young Socialist* had been in existence for fourteen and a half years, and the SSS movement for eighteen years. Throughout this time the journal and the movement had propagated internationalism and cooperation in its pages and its schools. However, considering the reaction of many socialist organizations both in Great Britain and elsewhere to the outbreak of hostilities, the magazine's reaction to events was not necessarily predictable.[2] To add to the moral dilemma, four days after the outbreak of war, the government passed the Defence of the Realm Act (DORA). This legislation attacked civil rights by allowing imprisonment without trial and limiting press freedom. For example, the reporting of information that might weaken morale and impede the course of the war was forbidden.

The first issue of the war for September 1914 had on its front page a poem, "Liege," by Dorothea Hollins, marking the invasion of Belgium. In the mood of the day, this would not be unusual. What was remarkable was that it was not an outright condemnation of Germany but a call for peace and a listing of the contributions to world culture from both Germany and Great Britain:

> *You gave us Thought and Science, and Music heavenly-true;*
> *We gave you Shakespeare, Wiclif, noble, toiling Darwin too;*
> *Our children loved your fairies, your tales of troll and knight;*
> *Our lovers loved your Heine, our thinkers loved your Light! (193)*

The theme of September 1914's editorial is "Thou shalt not kill"; it addresses internationalism and urges a campaign for international arbitration. There is an article on German and English folksong, celebrating the links that join the two nations' music and that "will survive the present terrible and un-natural strife" (197). Nine pages of this issue deal with the war, and all of them are international and antiwar in content.

This approach continued throughout the war. DORA meant that *Young Socialist*'s editors had to be careful what they published, and the magazine indeed refrained from vociferous protests that there should be no fighting at all. The tone was of regret and of certainty that internationalism was the way forward, that arbitration was the way to peace. There was no condemnation of those scholars and members who enlisted in the armed services; their choice was respected. However, the journal never compromised on its efforts to instill and encourage a desire for peace in its readers, and this is reflected in the stories and poetry that continued to be printed during the war years. Reports came in from the various schools outlining the difficulties of continuing to operate because of the loss of men—and not just to the armed services. Because these were schools for the working class and many pupils were from families of skilled workers, the new munitions work required for the war effort meant employment for the adults—and for the pupils too.

As the war continued, articles and letters from both children and adults were published informing readers of work being done with Belgian refugees, of former scholars serving at the Front, and of wounded comrades. The magazine printed a resolution from the National Conference held in 1915: "That this Conference of British Socialist Sunday School Unions express the opinion that the only flag we recognise is the Red Flag and our only war is against Capitalism" (May 1915, 79).

In January 1916, the first Military Act was passed calling for the compulsory enlistment of unmarried men between the ages of eighteen and forty-one. The *Young Socialist* editorial of February 1916 was entitled "The Perils of Conscription" (18). It drew attention to the powers of DORA, the attacks on workers' rights, and the increased power of the military authorities. It stated: "[Conscription] means forcing an individual who holds views *diametrically opposed to war* to act contrary to his most cherished convictions and beliefs, to violate his soul and his conscience, and to commit the crime of murder" (18, italics in original).

From this issue forward, *Young Socialist* threw itself into the fight against conscription and into support for conscientious objectors, many of whom were and remained scholars of the Socialist Sunday Schools. In April 1916, the magazine reported receiving letters requesting testimonials of attendance at schools. Most issues covered the experiences of conscientious objectors at their tribunals, with accounts of scholars awaiting arrest, being jailed, and being mistreated by military authorities. There were also reports of physical attacks on scholars. The London Union's 1916 May Day demonstration outing had to be abandoned "owing to possible injury to the children, through molestation en route" (July 1916, 108). The editors reported in the same issue the case of a fifteen-year-old scholar of Marylebone School being "ducked in a pond and otherwise ill-treated" but happily concluded that his ardor was not dampened (108).

Not all of the SSS movement agreed with this stand (Fulham Socialist Sunday School Minute Book). Some felt that one's attitude toward the war was a matter of individual conscience and should be kept separate from the movement and the magazine, believing that these should be concerned only with the education of the children. However, the editors stood firm and argued that the magazine could not ignore the situation; they insisted that the magazine's content did not contravene the decisions of the National Conference, which had passed resolutions repudiating compulsory enlistment and pledging resistance to further conscription.

DORA meant that there could be no coverage of the Easter Rising of 1916 in Dublin, and it was not until May 1917 that reference was made to the February 1917 Russian Revolution. In the May issue, the editorial is entitled "A *Young Socialist* May-Day Greeting to Free Russia," and it welcomes the revolution and the inspiration it means for "workers for Freedom" (50).

Throughout the First World War, *Young Socialist* trod a principled and reasoned line. Opposed to militarism and conscription and aware that the war was being fought for economic reasons, the editors supplied a periodical that reflected these concerns and supported its scholars who were involved in the war machine, either fighting or working in munitions. It also provided support for its scholars who were conscientious objectors both through its pages and at the tribunals. It consistently propagated the ideas of internationalism and arbitration and provided an alternative voice for those who were opposed to the war. Although reduced to sixteen pages in 1916 due to paper shortages and price rises, the result of this stand was an increase in interest in the SSS movement and a boost in the circulation of the magazine.

At the end of the war, with the successful revolution in Russia and the development of the revolutionary movement in Britain, the magazine had the opportunity to expand; however, there were other issues to face. Fred Reid notes that those drawn into the SSS movement after the war were connected to the left wing of the ILP, and many of them were to join the emerging Communist Party in the 1920s (39). They were militant and, like Tom Anderson, interested in a revolutionary approach to the education of children. Although the Communist Party was to build its own youth movement, there were still many cases of individual party members active in the Socialist Sunday Schools. Alex Gossip, close to the Communist Party (although, contrary to Reid's assertion, he was never a member [Harrison]), encouraged comradely relations in the belief that all socialist organizations should be actively involved in the education of their children.

At the National Conference in 1918, proposals were made by the Tyneside Union suggesting the inclusion of more stories, an occasional play, and items for concerts (NCSSSU Minutes, Easter 1918, *Young Socialist* Report, 2–3).

May Westoby, the editor who succeeded Lizzie and Fred Glasier Foster, did try to fulfill some of these proposals. However, she was a proponent of socialism as a religion and had an antiquated style of writing that readers found patronizing. This was to bring her into constant conflict with more militant members, and various criticisms of her work were expressed at the National Conferences. Her tenure began with the euphoria of the victory of the Russian Revolution and ended with the Great Depression, leading to financial difficulties for the journal and the SSS movement in general. This reversal of fortune led to the reduction in pages from sixteen to twelve and to a steady decline in the magazine's circulation, as the schools and their supporters were unable to finance it.

During the Westoby editorship, the magazine began to publish more fairy tales and allegories. The allegories included serial stories by A. M. Redding recounting crusades to find utopias, reminiscent of John Bunyan's *The Pilgrim's Progress*. Socialism in all these stories is the final goal but the way traveled is often obscure, written in the language of high romance, often obfuscating to the reader. The tales of kings, queens, princes, and princesses continue, all royally aware that the socialism they kindly bestow on their subjects will conquer poverty and oppression and accepting in return the title of Supreme Comrade (Margaret H. Barber, "Lords and Comrades," *YS*, July and August 1920).

Strangest, though, is the Children's Page of April 1921. Written by Flora (Mrs. Edith Pearce), it is a report of a lecture on fairies. The report describes the types of fairies and asserts that people can see them if they are sensitive, while the camera can record them. Flora continues: "We are out to build the world anew with justice its foundation and love its law. In those happy days when love is the law of the land . . . we shall all grow sensitive again and see the fairies and all the wonders of Fairyland" (42).

The reference to the camera echoes Arthur Conan Doyle's championship of the Cottingley fairies. The trend toward this kind of article reflects perhaps the heightened interest in mysticism that began in the Victorian period and that enjoyed a revival during the immediate postwar period, as the nation tried to come to terms with the loss of a generation.

This is not to say that real events were completely ignored. There were articles on Russia, explaining the suffering of the Russian people under the czar and describing the current situation. Alfred Russell, a veteran member of the movement, produced an article on a rent strike in the October 1920 issue and took the opportunity to define the term "rent" (144). In April 1921, the editorial reported the "terrible wave of unemployment . . . sweeping over the whole world; a wave which means misery to millions of men, women and children" (38). Beginning in March 1922, appeals for donations to alleviate the famine areas in Russia appeared, and many schools contributed to the Save the Children Fund and its work in Russia.

March 1926 saw an expanded issue in which the central element was Westoby's story "Black Diamonds." This considered the plight of miners. She describes a group of miners trapped underground. They are ultimately rescued, and Westoby poses several questions at the end of the story—why are mines worked if they are dangerous, why are miners ready to risk their lives, and should they be paid small wages or enough for comfort? The most important question is, who should own the mines: "Since coal is, in one way or another, a necessity to us all, to whom should belong the mines made by Nature through thousands of years?" (183).

Two months later, in May 1926, the General Strike occurred. It lasted for nine days, and when the majority of the strikers went back to work, the miners stayed out for another terrible six months. There are references in *Young Socialist* to the General Strike and the continued lockout of the miners from May onward. Some of the competition questions in the Children's Pages relate to miners' leaders, and there is an acceptance that the scholars will be affected by the events: "I suppose it is because you have all been so excited about the Strike that I have received no solutions of last month's puzzle picture" (June 1926, 218). During this period there are reports in the school notes of contributions to the miners' fund.

After an absence during the First World War, probably caused by differences of opinion over the war, Frederick James Gould once more began to contribute articles on a regular basis. Many deal with notable individuals including Harry Quelch, member of the SDF and the publisher of its journal *Justice* (September 1920), and Booker T. Washington (November 1920), as well as articles on European history.

Contributors also included Andrew Fleming, the magazine's printer, who in March 1920 produced a story about a businessman who so successfully cuts himself off from his colleagues that he creates an insurmountable physical barrier and eventually commits suicide. Fleming then draws the conclusion that capitalism shuts itself off from the working class, and he relates this alienation to the situation in Europe: "A so-called victorious war has shut off the affections of more than half the people of Europe towards the Allies. . . . The hatred of the ruling classes here towards Socialism has shut off Russia, in whose virgin forests and vast mountain store-houses, and alluvial plains, there exists food and materials to make us all happy and comfortable. The Young Socialists of all lands will break the barrier" (44). He also contributed an account of his time in prison following his conviction for sedition along with the anarchist Guy Aldred (August and September 1926).

One of the major innovations of the Westoby period was the inclusion of articles in Esperanto. This began in 1920 and continued almost monthly throughout the period under consideration. There were also various pieces extolling the virtues of Esperanto including a contribution from the Esperantist Mark Starr of the Plebs League and later educational director of the International Ladies' Garment Workers' Union in New York (August 1924). Westoby also used articles written by scholars, mostly in their mid-teens, reprinted from the movement's manuscript magazine, *Youth*.

Westoby continued the tradition started by Archie McArthur of reprinting articles from U.S. socialist publications including the story "The Foreigner" by John Gabriel Soltis of the Socialist Party USA (June 1920). There were also letters from scholars from fraternal schools in the United States. These included one from Fanny Levy of the International Modern School in New York, who reported on their magazine and provided an essay from which Westoby quotes. Levy foresees the members of the House of Lords in poverty and announces that they will be sorry. To which Westoby replied, "Now, Fanny dear, you do not really mean that, do you?" (April 1922, 38). Westoby also commented on a report from a rally where a young scholar stated: "Unemployment, slums, and poverty in general were created by the idle rich" (October 1922, 120); she added in a footnote, "[o]ur little comrade was somewhat rash in his statements."

In the minutes of the National Conference of 1923, it was reported that Springburn School suggested that Westoby write a letter "on some current event in a fighting spirit." (NCSSSU Minutes, Easter 1923, *Young Socialist* Report, 1). Such criticism of the editor and editorial content continued at the 1924 conference. It was also at this conference that the Glasgow Union announced that it could no longer be responsible for the magazine, and it was agreed that the Yorkshire Union would take it over. Conference attendees also appointed an Editorial Ways and Means Committee, tasked with finding new material and cooperating with the editor to improve the magazine. Interestingly, the new committee's powers included the right to express disapproval of any article that appeared in *Young Socialist* and, most tellingly, to prevent similar articles from appearing in ensuing issues (NCSSSU Minutes, Easter 1924, *Young Socialist* Report, 1–3).

May Westoby first attempted to resign as editor at the 1926 National Conference, but her resignation was not accepted as the decision to appoint a new editor would rest with the conference. She therefore held her position into the following year (NCSSSU Minutes, Easter 1926). In her final report, she provided an overview of her tenure and mentioned the lack of suitable stories and articles and the inadequacy of funding, which limited the use of illustrations (NCSSSU Minutes, Easter 1927, *Young Socialist* Report, 1).

In conclusion, it should be noted that there was no period when *Young Socialist* was free from financial difficulties; its very existence was a constant struggle. From the first issues at the beginning of the twentieth century, when there was variety and rich experience of socialist thought and life, the magazine provided a forum where all the various parties and organizations could meet in the service of the education of the socialist child. As Ivy Tribe, president of the Socialist Fellowship, the successor to the Socialist Sunday School, said: "Why are we so proud of our little Magazine? Because it is unique in the history of the Working class Movement. No other organisation has ever produced a Socialist children's paper for so long and with such success. Success not by the number sold, or the profit made, but by getting our message of Socialism, as a way of life into the homes of the people and giving children food for thought" (1).

The magazine's primary concern was always determining the nature of its audience, the age and interests of its readers. Although from 1907 there was a Children's Page, later to be followed by an occasional piece for the very young child, there were always doubts as to whether this was enough. The magazine also had the purpose of communicating ideas and skills to the teachers and adults in the movement. When the journal had the luxury of twenty-four pages, this was acceptable; however, when the editor was limited to four or eight or even twelve pages, something had to be excluded, and often it was material suitable for younger children.

The Communist Party of Great Britain stated in its undated report *A Short History of the Working Class Children's Movement of Gt. Britain*: "It [the SSS movement] runs a paper called The "*Young Socialist*" edited by adults for the children, and no attempt is made to develop the paper as the children's own paper" (1). This is a shortcoming that the movement itself was aware of. The National Conference looked at every possible solution, aware that the magazine's format was not attractive to children, that it did not engage the young child or the adolescent. It was constantly hampered by constraints imposed by the nature of the magazine and its financial situation. Notes on the various schools' activities, advice on teaching, model lessons, all of these were required. There was never enough money for sufficient pages or illustrations. However, *Young Socialist* continued to appear, disseminating its message of building "the new world—its foundation to be justice; love to be the spirit of its inhabitants" (the magazine's banner from 1903 onward).

> *The Young Socialist* is, after all, not written wholly to amuse, but to help alter the life of the world, and that cannot be done entirely by comic pictures and jokes, or even wholly by charming stories and nothing more. It can only be done by tremendous and ardent effort on the part of everyone who thinks it necessary. (*YS* editorial, October 1924, 110)

NOTES

1. Socialist Sunday Schools were largely set up and influenced by the Independent Labour Party, the Social Democratic Federation, and the Labour Churches, organizations whose teachings and beliefs sprang from Christian socialist ethics. Tom Anderson first joined the ILP and then the SDF. However, by 1908 he was a member of the De Leonist Socialist Labour Party, which was based on Marxist principles. In a pamphlet, Anderson stated that the best method of educating children at a Socialist Sunday School was to "Teach them Revolutionary Socialism, based on the materialist conception of history" (Anderson 16). This goes some way to explain the differences between Anderson and the editors of *Young Socialist*.

2. The working-class movement was split in its reaction to the war, some elements supporting it and others in opposition. For example, the Labour Party was praised for

its commitment to the war effort; Henry M. Hyndman, formerly leader of the SDF, supported British involvement; and the Russian communist Peter Kropotkin, who was living in exile in London in 1914, was also pro-war. Among the well-known opponents of the war were Jean Jaurès of France, who was assassinated for his beliefs; Karl Liebknecht and Rosa Luxemburg in Germany; Lenin and the Bolshevik Party; Eugene Debs in the United States; and Errico Malatesta, Rudolf Rocker, Sylvia Pankhurst, and Fenner Brockway in Great Britain.

WORKS CITED

Anderson, Tom. *Socialist Sunday Schools: A Review, and How to Open and Conduct a Proletarian School.* Glasgow: Proletarian School, 1919. Print.

Blackburn, Alf. Letter to Jack Allam, March 16, 1955. TS. Labour History Archive (LHASC), Ivy Tribe Collection 239–244. People's History Museum, Manchester.

Communist Party of Great Britain. *A Short History of the Working Class Children's Movement of Gt. Britain.* N.d. TS. LHASC, CP/CENT/YOUTH/02/14. People's History Museum, Manchester.

Fleming, Andrew. Letter to Jack Allam, March 31, 1952. MS. LHASC, Ivy Tribe Collection 119. People's History Museum, Manchester.

Foster, Fred Glasier. *The Socialist Sunday Schools.* LHASC, Ivy Tribe Collection 2633-2638. People's History Museum, Manchester.

Fulham Socialist Sunday School Minute Book. June 24, 1916. LHASC, Ivy Tribe Collection box 10. People's History Museum, Manchester.

Harrison, Stanley. *Alex Gossip.* London: Lawrence & Wishart, 1962. Print.

National Conference of Socialist Sunday School Union Minutes. Easter 1911–1918. LHASC, Ivy Tribe Collection book 100. People's History Museum, Manchester.

———. Easter 1919–1927. LHASC, Ivy Tribe Collection 1E. People's History Museum, Manchester.

Reid, F. "Socialist Sunday Schools in Britain, 1892–1939." *International Review of Social History* 11 (1966): 18–47. Print.

Socialist Sunday Schools Potted History. N.d. TS. LHASC, Ivy Tribe Collection 148–164. People's History Museum, Manchester.

Tribe, Ivy. Presentation of a complete set of *Young Socialist* to the Marx Library, London. N.d. Address. LHASC, Ivy Tribe Collection 3096. People's History Museum, Manchester.

Yeo, Stephen. "A New Life: The Religion of Socialism in Britain, 1883–1896." *History Workshop* 4 (1977): 5–56. Print.

Young Socialist. London, Glasgow, Yorkshire, 1901–1926. Print.

Girls' Literature by German Writers in Exile (1933–1945)

JANA MIKOTA

Preliminary Remarks

When the Nazi regime came to power in Germany in 1933, numerous authors left Germany and devoted significant time and effort to opposing fascism and militarism in exile. Their writing for children, young people, and adults contributed to an antifascist, and sometimes also pacifist, literature for children and young persons. This article focuses on exile girls' literature (*Mädchenliteratur des Exils*) and its function for the reader. It asks whether this literature—by German writers exiled as a result of the Nazi regime—contributed to an antifascist and maybe even an international and pacifist upbringing.

Girls' literature has a long tradition in German. In typical *Backfischliteratur* (literature for adolescent girls), traditional gender roles were established and female readers were supposed to be preparing for their future roles as wives, housewives, and mothers. In the late nineteenth century, a contrasting girls' literature developed; this literature included new topics, subjects, and genres such as the colonial novel and travel stories. As it developed in the twentieth century, exile girls' literature was oriented to both forms: on the one hand, female authors in exile depicted girlhood as carefree and socially secure without eliminating gender-specific classifications; on the other hand, they included the topic of exile and expanded the domain of possible action for female protagonists, who could now act more independently and significantly than in earlier decades in German girls' literature.[1]

With their depiction of young female figures and their partial rejection of traditional constructions of gender, exile authors challenged the images of girls and women propagated by the Nazi regime. The images of girls and women depicted in exile literature opposed not only those of National Socialism but also those propagated by other dictatorships in the 1930s.

Exile authors tried to write against the National Socialists. Literature for children and juveniles in the Third Reich glorified the Nazi regime, the war, and the Nordic "race." Exile literature for children and juveniles, by contrast, supported "humanistic and cosmopolitan ideas about and views on human rights" ("humanistische, kosmopolitische und menschenrechtliche Gedanken"; Stern 300). The National Socialist "new" worldview and image of humankind was contrasted with the democratic and antifascist worldview and image of humankind of the exile. The authors of girls' exile literature supported this image of humankind as well.

Girls' literature in this essay is understood as literature explicitly addressed to female readers. Such an address is defined on a paratextual level by the cover, the title, publication as part of a series, or manner of advertisement. The subjects of girls' literature are those that interest young women and are taken from their milieu. While girls' literature is not exclusively written by female authors, most authors of girls' literature are women. All novels presented here have titles featuring girls' names, and the book covers display female figures and—as will be explained below—contain allusions to the female characters' personalities and virtues.

Some of girls' literature by female authors in exile could not be published until after 1945. Some authors like Hertha Pauli (1906–1973) and Erika Mann (1905–1969) published their novels in the language of their exile countries, but those novels were not published in the German language until decades after the end of the Nazi regime; other texts such as those of Maria Gleit are still awaiting translation into German. In autobiographical novels for girls such as *When Hitler Stole Pink Rabbit* by Judith Kerr, the defining changes caused by exile are picked up as a central theme, and the female protagonists' fears and sorrows are depicted in detail. Those texts were published after 1945; they were an important contribution to the enlightenment of girls about fascism and war.

Exile girls' literature was—like exile children's literature in general—heterogeneous, with different functions. Among the chief features and functions, (1) it tried to inform readers about the Nazi regime, in fact seeing readers as active fighters against fascism; (2) at the same time, it informed readers about the exile countries, treating their histories and diverse cultures; (3) it included, like adult literature, features of the historical novel, taking up not only German history but also the histories of the different exile countries; (4) it depicted the everyday life of children in the exile countries without explicitly presenting sociopolitical contexts to the readers; and (5) it led to the evolution of a firm sociocritical and political girls' literature. This essay focuses on functions (4) and (5). My analysis of exile girls' literature will reveal a host of different images of girl characters whose signal feature is that they take an active position against fascism; in this literature, girls are included in the fight against Nazi Germany. This firm political stance, which is presented to readers in different ways in these books, constitutes a modification of the view of the girl or girlhood as political, a view held by some during the Weimar Republic but, in exile, radicalized and understood as a given. Girls are depicted as active characters. Such topics as correcting "childish" and "contrary" behavior—a preoccupation of the German *Backfischliteratur* of the late nineteenth century—or marriage characterize only a small part of exile girls' literature. Girls' independence, and later the experience of having a career, are of course integrated into the texts.

Exile forced authors to leave Germany, and they experienced what it means to be on the run. The motif of travel, which had already found its way into girls' literature in the late nineteenth century, is used in different ways in exile girls' literature: (1) exile, and therefore involuntary traveling, are discussed in the context of the Nazi seizure of power; (2) girls are forced to leave their homes for various reasons, although the Nazis are not explicitly named as a threat; (3) girls have to go on a journey because of natural disasters or the loss of their parents; and (4) travel is seen as a vacation or recovery. While the first three points deal with involuntary travel, the last one takes up voluntary travel. Here, travel remains connected to adventure. Novels by Adrienne Thomas (1897–1980), Lisa Tetzner (1894–1963), and Kurt Held (1897–1959) illustrate these modifications in girl's literature by presenting active girl characters whose stance can be called antifascist. These novelists also present a construction of femininity that is an alternative to that promoted by National Socialism.

Girl's Literature of National Socialism: A Brief Introduction

To understand the relevance of girls' literature of exile, it is important to take a look at the girls' literature that developed under the influence of National Socialism. The Hitler Youth as well as the Bund Deutscher Mädel (League of German Girls) were characterized by military jargon and organized like troops of soldiers. Members had to subordinate themselves to and take, without question, orders from those with a higher rank. The aim of female education is "to prepare women for the unshiftable responsibilities of motherhood" (qtd. in Grenz 217), writes Adolf Hitler in *Mein Kampf*, defining the role of the woman in National Socialism.

Womanhood in the girls' literature of National Socialism is presented differently in three distinct periods, according to Dagmar Grenz. In the first period, girls are fighting for National Socialism. In the second, girls are integrated into the community. And in the third period, girls are part of the national struggle in the Second World War (Grenz 220–227). On closer examination, these three periods reveal that the concept of "girl" in National Socialism was contradictory and that a public role was definitely offered to girls. At the same time, as even this brief presentation of the texts will show, National Socialist girls' literature differed from girls' literature developed in exile.

First Period: Girls Fighting for National Socialism

According to Dagmar Grenz, all girls' novels published in Germany between 1932 and 1935 emphasize girls fighting for National Socialism and being consciously dedicated to National Socialism. Enemies of National Socialism such as Jews, communists, and social democrats are to be opposed. Grenz argues that the texts reveal a clear black-and-white thinking: supporters of National Socialism are positively presented, opponents negatively. The fight takes place on the street, and the girls often wear boys' clothes so that they can fight unhindered. However, although active girls are presented in the texts, in the end they return to their traditional role as women. For example, in *Hitlermädel kämpfen um Berlin* (ca. 1935) by Marga Möckel: "The Hitlerboy Max existed only for some hours, because the Hitlergirl Maxe has to carry out her duty!" (Möckel 70). In *Ulla, ein Hitlermädel* (1933) by Helga Knöpke-Jost, the duties of men and women in national socialist Germany are even more explicitly divided: "The man, the Hitlerboy and the SA-man, have to fight for the external freedom of our people by using all their strength and, if necessary, even sacrifice their lives. On the other hand it is the duty of women and girls to fight down the internal enemy that, all strange and wrong, has crept in the life of the nation, and has to vanish again. . . . The girl, wanting to become a mother one day must be able to educate her children in the way expected by Adolf Hitler from the next generation" (42). National Socialism needed girls, but they were to be active in the private sphere, passing on the Nazi ideology to succeeding generations.

Second Period: Girls' Everyday Lives under National Socialism

After 1935, the Nazi regime was stabilized and girls' literature responded by no longer depicting clashes between the National Socialists and others but instead describing the bright, practically sorrow-free daily routines of youth under National Socialism. Travels with the League of German Girls, but also the girls' duties under the regime—for example, the *Pflichtjahr* (year of compulsory service)—are described as positive achievements. The girls naturally subordinate themselves according to National Socialist ideology, and hierarchical structures—such as those of holiday camps—are not questioned. Suse Harms, in her novel *Sommertage in Heidersdorf* (1939), depicts cheerful everyday life in a holiday camp: "Then there was the morning run over the lawn wet with dew through a barbed wired fence into the wood, over trunks and through bushes. Everywhere birds were chirping, a cuckoo was calling, and over all this the sun was shining more brightly and brilliantly than in Berlin. It was great in Heidersdorf!" (39). Life in the countryside is idealized; the persecution of people resisting National Socialist ideology is not mentioned. This glorification of country life is consistent with National Socialist ideology, but it is also possible that the work in the countryside was represented as attractive for girls because there was a shortage of workers in Germany at that time and the girls' labor was needed.

That the girls should subordinate themselves and accept traditional female roles is made clear by these texts as well. For this reason it is not surprising that work plays only a secondary role. Motherhood, according to Grenz, included the idea of a woman as man's unpaid working friend "at home, in the family firm and on the farm" (227).

Third Period: Girls' Activities during the Prewar Period and Wartime

This group of texts written between 1937 and 1945 (Grenz 227) is closely connected with the war policy of the National Socialists; they also introduce girl characters in the German-speaking areas outside of the Third Reich, for example in Sudetenland and Austria. The wish to see the Führer and to openly wear the uniform of the Bund Deutscher Mädel at last is significant. This can be seen for instance in *Ostmarkmädel* (1939) by Herta Weber-Stumfohl: "The best and greatest part came on Friday Sept. 10 when we were allowed to see the Führer. We received the happy news that the Führer was prepared, at our request, to receive us. Once again the leaders of the illegal Austrian Hitler-Youth went to the Deutscher Hof" (qtd. in Wilkending 470; the Deutscher Hof is a restaurant). Novels in this third group describe the wish of the girls to belong to Germany, and, as in the first group, opponents to the National Socialist regime are presented.

At the same time, girls are shown to be involved in war activities, for instance as *Nachrichtenhelferin* (signal corps auxiliaries), nurses, or soldiers. The girls want to fight and are prepared to die for their country. However, the texts also make clear that such a function is only possible for women and girls during times of war. In peacetime, women should concentrate on motherhood. While girls are thought to be capable of fighting, finding satisfaction in work, and participating in public events—and thus to be equipped with male attributes—their place is beside and subordinate to their men, as is made clear by these girls' novels. Grenz summarizes this point: "She is allowed to work and to fight like a man, because her labor and her commitment are needed for political and economic reasons; she doesn't get male rights" (233). She can act in public; however, she gains neither greater freedom nor independence. As outlined below, girls' literature of exile can be seen as a reaction to girls' literature of National Socialism.

Girls' Literature by German Writers in Exile: Some Examples

Adrienne Thomas

Adrienne Thomas is one of the best-known German authors of novels for girls of the Nazi period. Born as Hertha Strauch on July 24, 1897, to a Jewish merchant family, she grew up speaking both German and French in Saint-Avold, Lorraine, and later in Metz. In her first novel, *Die Katrin wird Soldat* (1930), she reappraises her experiences during World War I, impressively describing the civilian population's and the soldiers' suffering. After the Nazi seizure of power in Germany, she was one of the first female authors to be banned in that country. Her novel was among those thrown into fires during the book burnings that took place on May 10, 1933. *Die Katrin wird Soldat* is characterized by a pacifism that Thomas had to abandon in her later works in reaction to National Socialist expansionism. With her texts, Thomas wanted to create a literary world that was democratically organized: she writes about "having to create the atmosphere of a book for young readers from a clean, democratic world order" (qtd. in Seeber 72). Her approach succeeded, especially in her novels for children.

In 1933, Thomas lived in Switzerland; in 1934 she moved to France, and in 1935 to Austria. She fled once again to France in 1938. With the help of the Emergency Rescue Committee she was able to emigrate to the United States in 1940 and lived in New York until 1947. She reflects on her experience in exile in France and the United States in her novels *Reisen Sie ab, Mademoiselle* (1947) and *Das Fenster am East River* (1945). She was comfortable living in America and, according to her letters, she only returned to Vienna in 1947 because her husband, Julius Deutsch, no longer wished to live in New York. (She died in Vienna in 1980.) Of her years in exile she writes, "Torberg said once that it was twelve lost years. For me it was twelve years gained. Everywhere I was I enjoyed being there. Everywhere I was able to cope with problems. I made the best of it and did not let things get me down. I lived modestly in America and worked for a paper" (qtd. in Kreis 224).

In exile she began writing again for children. She explained her task as follows: "There was a time when I put the manuscript I had started aside and thought that I could not reach my generation any longer. I did not see any solace or hope for us. But maybe I still had something to say to children. During that time, I wrote *Andrea*, *Viktoria*, and *Ein Hund ging verloren* for young readers" (Seeber 49).

In exile, unlike many other female authors in similar circumstances, Adrienne Thomas was able to continue writing. She was successful with her young-adult fiction published in the 1930s, 1950s, and 1960s. Those novels were published in several editions, and she partly revised her work of the 1930s after 1945. In her girls' novels *Andrea* (1937), *Viktoria* (1938), and *Von Johanna zu Jane* (From Johanna to Jane, 1939) she takes up young girls' everyday life experiences in a contemporary historical context. The contents of her novels correspond to the definition of girls' literature, but in their titles they differ from traditional girls' literature in Germany. Revealing, diminutive nicknames like *Backfischchen* (naïve young girl), *Nesthäkchen* (baby of the family), or *Goldköpfchen* (little fair-haired child) are traditionally used, but Thomas chooses first names that reveal very little about her female protagonists. While Andrea is a common name in German, the name Viktoria, on the other hand, hints at the nature of its bearer. *Viktoria* means victory, and—this much can already be revealed—the eponymous Viktoria is victorious in the novel: she gets a role in a movie and thus comes closer to her goal of becoming an actress. Both of the titles *Viktoria* and *Von Johanna zu Jane* indicate change.

In *Andrea*, Thomas describes the life of a group of teenagers in the fictitious duchy of Mannsburg. The girls Andrea and Viktoria together with their friends are the focus of the narrative's attention. The action is divided into three parts. The book opens in Mannsburg, where Viktoria's dog is kidnapped and killed; the second part describes the children's lives in a summer camp; in the third part, they return to Mannsburg and are able to unmask the dog thief. On their way to camp, however, the two girls get separated from their group and are forced to continue their way through the forest on their own. There, they meet Dan Martens. Already in their first meeting Andrea understands that Dan "nirgends mehr hin [gehört]" (no longer belonged anywhere; *Andrea* 46). Arriving at camp, he describes his experience to the young girls.

> Dan hatte nichts Böses getan und lebte doch wie ein Verbrecher auf der Flucht. Wenn er aber später dieses Jahr überdachte, stand nicht das im Vordergrund, sondern alles Gute, die tausend Freundlichkeiten, die ihm von Fremden, meist von Kindern, erwiesen worden waren. (Dan hadn't done anything bad, but still he lived like a criminal on the run. But when he thought back to these years later on, that wasn't foremost in his mind, but instead all the good things, the thousands of favors that strangers, mostly children, had done to him.) (53–54)

While at camp, the children decide to help Dan; they take him back to Mannsburg and found a secret society. In Mannsburg, Dan is at first suspected of being the dog thief, but he and his friends succeed in unmasking the real criminal. Herein Thomas's book differs markedly from the girls' literature of National Socialism, in which children are admonished to cooperate with authority. In the novel *Ulla, ein Hitlermädel*, for example, girls of the League of German Girls have to cook for the Hitler Youth boys at a holiday camp. The girls here are not the equals of the boys, and they have female characteristics. The eponymous Ulla objects to an order and is immediately reprimanded: "'What an imposition,' Ulla said, 'to make us play the kitchen maids for the boys. Otherwise, when they are underway they always cook for themselves.' That made Hilde angry: 'If you don't like it, you should have stayed at home. Our Gau-leader has ordered us to spend our time at camp this fall together with the boys. And when the Hitler Youth leader asks me if the BDM can be responsible for the food, then I can't say to him: 'No. Cook your stuff yourself. My girls are too good for this'" (Knöpke-Jost 65). In Thomas's *Andrea* we also see life in a holiday camp, but here the boys and girls spend their holiday together and handle the work in the camp cooperatively. A fifteen-year-old boy is responsible for the kitchen. Gender roles are not defined so rigidly as in *Ulla*.

The subject of travel is addressed twice in *Andrea*: Andrea and Viktoria go to camp voluntarily. Their parents do not see an educational purpose in the journey but want Viktoria to recover from the loss of her dog. With the character of Dan Marten, Thomas takes up the subject of the compulsory journey. Dan comes from South America and is looking for his father, who had to flee because of the radical political changes there. Thomas thus introduces a character who is stateless and homeless. The girls, who grew up in prosperity, learn about sorrows previously unknown to them: prosecution, jail, homelessness, and poverty. Dan embodies a situation that might have been familiar to some readers in the 1930s: exile, permanent flight, and being in need of help from other people. At the same time, children are the actual helpers. Thomas depicts people who carry the hope of a better future and who act in solidarity with their neighbor.

In *Viktoria*, the sequel to *Andrea*, the subject of traveling is taken up once again. Dan and his father, now reunited, invite the group to their estate in Salzburg, and the children travel to Austria with Aunt Karla. There they spend a carefree few days on vacation in a depiction of voluntary travel. Exile is no longer at the center of the story, and Dan's earlier statelessness and homelessness are only referred to in flashbacks. International boundaries and tolls barely play a role in the children's journey, although they are still checked when they cross borders. Central to the action instead are Viktoria's efforts to get into the movies as well as the growing friendship between Dan and Andrea. Viktoria wants to be a movie star, and her parents support this dream; this is in fact a common topos in girls' literature in the 1920s and 1930s.

In both novels, Thomas depicts a group of adolescents of both sexes who correspond to certain gender stereotypes. Even though she employs role clichés in her depictions from time to time, she also overcomes them. When Andrea and Viktoria arrive at the youth camp, they learn that a boy is in charge in the kitchen and that the girls working under him are jokingly called scullions: "Küchenchef war ein fünfzehnjähriger Bub. Er hielt gerade Instruktionsstunde mit den Mädeln, die ihm als Küchenjungen zugeteilt worden waren" (The person in charge of the kitchen was a fifteen-year-old-boy. He was instructing the girls working under him as scullions; *Andrea* 76). The group has no leader, and Frank, Andrea's brother, is indeed often criticized because of his authoritarian character: "'Du hast mir aber überhaupt nichts zu verbieten, Frank!' Das traf Frank fast noch mehr als der Einbruch und die leere Kasse. Andrea wagte es, ihm, dem großen Bruder und Hauptmann des Geheimbundes, in breitester Öffentlichkeit so zu begegnen?" ("You can't stop me from doing anything, Frank!" This hurt Frank even more than the break-in and the empty cash box. Andrea dared to stand up to him in broad daylight like that, to him, her elder brother and the chief of the secret society! *Andrea* 279). The authoritarian construction of masculinity represented by Frank is criticized by another character, Herbert Feller, a friend of Frank's who vouches for Dan Marten and gives him a home. He also defends Andrea: "'Zur Sache gehört aber wohl nicht, daß du mit Andrea so grob bist,' meinte Herbert, der diesen Einwurf schon lange auf dem Herzen hatte" ("It's pointless being so coarse to Andrea," remarked Herbert, who had nursed this objection for a long time; *Andrea* 117). Herbert's objection doesn't refer to the fact that the stronger man has to protect the younger girl but is meant as criticism of Frank's sometimes authoritarian behavior. Such assertions, made by the active characters and not by an intrusive narrator, emphasize the author's wish to model for her young readers a democratic world order.

Lisa Tetzner

Children's book author Lisa Tetzner treats the subject of exile in a sophisticated way in her nine-volume fictional work *Die Kinder aus Nr. 67*, the so-called *Kinderodyssee* (Children's Odyssey), thus contributing significantly to German exile literature in general. The work covers the years 1931 to 1946. The central characters are the children Mirjam Sabrowsky and Erwin Brackmann from house no. 67 in Berlin, who must leave Berlin immediately after the Nazi takeover, and Paul Richter, whose family joins the National Socialist German Workers' Party (NSDAP, later known as the Nazi Party) and lives through the war years in Berlin. These volumes depict the children's lives after 1933, including the new friends they make; adults play a role only in the background. The story describes how Erwin, Mirjam, and Paul grow up against the background of the National Socialist takeover and the Second World War. The novel's several volumes are connected by the children's compulsory journeys.

Tetzner, born 1894 in Zittau, Saxony, was already writing children's books in the 1920s. In 1933 she fled with her husband, Kurt Kläber, to Switzerland, where she died in 1963. Her books were banned in Nazi Germany. In her *Kinderodyssee*, Tetzner employs various genres and narrative forms.

In the fourth volume, *Das Schiff ohne Hafen* (1943; The ship without a harbor), the flight and the miseries of exile are depicted in great detail; the fifth volume, *Die Kinder auf der Insel* (1944; The children on the island), belongs to the genre of the Robinsonade; in the sixth volume, *Mirjam in Amerika* (1945; Mirjam in America), Mirjam's life in the United States is described in the form of a diary. Three volumes concentrate on Mirjam, who, as a Jew, was forced to leave Berlin with her aunt and is looking for a new home. While she acts as a member of a group in the first volumes and is supported by other children, she sets out on her own to find the relatives of a girl called Ruth in *Mirjam in Amerika*. While Thomas's Andrea and Viktoria are on vacation in Austria, Mirjam is not only confronted with the American way of life in New York but also experiences racism. She makes friends with an African American elevator boy, Jim, only to meet with strong criticism from her foster mother: "In the USA, no white woman or man can be seen with a negro. Never take a negro as your friend and never visit a restaurant with a black or eat with him at the same table. You have to know this once and for all. This was a big surprise and destroyed my respect for the USA. The day before the teacher had read to me part of the American Constitution in an emotional voice. According to it, all humans are equal, have the same rights and can say all they want to say, and even the poorest can become president" (*Mirjam in Amerika* 58). Thus, while showing that the United States welcomed refugees like Mirjam, Tetzner also represents the less positive aspects of Mirjam's new home, including racism toward blacks. Despite this aspect of life in the United States, Mirjam decides to stay rather than return to Germany after the war. Nevertheless, Tetzner's representation of American racism contrasts with works by other exile writers such as Erika Mann. Thomas and Tetzner offer divergent images of a girls' adolescence (*Backfischzeit*). Thomas shows the carefree lives of young middle-class girls; their fun is only interrupted by a dog thief. Otherwise they are financially secure, their families are intact, and their parents encourage their children's dreams. Tetzner, by contrast, creates a character who must confront adult problems at a young age; exile forces Mirjam into the role of a grown-up woman. Because Mirjam loses her aunt in exile and must take responsibility for other children whose parents are absent, she is burdened with a mother's role. Mirjam affectionately looks after them. When Mirjam and the children have been rescued, a mother thanks Mirjam exuberantly: "You prepared a bed for my boys and you even cooked for the boys and mended like a young good housewife. They have told me everything. They said you have been like their mother"

(*Mirjam in Amerika* 47). In other words, Tetzner depicts the disappearance of childhood in exile.

Like Thomas, Tetzner takes up the subject of travel in her novels. This topic was not included in girls' literature until the late nineteenth century but became common in exile literature. While travel is combined loosely with the plot in *Andrea* and *Viktoria*, it is a structural feature of *Mirjam in Amerika*. Because Mirjam has to leave Germany, travel is central to the volumes *Das Schiff ohne Hafen* and *Mirjam in Amerika*, and the plot depends on the journey. Mirjam gets to know new people and gains experience. Tetzner also takes up the topic of exile and life in foreign countries and discusses these topics more directly than Thomas does. The description of exile—being forced into emigration—is new to girls' literature, a result of political changes in Germany.

Kurt Held

Beginning in the 1920s, it was not only women who began rewriting traditional girls' literature but men as well, including Kurt Held (1897–1959), Lisa Tetzner's husband. Held published sociocritical works under his real name, Kurt Kläber, in the 1920s. He was arrested by the newly installed Nazi government in 1933 and soon released, after which he managed to emigrate to Switzerland with his wife. His novels were banned and burned in Nazi Germany. In Switzerland, he and his wife worked together and conferred with one another about their books. His Swiss publisher, Sauerländer, advised him to publish under a pseudonym. He and Tetzner decided on the name Kurt Held. In German, *held* means "hero."

Held's novel *Die rote Zora und ihre Bande* (Red-haired Zora and her gang) is one of the best-known exile girls' books in German, a classic among children's books that has been filmed several times; it is regarded as a model. In 1939, while on vacation in Senj, a town on the Dalmatian coast, Held met some youths who inspired him to write about them. He explained his task of writing for young people as follows: "Der Anlaß mein erstes Kinderbuch zu schreiben, kam von Kindern selber. Sie waren durch den Krieg heimat- und elternlos in unser Dorf geschwemmt worden. Wir hatten aber keine Bücher für sie, und so mußte ich ihnen jede Nacht etwas schreiben, denn am Morgen Punkt zehn standen sie unter meinem Balkon und schrien: 'Fortsetzung!' So entstand *Die rote Zora*" (The reason for writing my first children's book came from the children themselves. They had been brought to our village, homeless and parentless because of the war. But we did not have books for them and so I had to write something for them every night because in the morning at exactly ten they were standing under my balcony and shouting: "go on!" That's the way *Die rote Zora* developed; qtd. in Jentgens 502).

It is impossible to reconstruct today whether such stories are true or not. But their statements show that both Adrienne Thomas and Kurt Held used exile to write for a new target audience. Even as new possibilities opened up for them, both authors strove to create a new model with their children's novels that would resist the National Socialist worldview. Like Thomas, Held believed that children carried the hope of a better future. With his novels, he wanted to impress on readers his ideas of solidarity, equality, and freedom. Intentionally using literature didactically, he introduced a new topic into German children's literature. With *Die rote Zora*, he created characters who radically broke with earlier images of girls: "die Darstellung der Lebensverhältnisse einer Kinderbande ohne familiäre Bindungen, die durch die Schuld der Gesellschaft aus dem Gleis gerät und erst durch die Hilfe verständiger Erwachsener wieder in die Gemeinschaft integriert wird" (The depiction of living conditions in a children's gang without family attachments that is thrown out of kilter by society and that can only be integrated into the community with the help of understanding adults; Kümmerling-Meibauer 437).

When Held published *Die rote Zora* in 1941, this signified a new beginning for him. His new pen name protecting him against censorship and the police, he made his debut as an author of children's literature. As Kurt Held, he was also no longer the Kläber who had left the Stalinized Communist Party in 1938. His writing was influenced by his evolving sensibilities, and he achieved a point of view that combined "humanistische Anschauungen mit soziale[m] Engagement" (humanistic views with social commitment; Jentgens 503). Like the stories of Adrienne Thomas and Lisa Tetzner, in *Die rote Zora* Held presents the image of a democratic group of children, in which both girls and boys play equal parts.

The story of *Die rote Zora*, which takes place on the coast of Croatia, is told from the point of view of twelve-year-old Branko, who is driven out of the family apartment and has to fend for himself after his mother's death. Hunger leads him to steal bread. He is arrested, freed by Zora, and introduced to her gang, which consists of the boys Pavle, Duro, and Nicola. They live in the ruins of Nehajgrad, living on stolen food; the Uskoks, Slavs who held sway in that coastal region in the seventeenth century, serve as their model. The "Uskoken" fight again and again against a group of "Gymnasiasten" (high school students). The two groups represent different social classes: The Uskoken are poor and hungry and live on the fringes of society but—apart from having to steal the food they live on—they are honest. The Gymnasiasten are well fed, respected, and rich; they lie and are disloyal and tight fisted. The novel criticizes society repeatedly: "Die Menschen sind noch viel schlimmer. Die Menschen fressen ihre Brüder, weil es ihnen Freude macht, sie zu fressen" (Humans are even worse. Humans eat their brothers, because they enjoy eating them; 299). Zora's group supports and helps the poor while robbing those who are better off. Although the town authorities dislike them, the poor people, especially Gorian (a poor fisherman who often helps Zora), defend the group, and at the end of the novel all the children are taken in by various families. But the ideal of the Uskoken lives on. With the Uskoken, who are not organized militarily, Held presents a gang to the reader that offers an alternative model to National Socialist society, which employs strict the military organization of the Hitler Youth and the League of German Girls to prepare boys and girls for their future roles in the Third Reich. The group around Zora is characterized by solidarity, achieved especially by Zora. She doesn't subordinate herself to the male members, but is militant and at the same time free and independent. Such characteristics especially make clear that Held's Zora distinguishes herself from girlish characters in the girls' literature of National Socialism. As Dagmar Grenz emphasizes, girls depicted in National Socialist literature were likewise militant, but neither free nor independent; rather, they were subordinated and directed into their maternal role.

Travel also plays a role in *Die rote Zora*. Zora first must flee from Albania with her brother and mother because of a family feud in which Zora's father was killed. They travel north to the Croatian coast, where Zora's brother and mother die. Zora runs away from the children's home to which she is sent and, little by little, assembles her gang. Zora, the leader and founder of a gang of boys, is wild, freedom loving, and unruly. The attribute *rot* (red) refers to her hair: "Sommersprossen liefen über die Nase, brandrotes Haar lohte wie Feuer über ihr. Sie war barfuß und barhäuptig wie Branko, und sie streifte, genauso wie er, zwischen den Ständen hin und her" (She had freckles on her nose; flaming red hair blazed like fire over her. She was barefoot and bareheaded like Branko and she roamed around the stands as he did; 51). Her gang is not an authoritarian group; instead, everyone is allowed to represent his or her point of view, and ideas are then acted upon by the person who first suggested them. Because of Zora's red hair, the locals consider her a witch. At the same time, she is endowed with familiar female attributes: she provides security and cares for her friends. Held depicts Zora's troubled childhood and offers a complex portrait of her adolescence. She is permitted to have feelings for the opposite sex and becomes jealous when Branko expresses interest in Zlata, a rich and beautiful girl from the village.

Although Zora is accepted as a member of society at the end of the novel, she remains independent. With this depiction of a female leader, Held writes in opposition to the National Socialist ideal of femininity. In the village, nobody cares about the children; the gang functions as a family substitute and an alternative model to society. The children support and help each other, but there is also dissention and competition. In other words, Held does not depict a black-and-white world but shows that children have problems among themselves. The group has its own rules, but these do not correspond to the norms of the troubled adult society. They support justice and bravery and punish betrayal.

With Zora, Held created an interesting girl who impacted not merely girls' literature but German children's literature as a whole. Long before the discussion about emancipatory girls' literature in West Germany in the 1970s, he created a character that "zumindest tendenziell auf eine Überwindung geschlechtsspezifischen Rollenverhaltens hindeutet" (at least tendentially indicates the overcoming of gender-specific role behavior; Jentgens 506). Zora became a leading figure for a whole generation. Scholarship, however, often overlooks the novel's origins in exile and the concomitant changed awareness of childhood and gender. In Held's novel, sex-specific roles are dissolved. In the history of girls' literature, *Die rote Zora* marks a break. Since, however, the book was published in exile and reached Germany only after 1945, the changes in German girls' literature that it wrought were somewhat delayed. The girls' novel is characterized by girls acting in a sociocritical context. Zora's behavior is the result of social circumstances. It is her poverty that makes her become a female Robin Hood. She has a critical perspective on society, and her gang functions as a countermodel to the kind of society promoted in Nazi Germany. While Thomas shows how boys and girls act together and demand solidarity, Held breaks with traditions of girls' literature. Zora symbolizes a particular type of girl that Pippi Longstocking was to embody four years later.

Conclusion

The novels of Kurt Held, Lisa Tetzner, and Adrienne Thomas presented here show the heterogeneity of girls' literature in exile. While Tetzner's sociocritical series *Die Kinder aus Nr. 67* deliberately uncovers the strains of exile and portrays the land of the protagonist's exile, America, Held and Thomas forgo such specific descriptions. Yet all three texts encourage the reader to imagine a democratic world and depict diverse social structures, and are therefore still pertinent today.

The girls in these novels are marked by motherliness and caring, but they are also independent and active; both they and their opinions are accepted by their male friends. Brave behavior, independence, and motherliness are not in conflict with each other. This flavor of girls' literature no longer aimed to prepare readers for future roles as housekeeper, mother, and wife; instead, it showed girls their full range of chances and possibilities and assured them that they could act on equal terms with male protagonists. We can assume that the girls who read these novels were given some respite from the conflicts and problems of their everyday lives. They were able to join Zora's adventures without being directly confronted with her exile.

These girls' novels represent the social and political changes of an era. Girls like Mirjam were forced to leave Germany, and their ensuing experiences were shaped by economic poverty. Mirjam was in need of other people's help in her exile countries. *Andrea* picks up precisely this topic insofar as Thomas appeals to readers' humanity in her novels. Travel does not mean breaking free from dependence in these novels; when it does lead to a bit of autonomy, it is usually because the characters are forced into it involuntarily. Breaking with the family is depicted in painful terms, especially as it is often final. The break is caused by profound political changes: not all parents were able to leave Germany, and many died en route. Therefore, national affiliation, national pride, patriotism, and nostalgia for bygone days play a minor role. The protagonists instead open themselves up to new experiences in new countries.

Exile girls' novels vary the pattern of the traditional girls' novel, but they show that the importance of female socialization, as well as views of femininity in general, have changed. The girls' education that characterized the *Backfisch* novels vanished from exile girls' literature. Although *Die rote Zora* was written by a man, it effectively influenced German-language girls' literature. The analysis of the novels by Thomas, Tetzner, and Held has shown, furthermore, that there is no difference in men's concept of femininity. Like Thomas and Tetzner, Held also created independent, active girls' characters, perhaps due to his own exile and the wish to break away from Nazi Germany and its stereotypes of the sexes.

Despite the progressive depiction of gender by these exiled writers, they were not widely read immediately after World War II. Instead, children's

and youth literature written after 1945 again depicted traditional constructions of gender, in the tradition of *Backfischliteratur*. Only after 1968 did the
texts analyzed here begin to influence children's literature. After 1968, in the
context of the women's movement, an emancipated girls' literature emerged
that took up new themes such as education and work. Held's *Die rote Zora*
acquired exemplary status in this respect.

The girls' exile literature that proved useful after 1968 developed in response to the National Socialist depiction of girls, which aimed to open the
world of National Socialism for female readers and show them their duties
as women within this ideology. The exile writers, by contrast, conveyed to
their readers their idea of a humanistic world united against fascism.

NOTES

1. For the sake of elegance, in the remainder of this essay I will use the term German
rather than German-language or German-speaking (*deutschsprachig*).

WORKS CITED

Bock, Gisela. *Frauen in der europaeischen Geschichte: Vom Mittelalter bis zur Gegenwart.*
Munich: Beck, 2000. Print.

Fuss Phillips, Zlata. *German Children's and Youth Literature in Exile 1933–1950: Biographies
and Bibliographies.* Munich: K. G. Saur, 2001. Print.

Grenz, Dagmar. "Kämpfen und arbeiten wie ein Mann: sich aufopfern wie eine Frau;
Zu einigen zentralen Aspekten des Frauenbildes in der nationalsozialistischen
Mädchenliteratur." In *Geschichte der Mädchenlektüre: Mädchenliteratur und die ge-
sellschaftliche Situation der Frauen vom 18; Jahrhundert bis zur Gegenwart*, edited by
Dagmar Grenz and Gisela Wilkending, 217–239. Weinheim: Juventa Verlag, 1997. Print.

Harms, Suse. *Sommertage in Heidersdorf: Eine fröhliche Lagergeschichte.* Berlin: Junge
Generation, 1939. Print.

Held, Kurt. *Die rote Zora und ihre Bande.* 1941. Zürich: Unionsverlag, 1997. Print.

Hessmann, Daniela. "Der Beitrag jüdischer Autorinnen zur Kinder- und Jugendliteratur
der dreißiger Jahre, dargestellt an Beispielen von Anna Maria Jokl, Auguste Lazar, Ruth
Rewald und Adrienne Thomas." Unpublished thesis, University of Salzburg, 1999. Print.

Jentgens, Stephanie. "Eine Robin Hood der Kinderwelt: Kurt Held's *Die rote Zora und ihre
Bande.*" In *Klassiker der Kinder- und Jugendliteratur*, edited by Bettina Hurrelmann,
502–519. Frankfurt: Fischer, 1997. Print.

Knöpke-Jost, Helga. *Ulla, ein Hitlermädel.* Leipzig: Schneider, 1933. Print.

Koppe, Susanne. *Kurt Kläber – Kurt Held: Biographie der Widersprüche? Zum 100.
Geburtstag des Autors der "Roten Zora."* Aarau, Switzerland: Sauerländer, 1997. Print.

Kreis, Gabriele. *Frauen im Exil: Dichtung und Wirklichkeit.* Düsseldorf: Claasen, 1984. Print.

Kümmerling-Meibauer, Bettina. *Klassiker der Kinder- und Jugendliteratur: Ein internationales Lexikon.* Vol. 2, *H–P.* Stuttgart: Metzler, 2004. Print.

Möckel, Marga. *Hitlermädel kämpfen um Berlin: Eine Erzählung aus der Kampfzeit.* Stuttgart: Union Deutsche Verlags-Gesellschaft, ca. 1935.

Schmid-Bortenschlager, Sigrid, and Christa Gürtler. *Erfolg und Verfolgung: Oesterreichsche Schriftstellerinnen 1918–1945; Fünfzehn Porträts und Texte.* Salzburg: Residenz, 2002. Print.

Seeber, Ursula, ed. *Kleine Verbündete–Little Allies: Vertriebe oesterreichische Kinder- und Jugendliteratur.* Vienna: Picus, 1998. Print.

Sinhuber, Karin. "Adrienne Thomas." Master's thesis, University of Vienna, 1990. Print.

Stern, Guy. "Wirkung und Nachwirkung der antifaschistischen Jugendliteratur." In *"Wir tragen den Zettelkasten mit den Steckbriefen unserer Freunde": Acta-Band zum Symposion "Beitraege jüdischer Autoren zur deutschen Literatur seit 1945,"* edited by Jens Stüben and Winfried Woesler, 299–312. Darmstadt: Häusser Heinz-Jürgen, 1999. Print.

Tetzner, Lisa. *Die Kinder aus Nr. 67.* Vols. 1–2, *Erwin und Paul/Das Mädchen aus dem Vorderhaus.* 1933, 1948. Munich: Deutscher Taschenbuch, 1997.

———. *Die Kinder aus Nr. 67.* Vols. 3–4, *Erwin kommt nach Schweden/Das Schiff ohne Hafen.* 1941, 1943. Düsseldorf: Sauerländer, 2004.

———. *Die Kinder aus Nr. 67.* Vols. 5–6, *Die Kinder auf der Insel/Mirjam in Amerika.* 1944, 1945. Frankfurt: Sauerländer, 1989.

Thomas, Adrienne. *Andrea: Eine Erzählung von jungen Menschen.* Basel: Atrium, 1937. Print.

———. *Viktoria.* Basel: Atrium, 1938. Print.

Wall, Renate, ed. *Lexikon deutschsprachiger Schriftstellerinnen im Exil 1933 bis 1945.* Freiburg im Breisgau: Kore, 1995. Print.

Wilkending, Gisela, ed. *Kinder- und Jugendliteratur: Mädchenliteratur; Vom 18. Jahrhundert bis zum Zweiten Weltkrieg.* Stuttgart: Reclam, 1994. Print.

Different Tales and Different Lives

Children's Literature as Political Activism in Andhra Pradesh

NAOMI WOOD

In 1989, the United Nations approved the Convention on the Rights of the Child.[1] The convention defines childhood as a distinct status requiring moral and physical protection. According to the convention, children have a right not only to life, a name, and a nationality, but also to health care; adequate food, shelter, and clean water; and education, security, and freedom from exploitation. The convention states that children have the right to freedoms of expression, thought, conscience, religion, association, and access to mass media.[2] The UN's definition of childhood draws heavily on modern liberal thought. As Sharon Stephens explains, the original draft of the Declaration of the Rights of the Child, ratified in 1959, "was aimed at protecting and nurturing childhood, as defined by adults within the framework of Western modernity. It did not recognize that there might be cultural differences in what constitutes children's 'best interests,' or that children themselves might have something important to say about the nature of these interests" (35). Although the UN's 1989 convention addresses some concerns about cultural difference, the problems implicit in defining "the child" as an abstraction—a discrete individual, a member of a nuclear family, and a nationality—inadvertently erase or warp the self-understandings of the many children defined primarily by their ethnic group, caste, religious affiliation, or economic class.

So what does "childhood" mean in a country such as India? Well-received films such as *Slumdog Millionaire* (2008) and *Salaam Bombay* (1988) show India's children working in factories or on the streets, begging, and soliciting. The living conditions of these children reinforce in Western viewers "the colonial imagination of India as a country lacking a proper notion of childhood" and inspire would-be saviors to intervene through the UN, NGOs, and missionary initiatives (Nieuwenhuys 148). These groups may separate children from their families and communities to give them a higher standard of living and better educational prospects, thus pulling them out of the cycle of poverty.

Formerly colonized countries of the Global South such as India have a particularly fraught relation to Western-generated statements about universal rights. On the one hand, Indians reject colonial notions about their own benightedness and are eager to establish their credentials as economic and cultural equals in modern global society. On the other hand, many resist the dilution and compromise of traditional social values and structures. Childhood is a major area of contention, since children, as Anannya Bhattacharjee has written of women, are "inextricably linked to nationness" (20). Deepa Sreenivas and Deeptha Achar have observed: "From its very beginnings, children's literature has . . . assumed the responsibility of moulding a 'national child'" that represents the norm for others to copy. This ideal Indian child, often depicted on the educational charts sold in kiosks and distributed in schools, is male, Hindu, and hygienic (Rao, Geetha, and Wolf). Popular Indian children's writer Anushka Ravishankar depicts widely traveled children in confident rhymes. Kid-friendly movies feature lively children with all the technologies of the urban West, while the popular television show *Malgudi Days* (1987), based on the stories of R. K. Narayan, celebrates mischievous Swami's adventures—a veritable Tom Sawyer of preindependence southern India.[3]

Yet assertions of national identity exclude through definition, and many Indians recognize that the "one size fits all" definition of childhood derived from the UN reinforces the normative status of privileged children and fails, ironically, to help children from scheduled tribes and castes and religious minorities.[4] This essay shows that in India, the definition of childhood as a playful, innocent, and indulged state ignores or patronizes the many children whose fates are not so benign. This false picture of childhood is the legacy of colonialism and the colonial educational system, which continues to inform India's discourses of childhood and education. The definition institutionalizes structural and representational inequality that privileges the elite and disenfranchises those who do not "meet the standards." A first step in rectifying this situation is to critique this abstraction of the "ideal child" and instead depict the complex realities that belie his typicality. Feminist and Dalit[5] activists from Andhra Pradesh in south-central India have begun to dismantle these textual norms by commissioning and writing "Different

Tales" that recognize children's often complex status with regard to family, caste, school, work, and history. As noted by D. Vasanta, one of the project's initiators, the disjunction between the "ideal child" defined by the educational establishment and the actual children found in the seats of the school disables the very children who most need education (Vasanta 10–12). Low-caste, low-class Indian children do not see themselves as ideal children, with toxic consequences. The tales challenge normative childhood by resisting the temptation to depict underprivileged children as innocent or helpless victims, or as happily complicit in their oppression, instead showing children as rooted in their communities and capable of critical engagement with the material world.

Children, Education, and Literature: Ideal and Reality

Because representation in textbooks, fiction, and film is tacitly linked to political representation and agency, children's advocates have long promoted the inclusion of disadvantaged and/or minority children in educational and entertainment texts. In the United States, antiracist efforts began by identifying the problem—that an all-white, middle-class Protestant norm ignored the existence of minorities—then addressing the problem by encouraging the writing, publication, and celebration (through awards) of stories focusing on minority experience.[6] In India, representation of the child has been influenced by the legacy of British colonialism, the premises of the secular nation state, and the caste system. All three factors reify abstract notions of identity and thereby override the material and social conditions individuals encounter. They discourage critical thinking about the discrepancy between ideal and actual and promote what Marx would have called "false consciousness."

India's present government schools originated with the colonial British, who sought to train a native elite in the attitudes and values of the English rulers; in the words of Thomas Macaulay, "to form a class who may be interpreters between us and the millions whom we govern; a class of persons, Indian in blood and colour, but English in taste, in opinions, in morals, and in intellect" (430). As they replaced existing Indian educational institutions and practices with English ones, the British colonizers reinforced already existing social hierarchies, recognizing in the caste system an analogue for class distinctions at home. For the colonizers, Indian education served the same purpose as primary education did in England: to educate students to revere the values and epistemology of the upper classes that ruled them (Viswanathan 94–95).

Such an educational system did not advocate critical thinking; rather, it sought to indoctrinate students with the themes and tropes of an ideally English identity. Gauri Viswanathan shows how the texts selected for English instruction constructed the Englishman "as a symbol of free intellectual inquiry, religious noninterference . . . benign, disinterested, detached, impartial, and judicious" (99). Essay exam questions openly used English modes and customs as the norm: "On the internal marks of Falsehood in the Hindu Shastras"; "On the Physical Errors of Hinduism"; and "The Advantages India derives in regard to commerce, security of property, and the diffusion of knowledge, from its Connexion with England" (Viswanathan 102). As Viswanathan points out, abstraction overrode the concrete: "In a crude, parodic reworking of the Cartesian formula, production of thought defined the Englishman's true essence, overriding all other aspects of his identity—his personality, actions, behavior. His material reality as subjugator and alien ruler was dissolved. . . . [T]he blurring of the man and his works effectively removed him from history" (103).

This abstract universalism that ignored "often sordid history" (Viswanathan 103) continued to structure Indian curricula after independence. In his history of Indian education, Krishna Kumar notes that most state-sponsored primary education, implemented by low-status, poorly paid teachers restricted by their own limited education and autonomy, "removed what little possibility there might have existed in the curriculum of linking school knowledge with the child's everyday world" (15). School knowledge was "walled," as Kumar puts it, from the lived experience of the learners. Instead, school demanded memorization and rote repetition (14). In the early decades of the twentieth century, R. K. Narayan learned that "A was an Apple, B Bit it, C Cut it," and he understood the verbs, but no one could tell him what an apple was. The teacher speculated that it might be like *idli*, the favorite savory cake of southern Indian breakfasts (Mishra). The point of education was to memorize the "right" answer. According to Kumar, Indians educated in the English system became disconnected from their fellow Indians by design, becoming "enlightened outsiders" (14), disdainful of the masses and dismissive of indigenous knowledge. With no critical thinking taught in school, critical thinking about other aspects of civil society was also discouraged, Kumar charges.

Thus, the study of literature became another exercise in alienation from context and history, and English literature a preferred medium of class and national indoctrination (Viswanathan 94–95). For the aspiring Indian civil servant, knowledge of the English language was the only route to success, but it demanded ignoring the Indian context and the imperfections of actual Englishmen in favor of the idealized Englishness represented in schools' carefully selected literature. "[T]he English literary text functioned as a surrogate Englishman in his highest and most perfect state" (Viswanathan 103), discouraging criticism of the day-to-day administration of British India. Students were taught to ignore or accept contradiction rather than seeking to resolve or analyze it.

Opposing colonization of the mind was complicated, in the twentieth century, by the fact that no single program benefited all Indians. Elite Indians—often Brahmins—valorized ancient Indian Sanskrit texts to challenge European dismissal of native Indian philosophy. Others thought that technological progress provided the clearest route to independence and prosperity for India (K. Kumar 19). Historically marginal groups such as Dalits, or religious minorities such as Muslims and Christians, saw English education as an opportunity to redress caste-based injustice. Advocates such as Jyotirao Phule (1827–1890) and B. R. Ambedkar (1891–1956), with the encouragement of the English, seized upon English education "as a means of intellectual liberation from the tentacles of Brahminical mythology" (K. Kumar 103)—attacking one powerful ideal by means of another. However, the English curriculum was premised on a European liberal foundation that was insufficiently critiqued and adapted for an Indian context (K. Kumar 105), and thus, ironically, the school became an instrument that reinforced so-called backwardness rather than eradicating it (K. Kumar 109).[7] Krishna Kumar's account of the history of Indian education criticizes the failure of Indian schools to inculcate curiosity and a sense of civic responsibility because the goal has too often been to enforce order and submission to authority.

Indians continue to express reservations about the educational status quo and its focus on abstract learning and memorization as opposed to learning contextually and dynamically. The 2009 blockbuster film 3 Idiots,[8] set in India's (fictional) best college of engineering, critiques the pedagogy and exam practices that reward memorization rather than critical thinking and curiosity. Aamir Khan's character Rancho succeeds by being the most personally invested in learning, while his foil, the repellant and greedy sycophant Chatur, is interested only in how engineering can buy him the trappings of success. The film joyously advocates the familiar young adult theme of following one's passion (whether profession or life partner), although it remains true to its Indian roots by making parental reconciliation part of that process.

Indian parents recognize that education is important for their children's futures. The Indian Constitution of 1949 mandated free education for children through the age of fourteen, but government-run schools have not been successful in teaching children to read or indeed of even retaining students; India's literacy rates have lagged behind those of China and other Asian countries (Drèze 346). In this populous and diverse country with eighteen official languages and multiple scripts, literacy rates have been a continuing concern among government officials and for many parents. Despite increases in overall literacy confirmed by the 2011 census (up 9 points from 65 percent in 2001 to 74 percent), literacy is not universal (Chandramouli 98). Rates in individual states vary depending upon public investment in universal education, from a high in Kerala of 93.9 percent to a low in Bihar of only 63.8 percent. Moreover, gender discrepancies persist; female literacy is consistently lower than male (Chandramouli 126). Another, less visible disadvantage, given that the census does not track such records, is membership in the lower castes and other marginalized groups.

Government-run schools are frequently underfunded and understaffed and have limited resources. Textbooks are not written with the needs of a learner in mind—the chief mode of instruction is "copying and cramming" (PROBE 52)—and a dominant method of classroom management is beating. It is not surprising that many children cannot read even after attending school for several years (PROBE 48). Jean Drèze's 2001 description of the persistence and consequences of educational inequality in India has not been significantly outdated by new developments. Neither have attempts to open education to the private sector produced the desired results, as Ravi Kumar argues in *The Crisis of Elementary Education in India*. Contemporary movements to commodify education and deliver literacy at the cost of critical thinking, Kumar charges, fail to achieve "what [Rabindranath] Tagore[9] would have called 'freedom of the mind'" (34).

Government schools, moreover, are seen as part of the problem. In December 2011, Vikas Bajaj and Jim Yardley reported in the *New York Times* that "[i]n many states, government education is in severe disarray, with teachers often failing to show up. Rote drilling still predominates. English, considered a prerequisite for most white-collar employment in India, is usually not the medium of instruction." As Bajaj and Yardley recount, thousands of unregulated private schools have sprung up to respond to the demand for English instruction, but their approach is no less defined by the dominant model of rote teaching and memorization.

Further discouraging the children of Dalits, Muslims, and Adivasis from pursuing an education is their experience of discrimination in school. Researchers have observed "teachers refusing to touch low-caste children, children from particular castes being special targets of verbal abuse and physical punishment by the teachers, and low-caste children being frequently beaten by higher-caste classmates" (Drèze 352). Thus, even though education is a constitutional right of all Indians, educational and cultural factors discourage and even prevent many children of the scheduled castes and tribes from claiming that right.

Further, these children's identification with the project of schooling is discouraged by the dominant narratives of children's literature that define them—either by inclusion or exclusion—as abnormal, deprived, and marginal. Since the 1930s, Indian children's literature has reflected the concerns and values of a rising middle class establishing itself in relation to the rest of the world, especially Europe and America. Satadru Sen's study of Bengali literary childhood in the 1920s and 1930s shows how the Indian child was defined as modern and urban, with roots perhaps in the country but with a cosmopolitan orientation to the world similar to his (or sometimes her) peers in England and Europe (3). These trends have persisted in Indian children's literature. Literate Indians from dominant castes and classes have imbibed normative European notions of childhood and read Enid Blyton and J. K. Rowling. Budget-conscious publishers may be reluctant to produce contemporary fiction for children, arguing that parents are more eager to purchase informational books or retellings of traditional Indian myths and legends (Ramendra Kumar). Meena Khorana noted this tendency in the early 1990s, and it has continued to be an issue as texts that children demonstrably wanted to read were subordinated to those deemed more suitable because of their educational or religious value (Khorana xviii).

Even when India's marginalized children are represented in children's literature, their role is as foil to the wealthy child, as recipient of charity or other intervention to "save" them from their surroundings, depicting their interpolation into dominant society in terms of the values and norms that define them as Other and Abnormal. Some well-meaning texts attempt to evoke sympathy in the reader with the situation of the Othered child. In "Telling Different Tales: Possible Childhoods in Children's Literature," Deepa Sreenivas instances *Kali and the Rat Snake* (by Zai Whitaker, 2000), which tells of Kali, an Irula (tribal) boy from Tamil Nadu. The Irula traditionally are forest people, and Kali's father is a snake catcher. When the children in his schoolroom learn of his father's occupation, they ridicule him—until a snake invades their class, and Kali is able to catch it. "In that moment," recounts Sreenivas, "he becomes a hero in the eyes of his class-mates" (318). Yet this attempt to teach middle-class readers to value and accept an Other child mandates that Kali be separated from his own context (of the tribe, in the forest) and, in Sreenivas's words, be redefined as a liberal abstraction: the individual, a hero. He is represented, in other words, using the definitions of the class and culture that finds his existence as lacking because it is embedded in alien modes ("Telling" 318). The story exemplifies what Sims calls in the American context "socially conscious" multicultural literature; it "talks about" the minority child for the benefit of the majority. It does not recognize Kali's conflicts and challenges from within his own culture, and its resolution emphasizes acceptance by the majority not on his own terms, but on theirs. As Sreenivas points out, Kali's humiliation is not set "in the larger struggle of his family and community vis-à-vis unequal social relations and political marginalization" ("Telling" 319), and thus the solution to his acceptance is individualized and not related to the larger problem of social and cultural inequality: "In order to gain entry into the 'universal,' he needs to be abstracted from the concrete details of his exis-tence" ("Telling" 319). Thus, *Kali and the Rat Snake* recapitulates the larger problem of abstract normative discourses in education that privilege some children and alienate others and that fail to encourage recognition and understanding of social and economic realities. Children who share Kali's position as a culturally abjected Other are doubly excluded from represen-tation, both aesthetically and politically.

Children's Literature against the Grain

Worse, the knowledge of illiterate people was classified as ignorance: "None of the skills, crafts, arts and knowledge that the illiterate masses possessed could impress the educated Indian. . . . These forms of culture became sym-bols of ignorance and decadence and, as such, became irrelevant to educa-tion" (K. Kumar 15).

Krishna Kumar's critique of the reified content of education has been addressed by several recent initiatives in India. Since the early to mid-1990s, India's children's book publishing industry has burgeoned, with many presses, such as Tara Books (founded in Chennai, 1994), Pratham Books (founded in Mumbai, 1994), and Tulika Books (founded in Chennai, 1996), producing high-quality work with progressive or radical orientations. Rec-ognizing the importance of telling stories about many different kinds of children and rejecting the notion that children ought only to hear about happy or morally proper themes, these publishers see children's books as places to tell important—and traumatic—stories about the recent past, such as *Bhopal Gas Tragedy* by Suroopa Mukherjee (Tulika, 2002) and Sandhya Rao's *My Friend, the Sea* (Tulika, 2005), about the 2002 tsunami.

Activists such as Kancha Ilaiah[10] see children's education as a place to begin challenging ancient assumptions about value and work. In *Turning the Pot, Tilling the Land: Dignity of Labour in Our Times*, a nonfiction text, Ilaiah argues for the value and dignity of activities historically understood to be polluting and therefore beneath the dignity of the *varna* castes.[11] The book asserts parallels between sanitary workers and physicians (both deal with human waste and bodies); it shows that the lowly Dalit cobbler, disdained for his contact with animal hides, does the same work as a glamorous fashionista such as Manolo Blahnik; and it celebrates the chemical and agricultural discoveries made by dhobis (launderers) and Adivasis. Ilaiah attacks dismissive attitudes toward social inferiors and urges his readers, for example, never to use the dry toilets at railway stations because they are cleaned by hand by Dalit women who then are scorned for their service. With its focus on changing dominant groups' behavior, the book's implied audience is privileged. The book's zeal for correcting long-standing injustice is unmistakable, but its rhetoric nonetheless grates on implied readers and their opposites. It "talks about" marginal groups more than it "talks to" them, demanding that privileged readers change their behavior and their attitudes. While the book differs from the standard multicultural "politics of recognition" that merely "push[es] for the inclusion and acceptance of the subjugated culture's 'difference'" (Sreenivas, "Telling" 317), and while it does argue for structural social change and revaluation of so-called polluted activities, *Turning the Pot, Tilling the Land* still does not *speak to* the children whose condition and status it seeks to improve. Nevertheless, in its emphasis on Dalit and Adivasi intelligence and resourcefulness, it demonstrates why labor has its own epistemological integrity, history, and dignity.

The stories of *Different Tales* depict marginal children's lives, but without the sentimentality to which such depictions so often succumb. The *Different Tales* project invites children to understand themselves and their contexts in their own terms: telling stories of children's resourcefulness, initiative, and work; honoring their family and community lifestyles; and, finally, offering models for resistance. The project offers a model for other groups interested in children's literature and social justice. *Different Tales* comprise eight books containing thirteen stories each and are published in three languages (English, Telugu, and Malayalam). They are the brain-child of the Anveshi Research Centre for Women's Studies in Hyderabad, Andhra Pradesh. Founded in 1985, Anveshi is one of the foremost research centers for women's issues in India.[12] Among its many projects has been the study of the hegemonic function of children's textbooks. After assessing the books available to children in India and observing the alienating effects of conventional children's literature on young readers, chief editor of the series Deepa Sreenivas[13] and the Anveshi group have produced a series of beautiful books that tell other stories of childhood. Called *Different Tales*, the "series brings together stories from regional languages that talk about the life-worlds of children in communities that one rarely reads about in children's books" (Anveshi, "Anveshi Launches"). Individuals from Dalit, Muslim, and tribal groups wrote the stories, which were then illustrated by established and emerging artists from one of the premier art colleges of the country, Maharajah Sayajirao University of Baroda. The results are beautiful and provocative.

"History Doesn't Like Me!" Redefining and Revaluing the Normal

Anveshi's *Different Tales* project challenges the norms of Indian children's literature by reflecting Dalit, Muslim, and other marginalized children's re-alities and dreams without succumbing to the narratives of horrified pity that simply reverse and thereby reinforce them. The stories reflect the nega-tive and positive experiences of children with reference to *their* lives and aspirations rather than those of their more privileged compatriots. The text and especially the pictures convey respect for the children's distinctive ex-perience, and appreciation for the beauty as well as the challenges of their lives.

The individual stories of *Different Tales* are written by South Indians. Children of Madigas (Dalit leatherworkers), Malas (Dalit farmers), Mus-lims, and Christians are pictured in expressive and varied media that complement the stories. The *Different Tales* project represents these chil-dren's experiences without caveats. Some stories defy the conventions that insist childhood is happy and untroubled, that the best refuge for children is school, that all problems are psychological or micromanageable. Other stories acknowledge that children of Dalits and Muslims may experience social shaming and rejection based on their meat-eating diet and hereditary occupations; in school, their role in history may be elided and their poverty may be preemptively justified. Although not all these *Different Tales* have conventionally happy endings, all defy the narratives that normalize upper-caste experience and ignore, demean, or sentimentalize the rest.

As education researchers and memoirs attest, school is frequently an anxious place for children of Dalits and Muslims. The *Different Tales* depict exclusion and bias while affirming the marginalized groups' critical consciousness and their value. In Nuaiman's "Textbook," Saheer finds no Muslim names in the children's stories his class is given to read. Controverting the tradition that the textbook is always right, Saheer adds a Muslim name to his list of characters, risking a beating from the teacher for being incorrect. In Shefali Jha's "My Friend, the Emperor," Adil, the lone Muslim in his class, feels awkward when Jessy Teacher looks at him as she recounts the story of the battle between the first Mughal (Muslim) emperor, Babur, and the Rajput (Hindu) King Rana. "[T]he way she had told that story, each one of them had wanted the old Rajput king to win" (n.p.). To his father's query about why he doesn't like history, Adil counters, "history doesn't like me!" With the help of his father, Adil learns to relish the heroism of Babur, who triumphed against overwhelming odds. Babur himself manifests to teach Adil about the importance of a long perspective. The emperor challenges history's reductive binaries and asks subversive questions about heroism: "You mustn't worry about who was braver. Why must one be braver, more courageous, better than the other? The best battles are those where you cannot answer that question! It's a stupid question, really. One side won, the other lost, and so many things happened after that. Hundreds of years, people, events—history! And still we ask, who was braver? We should ask—why does it matter?" (n.p.).

Different Tales counters the abusive treatment of Dalits in two ways. First, stories depict discrimination to question it. Sara Joseph, also known for her subversive retelling of the Ramayana, wrote "Smells and Stenches," in which the protagonist Anni is publically ridiculed by her sweet-smelling teacher. The teacher assumes that Anni is dirty because of her status, even though she is very careful to clean herself with all the resources she has: water, harsh soap, tooth powder made from burnt rice husks, and neem twigs. The illustrations by Koonal Duggal depict Anni's many and varied efforts to be clean; she is depicted as white even though brown dung-like smudges obscure her classmates and teachers.

But Anni's story does not end happily; humiliated by her teacher's insults and smarting from arbitrary beatings, she runs home hungry with her

9.1. From "Smells and Stenches," in *The Two Named Boy and Other Stories*, written by Sara Joseph and illustrated by Koonal Duggal (Kottayam, Kerala: DC Books, 2008).

empty lunch plate. Although her actions demonstrate the falseness of her teacher's belief that she is dirty and that "all the kids from Kokanchira are greedy," alas, Anni is overwhelmed in the illustration by the dirt as she runs, brown smudges obscuring her clean face and body. The pictures indicate what the text does not openly state: that cultural definitions are more responsible for sullying Anni than any failure on her part or neglect by her family.

Joopaka Subhadra's "Friends in School" depicts Sreelatha and Suvarna. The tinted black-and-white photographs by Saumya Ananthakrishna underscore the girls' mutual love in the way their bodies, clothing, and red accents mirror each other. However, Sreelatha is a Madiga,[14] and when Suvarna's mother discovers that her daughter has lent Sreelatha a brand-new dress, she violently insists that her daughter burn it. Without resolving the conflict, the story concludes with Suvarna's refusal. The text says that she is running to her friend's house carrying the kerosene-soaked uniform, but the illustration suggests a larger repudiation of such prejudice, as an open-armed Suvarna runs beyond the borders of the white page, defying its boundaries just as her actions in the story have defied caste barriers.

The second way the tales challenge discrimination against Dalits is by redefining polluting activities as normal and valuable, amplifying through fiction and illustration what Kancha Ilaiah does with nonfiction. Rashmi Mala's gorgeous illustrations of Gogu Shyamala's story "Braveheart Badeyya"

9.2. From "Friends in School," in *Untold School Stories*, written by Joopaka Subhadra and illustrated by Saumya Ananthakrishna (Kottayam, Kerala: DC Books, 2008).

transform the despised emblems of the leatherworkers into valuable and life-affirming symbols. Badeyya is introduced in his disadvantaged place at school, set in the back, away from the other scholars and shunned because of his association with dead cattle. In Mala's illustration, all the students are contained by the outline of a cow, but Badeyya is positioned near the cow's anus, metonymically signifying his status at school.

However in this story, the bones, hides, and animal waste so crucial to survival and productivity are rendered textually and visually as toys, protection, and tools; Badeyya uses a "bone cart" to collect the dung that fertilizes the fields, and the bones also serve as toys.[15] In a culminating demonstration of leather's importance and the value of leatherworking, Badeyya intervenes to help his mother. She has been forced to remove her shoes to honor a man of a higher caste, and a dog then eats them, causing her feet to become pierced by sharp thorns as she subsequently walks barefoot. Mala's illustration aptly conveys the frustration, pain, and anger mother and son experience by exaggerating the size of the sharp thorns against a vivid red background, one of the most striking images in the series.

But a blue-lit Badeyya sits up all night to make his mother a new pair of shoes. Her injured feet now protected with strong leather shoes, the story

9.3. From "Braveheart Badeyya," in *Tataki Wins Again and Braveheart Badeyya*, written by Gogu Shyamala and illustrated by Rashmi Mala (Kottayam, Kerala: DC Books, 2008).

ends with Badeyya's mother praising him to the entire village: "You have done such a wonderful job!" Badeyya's "brave heart" is expressed not in violent confrontation in the manner of Mel Gibson fighting the armies of Edward Longshanks, but in the Gandhian spirit of *ahimsa* (nonviolence), resisting oppression with love and attention to his mother's needs. Noteworthy as well is the validation given to a child's productive work—Badeyya's skill with leatherworking is crucial to the psychological and physical support he gives his mother. The validation of work over school experience is deliberate, given the pervasive devaluing of children's work contributions to their family's welfare and the fact that Dalit children's school time is too frequently unhappy.

In another flouting of taboo, *Head Curry*, by Mohammed Khadeer Babu, describes meat eating as normal and pleasurable—a shocking sentiment in the highly vegetarian context of Hindu India where "veg" is the default buffet option as opposed to "non-veg." The dominant red tones of Gulammohammed Sheikh's rich illustrations convey, in Susie Tharu's words,

9.4. From "Braveheart Badeyya," in *Tataki Wins Again and Braveheart Badeyya*, written by Gogu Shyamala and illustrated by Rashmi Mala (Kottayam, Kerala: DC Books, 2008).

"anxieties about blood and the fraught status of meat" (284), but they also suggest warmth and plenitude. Sheikh's illustrations depict Khadeer's family and community by cutting one wall away from the buildings, showing daily activities alongside the special preparations for head curry. The strategy allows glimpses into a coherent religious and cultural community, depicting children in their contexts of family and neighborhood rather than isolating them as abnormal objects to be rendered in terms of outsiders' norms. The story, in the words of reviewer Shirly Mary Joseph, raises new possibilities for breaking down the boundaries of conventional thought. Joseph writes: "The boy's walk home with the ram's head-piece and legs in the wire basket 'making a pattern with the water dripping from the freshly cut meat pieces on the road,' is my favorite image in the story. Talk about tracing new trails! If only one such story were included in my school textbooks! All those questions (and the expected answers) for our exams wouldn't have been so blandly vegetarian." Joseph's link between dominant vegetarianism and blandness, the tacit rigidity requiring the "right answer," confirms that what

In the village the *mala* and *madiga* women giggled through their pallus as they shared the news. "The landlord wanted to catch our Balamani. She kicked him in the groin!"

9.5. From "Tataki Wins Again," in *Tataki Wins Again and Braveheart Badeyya*, written by Gogu Shyamala and illustrated by Puja Vaish (Kottayam, Kerala: DC Books, 2008).

many desire is acknowledgment of the messy yet piquant variety of their lives and experiences.

From a Western perspective, one of the most radical projects of *Different Tales* is to reexamine the role of work, both paid and unpaid, in these children's lives. As D. Vasanta writes, children's work is not always disempowering, nor is school invariably a "benign" and better place for children (5). In "Tataki Wins Again," Gogu Shyamala recounts the story of Balamma, an eleven-year-old girl, based on her recollection of her own oldest sister. Shyamala, who was the one child in her family chosen to attend school, "recalls with feeling that she was the one from her family who tired of carrying a heavy load under the hard sun before anyone else. . . . Her sister, on the other hand, could work in the fields with a rare stamina and involvement. . . . [After m]any years and an extremely difficult journey through school and college as a dalit girl/woman . . . she pays tribute to the sister and the family and the community that are the absent Others in the mainstream discourses of childhood" (Sreenivas, "Forging" 272). Balamma is a hard worker who gets up early to irrigate her family's fields. At play, Balamma scares up a rabbit and catches it to add valued calories, nutrition, and variety to her family's diet. In the last episode, the *karnam*, a higher-caste

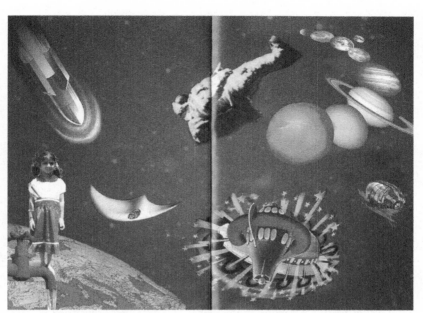

9.6. From "Shaija's Space," in *The Two Named Boy and Other Stories*, written by S. Sanjeev and illustrated by Lavanya Mani (Kottayam, Kerala: DC Books, 2008).

landlord, objects to her diligence and effective labor, chastises her for using too much water, and threatens her with rape. However, Balamma prevails: "In the village the *mala* and *madiga* women giggled through their pallus as they shared the news, 'The landlord wanted to catch our Balamani. She kicked him in the groin!'" The illustration shows a wall of strong women who, complementing their verbal description, look ready to invite Balamma into their midst as an equally strong woman, a contributor to the community good.

It is fitting that Balamma embraces her demonic label; to be called "Tataki," a she-demon "of colossal strength from Ramayana" who opposes the Hindu pantheon, is no insult. As Sreenivas writes, "In the mythologies of the upper caste, Tataki is an excessive sign—both in terms of her bodily size and in her non-recognition of territorial limits" ("Forging" 273). Rather than internalizing the pejorative and degrading connotations of the name, Balamma critically reframes the discourse that marginalizes her, instead confirming her power to resist.

Finally, *Different Tales* challenges normative discourses by considering children worthy of art that goes beyond simpleminded realism (itself another mode of idealism). Artists, like the writers, were encouraged to critique conventional children's picture books and think about what those norms convey: "The artists looked at a wide range of illustrations, both from India and abroad, to try and understand the manner in which illustrations reinforced stereotypes and normativity. Much of the dialogue centred on the question of visual language and its relationship to the norm. For instance, artists looked at the choices in play in the ways in which African-American bodies had been represented, the visual language involved, the manner in which skin colour was rendered and so on" (Sreenivas and Achar). Foregoing conventional heroism (in the style of socialist realism) or images of abjection, the artists capture something distinctive about each story and vividly render emotional as well as physical truths. In "Shaija's Space," Lavanya Mani's collages gloriously render the multiple meanings of Shaija's story. A little girl patiently queuing for her turn to fill her plastic jug with water for the family, Shaija nonetheless thinks in terms much larger than the space society has allotted her.

Mani's illustrations show Shaija's sense of space expanding with her thoughts—going out all the way to the solar system, peopling it and imagining other worlds. Drawing the reader in, such pictures reward study and critical thought through medium, color, and design. Their range—from the pencil drawings of Chinnan for "My Friend, the Emperor" to the photography of Saumya Ananthakrishna in "Friends in School" to the collages of Lavanya Mani in "Shaija's Space," all connect with the tales in distinctive and thoughtful ways.

Conclusion

The editors of Tulika Books write that children's books can "bring together the exterior and interior in different proportions, to present, through texts in different languages and pictures, the many realities lived and imagined in different corners of India and, gradually, the world" (Menon and Rao 18). For Western readers interested in positive intervention in children's lives, *Different Tales* reveals new aspects of the overexposed but undercomprehended lives of India's Other children. The Anveshi Centre has succeeded in producing meaningful and attractive books. The stories speak emphatically and empathetically to their intended audience of nine- to thirteen-year-old government-school students. But they also reach others, communicating these children's challenges and triumphs through mesmerizing images and remarkable stories. The stories see the children not as pathetic victims but as strong and resourceful agents in the context of their communities. The books demand that outsiders revise their impressions of the impoverished children they may see on the streets, who might, like Shaija, be imagining a place in history, time, and space. The space allotted by the series to imagination and beauty despite poverty and pain is thus one of its most powerful tools. Even as the stories tell true tales of sorrow, pain, and daily frustration and, in the words of American Mildred Taylor, of the difficulties of maintaining "human pride and survival in a cruelly racist society," they still celebrate "small and often dangerous triumphs" (Taylor 404). Taking risks to go beyond the school texts, challenging their own exclusion, redefining and revaluing work, *Different Tales* shows children willing to see what is not seen, say what is not said, and acknowledge the lives they actually live rather than the fantasies outsiders construct about them.

NOTES

1. India ratified the convention, with some provisos, in 1991. India's statement: "While fully subscribing to the objectives and purposes of the Convention, realising that certain of the rights of child, namely those pertaining to the economic, social and cultural rights can only be progressively implemented in the developing countries, subject to the extent of available resources and within the framework of international co-operation; recognising that the child has to be protected from exploitation of all forms including economic exploitation; noting that for several reasons children of different ages do work in India; having prescribed minimum ages for employment in hazardous occupations and in certain other areas; having made regulatory provisions regarding hours and conditions of employment; and being aware that it is not practical immediately to prescribe minimum ages for admission to each and every area of employment in India—the Government of India undertakes to take measures to progressively implement the provisions of article 32, particularly paragraph 2(a), in accordance with its national legislation and relevant international instruments to which it is a State Party" (UN General Assembly 3).

2. The United States has yet to ratify the convention in part because of these assertions of children's autonomy.

3. A better comparison is probably Rudyard Kipling's Stalky (from *Stalky & Co.*, 1899), because Narayan read Kipling. Stalky, like Tom Sawyer and Swaminathan, is a "good bad boy."

4. Scheduled castes and tribes or "backward castes" denote the low-caste groups formerly known as Untouchables. Minorities include Adivasis or tribals, Muslims, and Christians. Adivasis are the aboriginal people of India, displaced and marginalized by multiple invasions over the millennia; they are defined by the Indian Constitution as "Scheduled Tribes."

5. Formerly "Untouchables," called by Mahatma Gandhi "Harijans" or "Children of God," Dalits are the lowest castes of India, who historically have done the "polluting"

labor—working with waste, animal carcasses, dung, and the like. Along with Adivasis (see note 4), they are "scheduled" for special affirmative action policies by the Indian Constitution, although most continue to be excluded from the benefits of India's economic boom. For more, see Kurian.

6. Rudine Sims's *Shadow and Substance* has developed a useful classification system for evaluating the effectiveness of such efforts: socially conscious, melting-pot, and culturally conscious texts, so named for their attitude toward the implied reader of the text, from most distant from the minority child to closest to the minority being depicted. She recommends that minority children be "spoken to" rather than "spoken of," as subjects rather than objects, and that they be represented as part of a larger community; texts that do this she calls "culturally conscious" fiction, fiction that represents minority children as subject rather than object of the story's plot.

7. Deepa Sreenivas, like Kumar, sees unquestioning adherence to abstract liberal ideals of the individual harming aspiring Dalit children by implicitly and explicitly dividing them from crucial community support ("Forging" 276).

8. Based on the novel *Five Point Someone* by Chetan Bhagat (2004).

9. Rabindranath Tagore (1861–1941) was a pioneering educator, poet, and philosopher, and India's first Nobel laureate.

10. As of this writing, Kancha Ilaiah is professor and chair of political science at Osmania University in Hyderabad, Andhra Pradesh, and author of *Why I Am Not a Hindu* (1996) among other texts.

11. "According to the Rig Veda, . . . progenitors of the four ranked *varna* groups sprang from various parts of the body of the primordial man. . . . Brahmans, or priests, were created from the mouth. . . . Kshatriyas, warriors and rulers, were derived from the arms. . . . Vaishyas—landowners and merchants—sprang from the thighs. . . . Shudras—artisans and servants—came from the feet" (Jacobson).

12. Anveshi's academic activism has six areas of concern: education; health and health care systems; law and critical legal theory; Dalits and minorities; development; and public domain (Anveshi, homepage). Its library contains a large collection of women's and children's literature and serves as a resource for researchers interested in women's and children's issues in India and elsewhere. It publishes position papers in national journals and distributes them as pamphlets.

13. Deepa Sreenivas, a fellow at Anveshi, earned her Ph.D. at the English and Foreign Languages University, Hyderabad.

14. Madigas (a Dalit subcaste or *jati*) work with animal hides and leather, and are considered "polluted" by many higher-caste Hindus.

15. Kancha Ilaiah similarly redefines the Madigas' knowledge of working with and processing hides as scientific (see above, p. 177).

WORKS CITED

Anveshi Research Centre for Women's Studies. "Anveshi Launches 'Different Tales': A Series of Children's Books." Accessed May 29, 2010. Website.

————. Homepage. Accessed May 29, 2010. Website.

Babu, Mohammed Khadeer. *Head Curry.* Illustrated by Gulammohammed Sheikh. Kottayam, Kerala: DC Books, 2008. Print.

Bajaj, Vikas, and Jim Yardley. "Many of India's Poor Turn to Private Schools." *New York Times,* December 31, 2011. Accessed January 11, 2012. Website.

Bhattacharjee, Anannya. "The Habit of Ex-Nomination: Nation, Woman, and the Indian Immigrant Bourgeoisie." *Public Culture* 5:1 (Fall 1992): 19–44. Print.

Chandramouli, C. "Chapter 6: Status of Literacy." *Provisional Population Totals, Paper 1 of 2011 India.* Series 1, *Census of India,* 97–136. New Delhi: Office of the Registrar General and Census Commissioner, 2011. Accessed January 31, 2012. Website.

Different Tales. Series Editor, Deepa Sreenivas. Kottayam, Kerala: DC Books, 2008. Print.

Drèze, Jean. "Patterns of Literacy and Their Social Context." In *Handbook of Indian Sociology,* edited by Veena Das, 345–361. New Delhi: Oxford University Press, 2004. Print.

Ilaiah, Kancha. *Turning the Pot, Tilling the Land: Dignity of Labour in Our Times.* Pondicherry: Navayana Publishing, 2007. Print.

Jacobson, Doranne. "India: Social Systems; Class and Caste." In *India: A Country Study,* edited by James Heitzman and Robert L. Worden. Washington, D.C.: Federal Research Division, Library of Congress, 1995. Accessed May 23, 2010. Website.

Jha, Shefali. "My Friend, the Emperor." Illustrated by Chinnan. In *Spirits from History.* Kottayam, Kerala: DC Books, 2008. Print.

Joseph, Sara. "Smells and Stenches." Illustrated by Koonal Duggal. In *The Two Named Boy and Other Stories.* Kottayam, Kerala: DC Books, 2008. Print.

Joseph, Shirly Mary. "Different Tales: Review." Anveshi Research Centre for Women's Studies, August 16, 2009. Accessed April 19, 2012. Website.

Khorana, Meena. *The Indian Subcontinent in Literature for Children and Young Adults: An Annotated Bibliography of English-Language Books.* Westport, Conn.: Greenwood Press, 1991. Print.

Kumar, Krishna. *Political Agenda of Indian Education: A Study of Colonialist and Nationalist Ideas.* New Delhi: Sage Publications, 1991. Print.

Kumar, Ramendra. "Children's Writing in India: A Catch-22 Scenario." Desicritics.org, April 5, 2010. Accessed April 6, 2010. Website.

Kumar, Ravi, ed. *The Crisis of Elementary Education in India.* New Delhi: Sage Publications, 2006. Print.

Kurian, N. J. "Widening Economic and Social Disparities: Implications for India." *Indian Journal of Medical Research* 126:4 (2007): 374–380. Print.

Macaulay, Thomas. "Minute on Indian Education." 1835. Reprinted in *The Post-Colonial Studies Reader,* edited by Bill Ashcroft, Gareth Griffiths, and Helen Tiffin, 428–430. London: Routledge, 1995. Print.

Menon, Radhika, and Sandhya Rao. "The Culture and Politics of Stereotyping in Children's Books." *Wasafiri* 24:4 (2009): 16–22. Print.

Mishra, Pankaj. "The Great Narayan." *New York Review of Books,* February 22, 2001. Accessed January 3, 2013. Website.

Nieuwenhuys, Olga. "Is There an Indian Childhood?" *Childhood* 16 (2009): 147–153. Print.

Nuaiman. "Textbook." Illustrated by Chithra K. S. In *Untold School Stories*. Kottayam, Kerala: DC Books, 2008. Print.

PROBE. *Public Report on Basic Education in India*. New Delhi: Oxford University Press, 1999. Print.

Rao, Sirish, V. Geetha, and Gita Wolf. *An Ideal Boy: Charts from India*. London: Dewi Lewis Publishing; Chennai: Tara Books, 2001. Print.

Sanjeev, S. "Shaija's Space." Illustrated by Lavanya Mani. In *The Two Named Boy and Other Stories*. Kottayam, Kerala: DC Books, 2008. Print.

Sen, Satadru. "A Juvenile Periphery: The Geographies of Literary Childhood in Colonial Bengal." *Journal of Colonialism and Colonial History* 5:1 (2004), n.p. Project Muse. Accessed April 6, 2010. Website.

Shyamala, Gogu. *Tataki Wins Again and Braveheart Badeyya*. Illustrated by Puja Vaish and Rashmi Mala. Kottayam, Kerala: DC Books, 2008. Print.

Sims, Rudine. *Shadow and Substance: Afro-American Experience in Contemporary Children's Fiction*. Urbana, Ill.: National Council of Teachers of English, 1982. Print.

Sreenivas, Deepa. "Forging New Communities: Gendered Childhood through the Lens of Caste." *Feminist Theory* 11:3 (2010): 267–281. Print.

———. "Telling Different Tales: Possible Childhoods in Children's Literature." *Childhood: A Journal of Global Child Research* 18:3 (2011): 316–332. Accessed May 5, 2012. Website.

Sreenivas, Deepa, and Deeptha Achar. "Beyond the 'National Child.'" *Himal Southasian*, May 2010. Accessed May 5, 2012. Website.

Srinivasulu, K. "Caste, Class and Social Articulation in Andhra Pradesh: Mapping Differential Regional Trajectories." Working Paper 179. London: Overseas Development Institute, 2002. Accessed May 5, 2012. Website.

Stephens, Sharon. "Children and the Politics of Culture in 'Late Capitalism.'" In *Children and the Politics of Culture*, edited by Sharon Stephens, 3–48. Princeton: Princeton University Press, 1995. Print.

Subhadra, Joopaka. "Friends in School." Illustrated by Saumya Ananthakrishna. In *Untold School Stories*. Kottayam, Kerala: DC Books, 2008. Print.

Taylor, Mildred. "Newbery Award Acceptance." *Horn Book Magazine* (August 1977): 401–409. Print.

Tharu, Susie. "'Different Tales' for Children." *Contemporary Education Dialogue* 6:2 (Spring 2009): 279–284. Print.

UN General Assembly. Convention on the Rights of the Child. United Nations, November 20, 1989, Treaty Series, vol. 1577. At http://www.unhcr.org/refworld/docid/3ae6b38fo.html. Accessed March 1, 2012. Website.

Vasanta, D. "Childhood, Work and Schooling: Some Reflections." *Contemporary Education Dialogue* 2:1 (Monsoon 2004), 5–29. Print.

Viswanathan, Gauri. "Currying Favor: The Politics of British Educational and Cultural Policy in India, 1813–1854." *Social Text* 19-20 (Autumn 1988): 85–104. Print.

A Multicultural History of Children's Films

IAN WOJCIK-ANDREWS

Toward a Definition of Multicultural Children's Films

In his book *Multicultural Literature for Children and Young Adults,*
Mingshui Cai comments on the difficulties involved in producing a
"category of books" (xiii) called multicultural children's literature. His
comments are relevant to this essay, especially as at least one or more of the
films discussed might not typically be defined as multicultural, let alone
appropriate for children. Before proceeding, therefore, it is appropriate to
spend a few moments on the question of definition. You can't write a history
of a topic that you can't define. And when questions of children's material
culture and cultural hegemony are involved, the tendency is to simplify matters of race, class, and gender and their relation to history by assigning, in
this instance films for young people, to preexisting narratives of ownership
constructed around questionable, contradictory positions on nationalism:
Aladdin (1992) is American? *Children of Heaven* (1997) is Iranian? Neither is
multicultural? Like Alice tumbling down the rabbit hole asking "Who in the
world am I?" and answering, "I'm sure I'm not Ada ... and I'm sure I can't be
Mabel" (Carroll 37), a discussion about the issues and parameters involved
in defining a multicultural children's film is relevant at this juncture, even if
we define what it is not! What is a multicultural children's film?—"Ah, that's
the great puzzle!" (37).

To return to Cai's comments: one obvious way of interrogating simplis-
tic, binary approaches to questions of definition is to look at how similar,
frequently contentious but always vigorous debates informed the historical
development of multicultural children's literature. These days, the latter is

broadly defined as texts for young readers that focus on culturally diverse, typically underrepresented groups in American-produced children's litera- ture such as African Americans, Asian Americans, the elderly, the disabled, and religious and regional communities.[1] If we simply copy this definition, then set aside momentarily questions of commodity production, sovereign- ty, hegemony, and the like, a tentative list of multicultural children's (and young adult) films that might fit more or less neatly into our category would include in no particular order *Up* (age), *Pocahontas* (Native American In- dian), *Ponyo* (Asian American), *Akeelah and the Bee* (African American), and *The Karate Kid* (Chinese American).

But perhaps this list is a little too neat, a little too tidy! Websites like www.journeysinfilm.org argue that films from around the world such as *Children of Heaven* (Iran, 1997) and *Whale Rider* (New Zealand, 2002) should be used in American schools to prepare otherwise culturally insular American kids for twenty-first-century living, a life of globality, hybrid- ity, polycentrism. Any discussion of multicultural children's film therefore should talk about films produced in the United States for a domestic audi- ence as well those from abroad. Indeed, what about Vittorio De Sica's 1948 *The Bicycle Thief* (Italy), Jean Cocteau's 1946 *Beauty and the Beast* (France), or René Clément's 1952 *Forbidden Games* (France), European film classics that star mostly forgotten child actors but are nonetheless entirely appro- priate for young viewers of any nationality and culture? Some of the films mentioned above are filmic adaptations of literary works. However, while we might think of Disney's *Pocahontas* (1995) or *Aladdin* (1992) as adapta- tions and age-appropriate multicultural viewing for children, the historical distortions, the imperialist and hegemonic assumptions about culture, and the sheer ethnocentrism present in them and in Disney movies in general suggest that they are precisely the kind of multicultural children's films young viewers should not see!

"Who am I then?" (Carroll 39), a slightly distraught, frustrated Alice asks herself in the Pool of Tears. We might ask a similar question about multicultural children's films. Should Louis Malle's *Au Revoir, Les Enfants* (1987) be identified as a multicultural children's film or a French film whose focus happens to be childhood? What about Lasse Hallström's quirky, in- dependent *My Life as a Dog* (1985) from Sweden? Presumably films such as George Stevens's *The Diary of Anne Frank* (1959), Yurek Bogayevicz's *Edges of the Lord* (2001), and Mark Herman's *The Boy in the Striped Pa- jamas* (2008) require their own Jewish American children's film history. Are American multicultural children's films such as *Our Gang* (1922), *The*

Karate Kid (2010), and *The Princess and the Frog* (2009) less authentic than Iranian films such as the award-winning *Children of Heaven* (1997), or *Osama* (2003) from Afghanistan, or is authenticity really just a question of marketing, of production and postproduction values and strategies? If *Children of Heaven, Osama,* and *Turtles Can Fly* (2004) become more commercially and critically successful than they already are, does that make them less authentic than American multicultural children's films like the family-friendly *Because of Winn-Dixie* (2005), as culturally neutral and generic a multicultural film for the young that one is likely to find (Cai 24)? There is, of course, the issue of cultural difference, of what constitutes childhood in different societies. About the real, war-ravaged children in his film *Turtles Can Fly* (2003), Kurdish director Bahman Ghobadi writes: "[T]he children of Kurdistan are not children. They do not act like children in the West because they do not have the luxury of having that time to be children. They act like they are thirty or forty years old" (qtd. in Garcia 1). Having lived through and survived a range of horrendous experiences, many children around the world are grown up, hence Robin Wood's reflection that American films are in fact frequently childish (163). Finally, some critics proclaim that all children's literature is multicultural (Cai 11).[2] Perhaps all films starring children are multicultural, although most likely parents would not want their kids watching *Kids*!

At this point we have traveled far enough down the rabbit hole where there is an uncomfortable parallel between the guests at the Mad Hatter's tea party squabbling over a riddle and academic critics fighting over a definition. Given the incredible range and diversity of films, genres, styles, periods, and eras, I would suggest the following: The phrase "multicultural children's films" is a working hypothesis, an umbrella term sheltering films from around the world starring children and young adults. Some silent-era films such as *Broken Blossoms* (1919) and *Our Gang* (1922) should be viewed retrospectively as relevant to a growing academic discipline of Asian American and African American children's cinema and film whose future development and growth requires acknowledging the way the trope of the child has been used in the past with regard to questions of race. At least that is one of the broad, historical arguments implied in this essay. Some films are complex meditations on childhood, the loss of innocence, and the brutality that exists in children's cultures around the world at any given historical moment. *A Time for Drunken Horses* (2000), *The Spirit of the Beehive* (1973), *Pan's Labyrinth* (2006), and *Grave of the Fireflies* (1988), as well as *Empire of the Sun* (1987), *Radio Flyer* (1992), and *The Boy in the*

Striped Pajamas (2008) might be relevant in this regard. As children frequently do to parents, the above films push the critics' buttons, challenging
them to step outside their intellectual box and reconsider what constitutes
the territory of children's visual culture. In totality, all constitute the discipline of children's cinema and film, and the emerging genre of multicultural
children's films that are similar yet in the end fundamentally different from
mainstream children's films.

With these issues in mind, this article addresses the relationship between
children's films, history, and critical theory. It looks at Western-produced,
profit-making movies such as *Broken Blossoms*, *The Karate Kid*, and *The
Princess and the Frog*. It argues that discussing the contributions of these
and other Asian American and African American films starring children
is crucial to the establishment of an authentically diverse multicultural history of children's cinema and film consistent with, but interrogative of, the
power and reach of global capitalism. Such a world history, to rework the
title of Ella Shohat and Robert Stam's *Unthinking Eurocentrism: Multiculturalism and the Media* (1994), "unthinks" Hollywood and revolves around
questions of race, class, gender, and age, reflecting the multiple differences
in children's media culture as it has developed from the silent era to the
twenty-first century. It combats the cultural stereotypes produced by Hollywood, whose tendency in films for young people is to assume as hegemonic
the normative values of white middle-class society. In this regard, Disney
is particularly egregious. Beyond the question of cultural stereotyping, the
various histories of multicultural children's films that exist reflect specific
class struggles and remind us of the power of children's films in their totality to effect social, cultural, and political global change, hence the importance of incorporating them into school curriculums where they might
offer students more accurate images of the East and Africa, of other nations
and peoples whose cultures have been plundered militarily and visually by
weapons and by the violence of the colonial gaze. In this context, this essay
examines the relationship between multicultural children's films, history,
and critical theory from a Marxist perspective, beginning with silent-era
films such as *Broken Blossoms*. Although we might not think of *Broken
Blossoms* typically as belonging to a multicultural children's film history, as
previously suggested the complex range of images of the child deployed by
the film makes it a useful, indeed appropriate starting point. At least we are
out of the Pool of Tears!

Marxist Theory, Postcolonial Studies, and Asian American Children's Films: *Broken Blossoms* to *The Karate Kid*

Any historical materialist discussion and understanding of children's film history from *Broken Blossoms* (1919) to *The Karate Kid* (2010) must start with the social, political, and cultural discrimination faced by Asian populations migrating to the United States in the late nineteenth century, the precarious economic conditions and class positions in which they suddenly found themselves, and the degree to which the alternating absence and presence of those discriminatory practices shaped films starring young actors from the silent era, from 1895 to 1927. From a classic Marxist point of view, life determines consciousness, rather than the Hegelian idea that consciousness determines life (Marx, *German Ideology* 23). If we give credence to Marx's materialist, determinist approach, then the violent, discriminatory legal and political ideologies (the superstructure) imposed on migrant Asian workers in late-nineteenth- and early-twentieth-century England, Australia, and America were clearly produced by the economic conditions (the base) specific to capitalism and its alliance with colonial rule at that historical juncture.

Kevin Brownlow reports: "The Chinese first came to America as servants aboard Spanish galleons" (320). More came when gold was discovered in California in the mid-nineteenth century, and they faced discrimination as a function of a range of social, cultural, and economic issues. White America, caught up at the time in the discourse of anti-Asian sentiment, saw oriental culture as "a confusion of severed heads, temple bells, and screaming mobs" (320). Unsurprisingly, white America was anxious about cheap, dispensable Chinese labor eliminating American jobs, although, in one of the many ironies of the nineteenth century, it was Chinese (and later Japanese) workers who helped build the transcontinental railroad. As a result of these economic anxieties and strange contradictions, race relations between Americans and Asians deteriorated. Brownlow argues that although *Broken Blossoms* is one of a few movies that treat Chinese characters with some sympathy, most, including *Broken Blossoms*, reflect white anxieties, fears, and contradictory attitudes to what was pejoratively known as the Yellow Peril. Thus, *Broken Blossoms* offers a glimpse into the ways in which colonial powers at the turn of the twentieth century used film to infantilize the other through the trope of the child.

Adapted from British writer Thomas Burke's *The Chink and the Child*, D. W. Griffith's *Broken Blossoms; or, The Yellow Man and the Girl* (1919), starring Lillian Gish as fifteen-year-old Lucy Burrows (Lucy is twelve in the original story), has Cheng Huan, a Chinese student priest, emigrate to London's Limehouse District to preach Buddhism to Europe's "warring nations" (Brownlow 324). Cheng, played in "yellowface" by Richard Barthelmess, encounters Lucy, who is physically and emotionally abused by her working-class father, Battling Burrows. Cheng develops a fatal attraction to her. Enraged when he discovers the interracial relationship, Battling beats Lucy to death. Stricken by grief when the tragedy is discovered, Cheng shoots Battling, takes Lucy's lifeless body back to his dingy room, and kills himself by committing hara-kiri. By the end, Cheng, referred to as the Yellow Man; Lucy, the beaten and abused girl; and Battling, the violent, pugilistic, working-class father described as a "gorilla of the London jungle," have all died: in reel wars, as in real wars.

Although *Broken Blossoms* sympathizes with Cheng in many ways—after all, his Buddhist teachings urge nonviolence and his brave but tragic death stands in marked contrast to Battling's cowardly beatings of his frail, childlike daughter—the movie nonetheless stands as a clear reflection of America's cultural insularity and economic xenophobia by constantly invoking the discourse of yellowface to belittle Cheng and make him as childlike as Lucy. In the imperial imaginary, both become what Donna Haraway describes as "perpetual children" (qtd. in Shohat and Stam 107).

Yellowface, like blackface, occurs according to Yayoi Lena Winfrey when "Caucasians [yellow] their skin with makeup and tightly [tape] their eyelids to appear Asian" (1). I would argue that yellowface might also be viewed structurally as the overall "propagation of racist Asian stereotypes and caricatures" such as the coolie, the model minority, the nonthreatening Oriental, the evil Dr. Fu Manchu Asian, the silly Asian sidekick, the China doll, the dragon lady, or the geisha girl (Yellowface!). In other words, yellowface functions as a mark, or trope, of racial discrimination on different levels. First, textually speaking, these cultural stereotypes are passed down to movie generations and audiences through what Shohat and Stam and others call "tropes of empire" whereby invading colonial powers perpetuate their illusions of superiority through a racist discourse within literature or film that includes language, body, humor, comic and dramatic situations, and mise-en-scènes. One such trope might be the tokenistic conflation of multiple Asian countries into one undifferentiated, homogeneous oriental group subsequently used to represent whatever specific Asian or Eastern culture, customs, and geographical settings are demanded by the film's plot, storyline, and themes. Second, white actors playing Asian roles literally and concretely deny work to Asian actors and actresses, one labor issue among many that clearly affected Asian and American relations at the turn of the twentieth century. Third, more broadly, yellowface denies audiences access to the specific Asian culture being presented within the narrative. Ironically a form of censorship, as yellowface most frequently occurs in Western democracies that supposedly celebrate artistic freedom but in reality only pay lip service to it, yellowface in fact reinforces the ideological notion of cultural gatekeepers patrolling the geographical and imaginative borders of a dominant nation and its citizens, permitting and refusing entry to undesirables in the name of national security, economic expediency, cultural purity, and other ideological state apparatuses such as church, school, and family. Put simply, the discourse of yellowface, allied with other discriminatory social practices and grounded in the politics of economic inequality and the class conflicts generated by competitive capitalism, produces and perpetuates racism on behalf of colonial powers.

In the opening credits, Cheng is announced as the Yellow Man, a slur repeated throughout the movie to constantly remind audiences precisely who Lucy is involved with and all the implications of that miscegenation. Next, the "skylarking" American sailors, behaving like spoiled children, are seen enjoying some R&R at the "turnstiles of the East." This is followed by images of an extremely serious, contemplative "Yellow Man in the Temple of Buddha" before he leaves for a "foreign land" to bring a "message of peace to the barbarous Anglo-Saxons." Once in the Limehouse District of London, Cheng is known only as a "Chink storekeeper" who frequents opium dens where Orientals such as the Chinese, Malays, and lascars mix with prostitutes, all of whom the film tells us "squat at the portals of the West." Cheng's countrymen back home are described by two British clergymen as "heathens," a term frequently used at the turn of the century to discriminate against and exploit the Chinese, whose Buddhism the film makes clear differs radically from Christianity. There is a nice irony here: pacifistic Buddhist priests giving their life for freedom are heathens, while warring European nations slaughtering one another by the millions are Christians. In any event, when Cheng's forbidden relationship with Lucy is discovered, the anti-Asian rhetoric escalates and he is described as a "dirty Chink." Given the lack of evidence for this statement, we can only assume it originates from a kind of racialized politics of hygiene in which white, Christian, and Euro American signifies cleanliness and everything else signifies filth. In short, despite Cheng's attractive sensibilities—he is religious, sensitive, articulate, hard working, honorable, peace loving, and able to quote poetry—the slurs, the idea of him squatting, the half-bent body postures dehumanize him, mark him as different, unfamiliar, and untrustworthy; in short, a threat to white girls (Lucy) and white (British/American) culture. Beyond the racial slurs and Cheng's body positions is the employment of hara-kiri. In one of the final mise-en-scènes, Cheng mourns the death of Lucy. The use of a specifically Japanese ritual by a Chinese Buddhist missionary for dramatic effect suggests the conflation of cultural diversity and audience expectation in the name of artistic expediency—or perhaps it was just sloppy research. And, as is well known, there were many well-qualified Asian actors available for Cheng's role, but Griffith chose a white actor for the part, thus making the convention of yellowface highly visible not just through discriminatory labor practices but in the very material presence of the body, which is, after all, at the heart of historical materialism and the discourse of race.

A similar argument, that the openly racist discourse of yellowface in silent-era films starring young actors produced in the United States for do-mestic consumption are projections of white America's feelings about Chi-nese culture, which was seen as economically invasive and culturally threat-ening, might be made in relation to post–World War II movies such as *Lady and the Tramp* (1955), *The King and I* (1956), *Swiss Family Robinson* (1960), and *Breakfast at Tiffany's* (1961). Each of these classics contains instances of yellowface and other negative stereotypes, fuelled this time largely by anti-Japanese sentiment that washed up on American shores after Pearl Harbor. Often considered the most egregious example of yellowface in the aftermath of Word War II, *Breakfast at Tiffany's* has Mickey Rooney play-ing Mr. Yunioshi, the buck-toothed Japanese neighbor of Audrey Hepburn's character, wealthy socialite Holly Golightly. *Swiss Family Robinson* is an equally interesting example of yellowface, especially in connection to Asian American children's cinema and especially because critics such as Douglas Brode have tried to defend it, and other Disney offerings from this period, as progressive.

The arrival of postcolonial and Asian American studies, which roughly parallels the emergence of the civil rights movement, the women's move-ment, and the institutionalization of multicultural children's literature largely as a result of Nancy Larrick's famous essay "The All-White World of Children's Books," was extremely important in the history of multicultural children's films. In their introduction to a special issue of *Jouvert: A Journal of Postcolonial Studies*, Viet Thanh Nguyen and Tina Chen take a retrospec-tive look at the field and make a number of relevant points about Asian American, Marxist, and postcolonial studies that might be employed for a discussion of more recent Asian American films starring children such as the 2010 remake of *The Karate Kid*. Nguyen and Chen first note that Asian American studies, deeply influenced by Edward Said's 1970s research on orientalist studies, now includes discussion not just of Chinese and Japanese cultures (basically the focus of *Broken Blossoms*) but also those of Filipinos, Koreans, Pacific islanders, and South Asians. Like Marxist, feminist, and diversity or multicultural studies, Asian American studies has broadened, specifically from a preponderance of attention on the two main Asian cultures related to the United States, China and Japan, to a belated recognition of other cultural presences and influences: in a word, they have become more inclusive. For example, initial discussions in Asian American studies when it first appeared as an academic and professional discourse saw the early-twentieth-century immigration of Chinese and Japanese workers to the United States as mainly revolving around questions not just of assimilation and exclusion but also of national—American—identity. Nguyen and Chen argue that for historical, economic, and cultural reasons Filipino and Korean populations, for example, living in America today do not find "claiming America to be of utmost need" (n.p.). Nationhood, community, and home are important—of course they are—but not necessarily equated entirely with being American, Chinese, or Japanese. Furthermore, without "nation as a key unit of political, economic, and cultural organization" (n.p.), other areas of social and cultural identity such as place, borders, class, and racial identity are less effective as tools "of mobilization and change" (n.p.). Apart from anything else, Nguyen and Chen argue that many Asian populations in America today migrated from countries not colonized by America and thus adopt a different, perhaps contradictory, perspective on the politics of national identity from the movies in which such issues are dramatized, such as the 2010 remake of *The Karate Kid*.

The opening scenes of *The Karate Kid* (2010) require Dre and his (single) mom to gather their life's belongings, leave behind their friends, family, and neighborhood, and move to China for work-related reasons. These beginning images of Dre and his mom preparing literally for flight are instructive and suggest the movie's concern with uprootedness, shifting identities, and the excitement and apprehension that accompany relocation to a country whose history, culture, and language differ radically from those of America. Dre especially is bothered by the impending move. In his hometown, his identity is secure. Unsurprisingly he has no desire to leave, afraid, like Alice, that the further he travels from home the less he will retain his sense of identity. While sitting in their seats on the Air China flight waiting for takeoff, Dre's mother, who has clearly decided not to be a victim of her circumstances but still senses her son's uncertainty, determines that, to prepare for his new life in a foreign land, Dre should practice his Chinese conversation skills by speaking to someone on the plane. In some ways the classic, unwilling hero of the traditional monomyth, forced on a journey to a new world (the airplane is an interesting variation on the liminal space, or threshold), Dre reluctantly turns to an Asian-looking man in the adjacent aisle seat and introduces himself, in Chinese. The passenger, who listens patiently to Dre's halting but passable Chinese, quips: "Dude, I'm from Detroit." It's an ironic, amusing moment with serious, lasting implications for the film's narrative of identity. Dre's naïve, childlike mistake in thinking that skin color and physical features are the sole markers of racial and ethnic identity in today's world might be forgiven. As a black American kid from Detroit who has never traveled abroad, Dre's racial identity at home is marked, confirmed, and validated by the presence of other African Americans in his neighborhood and by the national discourse of race in the United States, which tends to polarize questions of racial identity. However, in a postcolonial world with an increasingly decentered, alienated, and fragmented sense of community and family—the airport here is an appropriate symbol of change, flux, impermanence, and the comings and goings of people—skin color and facial features are only partial markers of identity, as Dre continues to learn soon after he and his mom land in Beijing, take a taxi to their new home away from home (an apartment complex), and get to know the neighborhood. Dre's first friend, before he meets the local Kung Fu bullies and is subsequently rescued by Mr. Han, is a white expatriate kid about Dre's age who speaks perfect Chinese: Dre is indeed a stranger in a strange land. Even his peers look and sound nothing like he expected. Dre is invited by his friend to play basketball in the park adjacent to his apartment building. Dre's basketball skills are shown to be minimal. He dribbles the ball confidently but completely misses the net when he shoots. Embarrassed, he shuffles over to play table tennis with a few senior citizens who, contrary to the perceived stereotypes that surround the elderly, turn out to be ferocious, highly energetic competitors completely unfazed by the presence of the upstart African American kid from Detroit. That Dre loses even to the senior citizens is again amusing but important from the point of view of spectatorship. If young African American audiences are seeing Chinese culture for the first time through the eyes ofiDre, all the traditional, stereotypical markers of African American identity are foreclosed, shut down, and taken away. It turns out he can't play any sport, the locals can't understand him, and, contrary to the cultural stereotypes surrounding African American boys, Dre lacks the physical size and presence to protect himself against the local bullies who mercilessly beat him at any chance they can. Young audiences, black or white, have little with which to identify. Dre's lack of identity confirms what Asian American studies recognize—the continuing dislocation of home and the destabilization of national and personal identity.

However, the themes at the heart of *The Karate Kid* are economic issues, worker displacement, cultural migration, alienation, and loss of racial identity as a function of the kind of class conflict that comes along with global capitalism, and thus a historical materialist reading of the film remains compellingly relevant. *The Karate Kid* may well be about Dre's journey to a new land, but this journey of the child also functions as a trope of empire deployed by Western studios to help Western governments assert political, economic, and cultural hegemony over the East. The "flimsy integrationist" (Shohat and Stam 122) tendencies of the movie—Dre wins the hearts and minds of the locals—cannot conceal *The Karate Kid*'s true purpose. It is less about cultural authenticity or accuracy than it is commodity production, with Dre, an "American Adam" (Shohat and Stam 142), freed from the Old World of Detroit and all that that iconic city represents in terms of history and race relations and the cultural politics of identity, paving the way for the next generation of global consumers who live in the New World of Beijing. Of course, Dre is not buying any particular Chinese product: he could do that in Detroit using the Internet. The commodity, or product, being consumed by American audiences through Dre's eyes is China reduced to what is acceptable for Western audiences. Like much contemporary commercial cinema aimed at young viewers, *The Karate Kid* is a travelogue, a glossy National Geographic study whose skilled cinematography constructs China as a product that is then sold to young audiences in the West who marvel at and consume the beautifully photographed picture-postcard spectacles of the Olympic Park, the Great Wall of China, and the Forbidden Palace, to name but a few destination spots offered by the film. In this regard, *The Karate Kid* is profoundly ideological. In Said's terms, it is Occidentalist. *The Karate Kid* implies that America still thinks of the Orient as no more civilized today than it was in 1919, the year that *Broken Blossoms* was produced.

Summary

Asian American children's cinema as I have identified it runs roughly from *Broken Blossoms* in 1919 (modernism, silent era) to *Karate Kid* in 2010 and beyond (postmodernism, talkies). In between these films and dates can be found numerous examples of children's films and topics across a range of visual genres and media that reflect Asian American multicultural issues. During the silent era, images of the evil criminal mastermind, Dr. Fu Manchu, and his opposite, the benevolent detective Charlie Chan, flourished as examples of the Yellow Peril stereotype that in turn grew as a response to the fears of white Americans concerning Asian immigrants in the United States. In the 1940s, the cross-fertilization of American and Asian culture that occurred during World War II and its aftermath created the seeds for the growth of Japanese manga. Osamu Tezuka created the manga series *Astro Boy* in 1952. A computer-animated film featuring Astro Boy was released in 2009, although not to critical acclaim. *Empire of the Sun* (1987) and *Grave of the Fireflies* (1988) from the United States and Japan, respectively, deal seriously with World War II and its tragic consequences on children. At this time, the original *Karate Kid*, which established the franchise, was made (1984), with sequels cashing in on the original quickly following in 1986, 1989, and 1994. Disney made *Mulan* in 1998. Since the 1990s, perhaps the greatest Japanese influence on Asian American children's visual media has been director and animator Hayao Miyazaki, an auteur whose films such as *Princess Mononoke* (1997), *Spirited Away* (2001), and *Ponyo* (2008) are commercially successful and critically renowned. As discussed, the most recent Chinese American contribution to Asian American children's cinema is Columbia Pictures' *The Karate Kid*, released to coincide with the 2010 Summer Olympics held in Beijing.

The United States has maintained a military presence in the Pacific to protect American interests since the nineteenth century; in recent years, this military presence has sought specifically to counter China's increasing, and increasingly capitalist oriented, economic prosperity and political and cultural influence in that region. Setting aside the irony that almost a hundred years ago the situations of the United States and China were completely reversed (a growing American economy then, a growing Chinese economy now), an American military and political presence in the Pacific designed to counter Chinese strategic forays into the area continues to situate American Asian films for the young amid debates about American and Asian political, economic, and cultural influences and relations. *Broken Blossoms* (1919) and other movies from the silent era reflected early-twentieth-century American anxieties about how a growing Asian workforce within the United States threatened American jobs (hence the creation of Chinatowns, immigration ports such as Angel Island, the Chinese

Exclusion Acts, and the Chinese massacre of 1871 in Los Angeles), and the same argument about American anxieties might be made in relation to *The Karate Kid*, given Washington's ongoing protectionist strategies in the Pacific and the film's representation of an African American family uprooted from Detroit and planted in Beijing for work. This plot line suggests the intertwined roles that American and Asian cultures have consistently played on the world's political, economic, and philosophical stages. Culturally, but no less politically, it suggests the strategically important role that images or representations of the child in film, in our context children's films from *Broken Blossoms* to *The Karate Kid*, play when capitalism leads to clashes over economic resources, social relations, and art among countries where it operates as the "ruling material force" (Marx, *German Ideology* 44), all the while searching ceaselessly for a body, a child's body if necessary, in which to nestle.

Marxism, Race Studies, and African American Children's Films

In *Framing Blackness: The African American Image in Film*, Ed Guerrero writes that "slavery is the founding historical relationship between blacks and whites in America and, many would argue, lingers in subterranean forms today" (3). The legacies of slavery, blackface, and other forms of caricature and cultural stereotyping that constitute the discourse of racism I would argue linger today in the not-so-subterranean form of Western cinemas and films for the young such as *The Princess and the Frog*, successors to silent-era productions such as *Ten Pickaninnies* (1904), the original *Our Gang* shows, and the child stars who populated them.

In *Toms, Coons, Mulattoes, Mammies, and Bucks: An Interpretative History of Blacks in American Films*, Donald Bogle notes that from the very beginning of film in the silent era, African Americans were both stereotyped and cruelly caricatured but also celebrated. According to Bogle, by 1918, "the villains had come and gone. And the jester was about to be enshrined" (19). In the 1920s, the black jester figure and the child versions of that figure appeared with the "cornball names" (21) of Farina, Stymie, and Buckwheat. Bogle writes, with some irony, that while these three were stereotyped in the pickaninny tradition (23), they nonetheless had some individuality: "Farina was noted for his commonsense and heroic demeanor. Often he came to the rescue of little white damsels in distress" (23). It is frequently noted that *Our Gang*'s use of lower-middle-class black and white children, especially the pickaninny figure, was ahead of its time. Unlike the Uncle Tom stereotype of Edwin Porter's 1903 film version of *Uncle Tom's Cabin*, African American kids in *Our Gang* were not in blackface, to be sure; white and black boys and girls for the most part mingled freely as a group.

However, as in Asian American cinema at this time, the kids in African American films suffered doubly throughout the silent era. First, *Our Gang* was praised for its liberal tendencies, but we must remember that only three of its stars—Farina, Stymie, and Buckwheat—were African American. And a glance at the pages of relevant websites such as www.younghollywoodhof. com and www.imdb.com reveals that a only a minuscule number of child stars of the era were African American, and they acted in just one show! The former website, for example, starts listing child stars from 1908, but not until the 1920s and 1930s do Ernie "Sunshine Sammy" Morrison, Allen "Farina" Hoskins, and Billie "Buckwheat" Thomas appear. Second, African American child actors and actresses were not chosen to highlight the profound socioeconomic, cultural, and legal disadvantages under which they, or any working-class children at this point in history, lived. They were chosen so that their antics could sell the show to an emerging, middle-class, liberal audience. As such, they are the solution to class conflict: that they all play happily together suggests the universal state of childhood whereby class, race, and gender differences great and small are no barrier to friendship. But the solution of playing happily together is portrayed as childlike, not serious enough to be real, and thus marginal to the real politics of race relations. Third, the situation in which African American child actors found themselves is especially egregious as we recall that many silent-era movies that starred children took an active stance against the exploitation of child labor. Think here of films such as *Why?* and *Children Who Labor* (1912). Although sensational and sentimental, they at least spoke out against the appalling economic conditions under which children labored at the turn of the century and the political resistance to changing the laws that governed such practices. Granted, the African American child actors in *Our Gang* were gainfully employed and thus slightly better off than other, similar kids. Nonetheless, it might reasonably be argued that in regard to mapping out a tentative history of multicultural children's films produced in the United States, the social, economic, and cultural discrimination faced by African Americans in general at the turn of the twentieth century was clearly reflected in African American children's films. *Our Gang* can only be seen as progressive if all else is ignored, "as if there were no such things as race at all" (Bogle 23).

African American children's films were at the center of a number of important debates in the 1980s and 1990s about history and multiculturalism. Space prevents an examination of all of these debates. Most obviously, though, just as the "end of history" was being declared by commentators such as Francis Fukuyama, so films and made-for-television movies such as *Ruby Bridges* and *Selma, Lord, Selma*, suggested quite the opposite. Both of these movies very much kept alive for young audiences the history of the civil rights movement. *Cinderella* starred a multiethnic cast. *Bébé's Kids* starred an African American cast. As Shohat and Stam argue, the real issue was whose history was supposed to be coming to an end and whose was just beginning (248).[3]

Two more recent movies, *The Princess and the Frog* (2009) and *Akeelah and the Bee* (2006), suggest something of the current, contradictory state of African American children's films, or at least those films geared toward young audiences that star a predominantly African American cast. In some ways the two movies are similar. Both chart an African American girl's coming of age. *The Princess and the Frog* historicizes Tiana's childhood dream of following in her father's footsteps and owning a successful restaurant, although it places her at that historical juncture when she was least likely to succeed: early-twentieth-century, Jazz Age New Orleans. *Akeelah and the Bee* historicizes Akeelah's dreams of winning the Scripps National Spelling Bee by using the contemporary setting of South Los Angeles and the concept of public education.

Despite their similarities, the two movies are ultimately quite different. Whereas *The Princess and the Frog's* animated, stereotyped characters show few signs of race or class consciousness even though they are surrounded by evidence of both, the characters in *Akeelah and the Bee* show that acknowledging the barriers of race, class, and gender is the first step in learning to overcome them. As Akeelah walks home from her South Los Angeles school we see boarded-up stores, broken fences, trash on the sidewalk, homeless men, and gang members patrolling the streets in wildly expensive cars: in short, all the stereotypically visible signs of an economically depressed inner-city community about to fall further into urban decline. Soon after this street montage, the film narrows its focus to a more domestic scene. When Akeelah and her family sit down to dinner, her eldest brother, on leave from his military base, says that he wants to fly helicopters; his mother, played by Angela Bassett, tells him to let the "white boys" fly. Granted, her main concern, like that of any parent, is her son's safety. Nonetheless, her words and the gritty setting of South Los Angeles suggest that she, and the movie as a whole, recognize the barriers of race, class, and gender Akeelah must cross. By comparison, *The Princess and the Frog* hides such issues.

The two movies differ markedly in ways other than genre (animation versus live action), setting (fantasy New Orleans versus actual South Los Angeles), and race and class-consciousness: they differ in their use of language and the power of words to effect change. In *The Princess and the Frog*, language is a marker of race played for laughs. In *Akeelah and the Bee*, however, language is a deadly serious affair, almost literally. As Akeelah becomes increasingly successful at memorizing more and more complicated words, she becomes increasingly outcast. In the beginning, her spelling knowledge brings the wrath of her less articulate schoolmates, who befriend her when she talks and behaves like them but become vicious bullies when she refuses to do their English homework. In short, her very real entry into language is achieved at the cost of cultural alienation. Her brother, whose own journey involves associating with Los Angeles gangs and negotiating and falling victim to their own linguistic codes, warns that she will be going up against a "bunch of white rich kids" who will, in terms of language, beat her senseless. Her coach, Dr. Larabee, refuses to work with her until she changes her attitude, drops the "ghetto-talk," annunciates clearly, and speaks properly. Even her best friend, who recognizes that competence in the English language ensures class mobility (she wants to be an air stewardess) turns against her. In short, *The Princess and the Frog* uses historical revisionism, setting, and crude, physical slapstick humor to reinforce negatively the connections between language, race, and identity, connections grounded in history. Always serious and high minded, *Akeelah and the Bee* harnesses the power of language to improve the lives of young people.

In multicultural children's films, endings are especially important because they offer viewers a momentary glimpse of what might come to pass. The ending of *Akeelah and the Bee* does this in its characterization of the last two contestants in the spelling bee: Dylan, the aloof, driven, Asian child who dares to fail, and Akeelah, the once sassy and now pulchritudinous African American child daring to succeed. At the final stage of the spelling contest, Dylan and Akeelah spell and misspell their way to becoming cochampions and in the process go some way to dispelling not just the stereotypes of the model minority and the pickaninny that have plagued Asian and African American characters in films for the young since the silent era but the binaries of race that plague American race relations in general. As such, *Akeelah and the Bee* offers what Shohat and Stam call a "nurturing space for the playing out of the secret hopes of social life" (358).

Summary

The Princess and the Frog is one of the low points in African American children's films, although it contains the first black princess. *Akeelah and the Bee* is one of its high points. *The Princess and the Frog* suggests a dead end, a cul-de-sac, a movie stuck in first gear, spinning its wheels and going nowhere. *Akeelah and the Bee* suggests an open road with unlimited vistas. *The Princess and the Frog* pretends that the past hundred-odd years of racial conflict can be resolved with a song, a dance, and a magic wand, whereas *Akeelah and the Bee* at least tries to come to terms with discrimination. *The Princess and the Frog* is a film for the politics of yesteryear. *Akeelah and the Bee* is a film for today's political climate.

A powerful sense of past and present history is true of all multicultural children's films from *Pocahontas* to *Billy Elliot*, *The Secret of Roan Inish*, and *Turtles Can Fly*. Foregrounding the actual historical conditions within which and against which characters from diverse cultures search for meaning in their life is a defining feature of multicultural children's films. The relationship between history and African American children's films is especially important. That relationship is marked by a profound sense of presence as well as absence. In the early days of cinema, African American children were present in films and shows such as *Ten Pickaninnies*, *Our Gang*, *Kid 'n' Africa* (1933), and *The Littlest Rebel*. But throughout the twentieth century they were also erased through unfair labor practices and racist caricatures that reflect white America's fears and anxieties regarding African Americans. There is still no blockbuster movie aimed at young viewers about the death of Emmett Till; there has been no film adaptation of Mildred Taylor's *Roll of Thunder: Hear My Cry*. Why *Jumanji*, *The Polar Express*, *The Cat in the Hat*, and *The Lorax* but not *Mufaro's Beautiful Daughters* or *Tar Beach*? These absences when seen in conjunction with movies such as *The Princess and the Frog*, *The Help*, *The Blind Side*, and the like suggests a disavowal of the socioeconomic, political, and cultural legacies of the past as they relate to slavery and racial discrimination. They suggest an amnesia, a deliberate forgetting in African American children's films that constitutes on the one hand a Black People Free Zone (Warner 1) but more significantly a sickness generated by the refusal to use film to examine the past in meaningful ways for young audiences already raised on multicultural ideas and therefore clearly ready to be resistant spectators. Instead, *The Princess and the Frog*, *The Help*, and so on use the trope of the child to produce what Ward Churchill calls "fantasies of the master race," whereby the dominant white culture constructs film versions of the history of black Americans in ways that resolve all the original conflicts and its legacies for the white master race and infantilized viewers. In Marx's terms, all that is solid melts into air, as the depth and breadth of the actual, factual historical past—the experience of the body under slavery, blackface, segregation, and so forth—are minimized and silenced, buried by the studios beneath yet another feel-good fantasy about a white heroine coming of age as in *The Hunger Games* (2012). The need for a Marxist analysis of African American children's films—one that examines those films in terms of the intersections of history, ideology, class, race, and gender—is readily apparent and long overdue, as there are few discussions of the legacies of slavery or Reconstruction in relation to African American children's films, and those that do exist tend to avoid questions of historical materialism and its critique of capitalism as a mode of production whose economic divisions pit cultural groups, including those to which children belong, against one another.

Toward a Marxist Theory of Multicultural Children's Films

A Marxist theory of multicultural children's film history does not mean just talking about the degree to which a particular film reflects, or alludes to, a historical era, time frame, or specific date. It does not mean simply acknowledging the film's setting as historically relevant. Rather, it emphasizes that the historically determined conditions of a film's production, distribution, and release are intrinsic to an understanding and appreciation of the film itself, the genre to which it belongs, and the film period of which it is an ironic and contradictory representative. A Marxist approach means seeing First World multicultural children's films and the studios that produce and finance them such as Pixar, Disney, and DreamWorks as both commodity and franchise (given the tendency toward film sequels and prequels in capitalist consumer cultures), and as part of the capitalist mode of production that exploits the social relations of child workers within and without the film. A Marxist viewpoint would see children's films, especially in connection to their multicultural component, as intersections of class, race, gender, and age, and these four topics must inform any analysis of specific films or representative film periods. We would want to see the extent to which the social relations in the film—the theme of friendship—are formed and develop organically or develop as a function of the alienating tendencies of capitalism. From a Marxist point of view, understanding the pedagogical function of children's multicultural films is crucial to understanding how capitalist modes of production are truly divisive even as they proclaim their desire for unity. The world might be a stage upon which actors recite well-learned lines and play well-rehearsed roles. But it would be more accurate to say that the truly dramatic moments of revolt and contestation in history are precisely when the otherwise unrehearsed lines of the young, their unwanted and inappropriate stares, their cries, their laughter, their outbursts, the physical movements of their bodies echo and resonate with the sheer abject materiality of their existence and are heard clear above the polished, practiced, politely controlled conversations and performances of adults.

Marx wrote that the bourgeoisie must create ever-expanding markets to maintain its dominant economic and ideological position in the world: it must "nestle everywhere and settle everywhere" (Marx, *Manifesto* 87). Having made films about Native America (*Pocahontas*), the Middle East (*Aladdin*), China (*Mulan*), and so forth, it is easy to argue that corporate Hollywood has nestled and settled everywhere and that Disney's shareholders are no doubt pleased with the corporation's Fordist-like ability to transform the raw materials of a nation's history and culture into an American multicultural children's film genre exported around the world. But if history is where we all end, then it is appropriate to conclude this paper by noting Marx's comment that the "ever-lasting uncertainty" (*Manifesto* 87) created by the bourgeois epoch would eventually conclude and humanity would ultimately have to confront the "real conditions of life" (87); otherwise it would be destroyed completely by the magical spells it conjures, Disney's *Aladdin* a perfect metaphor for this state of affairs. The demand for concrete social, economic, political, and cultural change—think here of the recent Occupy Wall Street/Occupy the Earth movements—as a function of the dialectical view of history suggests that, while balancing precariously on the precipice of movie history, meaningful, challenging, multicultural children's films from within the United States, from postcolonial countries such as New Zealand and Australia, and from emerging nations such as Iran, see in the figure of the child a life worth living and are prepared to examine the "real conditions of life" (Marx, *Manifesto* 87). They are prepared to do so by producing child- and youth-oriented films that can be studied seriously as both aesthetic objects and as vehicles for social change. Authentic rather than corporate multicultural children's films—the 99 percent rather than the 1 percent—might actually change rather than merely interpret the way we see the world.

NOTES

1. Donna E. Norton's *Through the Eyes of a Child* states: "Multicultural literature is literature about racial or ethnic minority groups that are culturally and socially different from the white Anglo-Saxon majority in the United States, whose largely middle class values and customs are most represented in American Literature" (457).

2. In the chapter "Defining Multicultural Literature" in *Multicultural Literature for Children and Young Adults,* Cai quotes critics such as Patrick Shannon and Andrea Fishman, both of whom argue that all literature is multicultural. This seems to me a plausible approach to multicultural children's films.

3. We should also remember films from this period as different as *The Wiz* (1978) and *Sounder* (1972).

WORKS CITED

Akeelah and the Bee. Directed by Doug Atchison. Lions Gate Films, 2006. Film.

Aladdin. Directed by Ron Clements and John Musker. Walt Disney Pictures, 1992. Film.

Althusser, Louis. "Ideology and Ideological State Apparatuses." In *Lenin and Philosophy,* translated by Ben Brewster. New York: Monthly Review Press, 1971. Print.

Arora, Poonam. "The Production of Third World Subjects for First World Consumption: Salaam Bombay and Parama." In *Multiple Voices in Feminist Film Criticism,* edited by Diane Carson, Linda Dittmar, and Janice R. Welsch, 293–304. Minneapolis: University of Minnesota Press, 1994. Print.

Au Revoir, Les Enfants. Directed by Louis Malle. NEF Productions, 1987. Film.

Beauty and the Beast. Directed by Jean Cocteau. DisCina Productions, 1946. Film.

Bell, Elizabeth, Lynda Haas, and Laura Sells. *From Mouse to Mermaid: The Politics of Film, Gender, and Culture.* Bloomington: Indiana University Press, 1995. Print.

Bogle, Donald. *Toms, Coons, Mulattoes, Mammies, and Bucks: An Interpretative History of Blacks in American Films.* 4th ed. New York: Continuum, 2010. Print.

Boy in the Striped Pajamas, The. Directed by Mark Herman. Miramax, 2008. Film.

Breakfast at Tiffany's. Directed by Blake Edwards. Jurow-Shepherd Productions, 1961. Film.

Brode, Douglas. *Multiculturalism and the Mouse: Race and Sex in Disney Entertainment.* Austin: University of Texas Press, 2005. Print.

Broken Blossoms; or, The Yellow Man and the Girl. Directed by D. W. Griffith. United Artists, 1919. Film.

Brownlow, Kevin. *Behind the Mask of Innocence: Sex, Violence, Prejudice, and Crime; Films of Social Conscience in the Silent Era.* Berkeley: University of California Press, 1990. Print.

Burke, Thomas. "The Chink and the Child." In *Limehouse Nights.* London: Robert M. McBride, 1917. Print.

Cai, Mingshui. *Multicultural Literature for Children and Young Adults: Reflections on Critical Issues.* Contributions to the Study of World Literature, no. 116. Westport, Conn.: Greenwood Press, 2002. Print.

Carroll, Lewis. *Alice's Adventures in Wonderland and Through the Looking-Glass: The Annotated Alice*. Introduction and notes by Martin Gardner. New York: Meridian, 1960. Print.

Children of Heaven. Directed by Majid Majidi. Intellectual Development of Children and Young Adults, 1997. Film.

Children Who Labor. Directed by Ashley Miller. Edison Productions, 1912. Film.

Churchill, Ward. *Fantasies of the Master Race: Literature, Cinema, and the Colonization of American Indians*. Boulder, Colo.: Common Courage, 1992. Print.

Comolli, Jean-Luc, and Jean Narboni. "Cinema/Ideology/Criticism." In *Film Theory and Criticism*, edited by Gerald Mast et al., 682–689. 4th ed. Oxford: Oxford University Press, 1992. Print.

Crook, Eugene, Maricarmen Martínez, and Jessica Lowe. *Multicultural Film: An Anthology, Spring/Summer 2006*. Boston: Pearson, 2006. Print.

Delphy, Christine. "For a Materialist Feminism." In *Materialist Feminism: A Reader in Class, Difference, and Women's Lives*, edited by Rosemary Hennessy and Chrys Ingraham. New York: Routledge, 1997. Print.

Diary of Anne Frank, The. Directed by George Stevens. Twentieth Century Fox, 1959. Film.

Eagleton, Terry. *Marxism and Literary Criticism*. Los Angeles: University of California Press, 1976. Print.

Edges of the Lord. Directed by Yurek Bogayevicz. Braun Entertainment, Canal, 2001. Film.

Fantasia. Directed by James Algar et al. Walt Disney Pictures, 1940. Film.

400 Blows, The. Directed by François Truffaut. Les Films Du Carrosse, 1959. Film.

Fukuyama, Francis. *The End of History and the Last Man*. New York: Avon, 1992. Print.

Garcia, Maria. "Through a Kurdish Lens." *The Progressive*, March 2005. Accessed March 3, 2012. Website.

Gnanalingam, Brannavan. "Get That Camera Out of Here, We're Making a Film." *Werewolf*, no. 29. Accessed March 12, 2012. Website.

Gremlins. Directed by Joe Dante. Warner Brothers, 1984. Film.

Guerrero, Ed. *Framing Blackness: The African American Image in Film*. Philadelphia: Temple University Press, 1993. Print.

Haraway, Donna. *Primate Visions: Gender, Race, and Nature in the World of Modern Science*. New York: Routledge, 1992. Print.

Hartmann, Heidi. "The Unhappy Marriage of Marxism and Feminism." In *Women and Revolution: A Discussion of the Unhappy Marriage of Marxism and Feminism*, edited by Lydia Sargent. Boston: South End Press, 1981. Print.

Jackson, Kathy Merlock. *Images of Children in American Films: A Sociocultural Analysis*. London: Scarecrow Press, 1986. Print.

Jameson, Fredric. "Periodizing the 60s." In *The Ideologies of Theory: Essays, 1971–1986*, vol. 2, *Syntax of History*, 178–211. Minneapolis: University of Minnesota Press, 1988. Print.

Journeys in Film: Educating for Global Understanding. Homepage. University of Southern California, Annenberg School for Communication and Journalism, Norman Lear Center, 2003. Accessed October 1, 2012. Website.

Karate Kid, The. Directed by Harald Zwart. Columbia Pictures, 2010. Film.

King and I, The. Directed by Walter Lang. Twentieth Century Fox, 1956. Film.

Lady and the Tramp. Directed by Clyde Geronimi. Walt Disney Pictures, 1955. Film.

Larrick, Nancy. "The All-White World of Children's Books." *Saturday Review*, September 11, 1965, 63–65. Print.

Littlest Rebel, The. Directed by David Butler. Twentieth Century Fox, 1935. Film.

Macherey, Pierre. *A Theory of Literary Production.* 1966. Translated by Geoffrey Wall. New York: Routledge, 1978. Print.

Mandel, Ernest. *Late Capitalism.* 1972. Translated by Joris de Bres. London: Verso, 1975. Print.

Marx, Karl. *The German Ideology.* In *Marx, Engels, Lenin: On Historical Materialism.* New York: International Publishers, 1972. Print.

———. *Manifesto of the Communist Party.* In *Marx, Engels, Lenin: On Historical Materialism.* New York: International Publishers, 1972. Print.

Mulan. Directed by Tony Bancroft and Barry Cook. Walt Disney Pictures, 1998. Film.

Nguyen, Viet Thanh, and Tina Chen. Introduction to "Postcolonial Asian America." Special issue, *Jouvert: A Journal of Postcolonial Studies* 4:3 (2000). Website.

Norton, Donna E. *Through the Eyes of a Child: An Introduction to Children's Literature.* 6th ed. Upper Saddle River, N.J.: Merrill/Prentice Hall, 2003. Print.

Our Gang. Directed by Robert F. McGowan. Hal Roach Studios, 1922. Television.

Princess and the Frog, The. Directed by Ron Clements and John Musker. Walt Disney Pictures, 2009. Film.

Said, Edward. *Orientalism.* New York: Pantheon, 1978. Print.

Secret of Roan Inish, The. Directed by John Sayles. Columbia Pictures, 1994. Film.

Shohat, Ella, and Robert Stam. *Unthinking Eurocentrism: Multiculturalism and the Media.* London: Routledge, 1994. Print.

Snead, James. *White Screen, Black Images: Hollywood from the Dark Side.* Edited by Colin MacCabe and Cornel West. New York: Routledge, 1994. Print.

Stam, Robert. "Beyond Third Cinema: The Aesthetics of Hybridity." In *Rethinking Third Cinema,* edited by Anthony R. Guneratne and Wimal Dissanayake. New York: Routledge, 2003. Print.

Swiss Family Robinson. Directed by Ken Annakin. Walt Disney Pictures, 1960. Film.

Ten Pickaninnies. Directed by Thomas A. Edison. Edison Productions, 1904. Film.

Warner, Tony. "Lack of Black Characters in Children's Films." People with Voices, February 18, 2011. Accessed June 5, 2012. Website.

Weird Science. Directed by John Hughes. Universal Pictures, 1985. Film.

Why? Éclair American Productions, 1913. Film.

Williams, Raymond. *Marxism and Literature.* Oxford: Oxford University Press, 1977. Print.

Winfrey, Yayoi Lena. "Yellowface: Asians on White Screens; Is Charlie Chan Really Dead?" IMDiversity. Accessed May 6, 2012. Website.

Wood, Robin. *Hollywood from Vietnam to Reagan.* New York: Columbia University Press, 1986. Print.

Yellowface! "Yellow Face: The History of Racist Asian Stereotypes." Accessed April 3, 2012. Website.

Young Hollywood Hall of Fame. "Silent Film Artists, 1920s," 1997. Compiled by Drina Mohacsi. Accessed January 10, 2012. Website.

Bloodthirsty Little Brats; or, The Child's Desire for Biblical Violence

ROLAND BOER

Why are children drawn to the gory and bloodthirsty stories of the Bible? Given a choice in a decent children's Bible, why do they ask for the story of Absalom catching his hair, Jael pegging Sisera's head to the ground, Ehud losing his sword in Eglon's gut, Korah sliding into the chasm, or David adding a third eye to Goliath's forehead? Of course, in putting the questions this way I have implicitly taken up positions in ongoing debates. They are easy to identify: the question of whether children are devils, angels, or blank pages; the contrast between beneficial and harmful violence, or indeed between violence and nonviolence; the problem of whether texts (and other cultural products) incite violence, desensitize us to violence, or have no direct effect on us at all; the question of the nature of childhood itself, whether it is a construction as a distinct phase of life as defined only at the end of the seventeenth century or whether "childhood" goes back much further; and the question of its plasticity—does it end with the onset of puberty? Are teenagers still children or do they grow into a distinct group?

In light of these well-worn and somewhat tired debates, let me outline the assumptions with which I begin before considering in some detail the biblical stories I mentioned earlier. I operate with a modified version of the argument of Philippe Ariès. He contends that childhood as a distinct phase of life was gradually invented by the bourgeoisie from the eighteenth century onward. Riveted onto the nuclear family, which itself had been undergoing its own shaping, the crucial feature of this new part of our lives was fixed in place by the eventual extension of education to all classes—children went to school and emerged adults, trained and ready for adult society. Even though the working classes were the last to be swamped by childhood and education, eventually they too succumbed. So children became the objects of intense concerns in regard to moral, physical, and sexual problems, which in their own way reinforced the relatively new phase of childhood. How may such a materialist position be modified? I would like to deploy the simple point that distinct items within a mode of production are not necessarily unique to that mode.[1] As with money, private property, or classes (to name but a few), they have clearly existed before capitalism—so also with what is called "childhood." However, the role of such an item differs substantially and even qualitatively in different modes of production, specifically in relation to the other items, or what the Régulation theorists call "institutional forms" (Boyer 38–42). In this light I would suggest that Ariès's proposal may be reshaped, for childhood did become, within capitalism, something quite distinct from what it was before: a distinct concern of the bourgeoisie and the valorization of the nuclear family, with profound implications for approaching physical and mental development, sexuality, and moral concerns. Here the Bible played a crucial role.

I also assume that children are not devils, smitten with original sin; nor angels, given to an innocence eventually sullied by the grim world of adults; nor blank pages on which parents and educators need to make the best imprint.[2] I understand children as complex human agents, with their own concerns regarding sex, death, and life, who negotiate the world in ways that belie the constructs placed upon them (see esp. Hoyles and Evans). This position informs the questions with which I began this discussion— children choose certain biblical stories because they are complex agents. Further, I assume that stories, like those from the Bible, produce, in interaction with their readers and listeners, imaginary worlds that may or may not have connections with the real world in which we live. In other words, texts do not simply incite action (even propaganda struggles to do so), nor do they necessarily desensitize us to violence.

This leads me to the final point: it is possible to distinguish between different types of violence, whether overt, covert, or symbolic (in the very language we use). The violence of imaginary worlds produced by art, literature, and culture may not necessarily be a bad thing, in that it may address negative emotions and facilitate empowerment (see Jones); nor is the violence of a brutally oppressed group—a violence arrived at through absolute desperation—necessarily wrong, for it comes as a response to the systemic and covert violence of existing class and imperial relations.

Bloody Stories

With this theoretical framework gleaned from existing debates—the discursive and material constructions of "childhood," children as complex agents, the production of imaginary worlds, and the possibility of a good violence—I analyze a number of biblical texts. My analysis focuses on children's Bibles of the second half of the twentieth century, leaking over into the twenty-first.[3] These stories manifest some distinctive features, so much so that they may be described as generic expectations (Jameson): the stories are broken down into bite-sized pieces, not too long so that they can be read before sleep; any hint of sex is carefully airbrushed out (Mrs. Potiphar merely wants to kiss Joseph on the cheek; Rahab is a "friendly," perhaps too friendly, woman, and so on); these Bibles play an active role in "orientalizing" the Bible, depicting a faraway ancient East with its flowing robes and extraordinary, often magical, happenings; no matter how hard the authors might try, they cannot avoid the occasional moralizing comment; and the pervasive illustrations are usually insipid, following in the tradition of a certain style of religious art that is quite bad.

Yet in some cases one feature survives the passage from biblical text to children's Bible: violence. Here a distinction must be made, for in one group of retellings the more violent episodes are carefully excised, much like those concerning sex. For instance, stories of the birth of Jesus may remove the gruesome account of Herod slaughtering the children under two years of age (Davidson and Marshall, *Story of Baby Jesus*), or the Psalms appear without the grim petitions for the destruction of one's enemies (Davidson and Marshall, *Psalms and Proverbs*), or synopses of some of the stories of the Bible compiled for very young children simply skim over any item that is too frightening (Lloyd-Jones). By and large, such retellings are insipid and full of moralizing, which quickly leads to boredom among young listeners, as I have found from countless such readings with a large range of children.

By contrast, a good number of others are more willing to tackle stories of the danger of death, if not a violent end itself. Here are the people drowning as Noah and the ark sail away; Abel dying at the hands of Cain; the Ten Plagues on the Egyptians and then their drowning in the Red Sea; the Israelites in one of their many punishments; the inhabitants of Jericho as their walls tumble; King Eglon with the sword buried in his extended belly; Siserah and the tentpeg through his temple; the destruction of the Philistines, the Moabites, and anyone else who gets in the way of the Israelites; Solomon's call to cut the single disputed baby in two; Jezebel being thrown to the dogs; Daniel in the face of conniving opponents and hungry, sharp-clawed lions; John the Baptist's head on a plate; Stephen's stoning to death; Saul's persecution of the early Christians; Herod's slaughter of the young children in Bethlehem; and of course Jesus and his death (Chancellor and Leplar, Davison and Marshall, Tutu, Lloyd-Jones, Delval, Peale).[4] Gripping though the stories are, the illustrations play a crucial role. Occasionally they may let one down, alluding to violent ends but without overt depiction. More often than not they do not shy away from such images. The persistence of these engagements with violence undermines at least one facet of Ruth Bottigheimer's thesis in *The Bible for Children*, namely that there has been, since the sixteenth century, a shift away from staying "closer" to the biblical text, moving through more substantial revisions of troubling passages, and ending with complete amendments if not simply dropping certain stories entirely. On the question of violence, this is not the case, for a good number of children's Bibles continue to tell such stories.

I would like to compare two of these bible story collections, the comprehensive work by Norman Vincent Peale and an older book from my own childhood.[5] Peale makes no effort to airbrush the grimmer side of biblical stories. All the stories I mentioned above may be found here, plus a few more. These include the destruction of Sodom and Gomorrah, Jacob's theft of Esau's birthright, the violent feats of Samson, and the beheading of John the Baptist, as well as the New Testament's central, extended narrative of violence, namely the trial and death of Jesus, which includes the betrayal by Judas, the bloody whipping, and then the grimness of the cross. Peale is far from afraid to speak of sex and seduction, punishment and torture, and the violence of death. Connected to these stories is a significant collection of illustrations. Hardly the bland images of many children's books, they are often stark and strong, watercolors that enhance the effect. Let me focus on one of these stories, in order to compare it with my own experience below.

The story concerns the destruction of Sodom and Gomorrah (Gen. 13:18–19). Those cities had become, Peale writes, "evil places, full of sexual perversion and corruption of every kind" (38).[6] With an eye on the present, he observes that no doubt people believed that morals were relative, suiting their own needs, and that intellectuals had declared God dead. As with the other stories in Peale's work, the accounts are long and involved, requiring significant attention from the listener. We read of Abraham's drawn-out haggling with the angels (one of whom is God himself in disguise) in order to reduce the number of righteous to ten, so that the cities might be saved.

When two of the angels visit Lot and his family in Sodom, they barely escape "being maltreated by the evil-minded citizens of that evil-minded place" (43). The angels warn Lot, his wife, and his daughters to flee (although his sons-in-law opt not to do so), and the two cities are utterly destroyed with fire and brimstone. Gruesome enough, but the image that accompanies the story is transfixing. Roiling black smoke frames the picture, with red and yellow flames engulfing the teetering towers and crumbling buildings. Broken bodies lie on the ground. But the eye is drawn to a falling figure, on fire, who has leaped from a burning window high in a tower.

What is perhaps most intriguing about Peale's book is that it is based on stories he has told countless times to his own children and grandchildren. Indeed, his book and images, like the one I have just described, remind me uncannily of an old children's Bible from the same era, one read to me by my parents (my mother mostly). Let me invoke the literary trope of the lost manuscript, for the work that is so strongly imprinted on my memory is also one that has since disappeared. So I draw upon an adult's memory as a child, with its mix of deeper insights gleaned over time, embellishments, and features that have been forgotten. The lost Bible was full of lurid images, much like those in Peale's book, images that transfixed me and my brothers and inspired this essay in the first place. They were magnetic, a single picture on the left page with the text of the Bible story on the right. Absalom hangs from the tree branch, his luxurious hair hopelessly tangled as Joab moves forward to thrust those darts into his heart (2 Sam. 18:9–15). Korah's household slides into a yawning chasm, terror on their faces as the fearful Israelites look on, unable to turn away and yet horrified by the sight (Num. 16:31–35). Goliath begins to tumble to the ground, eyes wide, a hole between them where the stone had gone in, David standing by with an empty sling (1 Sam. 17). Jael hammers a tentpeg into the sleeping Sisera, who unaccountably does not wake (Judg. 4:21); the sword of Ehud disappears into the fat gut of the oppressive Eglon of Moab (Judg. 3:15–25); and John the Baptist's head, eyes closed and disheveled hair spread out, sits in a pool of blood on a large plate carried by the daughter of Herodias (Matt. 14:1–12).

Lurid, startling, exotic, and mesmerizing—these were stories that we wanted to hear again and again and again. Given half a chance, other children, as I have found, have the same response, whether my own children (in good Freudian analytic style, for Freud did much of his analysis on his own children and grandchildren), those I once taught in infant scripture classes at local schools, and those I encountered in Sunday schools. Forget

protecting supposedly innocent and vulnerable children against the evils
of the adult world; these apparent angels certainly let out the devil within
them whenever they had the chance.

What do these stories and images tell a child? That kings can be cruel?
That God will punish you with death for a misdemeanor? That the earth
will swallow you up should you disobey? How do kids negotiate the omni-
presence of gruesome death? I would suggest that we distinguish between
two types of gruesome stories, one dealing with punishment for sin and
rebellion, the other celebrating the often wily victory of the underdog. In
the first group we can gather the hairy end of Absalom and the yawning
destruction of Korah and company. In the second group come the stories
of dead-eye David, the outdoorsy Jael, and the disappearing sword of Ehud.
Only the loose head of John the Baptist does not quite seem to fit, but I
would suggest that it belongs to the second group, for reasons that will become clear soon enough.

Let us consider these stories more closely. As for Absalom, my childhood recollection of this story begins with the rebellion of the proud and
reckless Absalom against David, the son against the father, wanting the
kingship before it was due. It then moves swiftly to Absalom's end, after
a few choice comments on his vanity. The mule he is riding passes under
the thick branches of a massive tree, his mass of hair gets caught, the mule
quietly keeps going, and Absalom is suspended between heaven and earth.
And this is where the picture captures him, fright and pain on his face,
mule (although often a horse) rearing in fright and galloping on, Absalom's
hair knotted in the tree branches, a dart or three about to be thrust into his
heart. Absalom is perhaps a figure with whom a male child can identify,
for he challenges a dominating father whom the child may quietly wish
were out of his life. But this glimmer of identification soon passes with the
way the story is presented, for Absalom receives the grim reward for his
rebellion, as will the young son should he challenge the father too much.
Absalom is hardly one to cheer, for he fails in his quest, especially when the
conniving of Joab and the grieving of David in the biblical text (2 Sam. 19:1)
fail to make it into the children's story as it is retold.

Korah too falls—quite literally—to the same fate, if the story makes it
into a children's Bible at all. No matter how much this rebellion becomes
one that involves the whole people (Num. 17:10), it too becomes an upstart
rejection of God and his appointed leaders, Moses and Aaron. As disobedi-
ent and ungrateful rebels, Korah and his family are not those with whom
children can easily identify. The vertigo-producing abyss that opens up

beneath is enough to mesmerize any child (and perhaps generate a nightmare or three).

How different the stories of Jael and Ehud are, for the heroes can certainly be cheered. However, the key with these stories is that the victory comes unexpectedly through a ruse. Neither Jael nor Ehud come from a position of overt power, as do Moses, Aaron, David, and the Almighty himself in the previous stories. In each case, they win through from the weak position. The account of Jael usually appears in a children's Bible at the end of the story of Deborah and Barak in their battle with Sisera and the Canaanite army of nine hundred chariots (Judg. 4). Jael welcomes the fleeing Sisera into her tent, gives him some milk when he asks for water, and covers him so he can rest. Sisera asks her to watch at the tent flap and turn away anyone inquiring after him. But Jael takes a tent peg and a hammer, tiptoes over to the sleeping Sisera, and pegs his head firmly to the ground through his temple—as firmly as one might secure a tent. A little deception, an innovative use for some everyday campground equipment, and the enemy is vanquished.

So also with Ehud, who carries out his daring deed against the oppressive Moabites and Eglon, their king. I must admit that this story was one of my favorites as a child. The details are still imprinted in my mind from countless retellings. Ehud is slightly different from his peers, left-handed, so he carries his short sword concealed on his right thigh. The guards at the gate check his left side, assuming that he is a right-handed man (you will struggle to find this detail in Judg. 3:15–23, for while children's Bible stories often abridge, they also add narrative details).

Ehud presents the gifts that he has brought to Eglon, although we all know that the gifts are really a trick to get close to the king. And then Ehud mentions to Eglon that he has a secret message, perhaps some top secret information about a plot against Eglon, so the latter tells all his retainers to leave. (I never questioned why he would do something so stupid with a representative from a subjected and enemy people—my eyes were glued to the picture.) Add to this the glorious detail that Eglon was extremely fat, and a child can readily picture a wily Israelite standing before the vast spread of the king.

The next moment is the best of all, for as the king stands up, his massive gut hanging out, Ehud reaches for his sword and thrusts it deep into his belly. The short double-bladed sword disappears into the fat, even to the hilt, so Ehud lets go before his hand disappears too. Calmly, he closes the door of the room, the roof chamber, and walks off. What a ruse! Devious, smart, and against the odds, Ehud comes out on top. The last detail of the story continues to fascinate children. Seeing the doors closed, the king's servants don't dare to disturb him, for they think he is relieving himself.

At this moment an excursus is needed, explaining the ways people used to go to the toilet in the ancient world—kings would simply do it in the room, perhaps for the servants to carry out later, or perhaps while hanging over a plank to the general cesspit below (which would then be used for fertilizer). Common people would do it anywhere they could crouch in peace. And since they didn't wear underwear, all they needed to do was lift the robe. Toilet paper? Well, in the same way the Bible mentions that the left hand should not know what the right hand is doing (Matt. 6:3), so also the right hand should not be aware of what the left hand is doing.

Finally, the servants decide that even a constipated man would not take so long, so they break into the room only to find Eglon dead and rather stiff. My elaborate retelling of this story, full of its fascinating details, comes not merely from memory but from reading and elaborating the story for children, countless times. It is a winner each time.

Heroes who win through a ruse, the weaker ones who triumph by their own ingenuity—these are the gory stories children seem to enjoy. I have been deploying the reading strategy first proposed with such ingenuity by Ernst Bloch in *Atheism in Christianity* and followed by Jack Zipes in *Breaking the Magic Spell*.[7] Bloch's Marxist readings of myth, especially fairy tale and folktale, operate in terms of a process of discernment, in which the story of an underdog coming out on top, often through a trick or two, is an expression of the desire for liberation from oppression. Read in terms of class, these accounts become those of the unlikely success of oppressed classes, embodied in a clever class hero who manages to outsmart the brutal White Guard rulers. But how does discernment take place? For Bloch, one often finds such stories of rebellion contained within narratives that justify the powers that be. The Bible, a favorite for Bloch, is a classic case: too often does God side with the oppressor, with the pharaoh or Moses (the wilderness tyrant and not the liberator from oppression in Egypt), with kings and emperors. However, in the midst of these stories of oppression one finds continual rebellions, some of which manage to break through and win a temporary victory. I would suggest that these underdogs, the ones contained and oppressed, are precisely the characters with whom children can identify. In their own worlds they are the weaker ones who must negotiate not only the strange world of adults but also bullies within their own circles.

Yet Jael and Ehud are adults, at least as that category has developed in the past few centuries. Not so David in the story of David and Goliath; of course David wins against the odds, but he does so not so much through a ruse as through a child's own ways. For David too is a child, at least in this story. The subject of endless retellings, a staple in children's Bibles, even making it into the Little Golden Books series (Hazen)—along with *The Little Steam Engine*, *The Ugly Duckling*, *The Saggy Baggy Elephant*, and *The Princess and the Pea*—David is a child with whom children can identify only too well. The overlooked youngest member of the family of Jesse, who has to be called from tending the sheep to be anointed by Samuel (1 Sam. 16:1–13), the one who comes onto the battlefield to bring his three older brothers some grain and loaves (1 Sam. 17:17–18), David is perceived as a child who is an onlooker and interloper in the world of adults. The rooms of high priests, the king's court (where David plays the lyre), and above all the battlefield, where men gather for serious adult business—these are seen as adult realms, blocked to the children who have this story read to them. Of course, the effect of the story relies upon and reinforces the separation of such worlds, which have their own history of invention and maintenance, as we saw above. But in this story, the child does not peek through a door late at night, curious about the visitors with their loud talk, drinking, and smoking, desperately wishing to be able to enter that world, waiting for the long distant moment when he or she too will be an adult. In the story of David and Goliath, the child peeks in and is then called to center stage. And what does he do? He achieves what no adult could—he slays Goliath. He does so not in an adult way (armor and weapons are useless to David [1 Sam. 17:38–39]), but in a way with which he is accustomed, namely smooth stones and a sling. These are a child's toys, the homemade slingshot (or perhaps a purchased super-soaker these days) fired at makeshift targets such as tin cans on a fence. David triumphs in a world of adults by using the ingenuity of a child (the children's stories conveniently cut out the somewhat painful bragging of David in 1 Sam. 17:24–30).

Jael, Ehud, and David against Goliath—these are all characters with whom a child can identify. What then of John the Baptist? This story is really a mix of the various features I have traced thus far. The "child" in question, or at least the younger person (for she dances before the lascivious gazes of the men), is hardly a sympathetic figure, one with whom a child hearing the story would identify. So there is no tricky hero, no child who conquers the world of adults in a child's ways; the child in this story does not come out so well. She is more like a member of the gang of bullies at school (male or female), or perhaps the scheming girl or boy who has re-peatedly stabbed you in the back. Unlike Absalom or even Korah (although I must admit to having a soft spot for Korah), sympathies go to John the Baptist, who comes to a gruesome end. Here the hero is a tragic one, one who suffers at the hands of evil adults and a wicked child.

The Invented Worlds of Children and Fairy Tales

How do we assess the complex patterns in these gory children's stories? I would like to make four observations. I begin with a common insight but seek to give it a subversive, Marxist twist: the appeal of narratives like that of Jael, Ehud, and especially David with his slingshot, at least in the way those stories are told to children, may be found in the way the weaker person wins, usually through a ruse, although in David's case by using ways known only too well by children. These stories are of the same ilk as those by Roald Dahl: selfish, mean, and nasty adults populate Dahl's stories, which are told from the perspective of a child. That child often suffers at the hands of adults and other nasty children, but the child resorts to his or her own ways to come out on top.

So Matilda, in the work of the same name, finds that her strange powers enable her to deal with greedy parents and a horrendous headmistress, Miss Trunchbull; and James must negotiate the avaricious adults who wish to make money from the magical peach in *James and the Giant Peach*. Often a sympathetic adult assists the child, such as the rough, cigar-smoking, take-no-crap grandmother in *The Witches*, who must help foil the evil witches' plot to get rid of all children, or perhaps a grandfather who does not so much shelter Charlie as become his sidekick in *Charlie and the Chocolate Factory*.

Far less successful in constructing such a world of children is the phenomenally popular Harry Potter series created by J. K. Rowling. Taking its cue from the endless novels valorizing the British private school system such as those by Enid Blyton (some propaganda was certainly needed for such a dreadful system), the Harry Potter series produces a child's own world in a boarding school milieu, full of magic, evil adults, obligatory bullies, and then, as a twist, the horrible world of everyday adults (the Muggles) who make Harry's life hell. These novels fail when Harry wins time and again, achieving amazing feats that grow tiresome all too soon. More than one child has told me (through an informal survey) that they have read Harry Potter books, but that they are by no means the best books they have read.

However, biblical stories as they are told to children also touch on a far more powerful genre, namely fairy tales. A subgenre of myth, the fairy tale celebrates time and again distinctly subversive themes, no matter how much they may have been watered down for widespread consumption and no matter whether they come from ancient folktales or were written by the likes of Charles Perrault, Oscar Wilde, or Hans Christian Andersen. The three little pigs finally win out over the big bad wolf, the ugly duckling turns into a beautiful swan, the child calls the bluff on the emperor's new clothes, Jack wins out over the giant at the top of the beanstalk, and so on.

As I mentioned earlier, it was Ernst Bloch who first uncovered the subversive dimensions of fairy tales, in which the "little folk" seem to triumph again and again, often through their wiles and clever reasoning, sometimes through simple patience and often unaccountable magic, and sometimes through bloodthirsty violence (*Principle of Hope* 352–369). Jack Zipes has built on Bloch's initial thesis, developing a social history of fairy tales and arguing that they often were composed or perhaps recycled in times of social unrest and revolutionary turmoil, only to be domesticated and instrumentalized through mass market production (*Breaking the Magic Spell*). However, Bloch's insight is that even as fairy tales are relegated to serving as children's bedtime stories, they may still contain traces of subversion, an excess content that cannot be completely eradicated. And children, finding themselves relegated to "minor" status, can identify with those who share their condition, albeit in different ways. In other words, this excess or surplus content becomes a point of unwitting class identification. And if the "little folk" of the story resort to violence against a system that seems omnipresent, then that violence too is celebrated through the child listener's fascination and desire to hear the story, again and again.

I would suggest that we find this pattern too in some of the more bloodthirsty stories that are so attractive to children in the Bible. Those of Jael, Ehud, and David are narratives of violence and bloodshed, but it is in response to the oppressive violence already prevalent in those stories: Jael undertakes her tent maintenance in the context of the much greater violence of battle; Ehud responds to the systemic violence of occupation with a single act that would now be dubbed "terrorist"; and David's stone silences the blustering violence of men and their armies.

We may understand this desire for biblical violence in two ways. First, I have always been struck by the way biblical narratives in general provide ways to negotiate the complex patterns of human (and indeed nonhuman, that is, animal and natural) interactions. The mother who welcomes back her runaway daughter with a barbecue for the wider clan unwittingly invokes the story of the Prodigal Son; or the child who swears in a fit of jealous rage, "I'll kill him," touches closely on the account of Cain and Abel. So also these children's Bible stories enable a child to negotiate, sometimes successfully and sometimes not, the complex relations and issues involved in growing up. They are of course not the only means by which a child does so, not the least because many children simply do not hear or read such stories, but they do provide one mode of negotiation and perhaps also of empowerment (see Jones).

Yet this position takes us only so far, so let me pick up on my earlier comments concerning identification with the oppressed "little people" in these biblical stories, although now with a dialectical twist. To begin with, we may read these children's Bible stories not as post factum, taking shape within a context of developing bourgeois ideology and its underlying capitalism, finding a niche within that type of literature most appropriate to the reshaped category of childhood. Instead, biblical children's stories played a vital role in the reconstruction of that category in the first place. Indeed, they continue to provide a major foundation for maintaining the sense that childhood is a distinct phase of life. After all, these stories separate themselves from the world of adults in the very act of being written, illustrated, published, and consumed. At this level, these Bible stories become part of the ideological and social construction of the bourgeois project, offering little that is liberating (see Bottigheimer, "God and the Bourgeoisie").

Yet this is one side of the dialectic, leading to a position that closes down any liberatory possibilities. The earlier readings of bloodthirsty biblical stories suggests otherwise. The key is that these stories, like the fairy tales that interested Bloch so much, are imported from outside the construction of childhood as a phase of life. Even watered down, moralized, and made palatable for children, they cannot be completely contained. They carry with them a revolutionary surplus that persists, especially in their portrayals of the downtrodden and unlikely hero with whom children, or indeed any oppressed group, can identify. In this respect, these stories carry with them the same rebellious impulse that refused to be silenced even in the editing process of the Bible itself, in which the intellectual elites sought to provide a collated text that was acceptable to their ruling-class patrons. This impulse or surplus is found with surprising frequency even in Bible stories edited and retold for children. At this level, the stories become elements in the agency of children in negotiating a world not initially of their own construction. And in that act, children who identify with such stories also inadvertently express their resistance to that constructed phase known as childhood. To gloss Bloch's observation that the "Bible is the church's bad conscience" (*Atheism* 21), I would suggest that children's Bible stories may well be seen as the bourgeoisie's bad conscience.

NOTES

1. On such a materialist register do I read the criticisms leveled at Ariès (see Adams 2–4 and the references cited there), which involve locating distinct senses of childhood before capitalism. Rather than seeing such criticisms as simple refutations, Ariès's position requires a more supple materialist reading.

2. See the excellent survey of the complex interchanges between these perceptions of childhood by Gill Valentine (583–587). See also Christopher Ellison and John Bartkowski.

3. Of course, such efforts at rendering biblical narratives into forms deemed appropriate for children is a practice that goes back to the relatively late (in comparison to China) discovery of the printing press in western Europe. For an excellent and comprehensive study that traces the changing perceptions of childhood in the West from the sixteenth century onward and thereby the nature of children's Bible stories, see Ruth Bottigheimer, *The Bible for Children.*

4. This focus on violence and the more gruesome side of life is more characteristic of children's stories of the Bible in the precapitalist period (Luttikhuizen).

5. In contrast to these two works, Sally Lloyd-Jones's *The Jesus Storybook Bible* (2007) lies somewhere in between, for it does not shy away from telling the more gruesome stories of the Bible, yet the copious illustrations tend to avoid depicting those moments, even with accounts such as David and Goliath or the drowning of the Egyptians in the Red Sea. The exceptions are few: the Ten Plagues on the Egyptians and the death of Jesus.

6. One cannot help wondering if one of the grandchildren might have asked, "Grandpa, what is sexual perversion?"

7. A text to be avoided here is Bruno Bettelheim's dreadful effort, in which he makes a mess of Freudian psychoanalysis and reshapes fairy tales for the sake of therapeutic moralizing. See further Jack Zipes, *Breaking the Magic Spell,* 160–182.

WORKS CITED

Adams, Gillian. "Medieval Children's Literature: Its Possibility and Actuality." *Children's Literature* 26 (1998): 1–24. Print.

Ariès, Philippe. *Centuries of Childhood.* Translated by Robert Baldick. London: Pimlico, 1996. Print.

Bettelheim, Bruno. *The Uses of Enchantment: The Meaning and Importance of Fairy Tales.* New York: Alfred A. Knopf, 1976. Print.

Bloch, Ernst. *Atheism in Christianity: The Religion of the Exodus and the Kingdom.* 1968. Translated by J. T. Swann. New York: Herder and Herder, 1972. Print.

———. *Principle of Hope.* 1959. Translated by Neville Plaice, Stephen Plaice, and Paul Knight. Cambridge: MIT Press, 1995. Print.

Bottigheimer, Ruth. *The Bible for Children: From the Age of Gutenberg to the Present.* New Haven: Yale University Press, 1996. Print.

———. "God and the Bourgeoisie: Class, the Two-Tier Tradition, Work, and Proletarianization in Children's Bibles." *The Lion and the Unicorn* 17:2 (1993): 124–134. Print.

Boyer, Robert. *The Regulation School: A Critical Introduction.* Translated by Craig Charney. New York: Columbia University Press, 1990. Print.

Chancellor, Deborah, and Anna C. Leplar. *Children's Everyday Bible.* London: Dorling Kindersley, 2002. Print.

Dahl, Roald. *Charlie and the Chocolate Factory.* London: Allen & Unwin, 1967. Print.

———. *James and the Giant Peach.* London: Allen & Unwin, 1967. Print.

———. *Matilda.* London: Jonathan Cape, 1988. Print.

———. *The Witches.* London: Jonathan Cape, 1983. Print.

Davidson, Alice Joyce, and Victoria Marshall. *Psalms and Proverbs.* Alice in Bibleland Storybooks. Norwalk, Conn.: C. R. Gibson, 1984. Print.

———. *The Story of Baby Jesus.* Alice in Bibleland Storybooks. Norwalk, Conn.: C. R. Gibson, 1985. Print.

Delval, Marie-Hélène. *Reader's Digest Bible for Children: Timeless Stories from the Old and New Testaments.* Translated by Ronnie Apter and Mark Herman. New York: Reader's Digest, 1995. Print.

Ellison, Christopher G., and John P. Bartkowski. "Religion and the Legitimation of Violence: Conservative Protestantism and Corporal Punishment." In *The Web of Violence: From Interpersonal to Global,* edited by J. E. Turpin and L. R. Kurtz, 48–67. Urbana: University of Illinois Press, 1997. Print.

Hazen, Barbara Shook. *David and Goliath.* A Little Golden Book. New York: Golden Books, 1974. Print.

Hoyles, Martin, and Phil Evans. *The Politics of Childhood.* London: Journeyman Press, 1989. Print.

Jameson, Fredric. "Science Fiction as a Spatial Genre: Generic Discontinuities and the Problem of Figuration in Vonda McIntyre's *The Exile Waiting.*" *Science Fiction Studies* 14 (1987): 44–59. Print.

Jones, Gerard. *Killing Monsters: Why Children Need Fantasy, Super Heroes, and Make-Believe Violence.* New York: Basic Books, 2002. Print.

Lloyd-Jones, Sally. *A Child's First Bible.* New York: Reader's Digest, 1998. Print.

———. *The Jesus Storybook Bible.* Grand Rapids, Mich.: Zonderkidz, 2007. Print.

Luttikhuizen, Gerard, ed. *Eve's Children: The Biblical Stories Retold and Interpreted in Jewish and Christian Traditions.* Leiden: Brill Publishers, 2003. Print.

Peale, Norman Vincent. *Bible Stories.* Carmel, N.Y.: Guideposts, 1973. Print.

Tutu, Desmond. *Children of God Storybook Bible*. Grand Rapids, Mich.: Zondervan, 2010. Print.

Valentine, Gill. "Angels and Devils: Moral Landscapes of Childhood." *Environment and Planning D: Society and Space* 14 (1996): 581–599. Print.

Zipes, Jack. *Breaking the Magic Spell: Radical Theories of Folk and Fairy Tales*. New York: Routledge, 1979. Print.

———. *Fairy Tales and the Art of Subversion: The Classical Genre for Children and the Process of Civilization*. New York: Routledge, 1988. Print.

Utopia and Anti-Utopia in Lois Lowry's and Suzanne Collins's Dystopian Fiction

ANGELA E. HUBLER

The vast majority of dystopian and utopian fiction for young adults is shaped by the Cold War horror of a collective. Generations of children, in the United States at least, have read Madeleine L'Engle's *A Wrinkle in Time*, in which the Murry children learn the value of individualism and freedom. In Camazotz, the novel's dystopia, "all of the children on the street bounce their balls in strictly exact unison" (Hintz and Ostry 7). The protagonist learns that conformity does not lead to happiness, and she returns home to the United States, the novel's real good place, where, despite the suffering that those who are different experience, difference is tolerated. L'Engle won the Newbery Medal for this novel in 1963. To ensure that children in the United States continue to treasure the ideology of individualism, the American Library Association awarded the 1994 medal to Lois Lowry's *The Giver*, assuring it, like *A Wrinkle in Time*, best-seller status and a semipermanent position in the classroom. In *The Giver*, Lowry warns that dystopia results from efforts to construct an ideal society, and that a loss of individual freedom is the cost of utopian striving. Rather than social change, then, in the third book of the tetralogy inaugurated by *The Giver*, she prescribes a religious remedy for social conflict. Thus, like L'Engle, Lowry stresses the dangers of mind control, affirms the current U.S. status quo, and discourages collective efforts to improve on it. Other old chestnuts typically assigned to middle and high school students—George Orwell's *1984* and William Golding's *Lord of the Flies*, for example—reiterate L'Engle's and Lowry's ideological themes. Some recent young adult dystopian novels offer a more radical perspective on the theme of mind control, demonstrating the way technology is used to enforce the capitalist imperative to consume, for example M. T. Anderson's *Feed*.

It's rare, however, to encounter a dystopian novel like Suzanne Collins's *The Hunger Games* (2008) and its sequels, *Catching Fire* and *Mockingjay*: what's targeted isn't Cold War–era mind control but economic inequality, totalitarian rule, and oppression maintained by brute force. Astonishingly, the novels also depict a revolution that overthrows this oppression. Even more surprisingly, *The Hunger Games* has been on the *New York Times* bestseller list of children's series for 161 weeks (at number one for 128 of those weeks)—and was released as a film in 2012, with the sequels in production. There are now twenty-three million copies of the book in print (according to Scholastic Press, the publisher), compared to more than five million copies of *The Giver*. Of the two writers, Lowry is the more established and lauded, and as such her books have a firm place in the school curriculum: one of my sons read *The Giver* in the sixth and ninth grades, and the other was assigned the book in two different classes as well! Collins's more recent 2008 publication of *The Hunger Games* has outsold *The Giver*, but her work has not garnered the prestigious awards that Lowry's has. While both series are enormously popular, they merit analysis not just because of their popularity but because they offer profoundly different—paradigmatically different—views about the possibility of social and political change.

Generically, Lowry's and Collins's trilogies are similar, and like most dystopian writers, both promote individual resistance to totalitarianism. But while both depict dystopian societies, the representation of these societies functions very differently in the respective writers' works. Collins, in fact, is both more pessimistic than Lowry in her assessment of the United States— suggesting a dystopian future if her warnings against dangerous tendencies are not heeded—and more optimistic in her assessment of the possibility of collective efforts to achieve social justice. Despite superficial generic similarities, then, Lowry and Collins represent two historical antinomies: Lowry that of Anti-Utopia and Collins that of Utopia.

Utopia and Anti-Utopia

The distinction between Lowry's and Collins's series as representing the Anti-Utopian and Utopian, respectively, is based on a critical framework developed by Tom Moylan to study dystopian narrative. Moylan distinguishes between terms that specify literary form—utopia, anti-utopia, dystopia, pseudo-dystopia—and those that refer to "historical antinomies"—Utopia and Anti-Utopia (157). Drawing on the ways that these terms have been utilized by Darko Suvin, Lyman Sargent, Fredric Jameson, and other critics, Moylan argues that literary texts must be understood both formally and in terms of the sociopolitical positions that they represent. Moylan calls Utopia an "impulse or historical force" that can be distinguished "from its various expressions (as texts, communal societies, or social theories)" (155). This "impulse" can be understood, Sargent explains, as "social dreaming—the dreams and nightmares that concern the ways in which groups of people arrange their lives and which usually envision a radically different society than the one in which the dreamers live" (3). While the proponents of Utopia imagine the possibility of a better world, Anti-Utopia, not surprisingly, is an "outright rejection of both Utopia and the historical changes it informs and helps to produce" (Moylan 134). In 1991, just after the fall of the Berlin Wall and the breakup of the Soviet Union, when Jameson gave the lectures published as *The Seeds of Time*, he noted that "it would seem that the times are propitious for Anti-Utopianism; and, particularly in Eastern Europe, but washing all the way back over the reactionary revisions of the French Revolution that have momentarily gained currency in Western Europe, the critique and diagnosis of the evils of the Utopian impulse has become a boom industry" (53). Jameson's comment appears to be relevant to the publication and popularity of Lowry's *The Giver*, which depicts a society that aimed to be utopian but went very wrong, and its dystopian sequels.

The Political Unconscious of Lowry's Fiction

Lowry claims: "I don't make political statements" (Hintz and Ostry 196). Jameson argues, however, that "there is nothing that is not social and historical—indeed, . . . everything is 'in the last analysis' political" (*Political Unconscious* 20). Thus, the imagination that we envision to be somehow walled off from the social and historical is in fact shaped by it, constituting what Jameson calls "the political unconscious" (20). In fact, Jameson insists that any attempt to distinguish between "cultural texts that are social and political and those that are not becomes something worse than an error: namely, a symptom and a reinforcement of the reification and privatization of contemporary life" (20). That is, the refusal to acknowledge the relationship between the "public and the private, between the social and the psychological, or the political and the poetic, between history or society and the 'individual'" does not free us "from the grip of Necessity" but conversely strengthens its power over us (20). As I will argue, this is, indeed, the case with Lowry's tetralogy. While the novels depict the horrors of collective and totalitarian societies, Lowry's desire to champion the individual while refusing to "make political statements" paradoxically suggests that the attempt to create a truly free society is futile.

The historical events shaping the novels' political unconscious include the Cold War horror of the collective and of the threat of a totalitarian society. Moylan notes that in the twentieth century, "Anti-Utopia . . . found its most powerful vocation in shaping the hegemonic reaction against communism and socialism" (131). Indeed, as Lowry herself remarks, "I think, on one level, the book [*The Giver*] can be read supporting conservative ideals—it challenges the tendencies in any society to allow an invasive government to legislate all lives" (Silvey). Her tetralogy is Anti-Utopian in suggesting in her depiction of the community of *The Giver* that the utopian attempt to create a better society is "more dangerous than it is worth" (Moylan xiii).

The protagonist of *The Giver*, Jonas, lives in a society that has been shaped by a utopian desire to achieve social harmony and safety. Strict population control has been instituted in order to eradicate hunger, which, Jonas learns, had led to warfare in the past (111). While the novel does not explicitly articulate that this has been done in part to eliminate racism, genetic engineering has made all skin color the same (94).[1] Potential sources of conflict—love, anger, pain, sexual desire, and other intense emotions—have also been repressed. Similarly, individuality and choice have been sacrificed for "Sameness" (94). It is "considered rude to call attention to things that were unsettling or different about individuals" (20). Color too, has been eliminated, symbolizing the sacrifice of that which gives beauty and meaning to life, the cost of utopian desire.

Jonas, however, is one of a very few people who have "the Capacity to See Beyond," which means that he can both perceive color and "receive memories"—telepathically presumably—of all that has been sacrificed in constructing the society (63). When Jonas discovers that those who are too much trouble to care for—the very old, newborns requiring excessive nurture, repeat criminals—are killed rather than innocuously "released," as he has been told, he escapes with the baby Gabriel, a fussy baby who has been scheduled for release (7–9). After days of searching without success for Elsewhere—another community in which they will be safe—Jonas and Gabriel find themselves starving, and Jonas questions his decision:

You have never been starving, he had been told. You will never be starving.

Now he was. If he had stayed in the community, he would not be.
... Once he had yearned for choice. Then, when he had had a choice,
he had made the wrong one: the choice to leave. And now he was
starving. ... If he had stayed, he would have starved in other ways. He
would have lived a life hungry for feelings, for color, for love.

And Gabriel? For Gabriel there would have been no life at all. So
there had not really been a choice. (173–174)

End of discussion. The novel, then, refuses to say "No to deprivation" (Bloch
5), sighing that while it would be nice to eliminate racism, sexism, war, and
hunger, the cost is too high: feeling, individuality, humanity itself. So, Lowry
suggests, we really do live in the best of all possible worlds, don't we? Here
in Elsewhere, also known as the United States of America.

In the conclusion of the novel, Jonas sees the lights of a village below,
and while his arrival and rescue there is not narrated in the novel, it is suggested. Jonas is spurred on by a memory of a sled, which he finds atop a
hill. As he sleds down holding Gabriel, "all at once he could see lights, and
he recognized them now. He knew they were shining through the windows
of rooms, that they were the red, blue, and yellow lights that twinkled from
trees in places where families created and kept memories, where they celebrated love. ... Suddenly he was aware with certainty and joy that below,
ahead, they were waiting for him; and that they were waiting, too, for the
baby" (179–180). The phrase "waiting for the baby" has more than one connotation here. One is indicated by the phrase "lights that twinkled from
trees"—Christmas trees decorated with colored lights, which suggests that
Elsewhere is a Christian community anticipating the birth of the baby Jesus
at Christmas. The syntax of the sentence also indicates that the "families"
are waiting for Jonas and Gabriel, the baby Jonas is rescuing. In an interview
about this novel, Lowry claims: "If I had begun to think in literally Christian terms, I would have backed off the project because I have no interest
in writing 'religious' books. Still, clearly, the theology is there, inherent in
the story" (Silvey). Paradoxically, then, while the deep logic of the novel is
Christian in that virtually all that is revealed about Elsewhere is its Christian character and thus, presumably, the factor determining the difference
between Elsewhere and the dystopia from which Jonas and Gabriel flee,
Elsewhere's Christianity is only obliquely indicated to the reader, particularly the child reader who may miss the subtle clues.

Although two characters escape a totalitarian society for "Elsewhere,"
that destination offers an alternative only to the dystopia within the novel,

but not to social reality outside of it. Indeed, the components of Elsewhere that define it as a refuge are central to U.S. ideology: seemingly unconstrained individual choice, the family, and Christianity. *The Giver* contains not a glimmer of Utopia, or as Ernst Bloch puts it, "hoping beyond the day which has become" (10). On the contrary, the dystopia functions to confirm the normative status quo of U.S. society.[2]

If the presence of Christianity promises utopia in *The Giver*, its impotence bespeaks dystopia in its sequel, *Gathering Blue*. This novel begins in a village that is neither the community that Jonah fled from, nor the Elsewhere to which he escapes, although it coexists in the same world with them. While the protagonist, Kira, knows that "the Worship-object, the mysterious wooden construction of two sticks connected to form a cross . . . was said to have had great power in the past," it has lost significance in this postapocalyptic society in which family life is devoid of marital and parental affection, the seriously injured are dragged to a field to die rather than cared for, girls are forbidden to read, and the gifts of a tiny group of artists are controlled by the ruling Council of Guardians (24). Kira is one of these artists, a weaver. But like the other artists, a singer and a carver, she has the power not just to represent what is, but to create the future. The Council of Guardians, however, "were forcing the children to describe the future they wanted, not the one that could be" (212). An alternative to this hell, the Elsewhere of *The Giver*, however, beckons: Kira's father, in fact, has been rescued by its inhabitants when he was injured and left for dead by a rival. He tells her, "There is no arguing. People share what they have, and help each other. Babies rarely cry. Children are cherished" (205). Thus, the unbelievable inhumanity of the dystopian society is countered by unbelievable harmony in the novel's seeming utopia.

In fact, the third novel in the sequence, *Messenger*, establishes human incapacity to create and sustain utopia. By the time the novel opens in the Elsewhere where refugees like Kira's father, Jonah, and Gabriel have been welcomed—called Village by its inhabitants—it is being transformed by "selfishness": a newcomer has opened a "Trade Mart" where villagers barter not material goods but "their deepest sel[ves]" to satisfy their greed and desire (34). As they trade away more of themselves, the villagers decide to close the town to newcomers. This offers a serious challenge to the utopian possibility that Elsewhere appears to offer in *The Giver* and *Gathering Blue*. The novel does not depict the political and economic factors that lead to immigration or that might result in hostility to immigrants. Instead, Lowry offers readers a religious allegory in which the "illusion" that has spoiled this utopian aspect of the Village is vanquished by the sacrificial death of a Christ-like figure, Matty, whose supernatural power of healing cures the village of evil at the cost of his own death.

Matty's death is not, however, analogous to the martyrdoms of people like Archbishop Óscar Romero or Martin Luther King Jr., understood by progressive Christians as Christ-like sacrifices. Unlike King and Romero, Matty is not murdered by the opponents of a collective social movement designed to transform the material conditions of an unjust society. Nor has he exhorted the villagers to act out of love rather than self-interest. Instead, he heals the villagers by pouring his strength out onto the earth: "He simply clawed at the earth, feeling the power in his hands enter, pulsating, into the ruined world. He became aware, suddenly, that he had been chosen for this" (166). As Matty dies, the village, villagers, and surrounding forest return to their previous state. So . . . apparently the mechanism to achieve—or in this case restore—the good (though not utopian) society is the self-sacrifice of supernatural individuals. Pertinent here is Lyman Tower Sargent's assertion that the "ideological roots of anti-utopianism" are found "in the Christian idea of original sin, with its implications that fallen humanity cannot, and in some versions, must not, improve its own condition in this life" (Moylan 134).

The logic of this sacrifice, however, is unclear. Is Matty's death atonement for the villagers' evil? How does his death remove conflict from the village? This confusion, or "misunderstanding," René Girard argues, is in fact a necessary part of sacrifice (7). In *Violence and the Sacred*, Girard rejects expiation (or atonement) as the logic of sacrifice: "Rather, society is seeking to deflect upon a relatively indifferent victim, a 'sacrificeable' victim, the violence that would otherwise be vented on its own members, the people it most desires to protect" (4). Sacrifice, then, functions to prevent uncontrolled violence potentially resulting from "dissensions, rivalries, jealousies, and quarrels" (8) within primitive societies without a judicial system. One wonders, then, given the fact that most readers of Lowry's novel live within societies with judicial systems, what the significance of this sacrifice—or the novel—might be. To assert the fallen nature of humanity: a proclivity to selfishness that makes violence inevitable? A consequent need for periodic sacrifice?

In any case, this conclusion locates the novel, if not the entire series, firmly within the realm of the mythic rather than the historical. Thus, conflicts in the novel are represented as irresolvable through political and social change, which is displaced by the demonstration of a universal truth about the selfishness of human nature that ensures social conflict regardless of social organization. This situation requires a divine intervention. The rejection of a utopian historical project, imagined by Lowry as "social engineering," in favor of the radical individualism reflected in *The Giver* creates a new problem for Lowry, which she must resolve supernaturally, given her rejection of social and political remedies.[3]

With this, Lowry places herself firmly within the tradition of Western dystopian fiction discussed by M. Keith Booker, who argues that this tradition is "quintessentially bourgeois" in that it tends toward "suppression of any positive (utopian) figuration of collective experience. After all, the paradigm of dystopian fiction is an oppositional confrontation between the desires of a presumably unique individual and the demands of an oppressive society that insists on total obedience and conformity in its subjects" (59).

Similarly, the authors of *New World Orders in Contemporary Children's Literature* assert that Lowry's constructions of community are more conservative than transformative (Bradford et al. 110). They note that "the qualities which distinguish Village as a utopian community echo national mythologies of the United States as a haven for those from dysfunctional and impoverished communities" (110). In keeping with this location of political threat outside of the boundaries of the United States, Lowry notes the similarity of Kira's village in *Gathering Blue* to Afghanistan, where the Taliban denied women the ability to read and are guilty of "subjugation of women, and brutality toward the weak" ("A Conversation" 7). With this, Lowry deflects any attention to women's oppression in the United States. Never mind that the United States' support for mujahideen efforts to overthrow the Afghan government set the stage for the Taliban to take power. Instead, social criticism implicit in the novel is deflected outward: American ideology is celebrated and the United States contrasted with countries lacking the traditional liberties we are supposed to enjoy.

The Material Basis of *The Hunger Games* Trilogy

Unlike Lowry, Suzanne Collins acknowledges that her writing is motivated by political and utopian desires. She says that she hopes dialogue about the wars represented in her *Gregor* and *Hunger Games* series will help eliminate war: "Obviously, we're not in a position at the moment for the eradication of war to seem like anything but a far-off dream. But at one time, the eradication of slave markets in the United States seemed very far off. . . . We can change. . . . It's not simple, and it's a very long and drawn-out process, but you can hope" (Margolis). In another interview, Collins says that she sees the series as "an exploration of 'unnecessary' war and 'necessary' war, when armed rebellion is the only choice" (Italie). Thus, while the media has described her trilogy as promoting an antiwar message and some even see it as pacifist, Collins's clear sympathy with those who rebel against their oppressors, even violently, suggests that her position is more complex than an unequivocal commitment to nonviolence.[4]

The Hunger Games trilogy is set in Panem, "the country that rose up out of the ashes of a place that was once called North America" (*Hunger Games* 18). Panem, "a Capitol ringed by thirteen districts," emerges from a war for survival after natural disaster, climate change, and famine (18). Those in the districts "battle starvation" as they labor to provide the elite inhabitants of the Capitol with the food and consumer goods that make it a material paradise (19). After a failed rebellion against the Capitol in which one of the rebelling districts, 13, is supposedly "obliterated" (18), the Hunger Games are imposed upon the twelve districts that remain. The games are a yearly televised spectacle in which twenty-four "tributes," a boy and a girl from each district, fight to the death, leaving just one victor alive. This brutal competition serves both to punish the districts for their attempted rebellion and to provide entertainment for the Capitol. However, when Katniss, the trilogy's sixteen-year-old protagonist, is selected as a tribute, she teams up with the male tribute from her district, Peeta, and with the aid of their mentor, Haymitch, a District 12 victor from an earlier games, both survive the games. When Katniss and Peeta are again selected as tributes in the next games, tributes from five other districts join in an act of rebellion against the Capitol and ally themselves with Katniss and Peeta. A full-scale armed rebellion ensues, which succeeds in overthrowing the Capitol and forming a democratic republic (*Mockingjay* 83).

Collins represents this rebellion as a response not to ideological but to material factors. The plot follows the trajectory outlined by Ernst Bloch in *The Principle of Hope*: "Hunger cannot help continually renewing itself. But if it increases uninterrupted, satisfied by no certain bread, then it suddenly changes. The body-ego then becomes rebellious, does not go out in search of food merely within the new framework. It seeks to change the situation which has caused its empty stomach, its hanging head. The No to the bad situation which exists, the Yes to the better life that hovers ahead, is incorporated by the deprived into *revolutionary interest*. This interest always begins with hunger, hunger transforms itself, having been taught, into an explosive force against the prison of deprivation. Thus the self seeks not only to preserve itself, it becomes explosive; self-preservation becomes self-extension" (75–76). Like Bloch, Collins represents the revolutionary force of hunger. Far from being a necessary evil, hunger is one of the deprivations that motivates those who rebel against Panem. In Panem, Collins indicts a country in which some are sick with excess and others starve. At a hedonistic party in the Capitol, Katniss is appalled by the contrast between excess and privation: "All I can think of is the emaciated bodies of the children at our kitchen table as my mother prescribes what the parents can't give. . . . Often . . . there was nothing to give and the child was past saving, anyway. And here in the Capitol they're vomiting for the pleasure of filling their bellies again and again" (*Catching Fire* 80).

Collins has made it clear that such scenes are extrapolated from contemporary society, saying that "real world events influenced the story. . . . I think it's crucial that young readers are considering scenarios about humanity's future. In *The Hunger Games* I hope they question elements like the global warming, the destruction of the environment. How do you feel about the fact that some people take their next meal for granted when some people don't have enough to eat?" (Tanenhaus). Collins may be referring here to the more than seventeen million U.S. children who lived in food-insecure (low food security and very low food security) households in 2009 (U.S. Department of Agriculture). Hunger is, of course, the result of poverty, which has been increasing in the United States in recent decades, along with income inequality, also problematized in the trilogy. Shockingly, the poverty rate for children in the United States reached its lowest level in 1969 at 14 percent, whereas by 2009 it had risen to 21 percent (DeNavas-Walt, Proctor, and Smith 56).[5] These statistics are a consequence of the current economic crisis, which is itself the culmination of long-term trends. Johanna Brenner says, "For all families headed by adults aged 25–54, the last thirty years have seen median family income plummet by 29 per cent in the lowest income families—the bottom 30 per cent of all families—and by 13.2 per cent for families in the middle 50 per cent of the income distribution. Meanwhile, rather than losing ground, median income rose for families in the top 20 per cent" (68).

The source of such economic hardship is hotly debated. While groups like the various Tea Party organizations see excessive taxation and government spending on social welfare as the origins of their economic hardship, the extreme inequality that Collins represents resonates with explanations like David Harvey's, who argues that the crisis has resulted from "the internal contradictions of capital accumulation." While thirty years of wage repression has filled the pockets of international finance capitalists, creating a host of new millionaires and billionaires, labor has struggled to maintain purchasing power by increasing credit card and mortgage debt.[6]

Whereas Lowry represents restrictions on individualism as totalitarian evil, Collins shows the way in which competitive individualism is mobilized by the ruling class to maintain relations of domination and oppression. Conflict in the Districts, for example, is fostered not only by the Hunger Games but also by the tesserae, tokens that allow the children of the "poor and starving" to receive a year's supply of grain and oil per family member in exchange for additional entries in the drawing to select tributes for the games (*Hunger Games* 13). Gale, an inhabitant of the Seam, the part of District 12 inhabited by coal miners, believes that the tesserae are a "way to plant hatred between the starving workers of the Seam and those who can generally count on supper and thereby ensure we will never trust one another. 'It's to the Capitol's advantage to have us divided among ourselves,'" he says (14).

The trilogy's Hunger Games remind readers of both our own reality television programming and the gladiatorial games of ancient Rome, referred to in the Latin word for bread, *panem*, which is both the name of the country in which the trilogy is set and part of a phrase, *panem et circenses* (bread and circuses), coined by the Roman satirist Juvenal. With this phrase, Juvenal identified the mechanism by which the state pacified its subjects and distracted them from political reality and civic responsibility. Reality television functions similarly, and, in fact, Collins has said that the idea for *The Hunger Games* came to her as she "was channel surfing between reality TV programming and actual war coverage. . . . On one channel there's a group of young people competing for, I don't know, money maybe? And on the next, there's a group of young people fighting an actual war. And I was tired, and the lines began to blur in this very unsettling way, and I thought of this story" ("Conversation"). Collins identifies several problems with reality television: "the voyeuristic thrill—watching people being humiliated, or brought to tears or suffering physically. . . . There's also the potential for desensitizing the audience, so that when they see real tragedy playing out on, say, the news, it doesn't have the impact it should" ("Conversation").

But there are other aspects of reality television relevant to the trilogy: one subgenre of such programming, the makeover variety (*What Not to Wear*, *The Biggest Loser*, *Bridalplasty*, etc.), reduces human needs to commodity consumption in pursuit of superficial self-transformation, while another, initiated by *Survivor*, promotes individualism and the profit motive. Thus, the potentially revolutionary human desire for freedom and authenticity, "the better life that might be possible," is "harnessed and manipulated . . . colored pink and tinged with blood" (Bloch 3, 13), that is, bought at the expense of the exploitation of someone else.

In Katniss, Collins depicts a character who increasingly challenges the competitive individualism promoted by the Capitol, and with it, its power. At the end of the first Hunger Games competition, Katniss and the other tribute still alive, Peeta, are incapable of killing one another to win. But Katniss initiates a game of brinksmanship with the gamekeepers when she suddenly realizes that the games must have a victor: she and Peeta begin to eat poison berries and are only halted by a last-minute announcement declaring them both to be victors.

Katniss's motives for her risky ploy aren't clear, even to her. What is clear, however, is that her action has been understood as an act of resistance to the Capitol, and her pin with a mockingjay is seen as the emblem of the growing uprising. Even when Katniss learns of this, however, she proposes not to join the rebels but to escape with her closest friends and family members. But Gale convinces her otherwise. She realizes, "it isn't enough to keep myself, or my family, or my friends alive by running away. . . . Even if I could. It wouldn't fix anything. It wouldn't stop people from being hurt" (*Catching Fire* 118). With this, Katniss's commitment to individual self-preservation shifts to political solidarity with those who share her condition.

Solidarity among the oppressed is the only force capable of overthrowing the domination of the Capitol, or of any brutal regime. Haymitch reminds Katniss of this in his last words of advice before she begins her second Hunger Games: "just remember who the enemy is" (*Catching Fire* 260). This insight is critical to the formation of solidarity and the instigation of rebellion as demonstrated in *Spartacus*, the semihistorical 1960 film by Stanley Kubrick that Collins says she "drew upon" in her trilogy (Blasingame 727). *Spartacus* depicts a slave rebellion against the Roman Republic as beginning at a school for gladiators, when Draba, the victor in a death match against Spartacus, asks his aristocratic audience to be allowed to show mercy to his opponent. When they give the thumbs down, rather than killing Spartacus, Draba throws his trident at his ruthless spectators and then leaps into their box to attack them. While Draba is killed, his action inspires Spartacus and other slaves in the school to rise up; the historical Spartacus, a Thracian gladiator who was a slave leader in the Third Servile War (73–71 BCE), has inspired revolutionaries through history. Collins surely refers to Draba in the character of Finnick, one of Peeta and Katniss's allies in the second Hunger Games, as she makes his weapon of choice the trident.

While the trilogy supports the necessity of the districts' rebellion, it also represents the cost of their victory. Some of the tributes who have allied themselves with Peeta and Katniss sacrifice themselves in the second Hunger Games in order to keep alive Katniss, the symbol of the uprising, and Peeta, whom she has dedicated herself to saving. For example, when Katniss is unable to carry Mags out of a deadly nerve gas attack, Mags walks directly into the gas—which immediately kills her—so that Finnick can carry Peeta. Unlike the religious sacrifice of Matty's life in *Messenger*, however, Mags's action is practical: she believes that by sacrificing herself, Katniss and Peeta will survive. Moreover, Mags hopes that their survival will allow them to lead a revolution that will end the Hunger Games and the oppressive rule of the Capitol. In fact, her sacrifice is rewarded, and the uprising succeeds.

The cost of this success, however, is high. Peeta "clutches the back of the chair and hangs on until the flashbacks are over" and Katniss "wake[s] screaming from nightmares of mutts and lost children" (*Mockingjay* 388). Such passages make it clear that war scars even the victors with wounds that continue to traumatize them decades later. Again, it may be appropriate to relate these passages to recent events, as Collins says that "our wars in Afghanistan and Iraq, the popularity of reality television, and the state of the environment have had an effect" on her trilogy (Tanenhaus). This realistic depiction of the consequences of violence suggests that Collins's support for violence is limited.

This critical depiction of violence is clearly linked to the construction of masculinity in Katniss's romantic dilemma: whether she should choose Gale or Peeta. The two are represented in sharp contrast. Peeta doesn't try to conceal his emotions when he bids his family farewell after he is selected as a tribute; Katniss observes that he "has obviously been crying and interestingly enough does not seem to be trying to cover it up" (*Hunger Games* 40). In fact, Peeta is characterized by emotion: his self-sacrificial love for Katniss. Gale, however, is characterized in terms of traditional masculinity: Katniss says that at fourteen, Gale "already looked like a man. . . . He's good looking, he's strong enough to work in the mines, and he can hunt. You can tell by the way the girls whisper about him when he walks by in school that they want him" (10). Gale is hot, but he is too hot. In the conclusion of the trilogy, Katniss describes her choice of Peeta as inevitable: "I know this would have happened anyway. That what I need to survive is not Gale's fire, kindled with rage and hatred. I have plenty of fire myself. What I need is the dandelion in the spring. The bright yellow that means rebirth instead of destruction. The promise that life can go on, no matter how bad our losses. That it can be good again. And only Peeta can give me that" (*Mockingjay* 388). Gale's virility is sexy but dangerous in his embrace of violence. Like Katniss, a postrevolutionary society may be threatened by the ruthless destruction that results from a single-minded pursuit of victory at all costs.

More than fifteen years after the success of the revolution, Katniss fears that what has been achieved can still be lost. Thus Collins, like Lowry, is aware of the ways that efforts to improve society can be betrayed. Consequently, the sober conclusion of the novel does not offer the closure of utopia achieved. Rather, the *possibility* of a society free of war and oppression is offered. But while Lowry does not offer even the hope that human society can avert dystopia without supernatural intervention, Collins does. Despite the fact that humans are "fickle, stupid beings with poor memories and a great gift for self-destruction," Plutarch, the new secretary of communication, offers the possibility that "we are witnessing the evolution of the human race" (379).

The many proponents of Lowry's dystopian fiction assert that it empowers readers as "potential agents of positive social change" (Latham, Hanson) and urges them to utopian commitments (Hintz). However, as I have argued, the ways in which Lowry's novels manifest suspicion of utopian projects and project a static view of human nature as selfish and therefore incapable of creating and maintaining a just society without supernatural intervention align her not with the forces of Utopia but those of Anti-Utopia. Thus, while her novels encourage individual acts of moral resistance, the characters who exercise such agency in her work are not ordinary but have some sort of extraordinary talent or power. Collins, however, offers the hope to readers that a better society can be created through the collective efforts of ordinary people. And this she does because the fundamental view of the world upon which her fiction is based is Utopian.

ACKNOWLEDGMENTS

I would like to express my gratitude to Tim Dayton, Michele Janette, and Naomi Wood for their invaluable support at all stages of the writing of this essay.

NOTES

1. Susan Stewart's analysis of the novel is especially interesting in its discussion of the topic of racial difference, which she highlights.

2. In this, my reading agrees with that of Susan Stewart in her essay "A Return to Normal." But while Stewart sees the novel primarily as an endorsement of "our cultural values" (23), I argue that the novel goes beyond an endorsement of U.S. society to reject Utopia as a project of human liberation as too costly. In this, my analysis conflicts with Carter Hanson, who argues in "The Utopian Function of Memory in Lois Lowry's *The Giver*" that "through her protagonist's alienation from his society and resistance to it, the novel offers hope for a better future" (45).

3. The recent publication of the fourth novel in this series, *Son*, which begins in the dystopia that Jonas and Gabe escape from and moves to Village, extends the logic expressed in the previous novels. In it, Gabe's mother, Claire, sacrifices her youth to Trademaster in order to find her lost son, Gabe. Gabe, however, saves her from untimely death by using his gift to confront and destroy Trademaster. Unlike Matty, he survives.

4. Domenico Losurdo argues that even movements and individuals that profess pacifism have violated the principles of nonviolence, especially in "great historical crises" (85).

5. Importantly, this statistic is based on official U.S. government measures of poverty. In 2009, for example, poverty for a family of four was defined as annual household earnings below $22,050. However, these earnings are significantly below the cost of even basic needs. In fact, then, many more people than those recognized by the official poverty rates actually live in poverty. According to the National Center for Children in Poverty at Columbia University, "research shows that, on average, families need an income about twice that level to cover basic expenses. Using this standard, 42% of children live in low-income families."

6. According to *Forbes*, 2011 broke the records both for the number of global billionaires and for their "combined wealth" (Kroll and Dolan). The high point for U.S. millionaires was 2007 (Ody).

WORKS CITED

Azizian, Carol. "Staying Power of 'The Giver' Surprises Author Lois Lowry." Michigan Live, April 2, 2008. Accessed March 30, 2011. Website.

Blasingame, James. "An Interview with Suzanne Collins." *Journal of Adolescent and Adult Literacy* 52:8 (May 2009): 726–727. JSTOR. Accessed January 6, 2011. Website.

Bloch, Ernst. *The Principle of Hope*. Translated by Neville Plaice, Stephen Plaice, and Paul Knight. Cambridge: MIT Press, 1986. Print.

Booker, M. Keith. "African Literature and the World System: Dystopian Fiction, Collective Experience, and the Postcolonial Condition." *Research in African Literatures* 26:4 (Winter 1995): 58–75. JSTOR. Accessed November 15, 2010. Website.

Bradford, Clare, et al. *New World Orders in Contemporary Children's Literature: Utopian Transformations*. New York: Palgrave Macmillan, 2008. Print.

Brenner, Johanna. "Caught in the Whirlwind: Working-Class Families Face the Economic Crisis." In *Socialist Register 2011: The Crisis This Time*, edited by Leo Panitch, Greg Albo, and Vivek Chibber, 64–85. London: Merlin, 2010. Print.

Collins, Suzanne. *Catching Fire*. New York: Scholastic Press, 2009. Print.

———. "A Conversation: Questions and Answers." Scholastic. Accessed March 7, 2011. Website.

————. *The Hunger Games*. New York: Scholastic Press, 2008. Print.

————. *Mockingjay*. New York: Scholastic Press, 2010. Print.

DeNavas-Walt, Carmen, Bernadette D. Proctor, and Jessica C. Smith. *Income, Poverty, and Health Insurance in the United States: 2011*. U.S. Census Bureau, September 2012. Accessed January 10, 2013. Website.

Girard, René. *Violence and the Sacred*. Translated by Patrick Gregory. Baltimore: Johns Hopkins University Press, 1972. Print.

Hanson, Carter F. "The Utopian Function of Memory in Lois Lowry's *The Giver*." *Extrapolation* 50:1 (2009): 45–60. Print.

Harvey, David. "The Crises of Capitalism." Lecture presented to the Royal Society for the Encouragement of Arts, Manufactures and Commerce, RSA House, London, April 26, 2010. Accessed January 1, 2011. Website.

Hintz, Carrie, and Elaine Ostry, eds. *Utopian and Dystopian Writing for Children and Young Adults*. New York: Routledge, 2003. Print.

Italie, Hillel. "Suzanne Collins Completes 'The Hunger Games.'" Associated Press, September 23, 2010. Accessed January 1, 2011. Website.

Jameson, Fredric. *The Political Unconscious: Narrative as a Socially Symbolic Act*. Ithaca: Cornell University Press, 1981. Print.

————. *The Seeds of Time*. New York: Columbia University Press, 1994. Print.

Jordan, Tina. "Suzanne Collins on Writing a 'Hunger Games' Movie: 'You Have to Let Things Go.'" *Entertainment Weekly*, February 24, 2011. Accessed February 24, 2011. Website.

Kroll, Luisa, and Kerry A. Dolan. "World's Billionaires 2011: A Record Year in Numbers, Money and Impact." *Forbes*, March 9, 2011. Accessed April 11, 2011. Website.

Latham, Don. "Discipline and Its Discontents: A Foucauldian Reading of the Giver." *Children's Literature* 32 (2004): 134–151. Muse. Accessed March 2, 2011. Website.

Losurdo, Domenico. "Moral Dilemmas and Broken Promises: A Historical-Philosophical Overview of the Nonviolent Movement." *Historical Materialism: Research in Critical Marxist Theory* 18:4 (2010): 84–134. Print.

Lowry, Lois. "A Conversation with Lois Lowry." In *Gathering Blue*, 4–7. New York: Dell Laurel-Leaf, 2000. Print.

————. *Gathering Blue*. New York: Dell Laurel-Leaf, 2000. Print.

————. *The Giver*. New York: Bantam Doubleday Dell Books for Young Readers, 1993. Print.

————. *Messenger*. New York: Walter Lorrain Books, 2004. Print.

————. *Son*. New York: Houghton Mifflin Harcourt, 2012. Print.

Margolis, Rick. "The Last Battle: With 'Mockingjay' on Its Way, Suzanne Collins Weighs In on Katniss and the Capitol." *School Library Journal*, August 1, 2010. Accessed January 6, 2011. Website.

Moylan, Tom. *Scraps of the Untainted Sky: Science Fiction, Utopia, Dystopia*. Cumnor Hill, Oxford, England: Westview, 2000. Print.

National Center for Children in Poverty. "Child Poverty." Columbia University, Mailman School of Public Health. Accessed May 11, 2011. Website.

Ody, Elizabeth. "U.S. Millionaires' Ranks Increase 8%, Remain Below '07 High of 9.2 Million." Bloomberg, March 16, 2011. Accessed April 11, 2011. Website.

Sargent, Lyman Tower. "The Three Faces of Utopianism Revisited." *Utopian Studies* 5:1 (1994): 1–37. Print.

Silvey, Anita. "The Edwards Award-Winner Talks about *The Giver*'s Controversial Past and, Yes, Its Enigmatic Ending." *School Library Journal*, 2007, n.p. Accessed December 14, 2010. Website.

Stewart, Susan Louise. "A Return to Normal: Lois Lowry's *The Giver*." *The Lion and the Unicorn* 31:1 (2007): 21–35. Print.

Tanenhaus, Sam. "*Book Review* Podcast: Suzanne Collins." *New York Times*, August 27, 2010. Accessed November 29, 2012. Website.

U.S. Department of Agriculture. "Food Security in the United States: Key Statistics and Graphics." January 15, 2011. Accessed May 11, 2011. Website.

Ursula Le Guin's *Powers* as Radical Fantasy

JUSTYNA DESZCZ-TRYHUBCZAK

The term "Radical Fantasy" first appears in Fredric Jameson's contribution to a 2002 issue of *Historical Materialism: Research in Critical Marxist Theory*, edited by China Miéville and Mark Bould under the title "Symposium: Marxism and Fantasy," in which the rejection of fantasy as a genre marked by the instrumentalization of imagination and the exhaustion of utopian energies was successfully challenged from a variety of perspectives. Jameson's article, "Radical Fantasy," focuses on the category of radical or materialist fantasy, that is "a fantasy narrative apparatus capable of registering systemic change and of relating superstructural symptoms to infrastructural shifts and modifications" (280). As Jameson explains, elements of historical changes in a fantasy text may transform "the ethical superstitions of good and evil forces into concrete social phenomena a good deal more horrifying that the older abstractions," thereby allowing for the presentation of "the concrete social worlds of alienation and class struggle" (280). This laconic proposition was later elaborated upon by William J. Burling in his essay "Periodizing the Postmodern: China Miéville's *Perdido Street Station* and the Dynamics of Radical Fantasy." Looking at radical fantasy as a new fantastic genre characteristic of late postmodernism, Burling shows that it is marked by an interest in ethnically diversified groups of the marginalized and the oppressed who collectively organize themselves in a struggle to effect social change. It is within the context of joint action that individual integrity and ethical quandaries become particularly consequential.

The radical trend in fantasy has also developed within children's and YA literature. Examples of such content can be found in China Miéville's *Un Lun Dun*,[1] Frances Hardinge's *Gullstruck Island*,[2] and Philip Pullman's *His Dark Materials* trilogy.[3] Yet, however helpful Burling's elaboration of

Jameson's ideas undoubtedly is, his approach excludes texts that can also qualify as radical fantasy in that they present "deep history" (Jameson 280) even if at the same time they problematize processes of collective action and young protagonists' involvement in them. This essay examines the process of building a utopian world in *Powers*, the third volume of Ursula K. Le Guin's YA fantasy series *The Annals of the Western Shore* (2004–2007), which can be seen as the author's critical intervention in the genre of radical fantasy for young readers.[4] In *Powers*, the slave boy Gavir is a child living, to use the words of Odo, Le Guin's reformer from *The Dispossessed*, in "the guilt of ownership and the burden of economic competition" (247). In his search for freedom Gavir rejects various faulty forms of collective resistance, which inescapably become as oppressive as the sociopolitical configurations they were meant to transform. As he learns, a better world can originate only from a constant evolution of individuals and societies, in the spirit of mutual aid and solidarity. Accordingly, as Gavir does not reach any ultimate conclusion of his quest, the closure of the novel may seem ambiguous and even anti-utopian. Nevertheless, its purpose is not so much to stress the difficulty of conceiving a liberating utopian solution, but to emphasize the necessity of seeing change as a permanent and open-ended negotiation between the preservation of autonomous, provisional, and contextual subjectivity and collective social action. Generalizing from the example of *Powers*, it can be argued that the category of radical fantasy delineated by Burling may be extended to texts that also focus on specific social worlds marked by alienation but whose radicalizing potential resides in the very discussion of the nature of oppression and mechanisms of revolutionary efforts. Finally, it is also argued that although radical fantasy may not be any more subversive than other cultural forms, it may provide young readers with patterns of radical political subjectivity adequate to deal with contemporary forms of domination and exploitation.

Radical Fantasy and Young Utopians

In opposition to traditionally ahistorical approaches to fantasy, which fail to take into account concrete conditions of material production in their emphasis on aesthetic or moral values, Burling analyzes the development of the genre from a historical materialist perspective and sees radical fantasy as a form emerging in response to individual and collective life in late postmodernism and multinational capitalism. As he contends, "[t]he significance of Radical Fantasy can be understood only by an approach that recognizes innovation in form as a response to a specific historical context affecting not just fantasy but the entire system of the arts. Likewise what authors, readers, and critics have been calling 'the fantastic' for the century prior to the emergence of Radical Fantasy can be seen as a series of historically distinct formal responses corresponding to three eras of cultural production we now identify as modernism, late modernism, and postmodernism" (327). Postmodernism, Burling further argues, has been "superseded by yet another distinct phase, late postmodernism, which has emerged following economic shifts of the mid-1990s. In this new period of late postmodernism, Radical Fantasy is a representative" (327). In its contents, as Burling shows with the example of China Miéville's *Perdido Street Station* (2000), radical fantasy abounds with innovative devices of setting and characterization—predominantly (but not exclusively) urban backgrounds reflecting the domination of hegemonic economic and political practices, biologically diverse fantastic characters whose existence is an integral part of communities including humans, and representations of collective identities—all of which enable the depiction of social and political activism. Hence radical fantasy can be seen as a utopian form (along with science fiction and cyberpunk) both by the very fact of positing the impossible as the radical difference from the real and by depicting transformation in the presented social order.

The utopian potential of radical fantasy is exceptionally tangible in contemporary radical fantasy addressed to young readers as it facilitates conceptualizations of historical change and alternative social orders, as evidenced by young characters' engagement in abolishing existing power structures and building new networks of social relationships. Moreover, the emergent oppositional social, political, and cultural practices are depicted in the context of a redefined conception of a child-as-utopian, namely an individual who remakes hegemonic structures not by private rebellion but by inspiring and leading collective social action. Moreover, through inviting young readers to enter imaginary worlds, fantasy texts provide specific images of social structures and changes they undergo both as believable elements of a given fantastic universe and as metaphors commenting on real phenomena, thereby enabling readers first to vicariously experience transformation and then to relate it to their own predicaments. In this sense, in radical fantasy, the modus operandi of fantasy involving readers in the dialectic of analogy and difference is enhanced by the analysis of the dynamics of material conditions of social life and personal consciousness.

What also strengthens the critical impact of radical fantasy is the lack of happy endings suggestive of closure; rather, it is in fact toward the end of a story that young protagonists use their new knowledge and experience to continue transformations they have initiated. Therefore, fantastic worlds remain ambivalent sites of contradiction and only promise the possibility of solving conflicts, thereby representing the acknowledgment that societies are not fixed entities but sites of a perpetual conflict. Le Guin's comments on the most crucial functions of fantastic texts as depicting "alternatives to the status quo which not only question the ubiquity and necessity of extant institutions, but enlarge the field of social possibility and moral understanding" ("A War without End" 218), suggest the possibility of locating her fantasy texts for young readers within the genre of radical fantasy. So does her belief that young readers enjoy reading fantasy "because in their vigor and eagerness for experience they welcome alternatives, possibilities, change" (218–219).

A Utopian Project without End

Powers is a memoir of Gavir, another fictional child of Le Guin's—along with Myra, Tehanu, Therru, and, first and foremost, the Omelian child locked in the cell—who has been psychologically and materially damaged. Having escaped from his life as a slave in Etra, one of the City States constituting Le Guin's fantastic realm of the Western Shore,[5] Gavir arrives in Mesun, a university city famous both for its culture and learning and for its egalitarian social order. There, Gavir becomes an assistant to Orrec Caspro, a revolutionary poet who, in *Voices*, a prequel to *Powers*, contributes to a peaceful emancipation of a conquered city.[6] As a story about youth told from the perspective of the adult self who may have achieved a relative critical distance from the past but is still grappling with traumas from childhood, *Powers* is a poignant insight both into the mechanisms and psychology of oppression and into the complexities of attaining genuine personal and collective freedom. Moreover, the time span between the very act of storytelling and the events recollected by Gavir encourages readers to speculate about what may have happened in between, in particular whether the Western Shore has become more egalitarian and whether Gavir used his experience to contribute to this transformation.

As Gavir and sister, Sallo, have been slaves almost from the beginning of their lives, they do not know any alternative social order to that of Etra and the House of Arca, in which they serve. Hence Gavir not only accepts his lot but deeply believes that this is the best possible place for him to be. As an adult, Gavir bitterly comments on this blind sense of loyalty: "Writing about our life in the House of Arcamand in the City State of Etra, I fall back into it and see it as I saw it then, from inside and from below, with nothing to compare it to, and as if it were the only way things could possibly be" (25–26). As a child, Gavir uncritically trusts his owners: "I was not afraid of the Father. . . . I was in awe of him. I trusted him. He was completely powerful, and he was just. He would do what was right, and if we had to suffer, we had to suffer" (21). The boy's identification with Arcamand is so strong that hardly anything could give him more pleasure than being called by his name and praised by the Mother of the House. This exhilaration on Gavir's part should not come as a surprise in a society in which a slave "mother may believe the child she bore is hers, but property can't own property; we belong to the family, the Mother is our mother and the Father is our father," which little Gavir intuitively realizes very well (43). It is only with the benefit of hindsight and numerous experiences revealing mechanisms of oppression that Gavir will be able to conclude: "Children see the world that way. So do most slaves. Freedom is largely a matter of seeing that there are alternatives" (26). Admittedly, as the protagonist recalls, the masters of Arcamand were relatively benevolent toward their slaves, providing them with much better living conditions than other Etran Houses. Furthermore, the loyalty and obedience of Arcamand slaves were also consistently solidified by the teachings of Everra, an educated slave deeply convinced of the absolute rightness of his mission of inculcating in both the slave children and the children of the House the belief in the superiority of tradition. Such power relations exemplify the aforementioned internalization of power owing to which the oppressed themselves perpetrate oppression in their minds, for, to use Le Guin's phrase, "they have no opportunity even to perceive as capable of being changed" ("A War without End" 219). Finally, the internalization of hierarchy and domination is evident not only in the unquestioning obedience of the Arcamand slaves but also among the free citizens of Etra. This is the case with the submission of free women, including those from the elites, best exemplified in the lot-awaiting Astano, "[s]ilent and proper and modest and self-contained, a perfect Senator's daughter" (10), who is married off to a noble of another House without being asked about her own preferences.

Yet this apparently seamless hegemonic order is not impervious to disruptions in the form of small enclaves of resistance, which testify to the feasibility of creating an alternative reality and to the human capacity for mutual aid and solidarity. In the novel, this potential emerges particularly clearly in secret readings of revolutionary poets praising liberty, popular among educated slaves, and in children's games involving both slaves and their masters. As Gavir recalls his meetings with the slaves working to preserve archives in an Etran temple, he felt confused by their ability to criticize the dominant order: "My companions here, more refined in their manners than many nobles, and honest and mild in daily life, were in their talk and thought shamelessly disloyal to their Houses and to Etra itself. . . . They talked of their masters disrespectfully, contemptuous of their faults. They had no pride in soldiers of their House" (121). Their dissent is to a large extent fueled by their readings: "Denios—the greatest of poets, all my companions said—had been born a slave. In his poems he used the word liberty with a tenderness, a reverence, that made me think of my sister when she spoke of her beloved" (137). Although Gavir cannot fully comprehend the radicality of the poems and even protests his companions' disloyalty, he cannot stop thinking about the possibility of an alternative social order. Even the teachings of Everra, who for Gavir is a figure of authority, do not prevent him from musing on freedom.

It is only in retrospect that Gavir realizes that in fact he often participated in such transgressive behavior himself, for instance when playing soldiers. Although the young slaves had to obey the senator's son, in becoming soldiers they could imaginatively occupy the position that in Etra was available only to free men. Yet the most illustrative instances of the suspension of injustice in Arcamand were the family's summer stays at their farmhouse in Vente, especially, and understandably, during the absence of Senator Arca. As Gavir recalls those days, "[t]here was a lack of hierarchy and protocol. Everything seemed to go along quite well without the formalities and rigidities of life at Arcamand. . . . We ate outside at long tables under the oak trees near the kitchen, and though there was a Family table and a slave table, setting wasn't all by status. Everra usually sat at the Family table at the invitation of the Mother and Yaven, while Sotur and Astano, self-invited, sat with Ris and Sallo at ours. We sorted ourselves out less by rank than by age and preference. . . . But it changed, it had to change, when the Father arrived for the last few weeks of the summer" (65–66). The fact that such happy moments occur only when the patriarchal authority is absent reflects Le Guin's conviction that the feminine principle is inherently subversive, and even anarchistic: "The *'female principle' has historically been anarchic; that is, anarchy has historically been identified as female. The domain allotted to women—'the family,' for example—is the area of order without coercion"* ("Is Gender Necessary?" 11–12, italics in original).

A particularly telling example indicating the potential destabilization of the dominant order through both individual critical reflection and the oppositional potential of women is that of Astano and her cousin, Sotur, considering the possibility of using the farm slaves to build a stone fort. Despite having the right to order their slaves as they wish, the girls immediately realize that, by resorting to coercion, they would destroy the exceptional atmosphere and experience of subversive play at Vente:

> "We'd have to ask the foreman," Astano said to Sotur, and they briefly discussed the chances of getting any farm slave released to us. "Only if we said they were to work for us," said Sotur, and Astano replied, "Well, they would. We worked as hard as any of them do! Digging that moat was awful. And we never could have done without Yaven."
>
> "But it would be different," Sotur said.
>
> "Giving orders . . ." Astano said, "Yes."
>
> And there they left it. The idea was not mentioned again. (79)

It is worth noting that Astano and Sotur's reflections may also be seen as an illustration of Le Guin's belief that "children have a seemingly innate passion for justice; they don't have to be taught it. They have to have it beaten out of them, in fact, to end up as properly prejudiced adults" ("Reading Young, Reading Old" 53). Nevertheless, Le Guin is far from idealizing children, as some of her young characters, including Gavir, are hardly capable of critical reflection, having either internalized oppression or become oppressors themselves.[7]

Albeit temporary, unstable, and in fact dependent on the benevolence of the system, the abovementioned enclaves provide emancipatory spaces transcending class divisions and marked by solidarity and equity that nurture their participants when they inevitably have to submit to the oppression of hierarchical and centralized social organization. Nonetheless, even these spaces of alterity may not be enough to rely on in the face of the logic of scapegoating as the fundamental principle of any dystopian society, illustrated so powerfully by Le Guin in her story "The Ones Who Walk Away from Omelas." Just as in the short story, in *Powers* the author also uses the image of the suffering child to unmask society's dependence on the acceptance of injustice. The first instance of the ill-treated child is Miv, who dies after being violently hit by Torm, one of the two sons of the Arcas.

His parents do not punish him for his brutality, trying to ignore the shame brought upon the family by their son's behavior. The acknowledgment of the boy's guilt would inevitably expose the falsity of the Arcas' claim that, in comparison to other Houses, their household is based not on exploiting the slaves but on benevolent stewardship. As Gavir reminisces about this event, although he was still full of trust in the justice executed by his owners, "[i]t seemed to open cracks and faults in the world, to shake things loose. I went to the anteroom of the Ancestors and tried to pray to my guardian there, but his painted eyes looked through me, haughty and uninterested" (45). The little boy's death is only a premonition of Gavir's and Sallo's becoming scapegoats themselves, when the former is offered money to accept that his beloved sister's suffering and death had resulted from an accident, although in fact they had been caused by Torm, avenging himself on his brother. Gavir thus recalls Everra's attempts to hide the truth: "An accident, last night, in the pools at the Hot Wells. A sad accident, a terrible thing, Everra said, tears in his eyes . . . Sallo had been drowned—had drowned, he corrected himself—had drowned, as the young men, who had drunk too much and gone past all decency, were playing with the girls in the pool" (149). However ashamed of himself the teacher is for lying to the boy, he is too loyal to the Arcas to admit the truth. Later, when Gavir insistently asks whether Torm would be punished, Everra unwillingly reveals the sham behind the Family's reliance on justice:

> Everra started back as if afraid of me. "Be calm, Gavir, be calm," he said placatingly.
> "Will they punish him?"
> "For the death of a slave girl?" (151)

Everra's resigned reply undermines the boy's idealistic perception of Arcamand, which in turn causes him to run away.

Gavir's ultimate deprivation caused by the loss of Sallo may be seen as one more example of the use of the abused and forlorn child for the narrative purpose of affecting readers, which, as Laurie Langbauer rightly remarks with reference to such writers as Dickens, Dostoevsky, and Le Guin, is precisely another act of scapegoating (103–104). As Elizabeth Parsons argues, one of the dangers of relying on "the underdog trope as vehicle of the left" (356), or on antihegemonic critique in general, is that it may be also useful "to the other side of the ideological equation" (356). In her discussion, she refers to the commentary of Perry Nodelman and Mavis Reimer on the underdog motif in *The Pleasures of Children's Literature*, who stress that the motif is very common in texts for young readers and manifests itself, among other ways, in the fact that "a truly happy ending occurs only when a person who was oppressed achieves a position in which it is possible to oppress others" (Parsons 356). Parsons claims that such a scenario is frequent even in Marxist-oriented texts. Yet, Le Guin's narrative challenges Parson's argument: Gavir is more than a helpless underdog. By allowing the boy to realize that Arcamand is far from ideal, then having him escape so as to experience various forms of rebellion, and finally sending him on his own quest for freedom, the author allows the child protagonist to attempt to question and redefine oppressive distribution of power instead of becoming another "top dog" (Parsons 356).

Before Gavir begins his own "social dreaming" (Sargent 3), he participates in two anarchic projects which fail when, to use Tom Moylan's phrase, "centralization of power in an elite group and the reduction of the ideals of the revolution into a dogmatic ideology" negate "further emancipatory activity" (100). In both cases—in the community of the Forest Brothers and in the Barnavites' town, the Heart of the Forest—Gavir encounters attempts to form fraternal attitudes intended to eliminate social and economic inequities. As in *The Dispossessed*, in *Powers* Le Guin explores the very origins of the human instinct for solidarity. For her, it may be a result of the shared experience of pain and deprivation. As Dan Sabia comments on this motif in the context of *The Dispossessed*, Le Guin's intention is to indicate "that recognition of the individual's weaknesses and vulnerability is most starkly felt when one suffers, or sees others suffering. On those occasions, human beings instinctively reach for aid or comfort, or try to provide it, and in that moment the need for others, and hence for brotherhood or solidarity, becomes particularly clear" (114). Gavir initially fully identifies with the Forest Brothers, who, as he realizes, also "had escaped, run away from something unendurable" (179). As he further comments, "[t]hey were like me. They had no past. Learning how to get through this rough life, how to endure never being dry or warm and clean, to eat only half-raw, half-burnt venison. I might have gone with them ... not thinking beyond the present hour and what was around me" (179). The same awareness of the common past seems to be the principal foundation of the Barnavites' community, whose members escaped oppression in various parts of the Western Shore. Yet the ethic of mutual aid and solidarity professed in both groups degenerates into a dystopia of coercion, regulated by the relations of command and servility.

In the case of the Forest Brothers, the germs of the inevitable failure are visible in the oath the newcomers have to take to be accepted in the community: "If you live with us you'll learn what fair sharing means. . . . It means what we do, you do. It's one for all with us. If you think you can do whatever you like, you won't last here. If you don't share, you don't eat. If you're careless and bring danger on us, you're dead. We have rules. You'll take an oath to live with us and keep our oath. And if you break that oath, we'll hunt you down surer than any slave taker" (173). As it turns out, Gavir can survive in the community only because he knows how to fish and how to recite poems to entertain his companions. Moreover, the falsehood of the ideal of "the friendship of the Forest Brothers" (174) as a collectivity respecting the perspective and predicament of all its individual members becomes particularly palpable when one of them falls sick and cannot hunt. As he no longer contributes to the community's supplies, he is denied food and any other help. Moreover, when Gavir protests against being bullied by some of the Brothers, his friend, Chamry, warns him: "Don't be smarter than your masters. It costs" (186), making the boy understand that the freedom the Brothers seem to enjoy is in fact another form of oppression to which they agree to submit. Gavir recalls his response to Chamry: "'They're not my masters,' I said furiously. 'We're free men here!' 'Well,' Chamry said, 'in some ways'" (186).

Escaping imminent persecution for his opposition, Gavir joins the Barnavites, of whom he heard when still in Etra. For Etran slaves, tales are just "impossible romances," for, as Gavir comments, "the idea that a band of slaves could live as if they were masters, turning the age-old, sacred order upside down, could only be a daydream" (123). However, Gavir enjoys listening to "these idylls of forest liberty" as they awaken in him a yet undefined longing for an alternative to the only order he knows and accepts. One of the slaves recounts what he knows about the Barnavites: they are "a band of escaped slaves living somewhere in the great forests northeast of Etra. Under the leadership of a man named Barna, a man of their own—a republic, in which all men were equal, all free. Each man had a vote, and could be elected to the government, and diselected too, if he misgoverned. All work was done by all, and all goods and game shared in common. They lived by hunting and fishing and raiding rich people's chariots and the traders' convoys that went to and from Asion. Villagers and farmers in the whole region supported them and refused to betray them to the governments of Casicar and Asion; for the Barnavites generously shared their loot and bounty with their neighbours in these lonely districts, who, if not slaves, were bondsmen or freedmen living in dire poverty" (123–124). Furthermore, as Gavir learns, they are "answerable to no master or senator or king, bound only by freely given allegiance to their community"; they "never steal from the poor," and the women living in farms and villages are not afraid of them, as "a woman was welcome among them only if she joined them of her own free will" (124).

When Gavir arrives in the Heart of the Forest and becomes both a participant of the community and its observer, he is very much in awe of Barna and his ideas for the growth of the settlement, which Barna himself summarizes as the "the Law of Barna": "I've brought the city into the forest. What's the good of freedom if you're poor, hungry, dirty and cold? That's no freedom worth having. . . . [H]ere in our realm no man will live in slavery or in want. That's the beginning and the end of the Law of Barna" (198–199). In order to present the potential of the ideal of fraternity and simultaneously to emphasize problems besieging any attempt at building utopian societies, Le Guin devotes much space to Gavir's musings on Barna, his leadership, and the functioning of the community he sets up: "Barna was the heart of the Heart of the Forest. His vision, his decision, was always the point of reference for the others, his will was their fulcrum. He didn't maintain this mastery by intimidation but through the superiority of his energy and intelligence and the tremendous generosity of his nature: he was simply there before the others, seeing what must be done and how to do it, drawing them to act with him through his passion, activity, and goodwill. He loved people, loved to be among them, with them, he believed in brotherhood with all his heart and soul" (211). However, the more Gavir witnesses the social life of the Heart of the Forest, the more he understands that the tales he had heard in Etra are far from the truth, while the Law of Barna itself is only an empty idea that Barna more and more conspicuously fails to implement. On one occasion, Gavir proposes the establishment of a school for children, arguing that instead of being allowed to "run about as they pleased and find out for themselves what best suited them to do" (207), as Barna would like, they should in fact be forced to work in the fields together with the adults. Barna refuses, perhaps not because he is preoccupied with other issues but because such an arrangement could give rise to a collective social effort that would not be directly under his control, revealing his inability to accept that any rules for his community should result from interactions and consensus among its members.

Another instance of Barna's failure is his idea for a widespread revolution that would involve slaves all over the Western Shore. Initially, this utopian horizon attracts Gavir: "All that ancient evil ordained by the Ancestors, that prison tower of mastery and slavery, was to be uprooted and thrown down, replaced by justice and liberty. The dream would be made real" (226). However, it turns out that the rebellion would in reality mean the replacement of one form of terror and oppression with another. As Barna imagines "the Uprising":

> In every house in the city, the masters will be penned up in the barracks, the way they penned us in when there was threat of war . . . but now it's the masters locked up while the slaves run the household, as of course they always did, and keep the markets going, and govern the city. In the towns and the countryside, the same thing, the masters locked up tight, the slaves taking over, doing the work they always did, the only difference is they give the orders. . . . So the army comes to attack, but if they attack, the first to die will be the hostages, the masters, squealing for mercy. . . . The general thinks, ah, they're nothing but slaves with pitchforks and kitchen knives, they'll run as soon as we move in, and he sends in a troop to take the farm. They're cut to pieces by slaves armed with swords and crossbows . . . trained men fighting on their own ground. They take no prisoners. And they bring out one of the squealing masters, the father maybe, where the soldiers can see, and say: You attacked: he dies, and slice his head off. . . . And it won't end until the masters buy their liberty with every penny they have, and everything they have. Then they can come outside and learn out how the common folk live. (214–215)

The obvious lack of any emancipatory potential in Barna's Uprising, whose victory would inevitably lead to oppression, fear, and suffering, can again be explained by the internalization of hierarchy and oppression. Le Guin thus acutely diagnoses the inevitable defeat of revolutions: "I see their failure beginning when the attempt to rebuild the house so everybody can live in it becomes an attempt to grab all the saws and hammers . . . and keep the others out. Power not only corrupts, it addicts. Work becomes destruction. Nothing is built" ("A War without End" 217).

Barna's inability to imagine a radical alternative to the order he is trying to abolish becomes particularly clear to Gavir when he finally realizes that the mechanisms of coercion, control, and manipulation pervade Barna's community itself. The most telling instance of the community's falling short of the idea of brotherhood is the status of women as second-class citizens. As Gavir comments on the lives of women in the forest town, "in fact there weren't many women in the Heart of the Forest, and every one of them was jealously guarded by a man or a group of men. Those you saw in the streets and garden seem all to be pregnant or dragging a gaggle of infants with them, or else they were mere bowed backs sweeping, spinning, digging, milking, like old women slaves anywhere. There were more young women in Barna's house than anywhere else, the prettiest girls in the town, and the merriest. They dressed in fine clothes the raiders brought in. If they could sing or dance or play the lyre, that was welcome, but they weren't expected to do any work. They were, Barna said, 'to be all a woman should be—free, and beautiful, and kind'" (210). Gavir also notes that not all women enter the community on their own accord but are abducted by Barna's raiders against their will, as is the case with the beautiful Irad and her little sister, Melle. Knowing no relation but that of possession and subjugation, Barna may claim that "men and women should be free to love one another with no hypocritical bonds of promised faithfulness to chain them together" (207), but in fact he is unable to imagine women as competent and independent members of his community. For him, they are commodities he can use or discard at his whim: "He loved to have them about him, and they all flirted and flattered and teased him assiduously. He joked and played with them, but his serious talk was always with men" (210). Significantly, like the Arcamand slaves who are complicit in their own oppression, Barna's women are not just victims of male domination but themselves participate in the mechanism of repression.[8]

The complexities of the relationship between power, freedom, and gender constitute one of the main themes in Le Guin's writing. In particular, Le Guin tries to dismantle the traditional polarization of genders into irrational versus rational, emotional versus intellectual, and so forth, seeing it as "a tremendous source of loss, a failure to integrate the best each gender has to offer, and a missed opportunity, missed countless times, to find common, human ground" (Welton 16). Analyzing the significance of Ged's masculinity in *Wizard of Earthsea*, Perry Nodelman refers to Eve Kosofsky Sedgwick's discussion of "male homosocial desire," namely men's desire for mutual acceptance from and domination over other males, achieved through the subjugation of women. As Sedgwick phrases it, as men establish power relations among themselves, they use women "as exchangeable objects, as counters of value, for the primary purpose of cementing relationships with other men" (qtd. in Nodelman 191).[9] These interdependencies of power and competition also manifest themselves in Barna's control over other males through his unwritten right to choose and keep for himself any woman he wants. As Gavir is warned by one of his peers, "[t]hough they were so pretty and apparently so available as to drive a boy my age crazy, their availability was sham, a trap, as men of the household had warned me early on. If he gives you one the girls, they said, take her, but only for the night, and don't try sneaking off with any of his favourites. And as they knew me better and came to trust my discretion, they told me dire stories about Barna's jealousy. Finding a man with a girl he himself wanted, he had snapped the man's wrists like sticks, they said, and driven him out into the forest to starve" (223). It does not take long for Gavir to understand that these practices do not differ from those in Etra, where some female slaves become gift girls, beautiful commodities to be traded as any other goods. Significantly, he recalls that in Etra, thinking about the fate of slaves girls made him "feel extremely lucky to be a man" (84). By making Gavir uninterested in romantic relationships and compassionate to women, and thereby presenting him as transcending masculinity defined by oppression of women and superiority over other men, Le Guin emphasizes the possibility of an individual dismantling the ideology of sexual difference and the male hegemony it sanctions. Barna's overall failure to genuinely reform his community may be seen as a consequence of his inability to combine revolutionary energy with social sympathy and consensus. Instead, his dependence on coercion is another form of inner enslavement, preventing him from comprehending his moral responsibility for all the members of his community.

Gavir's final realization of the failure of the Heart of the Forest is marked by his bitter self-castigating comment: "I had believed that the rule of the master and the obedience of the slave were a mutual and sacred trust. I had believed that justice could exist in a society founded on injustice" (226). He has learned, however, that "[h]onour can exist anywhere, love can exist anywhere, but justice can exist only among people who found their relationships upon it" (226). As typical of protagonists of utopian fiction who escape when utopias malfunction, Gavir eventually leaves Barna's town for Mesun, taking with him another underdog child, Melle, who has no one to take care of her after the Heart of the Forest is destroyed by Casicar soldiers. The boy's predicament is perfectly captured in Le Guin's comment from "A War without End": "What your eyes have seen they have seen. Once you see the injustice, you can never again in good faith deny the oppression and defend the oppressor. What was loyalty is now betrayal. From now on, if you don't resist, you collude" (216).Gavir's decisions to leave both of the degenerated communities he encounters can be seen as micropolitical acts of resistance to the abuse of power; they stress the importance of the individual's ongoing vigilance to injustice and the potential for recurrent deconstruction and reinvention of oneself.

Simultaneously, gaining awareness of the dangers of macropolitical action may condone not so much a rejection of such efforts but an encouragement to invent new forms of social consciousness and existence. The ending of the novel seems to suggest such a proposition. In Ansul, Gavir meets Orrec Caspro and his wife, Gry. Although not overtly stated in the text, it seems that the poet gathers around himself young people who may be ready to embark on their own projects of looking for new values and laws, which in the future may lead to broader social and political changes. Asking Gavir to become his assistant, Orrec mentions two young female students who returned to their hometown to "astonish the good priests with their learning" (389). Orrec and Gry also look after Memer Galva, the main protagonist of *Voices*, who is learning about modern poetry and enjoys, as she puts it herself, "the freedom of a child" (*Voices* 333), which can be understood as occupying no fixed ideological position but rather testing the existing ideologies and inventing new subjectivities and modes of radical thought.[10] One may also presume that in such an environment, the little Melle will be able to recover from the traumas of the past and imagine freedom, which, as Le Guin stresses in "A War without End," is the prerequisite of genuine liberation: "We will not be free if we cannot imagine freedom. We cannot demand that anyone can try to attain justice and freedom who has not had a chance to imagine them as attainable" (220). It is not clear what will happen to Gavir. For sure, he will become a free citizen of Urdile and study at the University of Mesun, which will enable him to follow his childhood dream to write a history of the City States exposing the unjust social fragmentation and stratification of the realm. Nor does Le Guin foretell the future of the Western Shore, but such an ambiguous conclusion of the tale is definitely not to suggest that an achievable utopia must unavoidably be an individual one. She rather indicates the importance of thinking about sociopolitical alterities as an ongoing personal and collective activity, which does not consist of following revolutionary leaders but rather of finding for oneself "a middle ground between defense and attack, a ground of flexible resistance, a space opened for change" ("A War without End" 216). Although, as Le Guin admits, "[i]t is not an easy place to find or live in" (216), by emphasizing the process of the reactualization of ideals, *Powers* affirms the sense and the desirability of both personal growth and solidarity with others. Even more importantly, the book illustrates that this autonomous "middle ground" is also, or perhaps especially, available to adolescents.

Conclusion

In praising *Tehanu*, Laura B. Comoletti and Michael D. C. Drout contend that the story shows "that after the rite of passage is completed the child must settle into the difficult, frustrating chore of being an adult, fighting the endless tiny existential social battles—be they struggles against gender oppression, inequities of power, illegitimate domination, and the enforcement of ideology on unwilling minds, or the crises of conscience, losses of motivation, and fears of failure—that make up adult life" (133–134). Furthermore, as Margaret M. Dunn notes, the Earthsea trilogy in general makes it clear that "the process of maturation is not something that ends at a given age or stage of life, and . . . is not something which, once successfully completed, is completed forevermore" (qtd. in Comoletti and Drout 134).[11] This can also be said about *The Annals of the Western Shore*, and especially *Powers*. Yet Le Guin's latest fantasy for young readers seems to focus much more consistently on modes of radical thinking in that it dramatizes the conclusion that any feasible and worthwhile utopian project should involve both collective efforts to introduce transformations and continual thoughtful choices preventing the likelihood of dystopia. As a metaphor of such an attitude, Gavir's youth illustrates that critical thinking about utopian alterities necessitates the awareness of the limits and possibilities of radical dissent. Hence, although *Powers* refrains from endorsing the validity of collective action, it can nevertheless be classified as an example of radical fantasy for young readers: its focus on problems inherent in oppositional efforts responds to a growing sense of disappointment and frustration, affecting both youth and adults, caused by the realization that, at least seemingly, there may be no alternative but to accept and participate in oppressive social and political configurations. Admittedly, not all fantasy texts have the potential for subversion. As Fredric Jameson argues, "[w]hether such fantasy can be any more politically radicalising than any other cultural forms . . . is not only a question of the immediate situation, it is also one of consciousness-raising as well—or in other words an awareness of the possibilities and potentialities of the form itself" (280). Undoubtedly, *Powers* is an example of a text criticizing what Le Guin calls "the lazy, timorous habit of thinking that the way we live now is the only way people can live. It is that inertia that allows the institutions of injustice to continue unquestioned" ("A War without End" 218). In its foregrounding of critical thought and the possibility of transformation, *Powers* may be taken as the indication of Le Guin's conviction that such a stance is also desirable in young people's engagements with current social and political issues and that it will find resonance with young citizens. It also testifies to the potential of radical fantasy as a form capable of articulating and encouraging both self-determination and activism.

ACKNOWLEDGMENTS

I would like to thank Angela Hubler and Tim Dayton for their input on earlier drafts of this essay.

NOTES

1. For a general discussion of radical fantasy, see Justyna Deszcz-Tryhubczak, "Utopianism in Radical Fantasy for Children and Young Adults." Spectres of Utopia: Theory, Practice, Conventions. Ed. Ludmila Gruszewska-Blaim and Artur Blaim. (Frankfurt am Main: Peter Lang Verlag, 2012), 204–214. For a discussion of *Un Lun Dun* as radical fantasy, see Justyna Deszcz-Tryhubczak, "'Minister,' said the girl, 'we need to talk': China Miéville's *Un Lun Dun* as Radical Fantasy for Children and Young Adults," in *Critical Insights: Contemporary Speculative Fiction*, ed. M. Keith Booker (Ipswitch, Mass.: Salem Press, 2013), 137–151.

2. In the United States, Hardinge's novel was published as *The Lost Conspiracy*.

3. This is the example of radical fantasy for younger readers mentioned by Burling. It is worth noting that while Burling stresses the importance of the urban setting as metonymic of class conflicts, in Pullman a substantial part of the plot involving struggles for freedom occurs away from the city. Hence it might be concluded that the urban milieu is not an indispensable element of radical fantasy. The partial location in the city is also the case in *Powers*.

4. In "Radical Fantasy," Jameson mentions the Earthsea cycle as marking the emergence of radical fantasy: "It is ... the informing presence of this deep history which is alone able to 're-function' ... the ethical superstitions of good and evil forces into concrete social phenomena a good deal more horrifying than the older abstractions: as witness the representational evolution from the evil 'shadow' of *The Wizard of Earthsea* to the truly chilling appearance of Jasper in *Tehanu* (1990), a character in which *ressentiment* and misogyny, class superiority and the dehumanising will to vengeance, are memorably compounded, affording a vivid experience of the oppression and paralysing force of the other's magic. Here the latter truly resituates us in the concrete social world of alienation and class struggle" (280).

5. Contrary to "the pseudomedieval matrix" of kings, aristocracy, merchants, and peasants (Comoletti and Drout 114) of Earthsea, the City States may bring to mind city-states of ancient Greece or Rome.

6. Together with his wife, Gry, Orrec Caspro appears in all the parts of the trilogy, himself representing the evolvement of individual radical dissent.

7. An example of the former is Ris, a slave girl, who finds it hard to imagine life in countries with no slavery. Hoby is an example of the latter.

8. The only example of female opposition in Barna's community is Diero's protest against his raping Irad in front of other men and women. Although Barna usually shows great respect to Diero, this time he simply strikes her unconscious, infuriated by any sign of female opposition.

9. See Eve Kosofsky Sedgwick, *Between Men: English Literature and Male Homosocial Desire* (New York: Columbia University Press, 1985), 137.

10. For a discussion of Memer's acquisition of an understanding of the mechanisms of oppression, see Marek C. Oziewicz, "Restorative Justice Scripts in Ursula K. Le Guin's *Voices*," *Children's Literature in Education* 42 (2011): 33–43. Although *Voices* could also be seen as radical fantasy, I do not discuss this issue here, as Oziewicz's article, albeit not presenting the novel in this light, nevertheless provides an exhaustive discussion of mobilization against oppression.

11. See Dunn's "In Defense of Dragons: Imagination as Experience in the Earthsea Trilogy," in *Proceedings of the Ninth Annual Conference of the Children's Literature Association*, ed. Priscilla A. Ord. (Boston: Children's Literature Association, 1983), 58.

WORKS CITED

Burling, William J. "Periodizing the Postmodern: China Miéville's *Perdido Street Station* and the Dynamics of Radical Fantasy." *Extrapolation* 50:2 (2009): 326–344. Print.

Comoletti, Laura B., and Michael D. C. Drout. "How They Do Things with Words: Language, Power, Gender, and the Priestly Wizards of Ursula K. Le Guin's Earthsea Books." *Children's Literature* 29 (2001): 113–141. Print.

Jameson, Fredric. "Radical Fantasy." *Historical Materialism: Research in Critical Marxist Theory* 10:4 (2002): 273–280. Print.

Langbauer, Laurie. "Ethics and Theory: Suffering in Dickens, Dostoevsky, and Le Guin." *English Literary History* 75:1 (2008): 89–109. Print.

Le Guin, Ursula. *The Dispossessed: An Ambiguous Utopia*. New York: HarperCollins, 2003. Print.

———. "Is Gender Necessary? Redux." In *Dancing at the Edge of the World: Thoughts on Words, Women, Place*, 7–16. New York: Grove Press, 1989. Print.

———. *Powers*. London: Orion Children's Books, 2007. Print.

———. "Reading Young, Reading Old: Mark Twain's *Diaries of Adam and Eve*." In *The Wave in the Mind: Talks and Essays on the Writer, the Reader, and the Imagination*, 46–56. Boston: Shambhala, 2004. Print.

———. *Voices*. Orlando: Harcourt, 2006. Print.

———. "A War without End." In *The Wave in the Mind: Talks and Essays on the Writer, the Reader, and the Imagination*, 211–220. Boston: Shambhala, 2004. Print.

Moylan, Tom. *Demand the Impossible: Science Fiction and the Utopian Imagination*. New York: Methuen, 1986. Print.

Nodelman, Perry. "Reinventing the Past: Gender in Ursula K. Le Guin's *Tehanu* and the Earthsea 'Trilogy.'" *Children's Literature* 23 (1995): 179–201.

Nodelman, Perry, and Mavis Reimer. *The Pleasures of Children's Literature*. 3rd ed. Boston: Allyn & Bacon, 2003. Print.

Parsons, Elizabeth. "The Appeal of the Underdog: Mr. Lunch and Leftist Politics as Entertainment." *Children's Literature Association Quarterly* 30:4 (2005): 354–367. Print.

Sabia, Dan. "Individual and Community in Le Guin's *The Dispossessed*." In *The New Utopian Politics of Ursula K. Le Guin's "The Dispossessed*,*"* edited by Laurence Davis and Peter Stillman, 111–128. Lanham, Md.: Lexington Books, 2005. Print.

Sargent, Lyman Tower. "The Three Faces of Utopianism Revisited." *Utopian Studies* 5:1 (1994): 1–37. Print.

Welton, Anne. "Earthsea Revisited: Tehanu and Feminism." *Voice of Youth Advocates* 14 (1991): 14–17. Print.

CONTRIBUTORS

ROLAND BOER is professor of literature at Renmin University of China, Beijing, and research professor at the University of Newcastle, Australia. His research passions are Marxism and religion, and to that end he has written numerous works. The most recent are *Lenin, Religion, and Theology* (2013) and *In the Vale of Tears: On Marxism and Theology, V* (2013).

HEIDI M. BRUSH is a doctoral student in children's literature at the Pennsylvania State University. She is interested in the intersections of orality, literacy, and "secondary orality" media practices such as digital storytelling and podcasts and especially in the ways in which non-Western orality and secondary orality complicate and redefine textual representations of non-Western cultures. Prior to her studies at Penn State, she was a professor of communications at the University of Wisconsin–Milwaukee.

JUSTYNA DESZCZ-TRYHUBCZAK is assistant professor of literature and director of the Center for Young People's Literature and Culture at the Institute of English Studies, the University of Wrocław, Poland, where she teaches English literature courses on children's literature and culture. She is the author of *Rushdie in Wonderland: "Fairytaleness" in Salman Rushdie's Fiction* (2004) and has published articles on Salman Rushdie, Angela Carter, fairy tales, and YA fantasy fiction.

DANIEL D. HADE is an associate professor of children's literature at the Pennsylvania State University. He has published in journals such as *Research in the Teaching of English*, the *Children's Literature Association Quarterly*, *Children's Literature in Education, Language Arts, Mythlore*, and *Horn Book*. He has taught and lectured in Sweden, France, Poland, the United Kingdom, Ireland, Italy, Ukraine, South Korea, and Taiwan.

ANGELA E. HUBLER is associate professor of women's studies at Kansas State University, where she teaches courses on the literature and culture of girlhood, gender, and class. She's published essays on the Dear America Series books, the feminist political novel for girls, girls as readers, the film *Girls Town*, and the writers Josephine Herbst and Linda Hogan.

CYNTHIA ANNE MCLEOD is a school librarian at Burney-Harris-Lyons Middle School in Athens, Georgia. Her dissertation explored representations of labor unions in American children's novels. She has taught children's literature at the University of Georgia and also served as a cofacilitator of the Red Clay Writing Project's Summer Institute.

JANA MIKOTA is a lecturer in the Department of Literary Didactics of the University of Siegen, Germany. Her dissertation focused on exile literature; her book in progress focuses on the reading canon as it was formed and reinforced in advice books and school curricula in the nineteenth century.

CARL F. MILLER received his Ph.D. at the University of Florida and is an assistant professor at Palm Beach Atlantic University, where his primary research interests are twentieth-century comparative literature, culture, and theory. He has recent publications on the influence of the Cold War in the 1980s graphic novel, the crisis of the Bildungsroman in Sherwood Anderson's *Winesburg, Ohio*, and the significance of philosophical ethics in Dr. Seuss's *Horton Hears a Who!*

MERVYN NICHOLSON is professor of English and department chair at Thompson Rivers University in British Columbia, and is author of *Male Envy: The Logic of Malice* and *13 Ways of Looking at Images: Studies in the Logic of Visualization*, as well as articles in many journals, including *Monthly Review*.

JANE ROSEN is a librarian at the Imperial War Museum, London, where she served as historical adviser for the exhibition "Once Upon a Wartime: Classic War Stories for Children." Her research interests include radical and working-class children's literature, and she has produced work on the publications of the Socialist Sunday School movement and the Proletarian Schools and Colleges at the beginning of the twentieth century. She is also working on a bibliography of working-class and radical children's literature in the twentieth century.

SHARON SMULDERS teaches in the Department of English at Mount Royal University, Calgary. Her interest in children's literature has led to articles on the poetry of Robert Service, Christina Rossetti, and Ann and Jane Taylor. She has also written on issues of race and representation in Laura Ingalls Wilder's *Little House* series and Beatrice Culleton Mosionier's *In Search of April Raintree.*

ANASTASIA ULANOWICZ is an assistant professor of English at the University of Florida, where she teaches graduate and undergraduate courses on children's literature, memory, trauma, and the historical novel. Her essays have been published in journals such as *Children's Literature, Children's Literature Quarterly,* and *The Lion and the Unicorn.* She is also the author of *Ghost Images: Second-Generation Memory and Contemporary Children's Literature.*

IAN WOJCIK-ANDREWS teaches courses in children's literature and film at Eastern Michigan University. He is the author of *Margaret Drabble's Female Bildungsromane: Genre and Gender* and *Children's Films: History, Ideology, Pedagogy, Theory.* Recent publications include "Elder Quests and Kid Ventures Equals Kid Quests" (*Journal of Education, Media, Memory, and Society,* 2013) and "Children in Film" (*Oxford Bibliographies in Cinema and Media Studies,* 2012). An essay, "Criticism and Multicultural Children's Films," coauthored with Professor Iris Shepard, is published in *Kidding Around: The Child in Film and Media* (Continuum, 2014).

NAOMI WOOD is a professor of English at Kansas State University specializing in literature for and about children, with a particular interest in Victorian literature and culture and fantasy. She has published on Victorian fantasists, Walt Disney's *Cinderella,* and Philip Pullman's *His Dark Materials.* She is currently writing a book on the theological aspects of children's fantasy. Since 2009, she has coedited *The Lion and the Unicorn* with David Russell and Karin Westman.

INDEX

Page numbers in **bold** indicate an illustration.

Made in the USA
Monee, IL
31 August 2021